Prisoners of War and their Captors in World War II

Prisoners of War and their Captors in World War II

Bob Moore and Kent Fedorowich

BERG
Oxford • Washington, D.C.

First published in 1996 by
Berg
Editorial offices:
150 Cowley Road, Oxford, OX4 1JJ, UK
22883 Quicksilver Drive, Dulles, VA 20166, USA

Berg is an imprint of Oxford International Publishers Ltd.

Library of Congress Cataloging-in-Publication Data

A CIP catalogue for this book is available from the Library of Congress.

British Library Cataloguing-in-Publication Data

A CIP catalogue record for this book is available from the British Library.

Cover photograph: reproduced courtesy of the National Archives of Canada.

ISBN 1 85973 157 0 (Cloth)
1 85973 152 X (Paper)

Typeset by JS Typesetting, Wellingborough, Northants.
Printed in the United Kingdom by WBC Book Manufacturers, Bridgend,
Mid Glamorgan.

Contents

Contents

Preface

The idea for this collection originated at a time when the editors were lecturers at the former Bristol Polytechnic. As specialists in the history of refugees in inter-war Europe, and ex-servicemen in the British Empire respectively, the shift to another category of the disempowered in the twentieth century was almost a natural step for both parties. It soon became apparent that, while there was a whole body of literature on civilians and internment during the Second World War, research on prisoners of war was somewhat fragmentary and spread among scholars across the globe. The primary purpose behind this publication is to bring together the work of scholars on this subject into a single volume for the first time, and in so doing, invite serious consideration of the experiences of many millions of servicemen taken prisoner by their enemies in all theatres of war.

As anyone who has ever attempted to edit a volume of essays will know, the possibilities for disaster are almost limitless. In this respect, this book was an exception. We would like to acknowledge in print the assistance and co-operation of all the contributors, who, although spread through four continents, met deadlines, answered queries and responded to criticisms and suggestions with good humour and often at very short notice. Their efforts meant that the manuscript was completed a little over two years after the project's inception – a remarkable achievement. We owe a special debt of gratitude to Drs Jeff Grey and Jeff Doyle (Departments of History and English, Australian Defence Force Academy), whose conference on prisoners-of-war history at Canberra in May 1994 was instrumental in bringing several of the contributors together for the first time. In addition, we should like to acknowledge the invaluable contribution of David Sissons of Canberra in effecting the excellent translation of the chapter by Ikuhiko Hata in a matter of weeks so that it could be included in this collection.

Given the number of libraries and record offices consulted by the contributors, it would be impossible to thank individually all the librarians and archivists who have given their time and expertise to the project as a whole. However, we are delighted to acknowledge their collective contribution here. We would also like to acknowledge the role of the Faculty of Humanities Research Committee of the University of the West of England, Bristol and the Department of English and History at the Manchester Metropolitan University, whose financial help has been an essential element in furthering our own work, and in the production of this volume.

Finally, on a personal note, we would like to thank our respective wives and families for their toleration of seemingly endless meetings and telephone calls discussing the minutiae of prisoner history and of the absences necessitated by research trips that brought this work to fruition.

Bob Moore
Kent Fedorowich

The publication of this book has been made possible by a grant from the Scouloudi Foundation in association with the Institute of Historical Research.

Abbreviations

AIF	Australian Imperial Force
BRC & StJJ	British Red Cross Society and Order of St John of Jerusalem
Btn	Battalion
CGS	Chief of the General Staff
DMI	Directorate of Military Intelligence
DPW	Directorate of Prisoners of War
FCNL	Committee of National Liberation
GHQ	General Headquarters
HD(S)E	Home Defence (Security) Executive
ICRC	International Committee of the Red Cross
IJA	Imperial Japanese Army
IJN	Imperial Japanese Navy
JCC	Joint Consultative Committee
NCOs	Non-commissioned officers
NEAS	Non-European Army Services
NFU	National Farmers Union
NMC	Native Military Corps
POW	Prisoner of War
POWs	Prisoners of War
PWE	Political Warfare Executive
SOE	Special Operations Executive
TUC	Trades Union Congress

Prisoners of War in the Second World War: An Overview

Bob Moore and *Kent Fedorowich*

During the course of the Second World War, around eighty million people served in the armed forces of the belligerent powers.[1] While exact figures will never be known, it has been estimated that as many as thirty-five million of them spent some time in enemy hands between 1939 and 1945.[2] Thus capture and incarceration as a prisoner of war during or immediately following the cessation of hostilities was certainly on a par with, if not exceeding, combat as one of the most common experiences for those in uniform. During the war, large concentrations of prisoners were created when the Germans interned the French Army after the armistice in June 1940, and when huge numbers of Soviet soldiers fell into their hands in the early campaigns on the Eastern Front in Europe. Similarly, large contingents of British and Commonwealth forces were compelled to surrender as the Japanese armies swept through south-east Asia. As the fortunes of war began to change, the Allied Powers also acquired large numbers of enemy captives. British and American operations in the Mediterranean theatre had netted more than 500,000 Italians and a significant number of Germans by the summer of 1943. Even this level of success was dwarfed by events on the Eastern Front, where the Red Army took the surrender of entire Axis armies, including around 100,000 on one day when Field Marshal von Paulus surrendered part of what remained of his Sixth Army at Stalingrad on 1 February 1943.[3] As the war in Europe and the Far East came to an end, so Allied prisoners were released while the remaining Axis and Japanese forces were taken into captivity.

Given that this experience was shared by so many, it is perhaps surprising that, in the voluminous literature on the Second World War, relatively little scholarly attention has been paid to prisoners of war (POWs) and their histories. Texts that concentrate on military affairs tend to deal with the victors in battle rather than the losers. Prisoners appear only when they are perceived to have had some positive (intelligence) or negative (obstructive) strategic importance. Yet if the military historians do not regard POWs as being within their remit, then there are few others to take up the challenge. With one or two honourable exceptions,[4] social historians have not chosen to analyse the captive experience, and what it meant for the prisoners or their families and dependants. Until recently, POWs have been perceived as a separate and discrete subject, studied by specialist historians devoted to uncovering the experiences of groups in particular theatres of war. In effect, there is a whole canon of work that can be described as prisoner-of-war history – important in its own right, but largely divorced from other areas of study.

This is not to imply that the literature is insignificant, merely that it has been confined within certain relatively narrow methodological and subject boundaries. Writing on POWs can be categorized under three main headings. First, and most numerous, are the accounts and analyses of prisoner experiences and behaviour. They are usually written 'from below', although many do attempt to link the workings of international conventions and captor policy to the everyday experiences of the prisoners. For the most part, these histories deal with one theatre of operations, one nationality of prisoner, or more commonly, one particular captor power.[5] As such, they draw from, and are complementary to, the wealth of memoirs and autobiographical material produced by ex-prisoners themselves. Collectively, these works do serve to highlight the multiplicity, variability and range of prisoner experiences in Europe, Africa and the Far East; yet their translation into other media, for example as documentary and feature films, has tended to narrow rather than broaden popular perceptions of the prisoners' experiences.

In the post-war world of the victorious powers, a culture and mythology has been constructed that focuses on stories of their servicemen in captivity. In the Anglo-American tradition, this centres on escape stories from camps inside Germany. While these may be based on fact, their admission into popular culture has usually been via the cinema, with the resultant embellishments insisted upon by Pinewood or Hollywood.[6] The film versions have encompassed stories of betrayal and of failed escape attempts, and stereotypical portrayals of German captors, usually including inefficient or biddable guards, upright unbending Prussian officers and a brutal SS. Rather fewer stories have emerged from prisoners of the Japanese in the Far East. Here the division between military and civilian captives is much less marked. There were few escape stories, and the popular image is based upon the brutality of the Japanese military regime, their treatment of the prisoners, the hostile environment and the psychological reactions to the extremes of a captive existence.[7] In some instances, for example in Australia, the image has been narrowed still further. Here, the prisoner-of-war experience has been focused almost entirely on the prisoners employed by the

Japanese on the Burma Railway, even to the exclusion of all the other places and circumstances where Australian troops were held captive. Among the victorious allies, only the Soviet Union has chosen to ignore its servicemen captured by the enemy. The severe retribution promised to any Red Army soldiers returning to the motherland having previously surrendered to the fascist enemy undoubtedly contributed to the willingness of some Soviet prisoners to join Vlasov's Army and change sides during the war.[8] Moreover, the heroic portrayal of the victory over Nazi Germany precluded any mention of those who had been captured. However, this did not prevent Stalin from demanding the return of all Soviet nationals at the end of the war, nor from including all those killed by the Germans in the total of Soviet victims for reparations purposes.

For the defeated powers, the recognition afforded to their servicemen taken prisoner was somewhat different. By the end of the war in Europe, all German forces had surrendered and been taken into captivity. While there were stories of heroic escapees, the prisoners' appearance in the post-war culture of West Germany was primarily as victims of the Soviet Union, kept in the *gulags* and work camps of Siberia into the 1950s and beyond. How many were taken prisoner but never returned from the East still remains a mystery. (This image of the prisoner as victim was reinforced by more recent claims of supposed atrocities committed against them by the Western Powers.) For the Japanese, falling into enemy hands was anathema, and there were few Japanese POWs before the last months of the war. For this reason, the shame attached to being a prisoner meant that those involved were ignored, and the POW experience does not feature at all in post-war Japanese culture. Suffice to say that whatever popularization of some specific aspects of the prisoner-of-war experience has taken place, it does no justice at all to the captivity endured by many millions of servicemen, both during and in the aftermath of the Second World War.

The second type of writing on prisoners of war encompasses all the general works written on particular nationalities of prisoner or those which are concerned with a particular theatre of war. The most extensive of these is the twenty-two-book series produced by the *Wissenschaftlichen Kommission für deutsche Kriegsgefangenengeschichte* (Scientific Commission for the History of German POWs). This deals with many aspects of German soldiers in captivity, both during and after the Second World War. Published between 1962 and 1974, and based primarily on German sources, the individual volumes contain a wealth of information, but suffer from the disadvantage of having been written before the archives of the captor powers became available.[9] Shorter, but nonetheless analytical and informative works have also appeared on the Italian POWs, most notably those by Conti and Rainero.[10] On the involvement of the United States, there are a larger number of works, both on their servicemen in captivity[11] and on their POWs.[12] Here again, the focus of these works tends to be on the prisoners in captivity, although some attempts have been made to link their experiences to the policies formulated at governmental levels. Thus far, there has been only one example of a work that takes policy as its central theme, namely that of Lewis and Mewha, whose *History of Prisoner of War Utilization by the United States Army 1776–1945* provides a long-term view of one particular aspect of prisoners' treatment by the United States.[13] While all these works have added enormously to our knowledge on specific aspects of prisoners' experiences in different theatres during the Second World War, even these specialist histories have not afforded much attention to the ways in which captor governments developed policies towards prisoners during that war in the light of their treaty obligations. To a large extent, this is not the fault of the authors, as it is only recently that government papers have been released, as in the case of the United Kingdom, or rediscovered, as has happened with German archives in the Soviet Union.

This omission from the historiography has been addressed in part by the third category of publication, namely the thematic and comparative works that have begun to appear since the mid-1970s. One of the earliest attempts to synthesize the prisoner experience in the Second World War was that of Barker, whose thematic approach provided a basis for the development of prisoner-of-war history.[14] Writing in the 1970s, he was unable to use much of the subsequently available archival material; but his lead has only recently been followed by one or two other scholars. On individual themes, one could point to the example of Gerald Davis's assessment of the impact of maintaining POWs on the economies of belligerent powers in the twentieth century;[15] but more extensive works have been sadly lacking. There is, however, one shining exception. S. P. MacKenzie, in a recent article in the *Journal of Modern History*, has succeeded in analysing captor policies in a comparative framework in an attempt to uncover the essential factors underlying prisoner-of-war treatment.[16] His conclusions are that in theatres of conflict where principles of humanity militated towards benevolence, it was possible for the principles of the 1929 Geneva Convention to be upheld. However, reciprocity, or rather concern for one's own prisoners in enemy hands, seems to have been the paramount determinant in the treatment of prisoners *where independent monitoring took place*. However, this was undermined when such monitoring did not exist, or where there was no possibility of retaliation, or where ideological malevolence overrode any of these more practical considerations. This analysis leads him to the conclusion that the Second

World War was a transitional phase in the treatment afforded to POWs, sitting uneasily between the primacy of humanitarian approaches in the First World War and the dominance of ideological considerations in post-1945 conflicts.

While these researches have shown the way for more extensive comparative analyses of prisoner-of-war experiences and their treatment by captors, both during the Second World War, and more generally in the age of total warfare, the subject has become channelled into a series of narrow areas that have had some sensational political, legal or historical notoriety. All might loosely be described as being in the realm of real or alleged war crimes; and, while this should not detract from their importance, this specialization has tended to skew academic and public perceptions of the wider and more general history of POWs in this particular conflict. In summary, there are at least four major examples where the treatment of particular groups of wartime prisoners has erupted into a major public debate via the popular press and media in the last twenty years.

In the late 1970s, Nikolai Tolstoy began a sustained campaign to highlight the case of the Cossacks, many of whom had fought for the Germans as part of Vlasov's Army, and who had surrendered to the British and Americans in 1945, but who had subsequently been forcibly repatriated to the Soviet Union under the terms of agreements reached at Yalta and at the behest of Stalin. Tolstoy claimed that this was an act of servility on the part of the Western Allies, and that it could have been largely avoided if the British Foreign Office had taken a different line.[17] While his conclusions were contentious, he also attempted to implicate some of the British officials involved in the deportations themselves, a course of action that ultimately led to a civil action for libel from one of those accused and the award of punitive damages against Count Tolstoy. While the legal action demonstrated the weakness of Tolstoy's case, it has been further undermined by the work of other historians, who have dismissed his accusations on the basis of all the available documentation and have also thereby exposed his methodology as defective.[18] While this particular controversy may have been laid to rest for the moment, it may yet be that new material from the former Soviet archives will encourage other historians to look at the evidence from the Russian side.

Almost contemporaneous with the publication of Tolstoy's work was the appearance of an important monograph by Christian Streit, who dealt specifically with the German Army's treatment of Soviet POWs.[19] He demonstrated quite clearly that the Wehrmacht and the Army command were implicated in all aspects of Hitler's war of annihilation, including the extermination of Jews and POWs. The whole debate on the conduct of the war on the Eastern Front was later taken further and enlarged both by Streit himself, and subsequently by Förster, Streim, Bartov and Schulte.[20] Streit's conclusions were more or less accepted by the historical profession; but the whole issue took on a political aspect in the 1980s as attempts were made to 'historicize' the Hitler period in German history. These included trying to equate Nazi genocidal policies with events in Stalin's Soviet Union and also to play down the role of most Germans in war crimes. In this context, Streit's conclusions did not correspond with the attempts of the former *Wehrmacht* and Army leadership to convince the world that they had fought a 'clean' war, even on the Eastern Front. Here again, a debate on the treatment of POWs went way beyond mere academic discussion and was planted firmly in the contemporary political arena.

A different, although equally sensational, debate began with the publication of the Canadian journalist James Bacque's *Other Losses: An Investigation into the Mass Deaths of German Prisoners of War at the hands of the French and Americans After World War II* in 1989.[21] His thesis was based on the terminology used by the Americans to tabulate and categorize their German prisoners during and immediately after the war, and the difficulties of reconciling the figures given in official reports. Bacque claimed that the 'other losses' were in fact prisoners who were either deliberately or accidentally killed through maltreatment at the hands of their captors. The accusations levelled against senior American military personnel, including the Supreme Allied Commander Dwight D. Eisenhower, and their extensive exposure in print and on television, inevitably provoked a storm of protest. However, most scholars of the period did not have sufficient pre-existing knowledge of the sources either to underwrite or refute Bacque's claims. Academic scepticism about the findings did exist, as the accusations certainly did not fit accepted pictures of the Allied occupation of Germany and western Europe. However, it took time for research to be carried out that could undermine the charges, which amounted to accusations of war crimes. In 1992, Bischof and Ambrose edited an entire collection of essays devoted to taking up and refuting Bacque's main claims.[22] While this may have satisfied the academic world, the fact remains that the original work will continue to have a substantial audience. This is due partly to the irrefutable nature of much of the narrative on camp conditions, partly to the continued closure of certain archives that might provide definitive evidence against the charges,[23] and also the publicity given to the book in the popular media.[24]

The final *cause célèbre* comes from the war in the Far East. Many aspects of Japanese treatment of POWs and captured enemy civilians in that theatre have been well documented and extensively discussed, both at an academic and a popular level. The Tokyo war crimes trials in 1949 dealt with some elements of Japanese criminality; but subsequent investigations have continued to unearth fresh accusations about actions against both civilians and prisoners that (under the criteria applied by the Western Powers) could only be described as criminal. The most notorious example of this concerns the activities of Units 731 and 100 of the Imperial Japanese Army. Their role in developing, testing and deploying methods of bacteriological warfare, coupled with their use of human vivisections to further their researches, all add up to a horrendous catalogue of crimes that it would be difficult to defend in any circumstances. The debate, as conducted by British and American historians, has centred not on the truth of the crimes carried out by Unit 731, but on the possible complicity of Western governments in covering up their existence, granting total or partial immunities to their perpetrators, and then keeping their files on the issue out of the public domain, even forty years after the event. The purpose behind this subterfuge was supposedly to protect the knowledge gained from these Japanese 'scientists' for the benefit of Western biological warfare projects. However, the charges of Western complicity were made all the more damning when it became apparent that some British and American POWs had been victims of the testing process, as well as the many thousands, and perhaps hundreds of thousands, of Chinese soldiers and civilians. In other words, the American, British and other Western governments had sought to protect those who had carried out a series of crimes against their own soldiers in captivity.[25] Although the specific activities of Unit 731 will never be the subject of further legal action (the vast majority of perpetrators and victims now having died) it remains the case that the actions of the Japanese authorities during the war continue to attract attention. In spite of the 1952 Peace Treaty, which supposedly settled all claims against the Japanese government, there have been recent attempts by individual victims to pursue claims for damages in the Tokyo courts.[26] Moreover, the supposed closure of the international legal case against Japan has not precluded further historical research on the subject by interested parties, both in the West, and in Japan itself.

The existence of this substantial body of work should not be allowed to obscure that fact that there is still much about the POWs and their captors of which we have remained ignorant – in the areas between the extremes of the Hollywood version on one hand and the sensationalism of James Bacque on the other – and it is to some of those areas that this volume is addressed. The contributors were not given specific tasks, but were asked to write on aspects of their chosen specialism that they considered of major importance to a greater understanding of the treatment of POWs in the various theatres of war. The results of these commissions can be loosely categorized into three groups: those that deal primarily with the development of national government policies towards prisoners during the war, those that examine the very different uses made of prisoners by the British and Japanese respectively, and those that deal with the experiences of specific groups or types of prisoner. Beyond the specifics of each individual contribution, the collection also has a wider purpose, namely to add fuel to the debate on the treatment of POWs in the twentieth century and to give further consideration to MacKenzie's view of the Second World War as an important formative but transitional phase between the armed conflicts in the early part of the century and those of the fifty years since 1945.

Detailed investigations of governmental policy-making on POWs have been sadly lacking to date, especially in relation to the Western Powers. The chapters by Bob Moore and David Rolf examine the two distinct elements of British POW policy, namely the treatment of captured enemies and the politics of trying to protect service personnel who had fallen into enemy hands. While painting rather different pictures of the same government (and in some cases the same officials), these chapters do demonstrate both the complexities of the issue and the compromises that had to be made as long as hostilities lasted. Whatever the contrasts between these two analyses, it is clear that there were times when the British government was prepared to relegate the well-being of its servicemen in captivity in favour of other, apparently more pressing interests. Also apparent in this survey is the fact that the British treated their German and Italian prisoners very differently. Whether this was the result of pre-existing cultural perceptions of their enemies, or based on experience during the war, there was undoubtedly a collective view that saw the Germans as ideologically committed and ruthless opponents who had to be treated with the utmost caution, but the Italians as basically honest and friendly people who had been led astray by Mussolini's fascism, but were nevertheless capable of redemption. Increasing contacts with the Italians in North Africa and in Britain itself helped to reinforce this view. To that extent, the treatment of the Italians mirrored that of captured Germans in the First World War; initial wariness followed by an increasing level of accommodation. In contrast, the Germans were not afforded similar treatment. Seen as inherently dangerous and deported to North America whenever possible, it was only near the end of the war that their treatment underwent some amelioration, only to be tempered once again when tangible evidence of German war crimes came to light as Europe was liberated.

While individual national studies of the POW question are undoubtedly valuable, they can serve to hide the international perspectives involved. The fact that the powers at war with the Axis and the Japanese were an alliance meant that there had to be collective planning and decision-making. In this respect, the treatment of prisoners was only one element among thousands of issues discussed by London and Washington during the course of the war. Yet it is equally important to realize that this was not just an Anglo-American affair. In her hour of need, Britain had called upon the services of her dominions and imperial territories to help prosecute the war. When their soldiers were captured, so the dominion governments acquired a direct interest in the whole question of POW welfare in German, Italian and Japanese hands.

Although the Germans regarded the British Empire and dominions as a single entity, the relationship between London and the dominion governments was an extremely complex one. In a detailed analysis of Canadian government attempts to free their servicemen from captivity, Jonathan Vance shows how that relationship operated in practice. He argues that the Canadians clearly thought they had choices available for negotiation with both the Germans and the Japanese. Closer military and economic ties with the United States led them to believe that their national interests might best be served by pursuing a parallel policy of hedging between American and British Commonwealth schemes for the reciprocal repatriation of their men, and thus having the best of both worlds. Ottawa was keenly aware of the possible political dangers involved if the United States negotiated the return of its soldiers while Canadians were not repatriated. In the event, as Vance demonstrates, Canada obtained few benefits from this policy, either for soldiers held by the Germans or the Japanese. Moreover, the Canadian reservations about Commonwealth schemes rendered them more or less inoperable. As Britain had sent large numbers of her German POWs to Canada, Berlin would not countenance any scheme that did not have complete Canadian support. Even allowing for the fact that the Canadians acted from the highest motives, it remains the case that their policy not only failed to produce any concrete gains but also served to hinder the repatriation of other Commonwealth POWs.

Nowhere in western Europe was the POW question more complex than in France. Mention of prisoners in that country inevitably brings to mind the French Army interned by the Germans in the summer of 1940 and its captivity for much of the war. This tends to over-shadow the civil war between pro-Vichy and Free French forces that was fought out in the Middle East and North and Equatorial Africa. Perhaps because the French have remained unwilling to address many aspects of their wartime history, the fact that both sides had prisoners who were their own countrymen has been largely ignored. In a highly original piece, Martin Thomas examines the strange history of the

French against the French and their treatment of prisoners. In doing so, he highlights the questions of status, and the reluctance of Vichy to treat Free French captives as anything other than traitors and liable to the full rigour of the law. He also shows how the holding of prisoners became an important element in establishing the status of de Gaulle's Free French movement and an important bargaining counter to protect its forces in Vichy and pro-German hands.

The second section of the book moves away from the high politics of international relations and takes a different perspective on POWs by looking at two very dissimilar case studies, one from Europe and the other from the Far East. Prisoners have long been seen as a potential asset by capturing powers in so far as they can be put to work. This had been common practice in the First World War and was enshrined in the 1929 Geneva Convention. However, this was not their only possible use. While prisoners had been used for propaganda purposes in the 1914–18 conflict, the idea of re-educating and 'turning' prisoners so that they could be used to help, and even fight, in the 'liberation' of their homeland was something entirely new.[27] In 1941, the British government sanctioned plans for its Political Warfare Executive to begin a programme of re-education among Italian prisoners held in India with a view to creating a group who would support the Allied cause against fascism, and at the very least help in the re-democratization of a liberated Italy. Here again, one can see British assumptions about the nature of their Italian captives coming into play. The whole plan was based on the view that most Italians were not committed to fascism and could be 'turned' to the Allies' advantage. In the event, the whole scheme was under-resourced and its objectives invariably sacrificed for more pressing needs such as labour supply. While little of any great value resulted, in part because the Italian surrender in September 1943 removed the need for 're-education', the scheme did represent the first attempt at a new type of political warfare that was to be repeated in future conflicts.

The second case study could not be more different. While much has been written about Japanese atrocities against POWs and civilians during the war in the Far East, most of this has concentrated on officially sponsored or sanctioned actions. While not wishing to diminish the appalling nature of the crimes committed by the Japanese, Charles Roland has chosen to examine a very specific form of war crime, namely the carrying-out of unauthorized medical experiments on Allied POWs by Japanese military personnel who were, or thought of themselves as, medically trained. In effect, he is examining the behaviour of the captors when there are apparently no constraints to their actions. For at least a few Japanese commanders in the field, this opportunity to use live human beings for experimental purposes proved too strong to resist. Some of the cases were brought to trial at the war's end, while others were not. From this limited sample, Roland attempts to make some sense of these crimes, trying to categorize the type of activity involved and unearth the motivation of the perpetrators. An important case study in its own right, this research also provides an insight into the behaviour of some marginal elements within the Japanese medical profession, with obvious potential comparisons with the actions of the SS doctors in the concentration and extermination camps of the Third Reich.

In the Anglo-American historiography, it has been the treatment of Allied prisoners that has been given most of the attention. This concentration on the mainstream experiences of Allied prisoners in captivity has nonetheless tended to marginalize the stories of the many non-white servicemen who fought in the French, United States or British Imperial forces. Given the racial precepts of German Nazi ideology, they were potentially at greater risk than their white counterparts. As David Killingray points out, the death rates among French colonial troops were proportionally much higher than among their metropolitan counterparts. This in itself deserves an explanation, but can be linked with the treatment meted out to British and American black soldiers in German captivity. What emerges is a mixture of indifference and downright malevolence by the Germans towards their non-white captives, a story which is partially mirrored by the behaviour of the Italians in North Africa. This neglect and worse of non-white captives indicates the German and Italian view of them as less important, both to the capturing power and to the governments whom they served. In other words it was assumed, usually quite correctly, that the Allied Powers would protest far more vehemently about mistreatment of white soldiers than of their black comrades in arms. In this respect, the experiences of black troops in captivity bear out MacKenzie's maxim that the protection of prisoners and the proper enforcement of international conventions depended largely on independent monitoring of conditions and the importance attached to specific groups of prisoners by their respective governments. For the most part, black prisoners in Axis hands seem to have fared worse than their white counterparts. In German hands, their experiences fall between the 'correct' handling offered to nearly all captured servicemen,[28] and the total disregard for treaty obligations that obtained on the Eastern Front. Nevertheless, the somewhat unpalatable conclusion is that in so far as these men were protected, that protection derived more from their nationality than from any specific attempts by their masters to plead their case with the German or Italian authorities.

In a totally different context, there are specific elements of the Italian prisoners' experiences in British hands that have been overlooked. Whereas the Maschke Commission devoted two volumes to the German prisoners held by the United Kingdom during and after the war, no similar survey exists for their Mediterranean allies. In many respects the Italian experiences of captivity were very different, not least because their homeland effectively changed sides in 1943, thus theoretically bringing their war with Britain to an end. The fact that the Italians were kept in Britain for three years after the overthrow of Mussolini is the starting-point for Lucio Sponza's assessment. His focus is not on the high politics of the issue, but on the men themselves, looking at their reaction to incarceration and use as a labour force in Britain, both before and specifically after the surrender of the Italian government in September 1943. While commenting on the British government's attempts to keep their Italian prisoners, through the development of the so-called 'co-operator' status for prisoners willing to be used for work outside the terms of the 1929 Geneva Convention, he concentrates primarily on the prisoners' morale and the ways in which they responded to changing political and objective local conditions in the later period of the war and the immediate post-war period. The comments of the captives he cites reinforce the difficulties of generalizing about any group of prisoners and demonstrate quite clearly the complex and often partially informed decisions that they had to make about their futures. Moving beyond the few published memoirs of Italian soldiers held in Britain, he provides a synthesis of what captivity in the United Kingdom was like from the prisoners' point of view, and in so doing, creates an essential counterweight to the 'view from above'.

One area of POW history that *has* produced more than its fair share of literature and myths is the Burma–Thailand Railway. Through a detailed examination of all the available sources, Jane Flower succeeds in demythologizing some of the more persistent fallacies about this most notorious project. While it has been widely accepted that the camps on the railway were not necessarily typical of Japanese treatment of POWs, this chapter demonstrates that conditions varied between different camps along the line. By charting the variations in Japanese behaviour between camps and over time, it is possible to show why certain types of prisoner were more likely to survive than others. Unlike many other works on the subject, this is a well-informed and detailed analysis based on solid primary research that does much to put the record straight about this most emotive of subjects.

Missing until now has been a Japanese perspective on Tokyo's policy towards POWs in the Second World War. In a highly original survey work, Ikuhiko Hata charts the development of Japanese treatment of

POWs from earliest times to the twentieth century. His conclusions are startling, and serve to undermine the beliefs commonly held in the West about Japanese attitudes to captured enemies. For example, it appears that the attitudes to captured Japanese soldiers returned after the Russo-Japanese and Sino-Japanese Wars were largely conditioned by an increasingly militaristic ethos that took pride in victory, and by public opinion. Yet Hata's research shows that treatment was neither consistent nor uniform across the country as a whole. Only in the 1920s and 1930s did the shame attached to being taken prisoner become a social norm shared by the entire community. In these same conflicts of the early twentieth century, the Japanese treatment of captured enemies had been exemplary and the cause for much international comment. However, Hata makes the linkage between the changes in domestic opinion about Japanese POWs and the widely differing attitude adopted towards Allied POWs in the Second World War in comparison with earlier wars. In assessing how this change took place, the article highlights the importance of the version of the Field Service Code in operation in 1941 as embodying the ideas of the military caste and of the moral precepts shared by the community as a whole. Thus it was not only military units who saw surrender as the ultimate humiliation, but even Japanese civilians who committed suicide rather than be captured. Following on from this, Hata makes some observations about the Japanese who did fall into Allied hands, and how they conducted themselves in captivity, again highlighting the contrasts in behaviour between the Japanese and their Allied counterparts.

The final chapter could have served as an introduction, but seems better placed as a postscript, as it directly addresses the effects of POW policies and experiences in the Second World War on subsequent international treaties and legislation, and provides a further commentary on their place in the overall history of POWs in the twentieth century. In summary, Joan Beaumont surveys the post-war developments in the light of the 1939–45 conflict and brings the debate up to date by looking at both the legislative changes and their practical operation in more recent conflicts, concluding with the problems facing the international community in upholding charges of war crimes against soldiers and politicians in the current crisis in the former Yugoslavia. While seeing the very serious problems inherent in this conflict, the conclusions suggest that some progress has been made, both in legislative and attitudinal terms, which makes a return to the excesses of the Second World War less likely. Given the parlous state of the situation in the Balkan region in the summer of 1995, one can only hope that this optimism is borne out by events.

Notes

1. Precise figures are impossible. Chris Cook and John Stevenson, *Longman Handbook of World History since 1914*, London, 1991, p. 50, give an estimate of 77,373,550 for all the belligerent powers in all theatres of war. While the overwhelming majority of service personnel were male, it should be remembered that most armed forces had some women in auxiliary and medical roles and that the Red Army had female service personnel who served in the front line as combat troops.
2. S. P. MacKenzie, 'The Treatment of Prisoners of War in World War II', *Journal of Modern History*, vol. 66, no. 3, 1994, p. 487 cites K. W. Böhme, *Zur Geschichte der deutschen Kriegsgefangenen des Zweiten Weltkrieges*, 15 vols, Munich, 1962–74, vol. 1, part 1, x. MacKenzie also suggests that approximately five million died in captivity.
3. R. A. C. Parker, *The Struggle for Survival: The History of the Second World War*, Oxford, 1989, p. 111.
4. Sarah Fishman, *We Will Wait: Wives of French Prisoners of War, 1940–1945*, New Haven, 1991.
5. A very limited example of such works might include R. Garrett, *P.O.W.*, London, 1981; D. Rolf, *Prisoners of the Reich: Germany's Captives, 1939–45*, London, 1988; M. Kochan, *Prisoners of England*, London, 1980; H. Nelson, *Prisoners of War: Australians under Nippon*, Sydney, 1985; A. K. Powell, *Stark Decency: German Prisoners of War in a New England Village*, Hanover, NH, 1988; Paul Carell and Günther Böddeker, *Die Gefangenen: Leben und Überleben deutscher Soldaten hinter Stacheldraht*, Berlin, 1980; T. Bird, *American POWs of World War II: Forgotten Men Tell Their Stories*, London, 1992; Maxwell Leigh, *Captives Courageous: South African Prisoners of War in World War II*, Johannesburg, 1992; D. G. Dancocks, *In Enemy Hands: Canadian Prisoners of War, 1939–1945*, Edmonton, 1983; Jonathan F. Vance, *Objects of Concern: Canadian Prisoners of War through the Twentieth Century*, Vancouver, 1994.
6. In this context, one thinks primarily of the films *The Wooden Horse*, 1950 or *The Great Escape*, 1963. One should also include the popular American television situation comedy *Hogan's Heroes*.
7. See *The Bridge on the River Kwai*, 1957 and *A Town Like Alice*, 1956 – the American title for the latter film was changed to *The Rape of Malaya*.
8. For this intriguing topic see George Fisher, *Soviet Opposition to Stalin: A Case Study in World War II*, Cambridge, MA, 1952; Catherine

Andreyev, *Vlasov and the Russian Liberation: Soviet Reality and Emigré Theories*, New York, 1987.

9. Erich Maschke (ed.), *Zur Geschichte der deutschen Kriegsgefangenen des Zweiten Weltkrieges*, 15 vols and two supplementary vols, Munich, 1962–74. On the unusual publication and distribution of these volumes, which has allowed conspiracy theorists to claim a cover-up of Allied mistreatment of German POWs, see also Rolf Steininger, 'Some Reflections on the Maschke Commission', in Günter Bischof and Stephen E. Ambrose (eds), *Eisenhower and the German POWs: Facts against Falsehood*, Baton Rouge, LA, 1992, pp. 171–4.

10. Flavio Giovanni Conti, *I prigionieri di guerra italiani*, Bologna, 1986; Romain H. Rainero (ed.), *I prigionieri militari durante la seconda guerra mondiale: aspetti e problemi storici*, Milan, 1985.

11. D. A. Foy, *For You the War Is Over: American Prisoners of War in Nazi Germany*, New York, 1984; E. B. Kerr, *Surrender and Survival: The Experience of American POWs in the Pacific 1941–1945*, New York, 1985.

12. A. Krammer, *Nazi Prisoners of War in America*, New York, 1979; Powell, *Stark Decency* (see Note 5 above); A. Frohn, 'Das Schicksal deutscher Kriegsgefangener in amerikanischen Lagern nach dem Zweiten Weltkrieg', *Historisches Jahrbuch*, vol. 111, 1991, pp. 466–92.

13. G. C. Lewis and J. Mewha, *History of Prisoner of War Utilization by the United States Army, 1776–1945*, Washington, 1955. For a comprehensive update of the American periodical literature on the employment of German POWs in the United States during the Second World War (primarily located in regional and state journals) see James E. Fickle and Donald W. Ellis, 'POWs in the Piney Woods: German Prisoners of War in the Southern Lumber Industry, 1943–45', *Journal of Southern History*, vol. 66, no. 4, 1990, pp. 695–725.

14. A. J. Barker, *Behind Barbed Wire*, London, 1974.

15. Gerald H. Davis, 'Prisoners of War in Twentieth Century Economies', *Journal of Contemporary History*, vol. 12, no. 4, 1977, pp. 623–34.

16. MacKenzie, 'Treatment of Prisoners of War' (see Note 2 above), pp. 487–520.

17. Nikolai Tolstoy, *Victims of Yalta*, London, 1977; idem, *Stalin's Secret War*, London, 1981; idem, *The Minister and the Massacres*, London, 1986, withdrawn from publication. For the claim that some British POWs were abandoned by their government after the Second World War and could still be in the former Soviet Union see Nigel Cawthorne, *The Iron Cage*, London, 1993.

18. Thomas M. Barker, 'A British Variety of Pseudohistory', in Bischof and Ambrose (eds), *Facts against Falsehood* (see Note 9 above), pp. 183–98; Anthony Cowgill, Christopher Brooker and Thomas Brimelow (eds), *The Repatriations for Austria in 1945: The Report of an Inquiry*, 2 vols, London, 1990; Robert Knight, 'Harold Macmillan and the Cossacks: Was there a Klagenfurt Conspiracy?', *Intelligence and National Security*, vol. 1, no. 2, 1986, pp. 234–54.

19. Christian Streit, *Keine Kameraden. Die Wehrmacht und die sowjetischen Kriegsgefangenen 1941–45*, Stuttgart, 1978.

20. Christian Streit, 'The German Armies and the Policies of Genocide' and Jürgen Förster, 'The German Army and the Ideological War against the Soviet Union', in Gerhard Hirschfeld (ed.), *The Policies of Genocide: Jews and Soviet Prisoners of War in Nazi Germany*, London, 1986, pp. 1–14 and 15–29 respectively; Omer Bartov, *The Eastern Front 1941–45, German Troops and the Barbarization of Warfare*, London/New York, 1985–6, and his *Hitler's Army: Soldiers, Nazis and War in the Third Reich*, New York/Oxford, 1991; Theo Schulte, *The German Army and Nazi Policies in Occupied Russia*, Oxford/New York/Munich, 1989; Alfred Streim, *Sowjetische Gefangene in Hitlers Vernichtungskrieg: Berichte und Dokumente, 1941–1945*, Heidelberg, 1982. See also the review by John H. E. Fried, 'The Fate of Soviet POWs in World War II', *Simon Wiesenthal Center Annual*, vol. 5, 1988, pp. 203–25.

21. James Bacque, *Other Losses: An Investigation into the Mass Deaths of German Prisoners of War at the hands of the French and Americans After World War II*, Toronto, 1989.

22. Bischof and Ambrose, *Facts against Falsehood* (see Note 9 above). For a commentary on the debate, see S. P. MacKenzie, 'Essay and Reflection: On the *Other Losses* Debate', *International History Review*, vol. 14, no. 4, 1992, pp. 717–31, and also Frohn, 'Das Schicksal deutscher Kriegsgefangener'; Arthur L. Smith, 'Der geplante Tod?', in Karl Dietrich Bracher, Manfred Funke and Hans-Peter Schwarz (eds), *Deutschland zwischen Krieg und Frieden: Beiträge zur Politik und Kultur im 20.Jahrhundert*, Bonn, 1990.

23. Steininger, 'Maschke Commission' (see Note 9 above), pp. 179–80, notes that at the time of his writing (1992), the International Red Cross Committee's (ICRC) reports on the Allied camps have been closed to researchers, in spite of their having been made available to the members of the Maschke Commission.

24. MacKenzie, 'Essay and Reflection' (see Note 22 above), pp. 730–1. It might be added that the book also has popularity in Germany, where it can cited by those on the right wishing to promote the image of a victimized German Army at the end of the war.

25. Peter Williams and David Wallace, *Unit 731: The Japanese Army's Secret of Secrets*, London, 1989; Sheldon H. Harris, *Factories of Death: Japanese Biological Warfare, 1932–1945, and the American Cover-up*, London, 1994.

26. For example, *The Guardian* of 1 July 1994 reported that more than 22,000 POWs and their widows were suing the Japanese government for £332 million compensation for 'cruel and inhuman treatment' between 1941 and 1945.

27. As ever, there is an exception to the rule, as the Russians and Bolsheviks did attempt re-education programmes of sorts amongst POWs from the Austro-Hungarian empire during the latter stages of the First World War. See Gerald H. Davis, 'The Life of Prisoners of War in Russia, 1914–1921', in Samuel R. Williamson, Jr and Peter Pastor (eds), *Essays on World War I: Origins and Prisoners of War*, New York, 1983, pp. 163–98.

28. The one possible exception here is the German victimization of captured Jewish servicemen from the British and American armed forces. See Mitchell G. Bard, *Forgotten Victims: The Abandonment of Americans in Hitler's Camps*, Oxford, 1994, pp. 71–6.

−1−

Axis Prisoners in Britain during the Second World War: A Comparative Survey

Bob Moore

In spite of being one of the major belligerent powers during the Second World War, the United Kingdom experienced little fighting on its own soil. For the most part, hostilities between British and German forces were confined to the skies above and the seas surrounding the British Isles. As a result, the number of enemy prisoners captured in or around Britain was relatively small, and consisted primarily of aircrew shot down over British soil, and of sailors and merchant mariners landed there by the Royal Navy. In March 1940, it was reported to the House of Commons that the total number of German prisoners held in Britain was a mere 257 officers and men,[1] and figures for mid-1941 suggest that the total captured in or around the United Kingdom was no more than 3,800.[2] This can be contrasted with the position at the end of the war in Europe, when there were 381,632 German and 153,779 Italian prisoners being held in Britain.[3] While this massive increase in numbers can be seen as a natural consequence of Allied success in the war in Europe, it does not explain why so many prisoners were deliberately brought to the United Kingdom. Moreover, a closer examination of the sources demonstrates that this was not by any means a straightforward accumulation, but involved both the export as well as the import of enemy servicemen at different stages of the war.

In order to explain these developments, this chapter surveys the government decisions that shaped the policy towards prisoners of war (POWs) in Britain during the Second World War. Taking as its starting-point the preparations made immediately before the outbreak of war to receive enemy prisoners, it focuses on four particular watersheds, each of which brought substantial changes to the numbers, types and nationalities of prisoner held on mainland Britain. The first major change in policy occurred in the summer of 1940, when the decision was taken to send German POWs, then held in Britain, to the dominions. The second involved the transfer of Italian prisoners taken in the Middle East to the United Kingdom as a labour force from the spring of 1941 onwards. This practice continued unhindered until the end of the war, but was modified by two further crises, which form the third and fourth elements in this analysis. The surrender of the Italian government in September 1943 prompted an Anglo-American debate on the status of captured Italian service personnel in the light of their country's changed allegiances, and the large-scale captures of German servicemen in North-West Europe after June 1944 led to large numbers of these men also being brought to camps on British soil.

I

In the months leading up to the declaration of war, some thought had been given to procedures for the reception and incarceration of POWs. Camps had been designated to receive enemy servicemen, and an inter-departmental meeting involving the Admiralty, Air Ministry, War Office, MI5 and Home Office had been convened on 9 June 1939, primarily to discuss how the interrogation of prisoners was to be carried out. Initially, the Tower of London had been set aside as the central interrogation centre; but it was recognized that this would be too small and could not provide the segregation between officers and men required by the British authorities. As a result, the centre was ultimately moved to Trent Park. It was this meeting's recommendations that formed the basis for a War Office directive sent out on 4 September 1939. This detailed all commands to use regimental depots as collecting points from which prisoners could be transferred to interrogation centres and finally to prisoner-of-war camps.[4] All captured enemy air force, military and naval personnel, together with those caught not wearing uniforms, were to be treated in the same way; but, at this stage, there was no expectation that a war against Germany would produce a large number of prisoners, at least not in the first weeks or months of hostilities.

For the most part, the early months of the war bore out the expectations of the British planners. Appropriate arrangements were made between the British and German governments for the implementation of the Geneva Convention and some subsidiary reciprocal arrangements, all to be overseen by their respective protecting powers, the United States and Switzerland. Enemy servicemen captured in or around the United Kingdom were mainly *Luftwaffe* aircrew, naval personnel or merchant mariners, but their numbers were small. Once they had been interrogated, the prisoners were taken to camps. Two of the earliest were Camp #1 for officers at Grizedale, near Ambleside in the Lake

District, and Camp #2 at Glen Mill, Oldham, Lancashire, where a disused cotton mill was used to house other ranks.[5] Reports on the behaviour of the prisoners at the end of 1939 showed that Grizedale contained fifteen German naval (U-Boat) officers plus some air force personnel, whose conduct was described as 'exemplary ... [and] ... without the slightest sign of defiance'.[6] The commander of Glen Mill camp had rather different problems with his charges. He noted that most of them were young, with 'little or no knowledge of any creed other than that of [the] Nazi-ism of Hitler's regime', and that eradicating this would undoubtedly take a long time. He also evinced a degree of sympathy for the U-Boat crews who had been bombed, but noted that they recovered quickly once they realized that they were going to be treated as human beings.[7] These individual reports seem to bear little or no relation to a Foreign Office memorandum to the War Cabinet on the German prisoners dated 18 December 1939 that described their morale as 'high' and their attitude as 'inclined to be defiant'.[8]

Even allowing for this rather idiosyncratic view, it was not thought likely that POWs would cause too much trouble for the British authorities in general or the War Office in particular. Plans were floated to place stool-pigeons among the prisoners, primarily to elicit information from captives that interrogations had failed to reveal, but also to prevent escapes.[9] While the system for registering enemy captives should have been foolproof, some prisoners did manage to slip through the net. An order reinforcing the requirement to report all captured enemy servicemen noted that one man had managed to spend five weeks in a naval hospital without being noticed.[10] In November 1939, there were no more than 150 POWs (excluding officers) recorded in the United Kingdom, and the number had only increased to 257 in early March 1940. The *Luftwaffe* were not mounting many operations over Britain, and the main source of captives continued to be the war in the Atlantic. Moreover, plans for the British Expeditionary Force (BEF) in France assumed that any prisoners taken on the European mainland would be kept there, rather than be transported across the Channel.[11]

There had been some discussion about the employment of prisoners on work permitted by the Geneva Convention, but, given the numbers involved, this remained at an academic level. Permission was given for inmates at Grizedale to undertake work inside the camp, which suggests that the officers there had been joined by men from the ranks. Things were to change only when British military operations began in earnest in the spring of 1940, and the focus of the war moved to North-West Europe. The end of the phoney war and the first threats to British domestic security prompted the first watershed in the perception of enemy prisoners and changes in their treatment by the authorities.

II

The slow accumulation of *Luftwaffe* and *Kriegsmarine* captives was augmented after the German invasions of Norway and the Low Countries and the fall of France. In the five days before their surrender on 14 May 1940, the Dutch contrived to ship approximately 1,200 German prisoners to Britain. These were mainly parachute troops captured by their armed forces during the abortive German attempt to surround The Hague and capture the Dutch Royal family.[12] Although captured by the Dutch, these men became the responsibility of the British once they had arrived in the United Kingdom. They were supplemented by an indeterminate number of prisoners brought back with Allied troops from Narvik at the end of May,[13] and by those evacuated with the BEF on its retreat from France. Yet even these numbers should not have caused any great problems for the British authorities. Before the outbreak of war, the War Office had earmarked a number of locations for prisoner-of-war camps, but only a few had been employed before the spring of 1940. Even then, there was no great pressure on space, and no apparent reason why the existing policy on the treatment of enemy servicemen needed alteration. Yet in the aftermath of the military defeats in Norway, the Low Countries and France, and under the burgeoning threat of a German invasion of Britain itself, major changes of policy were undertaken which led to large-scale deportation of German prisoners overseas.

To understand how this radical change of policy came about, it is necessary to examine the position of the British government in detail. From the beginning of 1940, anti-alien sentiments had been fuelled by the Rothermere and Beaverbrook presses. In April and May, as the military campaigns in North-West Europe reached their peak, reports of spies and the dangers of a fifth column were placed before the British public. Press demands for government action became more and more strident. While the benefit of hindsight and detailed investigation have shown that these reports and rumours had little validity, there is no doubting their impact at the time. Faced with having to explain a series of military disasters, the newly-formed Churchill government moved inexorably towards the internment of enemy aliens, and then to the removal of these 'dangerous' people overseas.

The story of internment has been well documented elsewhere, but one aspect concerns us here, namely how the German POWs came to be included in the measures taken against civilian enemy aliens, and how internment was transformed into a policy of deportation to the dominions (and specifically to Canada) in the summer of 1940. The decision to intern enemy civilians had been based on several factors, the fear of spies and a fifth column at a time of national crisis, coupled with a virulent press campaign and a new government determined to take some positive action, being the most important. As the scope of the internment policy was widened during the course of May, it soon became apparent that the authorities charged with carrying it out were unprepared for the sheer numbers involved. Many of the internees, rounded up at a few hours' notice, had to be 'housed' in tents or in partially completed council houses. Yet neither this, nor the general fear of internal subversion, can entirely explain why deportation was seen as the only viable alternative. On 24 May, Churchill had expressed himself 'strongly in favour of removing all internees out of the United Kingdom',[14] and this seems to have been the first indication that such a step was being contemplated. Three days later, Belgium surrendered and the War Cabinet were presented with a paper from the Chiefs of Staff indicating what should be done if France were to fall as well. Among its conclusions was that 'the most ruthless action should be taken to eliminate any chances of fifth column activities'. As a result, a new body, the Home Defence (Security) Executive (HD(S)E), was set up under the chairmanship of Viscount Swinton to deal with the whole question of aliens.[15] Its members represented primarily the War Office, MI5 and MI6, and its activities, and indeed its existence, were kept a secret from the public at large, Parliament, and indeed some members of the cabinet itself.

There had been no formal debate in cabinet, nor any official decision to deport the enemy aliens, as, once the issue had been transferred to this secret body, it ceased to be a matter for discussion, and became merely one for execution. The mechanics of transportation and deportation were arranged by the War Office in collusion with MI5, and much of the responsibility for what followed must rest with them. The first mention of POWs' being included in these deportations came with an HD(S)E suggestion that internees and POWs be transferred to islands off the coast; but this was deemed impractical.[16] Nevertheless, this lumping together of both groups was reiterated in the requests sent to the dominions at the end of May. The Canadian government expressed some reservations about housing large numbers of internees, but Viscount Swinton was already talking about the dangers of keeping alien internees *and war prisoners* in the United Kingdom. The pressure was maintained as a series of questions were asked in the House of Commons. On 30 May, MPs Roland Robinson and Henderson Stewart both asked for comment on the dangers of parachutists being dropped in the vicinity of, and then liberating, prisoner-of-war camps. Five days later Stewart made a specific suggestion that prisoners should be removed to Canada.[17] While these questions may well have been 'planted' to allow government spokesmen the chance to use these statements as justification for future actions, they nevertheless served to increase the fears about leaving prisoners in Britain while there was a danger of German invasion. This was also true outside the public domain, where one report from the Metropolitan Police circulated to the War Office purported to show collusion between the nurses at the German Hospital in Dalston and German prisoners held elsewhere in the country. Here the German matron of the hospital was accused of having purchased 'files, fretsaws and hacksaws [and having] despatched them to #13 internment camp at Lingfield, Surrey on the supposed pretence that German sailors needed them to manufacture model galleons'.[18] All these reports and accusations, both public and private, were symptomatic of the links being made between alien civilians and the POWs at the time.

Even before agreement had been reached with the dominions to provide space for the internees and prisoners, the position was complicated still further when the Italians joined the war on 10 June. This led to another wholesale round-up, this time of Italian nationals in Britain, and even more pressure on the authorities to accommodate them all. One further factor, if more was needed to persuade Swinton and the HD(S)E to include prisoners in the deportations, came from the dominions themselves. Both Canada and South Africa expressed reservations about internees, as they had civilian internment problems of their own, but seemed happier to take POWs.[19] One can only surmise that prisoners were easier to deal with and more acceptable because they could be portrayed as tokens of the dominions' participation and success in the war. As has been pointed out in studies of internment, there was a sinister side to this process. Enemy civilians were taken from their homes and placed in the hands of organizations such as MI5 that were neither accountable nor indeed had any official existence, under the control of a governmental committee, the HD(S)E, that was largely unknown and met entirely in secret. The only authority for the deportations seems to have been made explicit by a War Cabinet paper from Neville Chamberlain on 2 July, where he described the steps taken as 'on the direction of the Prime Minister'.[20]

In theory, the prisoners were better protected than their civilian counterparts. Their treatment was governed by the terms of the Geneva Convention and effectively safeguarded by the need for reciprocity in order to protect the interests of British prisoners held by the Germans. However, concern for British prisoners seems to have been overridden in the panic to remove the enemy from the United Kingdom's shores. Although the War Office was represented on the HD(S)E by the director of its Prisoner of War Department, Major-General Sir Alan Hunter, the Foreign Office, which was primarily responsible for the international negotiations on the workings of the Convention, was not. As a result, it was merely asked to comment on the measures being taken. The

Convention stipulated that prisoners could not be moved from the theatre of war in which they were captured, nor could they be exposed to danger in a war zone. While the Foreign Office officials were quite happy that moving captives to Canada could be interpreted as movement within one political unit, namely the British Empire, they were nevertheless fearful that the Germans might retaliate by transferring their British prisoners to (unpleasant places in) Poland.[21] However, the Foreign Office were little more than observers while the deportations were carried out, and had little notice of the first ship to sail, the SS *Duchess of York*, which left Liverpool on 21 June with 500 prisoners and 2,100 internees. The Foreign Office received protests from the Germans via the Swiss protecting power, and complaints from the United States Embassy in Berlin that the measure might well hamper their attempts to protect British nationals in Germany.[22] However, faced with the diktat from above, the diplomats could only try and produce *ex post facto* justifications for the policy. As one Foreign Office official remarked, if the risk had to be taken, at least it could be said that 'we are sending them somewhere where they will be safe from air-raids'.[23]

Given the exigencies of war, it is perhaps not surprising to find the policy of deportation being pursued with such single-mindedness. While these discussions took place, the BEF was being evacuated from Dunkirk and Churchill had made his now famous speech, exhorting the nation to prepare its own defence against the menace across the Channel. At the moment that the first transport set sail from Liverpool, the French were negotiating an armistice with the Germans, leaving Britain isolated. Protecting the interests and safety of British prisoners through reciprocal treatment of Axis prisoners had to be a secondary consideration to the security of the mother country. Only at the margins could there be some amelioration. In order to reassure or placate public opinion at home, it was to be stressed that the movement of prisoners *was* in accordance with the terms of the Geneva Convention. However, consideration was given to the transportation and accommodation of enemy servicemen. For example, it was reported that the POWs on the *Duchess of York* were allocated the best passenger cabins for their voyage to Canada.[24] Moreover, plans to house some prisoners and internees in Newfoundland were abandoned when it became clear that billets would not be ready and that the prisoners might have to spend a winter in tented accommodation.[25]

The outcome of this policy was that, in less than a month, some 1,958 German POWs were transported to Canada on three ships, the steamships *Duchess of York*, *Ettrick* and *Sobieski*. It was perhaps fortunate for the Churchill cabinet and the War Office in particular that a fourth ship, the SS *Arandora Star*, which was sunk by a German torpedo, carried only German merchant seamen and civilian deportees. Nevertheless, the sinking did prompt some discussion in cabinet on 3 July; but there was no apparent dissent to the deportations' being continued, and ministers sanctioned the voyage of the *Ettrick*, due to leave that day with 1,348 prisoners and 1,263 internees on board.[26] In fact, the ship took only 900 prisoners, and, with the *Sobieski* and *Duchess of York*, accounted for the 164 German officers and 1,794 men sent to Canada by the end of July. Thus on 8 August it was recorded that there were only 283 German prisoners remaining in Britain. They consisted of 127 *Luftwaffe*, 78 *Kriegsmarine* and 78 *Wehrmacht* personnel, including at least 11 who were medical staff. These were either recent captures or men who for medical or security reasons could not be sent overseas. While the transports in July 1940 were sufficient to meet immediate needs, the problem would not go away. While the Battle of Britain continued, Anthony Eden as Secretary of State for War reported to the cabinet on 24 September that there were 850 POWs in the country, and the total was increasing at the rate of about 100 a week.[27] Most of these were *Luftwaffe* personnel shot down over Britain and captured U-Boat crews. At this stage, the cabinet agreed to the general policy of sending POWs overseas, a policy that was to remain in force for German servicemen until 1944. The minutes and reports of the Imperial Prisoners-of-War Committee record the periodic shipment of German prisoners to Canada.[28] In March 1942 it was reported that all the prisoners available for transport would have been shipped across the Atlantic by May of that year. Finding space on ships returning to North America had presented no great difficulty; but the provision of guards was more problematic, and only solved when Canadian military personnel returning to the dominion were pressed into service.[29]

The effect of this policy can be seen in the Red Cross reports on the various prisoner-of-war camps designated for Germans. For example, Camp #2 had a designated capacity of 1,500 but contained only 229 NCOs and other ranks when visited in March 1942. In the same month Camp #8 (Oswestry), which could accommodate up to 3,000 men, had only 442 on the premises. Officer camps were similarly underpopulated. In October of the same year Camp #15 (Donaldson's School, Edinburgh), with space for 200, contained only 73 officers and 24 batmen.[30] It seems that as soon as a sufficiently large number of German prisoners had been accumulated in Britain, arrangements were made for their transfer to Canada.[31] The only exceptions were the sick and wounded, and prisoners who were perceived as useful either as possible exchanges for British prisoners in Germany or to the intelligence services. A few Germans who had shown anti-Nazi bias under interrogation were held back, but in order to interrogate these prisoners further without raising the suspicions of their comrades a 'nursing home' was set up at Broughton Rectory towards the end of 1941, where prisoners could be taken in civilian or hospital clothes 'for a rest'.[32] Towards the end of 1940 there had been a proposal that fit prisoners might also be exchanged with the Germans; but this was never seriously considered. At that time, Britain had few prisoners with which to trade, and would in any case be loath to hand back specialist servicemen like submariners. Moreover, as Air Marshal Sir Philip Babbington (Air member for personnel, Air Council) remarked at the time, this would be like having a game of snooker where all the balls were replaced, thus prolonging the game.[33]

It seems that the change in attitude towards German POWs and the measures taken to deport them after the summer of 1940 were predicated and excused entirely on the danger they posed to the security of the British Isles. At this stage, questions of reciprocal treatment for British prisoners in German hands were largely ignored, or at least relegated to secondary importance. Perhaps more important was the marginalization of the Foreign Office from the decision-making process and the effective transfer of control over prisoner-of-war matters from the competent ministries and the War Cabinet to the shadowy Home Defence (Security) Executive.

III

Just as the War Office was ensuring that all its superfluous German POWs were being shipped overseas, plans were being formulated to bring recently captured Italian soldiers into the country. This apparent paradox requires further explanation. Until the last months of 1940, Italian prisoners had not really figured in British military calculations; but all this was to change as the first campaigns were fought in North Africa. At the very beginning of 1941, the Commander-in-Chief, Middle East, General Sir Archibald Wavell, reported that his men had already taken prisoner more than 59,000 Italians and 14,000 Libyan (colonial) troops. His main concern was that he did not have the resources to guard, feed or administer such large numbers. Moreover, their presence in Egypt represented a potential threat to internal political stability.[34] In an attempt to alleviate the situation, Wavell had already begun to ship some Italian officers to India, but he needed War Cabinet sanction for a wider-ranging evacuation policy. In the following months, thousands of prisoners were moved to India, Kenya and South Africa. By August 1941, 120,603 men had been relocated in this way, but a further 77,674 were still in Wavell's hands.

In the meantime, another factor became linked to the problems of finding secure accommodation for POWs. By the end of 1940, labour shortages were becoming apparent in the British economy at a time when the government was insisting on increased targets for manufacturing in general and food supplies in particular.[35] As a result, the Ministry of Agriculture and Fisheries asked the War Cabinet to sanction the employment of 2,000–3,000 North Italian peasants selected from the prisoners taken in Libya to undertake essential drainage, ditching and reclamation work. The scheme was given cautious approval, subject to the agreement of the HD(S)E.[36] This committee stipulated only that the prisoners be kept in large numbers to limit the number of guards required, and away from protected areas. The Secretary of State for War also agreed to the proposal provided that 'the prisoners were carefully selected so that they would not include any violent or Fascist types'.[37] In this way, the first steps were taken towards supplementing the labour supply in Britain with enemy servicemen. Discussions took place with the National Farmers' Union and other trade unions to agree how the scheme would operate.[38] Transportation and accommodation for the initial 2,000–3,000 posed few organizational problems for the authorities; but Sir George Warner at the Foreign Office was at pains to point out the contradiction of bringing Italians *to* Britain only a matter of months after having justified the deportation of German prisoners to Canada on the grounds that they were being taken 'outside the area of hostilities'. The War Office merely replied that the Germans had been removed because they were hostile, and the Italians were being brought in because it was desirable to use them for labour purposes and convenient to remove them from North Africa.[39]

The civil servants at the Ministry of Agriculture based their demand for 2,000–3,000 men primarily on the numbers of prisoners it was thought might be successfully transferred to Britain and accommodated in existing camp facilities. It was only when requests were sent out to the various County War Agricultural Executive Committees that it became apparent that agricultural labour was in much shorter supply than had been thought. The prospect of a new source of labour proved to be an Aladdin's cave to hard-pressed regional committees, and resulted in a total demand for approximately 15,000 labourers.[40] The military were also keen to extend the scheme, suggesting that 15,000–20,000 prisoners 'of the type of good mechanic and workman fairly common among the Italians' might be used to conserve manpower resources at home.[41] In February, Churchill was still worried about the possible security implications of such a step;[42] but by May he had clearly changed his mind. In a memorandum to the War Cabinet secretary, Sir Edward Bridges, he outlined his reasons.

It occurs to me that we must now consider using these Italian white prisoners in Great Britain. A plan was set on foot to bring 2,000 over here for the Ministry of Agriculture. I was not myself attracted by the idea, as it seemed to be on such a small scale but raising all kinds of novel complications. However, it might be better to use these docile Italian prisoners of war instead of bringing in disaffected Irish over whom we have nothing like the same control. It would be worth while to make a plan for bringing in say 25,000 of these Italians, and employing them as an organised mobile body on the land.[43]

Churchill's comments about the disaffected Irish undoubtedly stemmed from the increasing difficulties that Britain had experienced in recruiting labour from this traditional source once the war had begun.

It was not long before Churchill's idea was presented to the War Cabinet by the Lord President, Sir John Anderson, suggesting that a further 25,000 Italians should be brought in from the Middle East at the rate of 5,000 per month.[44] Thus, even before the first Italians had arrived in the country, plans were already in hand to escalate the scheme substantially. From the spring of 1941, the speed with which Italian prisoners were brought to Britain was not to be dictated by demand, which seemed inexhaustible, but by the difficulties of transporting, accommodating and utilizing the manpower within the constraints dictated by security policy. Yet at the same time as more shipments of Italian prisoners were being sanctioned by the War Cabinet, it was also agreeing to send a further 2,000 German prisoners to Canada.[45]

Although the first group of Italians did not arrive until 26 July 1941,[46] there had already been some prior relaxation in the security provisions, as demonstrated by the fact that the first permanent camps were not to be in the north as originally planned, but exclusively in the southern half of England or in Wales.[47] After their arrival, reports at the end of August suggested that the selection process carried out in North Africa had been excellent and that the first group contained 'some very good material', of sound physique and with a willingness to work. While there were agriculturalists among them, few had had any experience with tractors and most had worked exclusively with oxen and ploughs. The remainder were of peasant stock, adept with sickle, scythe and spade, who were thought ideal for ditching and draining work.[48] In effect, the Italians had lived up to the British government's expectations of them as a docile and willing labour force. Within a month, the HD(S)E, which had been so insistent on the deportation of German prisoners, had agreed to relax the conditions on which prisoners worked in agriculture, to the point of allowing small parties of two or three men to work without escorts;[49] and the Minister of Agriculture was soon suggesting that prisoners be billeted on individual farms to overcome the shortage of camp accommodation.[50] A War Office report noted that, by April 1942, 438 prisoners had already been accommodated in hostels 'as an experiment' and that small numbers were being billeted on farmers with a view to extending the scheme during the following summer.[51] Moreover, a meeting held in November 1941 to discuss the employment of Italian prisoners suggested a further 50,000 should be brought to Britain during 1942.[52]

While the British authorities may have been pleased with their newly acquired labour force, conditions for the prisoners were not altogether satisfactory. An International Red Cross report in November 1941 on #4 General Hospital (Italian POWs) noted that there were 4 officers and 121 men as patients, most of whom had recently arrived in the country.

> Their journey took several weeks and took them through varied climates. A great number of those sick are suffering from dysentery and they arrived here in a destitute condition . . . The prisoners from the Middle East were lacking in practically everything and this situation particularly affected the sick, unable to earn money with their fellows in agricultural camps.[53]

If the early shipments of prisoners were carefully screened and selected, something had undoubtedly changed by December of 1942, when 1,316 Italians were sent to the United States, as they were either 'permanently sick, redundant or useless for labour purposes'.[54]

Although the Geneva Convention only allowed the use of prisoner labour in certain types of employment, there remained plenty of scope for disagreements between ministries about their quotas, and for realizing new tasks for which Italian servicemen could be used.[55] Although the difficulties of transporting large numbers of prisoners by sea continued to inform plans for their addition to the British labour supply, it was primarily home demand and available (or planned) accommodation that dictated the precise numbers involved. Pressure to bring in more prisoners continued unabated, and additional demand for 1943 was estimated at around 43,000.[56]

Given the numbers involved, it would be fair to say that Italian prisoner labour contributed to the non-military elements of the British war economy, most notably in agriculture. Their use as replacement for British workers was of major benefit, as was their apparent docility, which removed the necessity for close supervision and made the manpower gains even greater. Neither the supply of prisoners, which showed no signs of abating, nor the availability of shipping were insuperable problems. Indeed, the numbers of prisoners captured in late 1942 and early 1943 reached such levels that even the dominions and India could not be used to accommodate them all, and transports of

Italians captured by the British began to the United States.[57] At the same time that Italians were being widely used for labour and left almost unattended in Britain, the treatment of their German counterparts was heading in almost the opposite direction.

After the Anglo-Canadian raid on Dieppe on 18–19 August 1942, the Germans claimed to have found a British order that sanctioned the tying of prisoners to prevent their destroying documents. This was linked to a British raid on Sark on 3 October the same year, when five German prisoners were tied up in order to expedite their removal from the island.[58] The Germans threatened and then carried out reprisals by shackling British prisoners in their custody, and provoked a similar British response.[59] An International Red Cross report on POW camp #15 dated 15 October 1942 noted that six officers and 74 men were shackled daily between 9.00 a.m. and 9.00 p.m., but that 'this measure in no way affected the morale of these prisoners'.[60] While this tit-for-tat competition had petered out by the early spring of 1943, it was again indicative of the vast differences in treatment being afforded to German and Italian prisoners in Britain.

Other specific reciprocal arrangements with both the German and Italian governments did remain in force, even if there were problems in their negotiation and application. A report in December 1942 from the Prisoners-of-War Department of the Foreign Office noted the general agreements on rates of exchange for the payment of prisoners, and specific accords; with the Germans on the non-use of fortresses for camps, and free messing and appropriate bedlinen for officers, with the Italians on the free issue of tobacco and pay for army nurses. Other matters were considered too vague to require a formal agreement, although discussions on the numbers of postcards and the transmission of drugs in parcels for prisoners had been attempted; but the Foreign Office recorded that, to date, no reply had been received, 'which [was] quite in accordance with Italian methods'.[61] Of more importance were the attempts to implement the conventions on sick and wounded prisoners. The report noted that one exchange had taken place with the Italians in spite of the lack of a formal agreement.[62] On Germany, the conclusions were less encouraging. 'Whether it is necessary or advisable to attempt to record this in a formal agreement seeing that the German government have so far blocked the repatriation of all our sick and wounded I cannot say. Up to the present time, they have not even observed the convention.'[63] Only in 1943 did the situation improve, and the War Cabinet minutes of 18 October recorded the first exchanges of sick and wounded prisoners with the Germans.[64]

IV

The Italian surrender on 8 September was to be the catalyst that transformed the politics and economics of using POWs as labour in Britain. By that time, the British and Americans had accumulated about 450,000 Italian prisoners,[65] and decisions had to be made about their future. There were numerous legal complications created by the changed circumstances, not least the fact that Italy had effectively changed sides. The Geneva Convention made no provision for such an eventuality, and there were conflicting views on how the Italian servicemen captured in the war should be treated. Various possible designations were discussed, but all were ultimately rejected; and attempts to negotiate a formal agreement with the Badoglio government foundered on the Allied insistence that captured Italians would have to remain as prisoners until a formal peace treaty was signed. This impasse merely served to highlight the paradoxical position of personnel originally conscripted into the Italian army. Those recently captured in North Africa were being used for war work; others in Britain were employed in agriculture and other approved tasks; still more were in camps in the dominions; while many of those captured on the Italian mainland had already been paroled by the commander of the European Theatre of Operations, General Dwight D. Eisenhower, and allowed to return home to work in liberated areas. If this was not enough, Italian army units that had not been captured were fighting alongside the Allies against the Germans.

Ultimately, the Allies relied on a verbal agreement between Badoglio and Eisenhower that Italian prisoners in Sicily and North Africa could be used for certain types of war work. These volunteers were organized, first into British units and then as separate Italian service units as pioneer or transport companies.[66] While Badoglio remained intransigent at an official level, it became clear that he was not going to complain about the Allies changing the terms on which Italian prisoners were held. A system was devised where prisoners could opt to become 'co-operators', who would be willing to undertake a much wider range of work in exchange for better conditions.[67]

The War Cabinet also had to deal with the implications of the surrender for Italians already in the United Kingdom. The prisoners were beginning to ask questions, and the government feared that they might become discontented and their willingness to work would be affected. There was no question of an early peace settlement with the Italians, which would have made repatriation mandatory; but Eisenhower's attempts to offer the return of prisoners captured in Tunisia and Sicily in exchange for Allied servicemen held by the Italians was a much greater threat to the use of Italians for labour in Britain. In the event, the Italians were unable to prevent 2,500 of their British prisoners being taken by the Germans, which effectively meant that Eisenhower's offer had lapsed.[68] Nevertheless, it was clear that, with prisoners being paroled inside Italian territory, there was little chance of Eisenhower's agreeing to further large-scale transfers of POWs out of the Middle Eastern theatre. Nevertheless, Churchill remained adamant that the Italians should continue to be used to provide a labour supply.

> Where are the great mass (sic) that we have taken? Over 250,000 were captured by General Wavell alone. It would be rather difficult to move to England, men taken after the armistice who have done their best to help us or have not resisted at all, but we have these larger pools to draw on, and work in the UK is more important than in India or South Africa ... I certainly look forward to getting 100,000 more Italians into England for work purposes during 1944.[69]

Although the Prime Minister saw the difficulty in taking prisoners from the Italian and North African theatres to Britain now that an armistice and surrender had been agreed, he remained happy to countenance the shipment of prisoners from the dominions in order to meet the need for further labour.[70] South Africa was reported to have up to 40,000 prisoners who could be transferred for work in Britain, but, as the planners pointed out, it was not supply, but the lack of accommodation in Britain for prisoner labour that would dictate that only a further 11,000 could be brought in during 1943.[71] This continued to be the main stumbling-block into 1944, when the Lord President, Clement Attlee, reported to the cabinet that the Ministry of Labour thought that a further 250,000 prisoners could be usefully employed in Britain, but that there was only accommodation for 18,000, and then not necessarily where the work existed.[72]

The solution adopted in April 1944 was to offer Italian prisoners in Britain the chance to become 'co-operators', who would be employed in a much wider range of employment, including war work, in exchange for better conditions and other concessions. Those who chose not to co-operate were returned to camps, while co-operators were given greater freedom and financial rewards for their work.[73] This expansion of the use of Italian prisoner labour had advantages for many government departments; but the authorities continued to tread warily. Italian labour was only introduced into new trades with the agreement of the (local) workforce and the trade unions.[74] Although the government tried hard not to upset local opinion or create unnecessary social problems, the scheme did go ahead. By October 1944, there were some 140,000 Italian prisoners in Britain, of whom around 100,000 had volunteered as co-operators and were ultimately allocated to 'user departments'. The increase in total numbers had been governed by the changing war situation. In the build-up to the invasion of north-west Europe, the Ministry of War Transport had found it harder to provide shipping for the prisoners, and the arrival of American troops in Britain had put enormous strain on the availability of suitable accommodation. As a result, there was continued pressure to get the Italians to opt for co-operator status, so that security provisions could be relaxed. Further concessions had been made in August 1944, both to maximize the flexibility of prisoner labour, and to make space for German prisoners in camps.

V

In fact, the use of German POWs for labour purposes had begun in January 1944, when 969 'specially selected' Germans had arrived in Britain for work in agriculture. They were to be deployed in two counties on an experimental basis.[75] Their employment had been sanctioned by the Imperial Prisoners-of-War Committee as early as October 1943, but the summary minutes give no reason for this change of policy.[76] It is possible that this group had been singled out for their anti-Nazi views, as it seems unlikely that they had specialist skills in agriculture that could not be found elsewhere. However, it is more likely that the timing of the decision holds the key. In October 1943, there remained some considerable doubt about the future availability of Italian prisoners. Their removal from the Mediterranean had ceased to be politically expedient, and transfers from other parts of the empire were dependent on Allied shipping. If this first selection of Germans for work in Britain was an experiment, it did not represent a complete change in British thinking. A month after their arrival, the War Office were still arranging the transfer of other German prisoners to Canada.[77] Nevertheless, it could be argued that this represented the initial step towards the assimilation of German POW labour into the British war economy.

This remained the position until the Allied landings in Normandy on 6 June 1944. In the early stages of the campaign, there had been no space or accommodation to house prisoners in France, and they had been shipped across the Channel. This created two related crises. First of all, the authorities were desperately short of suitable camps and guards for these new captives. These could only be found by removing non-cooperating Italian prisoners into other accommodation. However, this could only be achieved if the Italians in question agreed to become co-operators. Appropriate incentives had to be found to make this attractive. At the same time, changing the status of these prisoners would mean that they could be employed on a much wider range of tasks, and this would inevitably denude the Ministry of Agriculture of much needed labour just when the harvest was due to be collected.[78] This in turn raised the question of whether these German incoming prisoners could be used as a labour force.

On 12 July, the War Cabinet discussed the possibility of German prisoners' being used as labour on a more extensive scale.[79] A subsequent report suggested that 17,200 suitably screened prisoners might be employed in Agriculture, Supply and War Transport, with the HD(S)E stipulations that they must always be under guard in groups of twelve or more, and must not include submarine crews or *Luftwaffe* personnel.[80] The scheme was accepted by the War Cabinet and implemented.[81] At this stage, there were still enormous reservations about the possible 'rehabilitation' or over-friendly treatment of German service personnel, as an Admiralty memorandum made clear.

> We must not forget the German initial deliberate aggression against Poland; the reduction of Warsaw and innocent Rotterdam from the air; their submarine warfare against our Merchant ships . . .; their numerous attacks on hospital ships; their devilish treatment of victims in their concentration camps, Jews and otherwise . . . these all being but the commencement of a ghastly list of crimes against the conscience of mankind. Prisoners, there-fore, while being treated not inhumanely, are to be shown very clearly that we regard them, Officers and men, as outcasts to the society of decent men and no friendly gestures whatever are to be made to them.[82]

Nothing was to be done that might increase the arrogance or confidence of the Germans, not least because it might complicate the future occupation of Germany.

If the captured Germans were still considered as pariahs in June 1944, this was to change in the following months. On 29 September, the War Cabinet received a report on the German POWs captured by British forces. They were not only 'being kept in France under extremely unsat-isfactory conditions', but it was also 'impossible to get the French authorities to construct better accommodation and the presence of these prisoners was an embarrassment to our Forces'.[83] To alleviate this embarrassment, it was suggested that the transfer of Italians from South Africa be suspended to make way for these Germans, although the War Cabinet retained the view that they would be more useful destroying military installations in France. Just over a week later, Churchill still attached importance to large numbers of German prisoners' not being brought to the United Kingdom.[84]

Further War Cabinet discussions on 30 November about the con-tinuing labour shortages in Britain centred on the need to use as much POW labour as possible. The employment of Italians was attracting press criticism, not least because the billeting of prisoners in London to carry out essential work in the capital was reputed to be limiting additional accommodation for the civilian population. Attempts were to be made to persuade the press to take a less hostile line. The employment of more Germans was also considered, although it was noted that existing security restrictions effectively made any material expansion of the programme impossible.[85] As a result of this meeting, changes were made to the policy on German prisoners. While it was still considered essential to have France and the United States accommodate as many as possible, a group of 20,000 were to be brought into the country to work in agriculture and forestry. To make this possible, security regulations were to be relaxed in line with suggestions made by HD(S)E. This included the possibility of small gangs of unescorted prisoners working outside the Eastern and London regions.[86]

The Allied advance into Europe only exacerbated the problem. By February 1945, 21 Army Group already had 56,700 German prisoners, but accommodation for only 39,000. The severe overcrowding was liable to be made worse by further captures and by transfers of prisoners from the Americans under the so-called 50:50 agreement.[87] Moreover, diphtheria had broken out in the Low Countries and there were fears that the poor conditions in which prisoners were held would encourage the spread of the disease. At the same time, all available hospital accommodation was being cleared in anticipation of future battlefield casualties as the Allied assault on Germany was pushed home.[88] Such was the severity of the crisis that the Secretary of State for War was prepared to countenance the continuation of the overcrowding in camps in Britain, and the use of tentage during the winter – in contravention of the Geneva Convention.

Until well into 1944, British government policy had been to ship all German prisoners who held extreme Nazi views to the United States or Canada.[89] Since the spring of 1940, they had been perceived as too dangerous to be accommodated in Britain, and it was only in 1944 that substantial numbers were retained in the country. Even then, it took a long time for them to be put to work. A report in November of that year suggested that there were around 100,000 of them in camps who had no work and were likely to become troublesome.[90] However, as has been demonstrated, the decision to bring them to Britain, and then to employ them, was forced on the government, partly as a result of the military successes in France and the Low Countries and the need to be seen to protect enemy prisoners, and partly to meet the burgeoning demand for labour as the war in Europe ended and attention was focused on the Far East. In the short term, the advantages of Italian labour had to be sacrificed to create space to deal with the Germans; but by 1945 the War Cabinet were already considering the effects of a peace treaty with Italy and the demands for repatriation that this would bring. In the longer term, it was widely recognized that the German prisoners would have to replace the Italians as a source of labour in the immediate post-war European world.

As had been the case with the Italians, after the initial experiment of using German prisoners as labour had been run for a few months, it was extended to allow the use of a further 20,000 unescorted Germans in agricultural and forestry work. By March 1945, 66,500 of the 70,000 employable Germans in Britain had been allocated to user departments.[91] This meant that in total there were 220,582 prisoners employed on the British mainland, and when government departments were asked to provide estimates for their needs after the war in Europe was concluded, their combined requirements totalled a staggering 730,000. While the logistics of such a large transfer of manpower were ruled out in the short term,[92] the figures look slightly less out of place when it is realized that the War Cabinet was expecting to be responsible for just over 700,000 German prisoners in Europe at the war's end.[93] In the event, the total demand for labour in Britain was reduced to a more manageable 182,000, although this took no account of the possible repatriation of Italians. After VE Day, restrictions on German prisoners were modified and they were also employed in a wider range of trades and occupations.[94] One might argue that, in spite of the strictures in June 1944 on treating captured Germans as pariahs, their rehabilitation to the point where they could be allowed to work freely and unescorted had been brought about by a combination of factors. On the one hand, the British authorities were anxious that prisoners' conditions should not be allowed to deteriorate below acceptable norms, not least to protect Allied prisoners still in German hands and the reputation of the Allied Powers. At the same time, if this meant bringing Germans to Britain, then further imports of Italian prisoner labour had to be sacrificed in order to bring this about. As a result, whatever the Germans might have done, it was essential that they be considered as a pool of labour that could be used to alleviate shortages.

VI

The story does not, of course, end with the cessation of hostilities in Europe. The use of POWs in Britain continued for some considerable time after 1945, raising a whole new series of international, political and social difficulties.[95] However, an analysis of the treatment of German and Italian prisoners in Britain demonstrates quite clearly that the perception of the captured enemy changed quite radically during the course of the war. From being a danger to security in 1940 and exported at the first opportunity, Italian prisoners were rapidly transformed into a welcome addition to an increasingly hard-pressed British manpower economy. It is clear from government records that the demand for labour throughout the war was always greater than the available supply, but also that POWs were never considered as a major solution to the overall problem, not least because their uses were so limited before the end of 1943.[96] Nevertheless, they did provide a welcome addition to the labour force for the Cinderella departments who were last in line for manpower allocations and the first to be denuded of personnel for the armed forces or essential industries.

Explaining why the Italians were treated so differently from the Germans, especially in the early stages of the war, is more difficult. The fact that the war situation was improving during 1941 as the immediate threat to the British Isles diminished could only have been of marginal importance. Certainly, it seems that the Italians were looked upon in an entirely different light from the Germans. Military reports on the morale and apolitical nature of their captives,[97] together with the sheer numbers involved, may have convinced everyone that it would be possible to find enough labour of 'a politically harmless character' from among them.[98] Even the Home Defence (Security) Executive made few stipulations about the proposed use of Italian prisoners. It is also possible that there was a general, but largely unspoken, feeling that the Italian character was entirely different from the German, and even that Italian Fascism was somehow different from Nazism. Comments about the Italians' usefulness and docility abound, although little contemporary empirical evidence was given in support of these views. Another clue comes from the Ministry of Agriculture and Fisheries. A report on the employment of POWs and enemy aliens during the First World War, circulated in November 1939, leads to the conclusion that the treatment of the Italians was the more normal precedent. During that conflict, prisoners had been allowed to volunteer for work in order to prevent 'idleness and unrest'. The conclusion of this report could easily double as a summary of what happened to the Italians in Britain during the Second World War.

> . . . the conditions under which the men were guarded became progressively more lax. This was due to the difficulty of providing guards, the constantly diminishing objections in the country to the employment of prisoners, the recognition that they were harmless and, as a rule, good workers – skilled agriculturalists were chosen as far as possible – and the increasing demand for their labour. Speaking generally, prisoners were guarded very lightly, if at all, when actually at work.[99]

Over time, the behaviour of the prisoners bore out British prejudices about the Italians as being docile and largely uncommitted to fascism. Between 1941 and 1943, the authorities felt their way towards a more liberal treatment of their charges, until the Italian surrender created a crisis that threatened their continued use as a labour force. The availability of transportation, guards and accommodation, as well as relations with local labour and trade unions, all served to limit the numbers involved. Undoubtedly the British government would have been happier to have continued to import Italian prisoner labour until the end of the war, but events in north-west Europe made it essential to replace the planned import of more Italians with Germans – with the result that a reappraisal of possible uses for German prisoners had to take place, albeit only in the final months of the war. Clearly, the course of the war had an effect on the way in which prisoners of war were perceived and used by the British government; but it remains difficult to escape the conclusion that their usefulness as a limited labour force in Britain did much to shape the policies adopted towards them, their governments and the international treaties and agreements that ensured their protection.

Notes

An earlier and shorter version of this chapter appears as 'Turning Liabilities into Assets: British Government Policy towards German and Italian Prisoners-of-War during World War II', conference paper presented at the Australian Defence Force Academy, Canberra, 12–13 May 1994.

1. Sir Victor Warrender MP, Financial Secretary to the War Office, in answer to a question from George Strauss MP, *Hansard*, House of Commons, fifth series (1939–40), vol. 358, col. 824, 8 Mar. 1940.
2. Public Record Office (hereafter PRO), Admiralty Papers (hereafter ADM), ADM 1/11640, statement on POWs by V. G. F. Bovenizer, War Office, 8 June 1941.
3. PRO, War Office Papers (hereafter WO), WO 32/9890, Imperial Prisoners of War Committee (IPOWC) report, sections 13 and 15, May 1945.
4. PRO, ADM 1/10579, War Office to all Commands, 4 Sept. 1939.

5. H. Wolff, *Die deutschen Kriegsgefangenen in britischer Hand: Ein Überblick*, Munich, 1974, pp. 3–4, 126–31. Glen Mill did not retain the #2. It was later designated as ETO PWE #3 and used as a transit camp for POWs who were transported to the US, and in 1944 handed back to the British authorities, who renumbered it as Camp #176.

6. PRO, ADM 1/10069, F. R. Cobb, Commander Camp #1, Grizedale, to Colonel Trench, Intelligence Division, Naval Staff, 25 Dec. 1939.

7. Ibid., H. A. Dennison, Commander #2 POW Camp, Glen Mill, Oldham, to Trench, 26 Dec. 1939.

8. Ibid., memo. by the Secretary of State for Foreign Affairs, 'German Prisoners of War in Great Britain', 18 Dec. 1939. Also see PRO, Cabinet Office Papers (hereafter CAB) CAB 67/3, WP(G)(39)157, memo. prepared by Sir Campbell Stuart's department, 18 Dec. 1939.

9. PRO, ADM 1/10069, memo. by John H. Godfrey, Director of Naval Intelligence, to Winston Churchill, First Sea Lord, 31 Dec. 1939. This policy was never very extensive, and only four stool-pigeons had been fully trained by the end of 1940: F. H. Hinsley, *British Intelligence in the Second World War: Its Influence on Strategy and Operations*, vol. 1, London, 1979, pp. 282–3.

10. PRO, ADM 1/10579, order no.3769 NL4062/39, 7 Dec. 1939.

11. PRO, Ministry of Agriculture and Fisheries (hereafter MAF), MAF 47/54, employment of POWs, agenda for meeting on 21 Nov. 1939.

12. Louis de Jong, *Het Koninkrijk der Nederlanden in de Tweede Wereldoorlog*, vol. 3, The Hague, 1970, p. 402.

13. Peter and Leni Gillman, *Collar the Lot! How Britain Interned and Expelled its Wartime Refugees*, London, 1980, p. 189.

14. PRO, CAB 65/7, WM137(40)11, 24 May 1940.

15. Gillman, *Collar the Lot!* (see Note 13 above), p. 141, cites CAB 66/7, WP(40)168, 'British Strategy in a Certain Eventuality', 25 May 1940 and CAB 65/13, WM141(40)9, confidential annexe, 27 May 1940.

16. Hinsley, *British Intelligence* (see Note 9 above), vol. 4, London, 1990, pp. 53–4.

17. PRO, Foreign Office Papers (hereafter FO), FO 916/2580, House of Commons questions from Roland Robinson MP and James Henderson Stewart MP, 30 May 1940 and then from Stewart again on 4 June 1940. See also, question from John Parker MP to Richard Law, *Hansard*, House of Commons, fifth series (1939–40), vol. 361, col. 392, 30 May 1940. Question from W. F. Higgs MP to Anthony Eden, 4 June 1940 and question from Henderson Stewart MP to Geoffrey Shakespeare MP, Parliamentary Under-Secretary

for Dominions Affairs, ibid. (1939–40), vol. 361, cols 751–2, 4 June 1940.

18. PRO, FO 916/2580, Metropolitan Police report, G Division, Islington station, 29 May 1940.

19. The Canadian government had thought of offering space for German POWs in February 1940, but had not pursued the idea: National Archives of Canada, Department of National Defence Papers, RG 24, vol. 6585, FD1, Dr E. H. Coleman, Under-Secretary of State, to Dr O. D. Skelton, Under-Secretary of State for External Affairs, 28 Feb. 1940; PRO, FO 916/2580, United Kingdom High Commissioner for Canada to Foreign Office, 6 June 1940, and to Viscount Caldecote (Dominions Office) 10 and 11 June 1940; Under-Secretary of State, Dominions Office to United Kingdom High Commission for Canada, 7 June 1940; Government of the Commonwealth of Australia to Dominions Office, 16 June 1940; United Kingdom High Commission for South Africa to Dominions Office, 17 June 1940.

20. PRO, CAB 67/7, WP(40)(G)170, memo. by the Lord President, Neville Chamberlain, 'Internees and Prisoners-of-War', 2 July 1940.

21. PRO, FO 916/2580, marginal notes by Harold Farquhar and H. W. Malkins of Foreign Office, 17–18 June 1940, which expounded the Foreign Office view that articles 25 and 26 of the Geneva Convention did not preclude the movement of prisoners within the Empire. Sir George Warner to C. W. Dixon, Dominions Office, 20 June 1940 on exposing prisoners in a war zone and note by Dixon, 26 June 1940 on the problems of retaliation if Britain sent prisoners to 'unpleasant spots in semi-tropical or sub-arctic regions'. Gillman, *Collar the Lot!* (see Note 13 above), p. 165 quotes Sir George Warner, also from FO 916/2580.

22. PRO, FO 916/2580, German Legation, Berne, to Foreign Office (via protecting power), 24 June 1940; US Embassy, London, to Foreign Office, 28 June 1940.

23. Ibid., memo. by D. J. M. D. Scott of Foreign Office, 15 June 1940.

24. Gillman, *Collar the Lot!* (see Note 13 above), p. 169.

25. PRO, FO 916/2580, memo. by P. J. Dixon, 1 July 1940; Gerhard P. Bassler, *Sanctuary Denied: Refugees from the Third Reich and Newfoundland Immigration Policy*, St John's, Nfld., 1992, pp. 163–7.

26. PRO, CAB 66/7, WP(40)(G)170, memo. by Lord President, 2 July 1940. The discussion noted that the voyage would be unescorted, CAB 65/8, WM192(40)12, 3 July 1940; but Gillman, *Collar the Lot!* (see Note 13 above), p. 204, suggests that the ship had a destroyer escort for the first thirty-six hours.

27. PRO, CAB 65/9, WM257(40)7, 24 Sept. 1940.
28. For example, PRO, WO 32/9890, IPOWC minutes, summary #3, Aug. 1941, notes cabinet approval for the transfer of a further 2,000 Germans to Canada; IPOWC minutes, summary #10, Mar. 1942, notes transfer of 216 German officers and 773 other ranks to Canada.
29. Ibid., IPOWC minutes, summary #10, Mar. 1942.
30. PRO, FO 916/308, International Committee of the Red Cross (ICRC) reports for Camp #2, 9 Mar. 1942, Camp #8, 10 Mar. 1942 and Camp #15, 18 Mar. 1942. All signed by ICRC delegate R. A. Haccius; Wolff, *Kriegsgefangenen* (see Note 5 above), p. 126.
31. See, for example, PRO, WO 32/9890, IPOWC minutes, summary #3, Aug. 1941, which recorded a War Cabinet decision to transfer another 2,000 Germans to Canada.
32. PRO, WO 208/3442, Colonel W. Sinclair to Brigadier G. H. Brooks, n.d.; Brooks to Valentine Williams, 30 June 1941.
33. PRO, ADM 1/11116, Air Marshal Sir Philip Babbington to Admiral Sir Charles J. C. Little, 24 Dec. 1940; memo. by Little, 2 Jan. 1941. See also FO 916/161, Foreign Office memo., 17 Feb. 1941.
34. PRO, Colonial Office Papers (hereafter CO), CO 968/45/1, C.-in-C. Middle East to War Office, 7 Jan. 1941.
35. PRO, CAB 118/65, PX(40)68, interim report by Manpower Requirements Committee, 8 Nov. 1940; MAF 47/54, R. Hudson, Minister of Agriculture, to Rt Hon. David Margesson MP, Secretary of State for War, 8 Jan. 1941.
36. PRO, CAB 67/9, WP(G)(41)6, memo. by Minister of Agriculture entitled, 'Italian Prisoners of War for Land Reclamation Work', 13 Jan. 1941; CAB 65/17, WM7(41)8, 16 Jan. 1941.
37. PRO, MAF 47/54, marginal index notes on attitudes of Secretary of State for War and Home Defence (Security) Executive.
38. Ibid., R. E. Stanley, Secretary of Agricultural Wages Board, Ministry of Agriculture, to H. J. Johns, Assistant Secretary, Man Power Division, Ministry of Agriculture, 5 Feb. 1941. The money would be paid to the War Office to offset the costs of paying and housing the prisoners. Also see memo. on meeting with NFU and other unions, 5 Feb. 1941.
39. H. Parkin, 'British Policy towards Italian Prisoners-of-War in Great Britain', unpublished BA (Hons) Humanities dissertation, Bristol Polytechnic, 1989, p. 8, cites FO 916/170, memo. by Sir G. Warner, 12 Feb. 1941.
40. PRO, MAF 47/54, Hudson to Margesson, 8 Jan. 1941. Notes on discussions with County War Agricultural Executive Committees, Feb. 1941; PRO, WO 199/405, Captain R. Fullerton, notes on a

meeting on the employment of Italian POWs in the United Kingdom at Hobart House, 12 Feb. 1941. Minutes of above meeting contained in MAF 47/54.

41. PRO, Prime Minister's Office Papers (hereafter PREM), PREM 3/363/1, Sir Desmond Morton, personal assistant to the prime minister, to Churchill, 24 Feb. 1941.

42. Ibid., Churchill to Sir Edward Bridges, Permanent Secretary of the Cabinet Office and Secretary of the War Cabinet, 28 Feb. 1941.

43. Ibid., 29 May 1941.

44. PRO, CAB 66/16, WP(41)120, 4 June 1941; CAB 65/17, WM7 (41)8, 16 Jan. 1941; CAB 65/18, WM57(41)8, 5 June 1941; CAB 123/136, War Office progress report on the transfer of POWs from the Middle East to the United Kingdom for labour purposes, 29 Apr. 1942.

45. PRO, CAB 67/9, WP(41)(G)75, memo. by Secretary of State for War entitled, 'Transfer of German Prisoners of War to Canada', 8 Aug. 1941; CAB 65/19, WM79(41)3, 11 Aug. 1941.

46. PRO, WO 165/59, IPOWC minutes, summary #2, July 1941.

47. PRO, MAF 47/54, War Office to W. C. Tame, Man Power Division, Ministry of Agriculture, 19 June 1941.

48. Ibid., report by A. Carr Williams, Man Power Division, to Labour Supply Branch, Ministry of Agriculture, 12 Aug. 1941.

49. PRO, WO 165/59, IPOWC minutes, summary #5, Oct. 1941; MAF 47/54, memo. by Johns, 25 Sept. 1941.

50. PRO, MAF 47/54, Hudson to Margesson, 28 Oct. 1941.

51. PRO, CAB 123/136, progress report on the transfer of POWs, 29 Apr. 1942.

52. Ibid., draft memo. to War Cabinet, 28 Nov. 1941.

53. PRO, FO 916/308, report signed by Haccius, ICRC, on #4 General Hospital (Italian POWs), 19 Nov. 1941.

54. PRO, WO 32/9890, IPOWC minutes, summary #19, Dec. 1942.

55. PRO, CAB 123/136, W. S. Morrison to Sir John Anderson, 1 July 1941; Board of Trade to Anderson, 6 Oct. 1941.

56. PRO, MAF 47/54, memo., 'Italian Prisoners of War: 1943 Programme – for meeting on 2 Dec. 1942', 30 Nov. 1942; memo. by Minister of Works and Planning, 14 Jan. 1943.

57. PRO, PREM 3/364/7, Lieutenant-Colonel L. C. Hollis, Senior Assistant Secretary (Military) to the Cabinet, to Churchill, 24 Apr. 1942, records the likelihood that the United States would agree to accommodate German and Italian prisoners taken by the British.

58. For a fuller version of the raid, see Charles Cruikshank, *The German Occupation of the Channel Islands: The Official History of the Occupation Years*, 7th edn, Channel Islands, 1988, pp. 240–1.

59. PRO, CAB 65/28, WM136(42)2, 8 Oct. 1942; WM137(42)1, 9 Oct. 1942; WM139(42)1, 12 Oct. 1942; WM140(42)2, 13 Oct. 1942; WM168(42)7, 14 Dec. 1942; CAB 65/33, WM33(43)3, 22 Feb. 1943. German POWs held by the Canadians were also included, see Cruikshank, *Channel Islands* (see Note 58 above), pp. 241–2.

60. PRO, FO 916/308, report by Haccius on visit to POW Camp #15 despatched by M. de Pourtalès on 15 Oct. 1942.

61. PRO, FO 916/271, draft agreements with Germany and Italy on POW treatment: Geneva Convention/Sick and Wounded Convention, POW Department, Foreign Office, 16 Dec. 1942, initialled by Sir Harold Satow. For compilation of lists of special agreements reached concerning the treatment of POWs with the German and Italian Governments, n.d., see FO 916/556.

62. In April 1942, 129 British sick and wounded were exchanged for 919 Italians in Smyrna Harbour under the auspices of the ICRC and Turkish military authorities. A. J. Barker, *Behind Barbed Wire*, London, 1974, p. 181. For a complete summary of the negotiations, see Sir Harold Satow and M. J. Sée, *The Work of the Prisoners of War Department during the Second World War*, London, 1950, pp. 57–8. This semi-official publication was found in the Canadian Department of National Defence Archive in Ottawa.

63. PRO, FO 916/271, draft version of report on special agreements with Germany and Italy on POW treatment initialled by Satow, 16 Dec. 1942.

64. PRO, CAB 65/36, WM142(43)4, 18 Oct. 1943; Satow and Sée, *Prisoners of War Department* (see Note 62 above), pp. 50–5.

65. C. R. S. Harris, *Allied Military Administration of Italy, 1943–1945*, London, 1957, p. 151. PRO, PREM 3/364/2, Resident Minister in Algiers to Foreign Office, 5 Feb. 1944, quotes the Italian government figure of around 27,000 officers and 420,000 NCOs and men. A table in PREM 3/364/2 gives a total of 556,780 prisoners, but this may have included a large number of Italian colonial troops.

66. For the development and extent of this use of Italian labour by the British Army see CAB 106/452, 'Report on Italian Co-operators and GHQ 2nd Echelon in the Mediterranean Theatres', n.d. [1945].

67. Harris, *Administration of Italy* (see Note 65 above), pp. 152–3. PRO, ADM 116/5182, Foreign Office to Washington Embassy, 8 Apr. 1944.

68. PRO, CAB 66/40, WP(43)392, memo. by Lord President on Italian POWs, 17 Sept. 1943.

69. PRO, PREM 3/364/2, Churchill to Lord President of the Council, 16 Sept. 1943.

70. Ibid., Churchill to Eden, 29 Sept. 1943; Churchill to Foreign Office, 13 Oct. 1943.

71. PRO, PREM 3/364/2, W. L. Gorell Barnes to General E. C. Gepp, Directorate of Prisoners of War, War Office, 14 Oct. 1943.

72. PRO, CAB 66/45, WP(44)36, memo. by Lord President, C. R. Attlee, 18 Jan. 1944.

73. PRO, WO 32/11123, War Office note, 9 May 1944.

74. PRO, Board of Trade Papers (hereafter BT), BT 168/84, Committee for the Allocation of Prisoners of War, 19th meeting, 6 Nov. 1944.

75. PRO, MAF 47/54, ministry memo. to County War Agricultural Executive committees in England and Wales on agricultural labour in 1944, 25 Feb. 1944.

76. PRO, WO 32/9890, IPOWC minutes, summary #29, Oct. 1943 and summary #32, Jan. 1944.

77. Ibid., summary #33, Feb. 1944.

78. PRO, PREM 3/364/13, WP(44)421, memo. by Ernest Bevin, Minister of Labour and National Service, 'Employment of German and Italian Prisoners-of-War', 31 July 1944.

79. PRO, CAB 65/43, WM90(44)1, 12 July 1944.

80. PRO, PREM 3/364/13, memo. by Bevin, 31 July 1944.

81. PRO, CAB 65/43, WM101(44)3, 4 Aug. 1944; Wolff, *Kriegsgefangenen* (see Note 5 above), pp. 12, 27, 55.

82. PRO, ADM 1/16898, Flag Officer-in-Charge, Harwich, to C.-in-C., The Nore, 20 June 1944; Admiralty memo. 'German Prisoners of War', n.d. (June 1944).

83. PRO, CAB 65/43, WM129(44)5, 29 Sept. 1944.

84. PRO, CAB 65/44, WM147(44)3, 7 Nov. 1944.

85. Ibid., WM160(44)5, 30 Nov. 1944; CAB 66/58, WP(44)687, 'Transfer of Italian Prisoners to this country and increased employment of German Prisoners', 24 Nov. 1944; PREM 3/364/13, memo. on the above by Bridges, 30 Nov. 1944.

86. PRO, BT 168/84, 'Employment of German Prisoners of War', minute 6, 18th meeting, 13 Oct. 1944; Ministry of Production memo.: Prisoners of War, 30 Sept. 1945.

87. This agreement between the two Western allied powers involved dividing all captured service personnel equally, irrespective of the forces to whom they had surrendered. Wolff, *Kriegsgefangenen* (see Note 5 above), pp. 15–16.

88. PRO, CAB 66/61, WP(45)89, 'Disposal of Prisoners of War captured in North-West Europe', memo. by the Secretary of State for War, 10 Feb. 1945.

89. The locations of British-captured German prisoners are listed ibid. as 36,000 in the Middle East, 34,000 in Canada and 130,000 in the United States.

90. PRO, BT 168/84, memo. A. V. Judges, Ministry of Labour and National Service, to Hudson, 3 Nov. 1944; Wolff, *Kriegsgefangenen* (see Note 5 above), pp. 20–1, gives figures of 90,000 for the end of Sept. and 144,450 for the end of Dec. 1944.

91. PRO, BT 168/85, memo. on POWs by Ministry of Production, 30 Sept. 1945. Wolff, *Kriegsgefangenen* (see Note 5 above), p. 55, gives figures taken from *Hansard* that suggest that there were 66,000 German prisoners actually working in agriculture and 1,000 in other occupations by May 1945.

92. PRO, CAB 66/65, WP(45)292, 'Employment of German Prisoners of War outside Germany after the cessation of hostilities in Europe', memo. by the Secretary of State for War, 10 May 1945.

93. PRO, CAB 66/61, WP(45)89, 10 Feb. 1945.

94. PRO, BT 168/85, memo. of 30 Sept. 1945.

95. Although written before the opening of British government papers, Wolff, *Kriegsgefangenen* (see Note 5 above), pp. 25–68, sheds a good deal of light on the use of prisoners after the surrender in May 1945.

96. The Ministry of Labour reports to the Cabinet contain only two mentions of POW labour between 1941 and the end of 1943. See PREM 4/54/1, report of manpower mid-1942, survey by Ministry of Labour and National Service and PREM 4/54/2, memo. by Lord President, 27 Oct. 1941.

97. See, for example, FO 371/29920/R 23, C.-in-C. Middle East to War Office, 13 and 27 Jan. 1941.

98. PRO, FO 916/170, War Office to South African Chief of General Staff, Pretoria, 29 Aug. 1941.

99. PRO, MAF 47/54, 'Employment of Prisoners of War and Enemy Aliens', n.d.

'Blind Bureaucracy': The British Government and POWs in German Captivity, 1939–45

David Rolf

In common with many adjustments necessary in the transition from peace to war in the winter of 1939–40, the British government's tardy realization of new realities precluded any genuine thought about what it might do if faced with large numbers of its subjects in enemy hands. There had, in fact, been adequate warnings in the First World War, when petty squabbles between the Foreign Office, War Office and Admiralty had caused much public concern over who precisely was responsible for safeguarding the interests of British POWs in German captivity. The confusions associated with four Ministers of the Crown answering questions about POWs, and the refusal of the Foreign Office to have anything more to do with policy concerning them in 1916, forced the Home Secretary, Sir Herbert Samuel, to set up an Interdepartmental Committee in October of that year under the Assistant Under-Secretary of State for Foreign Affairs, Lord Newton. He took charge, thereafter, of a new Department of Prisoners of War independent of the Foreign Office. From February 1915 there was also a Directorate of POWs (DPW) at the War Office under Lieutenant-General Sir Herbert Belfield. Subsequently, this was responsible for almost all matters affecting British POWs, while Lord Newton's department dealt only with the transmission of communications about them to foreign embassies and answered questions in the House of Commons through the Treasurer of the Household, Captain J. F. Hope. Unfortunately, as Prime Minister Asquith observed: 'The question of prisoners [of war] is a complicated one, which, from the nature of the case, cannot be confined to one Department', and these arrangements failed completely to assuage public fears, so that the problem continued to fester until 1918.[1]

Yet, when Britain once more found herself at war in 1939, many of the same problems had to be solved all over again – and all in response to an unyielding and vicious regime that proved itself more than capable of using the lives of POWs as mere bargaining pawns whenever it conceived an advantage might be gained. At first, the responsibility for dealing with enemy POWs and the welfare of Britain's own POWs was that of the Secretary of State for War, Leslie Hore Belisha. A special section (AG3(b) – later AG3(c)) – was created in the Adjutant General's Department under a Director of Personnel Services.

This was an office *ad hoc* by nature, without any real power. While the fate of its own prisoners in enemy hands was necessarily a matter of grave concern to the British government – especially if they were maltreated – there were so few of them during the 'Phoney War' that the subject was not one that bothered Whitehall. Despite the fact that their well-being involved political as well as humanitarian considerations, there was only a muddled and hesitant approach to their welfare and, as Sir Harold Satow, at various times Head of the Foreign Office's POW Department, later remarked: '. . . it would have made the task easier . . . if from the outset it had been realised, both in the Foreign Office and in the War Office, that the protection of prisoners of war was a matter which would require continuous effort. The War Office was, like the Foreign Office, lacking in imagination . . .'.[2]

A total lack of urgency over POW matters was confirmed by Satow's predecessor, Sir F. M. Sheppard, who commented exasperatedly in February 1940. 'History seems to be repeating itself', he reflected, as he read a copy of the Belfield Report, which he found 'interesting and instructive' on similar experiences between 1914 and 1918.[3] In terms of getting immediate help to British POWs at this early stage of hostilities, the War Organization of the British Red Cross Society and Order of St John of Jerusalem (BRC & StJJ) had been nominated by His Majesty's Government as the only authorized body for sending assistance. However, little had been done to ascertain whether it lay in their power to do so.[4]

For a while this hardly mattered, since even the Germans had little idea what to do with Squadron Leader S. S. Murray and Pilot Officer A. B. Thompson, who survived after being shot down the day after war was declared while attacking German warships in their North Sea bases. They were interned like civilians until joined by a small band of aircrew, who were eventually sent to an ancient fortress at Spangenberg, standing guard over the old highway from Thuringia to the Main and Rhine.

Only when the mass internment of enemy aliens at a few days' notice was ordered on 12 May 1940, and the disastrous loss of the greater part of the British Expeditionary Force resulted in thousands of British prisoners trudging towards hastily assembled prison camps in Germany and

Poland, did the issue become a pressing one for the British government. The first reaction was to establish a Directorate of Prisoners of War (DPW) at the War Office on 25 May 1940, and to bring out of retirement Major-General Sir Alan Hunter to serve as its director some three weeks later. At the same time, responsibility for civilian internees was switched to the Home Office.[5] By the autumn of 1941 the DPW had assumed all the trappings of a major bureaucratic machine, with three official branches (PW3 dealt with the welfare of British POWs) that had also spawned three unofficial ones.

Not all the problems in coming to terms with the needs of British POWs can be assigned to the slowness with which the DPW operated. Since the responsibility for them could not be pigeonholed neatly into any single department but cut across numerous Whitehall boundaries there was much scope for muddle and some vicious internecine departmental warfare. Nevertheless, the creation of an inter-departmental POW Co-ordinating Committee in order to bring some semblance of order within Whitehall to the treatment of POW matters was long delayed.

The natural result was much confusion in such a basic requirement as notifying anxious relatives that a husband or son had been taken prisoner. Since it suited their own needs, the German authorities were generally careful about this except when the sheer numbers of captives overloaded their administrative arrangements, or, of course, in cases where atrocities were committed against newly-surrendered prisoners.[6] They provided periodically, at least until the latter stages of the war, a list of British POWs and dead combatants through the *Wehrmachtsaus-kunftstelle für Kriegsverluste und Kreigsgefangene* (Army Information Office for Casualties and POWS), which forwarded three copies. One set went to the Foreign Office Information Bureau in London – which had been set up specifically to deal with *enemy* POWs in British hands – another to the International Committee of the Red Cross (ICRC) at Geneva and a third to the Swiss as the Protecting Power.[7] The Bureau then passed on the information to the Casualty Branch of the War Office's DPW and the POW Department of the Foreign Office, and also sent lists to the BRC & StJJ. The result was much delay and confusion between the Foreign and War Offices, especially since the Bureau was clearly overstretched in being saddled with 'a task which was certainly outside its province, but which, unsought, had been thrust upon it'.[8] This had occurred despite official arrangements in force from 11 October 1940, whereby all work based on lists of British POWs was to be centred on the War Office's DPW at Hobart House. Moreover, as General Hunter observed, it was 'an irony of fate' – or sheer incompetence – that, since there was no one with any knowledge of French or

German within Section PW3 of the DPW, all documents received from the ICRC containing French and German expressions had to be submitted back to the Foreign Office's POW Department for translation.

The net result, especially in the early months of the war, was that news of individuals often filtered home more rapidly through unofficial than official channels. Somewhere in Belgium on the long march into captivity during the cloudless summer of 1940, Private Bowers managed to slip several hastily scribbled messages to Red Cross nurses. These missives eventually reached home, long before his mother received formal notification that he was a POW. 'She had received the official telegram to say I was missing', he wrote, '[and] took them to some official in St. James's [Palace] . . . There she was told to ignore them as they were probably forgeries and that our Regiment wasn't in France anyway. Blind bureaucracy of course.'[9]

Naturally enough, both the War Office and British Red Cross had to treat unofficial reports about POWs very cautiously; but the fact that next of kin often received news of POWs before the official organizations got round to informing them was considered a small triumph in the War Office. At least 'it means that the arrangements in the enemy country for censoring the mailing prisoner's correspondence are working satisfactorily', concluded a War Office spokesman in November 1941.[10] The inference here was that since censoring was taking place, then POWs' mail *was* being processed by the German authorities and the reciprocal scheme for prisoners to contact home, however imperfect and liable to sudden delays, was working.

By then other matters had been sorted out, though not before General Hunter had repeatedly attempted to disentangle the work of his own DPW – and especially that of PW3 – from the Foreign Office's POW Department. As he commented ruefully to his opposite number at the Foreign Office, 'I shall not be here if there is another war. But if it comes, I hope that the Department of my successor will have a more explicit title.'[11]

Since matters had not been thought through at any length, the somewhat cavalier way in which the government shuffled off part of its responsibilities to the BRC & StJJ without first ascertaining that those obligations could be met led to dissatisfaction among the general public even before Hunter was appointed; unfortunately for him, he was caught up in the resulting protests.[12] As early as February 1940, it was becoming clear that existing voluntary and charitable efforts would not be enough to cope with the demands posed by British POWs, and that government assistance would have to be provided.

Matters came to a head in the autumn when, consequent upon a great influx of British prisoners into camps and the closure of routes for relief through France and the Low Countries, the system for supplying them with food and clothing parcels nearly collapsed. A series of highly critical articles in the national press, especially in the *Sunday Express*, coupled with a vociferous campaign by Mrs W. Coombe Tennant – whose own son, Captain A. H. S. Coombe Tennant, Welsh Guards, was incarcerated in Oflag VIB – bitterly criticized the Red Cross and St John War Organization and the lack of governmental supervision.

Supporting her campaign with telling evidence from POWs themselves, she wrote to Mrs Churchill about the thousands of British prisoners taken during the fall of France. 'And this', she complained, 'was all their country could do for them – to leave them to rot in starvation and rags . . . Before handing over to the Red Cross the monopoly of supply of food and clothing to our Prisoners the Government should have made absolutely certain that it was competent and able to carry out an admittedly big undertaking, and from time to time it should have reviewed the working of this arrangement . . . It did neither.'[13]

This correspondence was passed on to the Permanent Under-Secretary of State for War, Sir James Grigg, while Churchill sat firm, refusing in the House of Commons on 5 November to institute an enquiry into the whole affair, as did the Secretary of State for War, Anthony Eden, later that same month. Privately, Grigg was worried: 'I have heard reports about the shortcomings of the Red Cross in this respect and if half of what is said is true it looks as if there might be a very considerable scandal brewing.'[14] As a first priority, Whitehall was anxious to limit the damage, and sent a 'simple acknowledgement' to Mrs Coombe Tennant, observing that her initial action in calling attention to delays in sending relief to prisoners was useful, but her continuing protests were 'now doing far more harm than good as the War Office and everyone else concerned are well aware of the facts'. Not everyone agreed: as one official noted, the War Office had been brought up against the realities of the situation through her actions, and the more she and others kept the issue alive, 'the sooner things will improve'.[15]

There can be little doubt that members of the government were more than happy to let the Red Cross and St John War Organization shoulder the blame in public for the parlous state of POW relief. They understood quite clearly that the General Post Office was entirely responsible for liaising with the ICRC for the onward transmission of parcels, and that this was not within the remit or control of the local Red Cross organization. Yet when the Lord Privy Seal, Postmaster-General and other Ministers had the chance to remove the erroneous impression that it was, they signally failed to do so.[16] Not until January 1941, did the Secretary of State for War, Captain David Margesson, admit to the

House of Commons that the dispatch of parcels was outside the remit of the ICRC.

In order to stem criticism and allay public unease, Sir Edward Grigg insisted that the chairman of the BRC & StJJ's Executive Committee, Field Marshal Sir Philip Chetwode, bring in Stanley Adams of Thomas Cook & Son on 28 January 1941 to beef up the parcel service.[17] This brought a temporary improvement; but further criticism led to Adams's abrupt departure in January 1942, complaining that he was 'conscious of the manner in which my authority is being whittled down'. Chetwode was equally annoyed, and told the Secretary of State for War that Adams had 'intended to hold a pistol at our heads . . . I am very sorry I ever took him [on].'[18]

The upshot was that the Lord Privy Seal, Sir Stafford Cripps, who was 'very anxious' to avoid any further public discussion of the issue, ordered an enquiry under the chairmanship of the Solicitor-General, Sir William Jowitt. At the same time he bought off Irene Ward, Member for Wallsend, a strong and consistent critic, by promising that the results of the private enquiry would be sent directly to the Secretary of State for War if she would desist from again raising the matter in the Commons. Sir James Grigg was entirely unamused when he discovered that Jowitt, who had 'no standing in the matter whatsoever', was in charge of the enquiry, and that Cripps was putting forward a written rather than a verbal report, since he had never agreed to delve into the domestic arrangements of the BRC & StJJ, which was essentially a voluntary society.[19]

While Chetwode took comfort from the essentially private nature of the examination into his organization's affairs – 'We were a little bit afraid that certain people thought we were in the position of defendants', he told Duncan Sandys – he soon took great exception to Jowitt's conduct of the enquiry.[20] Not only had Jowitt been rude to Major-General Sir Richard Howard-Vyse, chairman of the POW Department, but he 'would walk up and down the room, railing at what he called "the aristocratic ladies" who, he said, had made a demonstration against Adams in the office. He went to the length of saying that we should employ more people who sprang from the loins of the people', complained Chetwode indignantly, 'which he certainly does not himself.'[21]

There was some justice in Jowitt's criticisms, for the social make-up of the BRC & StJJ, certainly in its upper echelons, was limited to a well-connected social stratum. But the government was determined to bury the problem, and eventually suppressed Jowitt's report, much to the fury of the indefatigable Mrs Coombe Tennant, who blamed Grigg for this and accused him of shielding his friend, Philip Chetwode. Thereafter,

Grigg deliberately snubbed Irene Ward, commenting in May 1942, that 'it would be charitable to assume that she is cracked', and noting the following month, 'I don't propose, if I can help it, to send any more letters to Miss Ward. She can raise her stuff in the House if she wants to.'[22]

In the meantime, Mrs Stafford Cripps undertook to pacify the 'old campaigner', Mrs Coombe Tennant. Chetwode was satisfied with the general outcome and wrote thanking Sandys and Grigg: '... unless we had had very good friends like you, the public would have got a very wrong impression of the whole incident'.[23] What Grigg was about, however, was limiting the political damage that the affair could have caused and drawing to a close the protracted controversy over the activities of the BRC & StJJ, though the newly-formed POW Relatives' Association pursued the matter late into the year, 'which is more foolish than most of their work', commented Chetwode, 'and that is saying a good deal!'[24]

No doubt this acid comment was occasioned by the forceful criticism levelled by Dame Adelaide Livingstone – she had acted as honorary secretary to the government's Committee on the Treatment of British POWs during the First World War – who informed the Foreign Office, quite truthfully, that the general public still thought the BRC & StJJ was totally responsible for all POW matters and that it 'is persuaded that since the spokesperson of the principal Ministry concerned – i.e. the War Office – is a junior Minister, the Government as a whole take . . . little interest in POWs'. Unable to comprehend why no official announcement had ever been made to clear up the confusion, a Foreign Office spokesman admitted that 'There is much in what . . . [she] says.'[25] Nor could the President of the Board of Education, R. A. Butler, also approached by Dame Adelaide, understand the government's hesitancy in the matter, despite the fact that his own private secretary, G. W. Harrison, gave the game away: 'I am sure the "erroneous idea" is widespread. I don't think it would be easy to find many relatives of Br. Pr/W [British Prisoners of War] in Germany who have a good word to say for the B.R.C.S. [British Red Cross Society].'[26] Naturally, while public criticism was focused in one direction it did not fix upon the War Office's mandarins, who actually bore responsibility for the smooth regulation of POW affairs. A more convenient scapegoat would have been difficult to find, despite reassurances given by the Foreign Office to an official of the ICRC, Mlle Odier, who had to keep her visit and that of Marcel Junod to London secret because of what she termed the 'very unfair' press campaign waged against it.[27]

Indeed, despite the fact that British POWs were vitally dependent upon the good offices of the ICRC, which established a sea-route for sending them parcels containing the necessities of life in December 1940, and was later crucial in organizing various repatriation schemes, the War Office was unrelenting in its vigilance over its own rights and lines of demarcation, and was ever ready to defend what it considered to be its own territory from supposed or real incursions by the Red Cross.

This was true, too, of home affairs, where the War Office kept a 'steadily increasing watch and control over the actual work of the Society' (i.e. the BRC & StJJ), and ensured that it made no pronouncements on 'matters regarding prisoners of war which . . . do not come within their province at all'.[28] In fact, all information about British POWs was very carefully censored, prompted by the reluctance of the War Office, in common with other departments, to offer information 'which might be used as a stick with which to beat it . . .', and by a desire not to antagonize the German authorities during sensitive repatriation negotiations, nor to raise unduly the hopes of POW relatives.[29]

Following the upheavals in the early part of 1941, late in the same year Major-General E. C. Gepp, who had retired from active service, assumed the Directorship and re-organized the DPW into two main arms, PW1 dealing with the administration of enemy prisoners in British hands and PW2 with the welfare of British POWs together with policy questions on the treatment of enemy prisoners and all questions of reciprocity – which, as we shall see, was to become a difficult and dangerous question for the British government in the following year.

As the war progressed circumstances dictated the creation of other arms of the DPW, and by May 1945 it employed thirty-two military officers, nine junior civil assistants and no less than seventy-eight clerks. Essentially, the DPW was a reactive body, making such adjustments as seemed necessary in the light of new demands – hence the creation of PW5, which handled the planning and execution of repatriations and measures to be taken in returning British POWs at the conclusion of hostilities.

Although in course of time the DPW was supposed to deal in matters of detail with the ICRC through the POW Department at the Foreign Office, it actually had direct contacts with the ICRC's delegate in London and also with the British Red Cross representative in Geneva. But there were problems with the latter. 'I think the less said about . . . [him] the better', noted W. H. Gardner, 'I do not remember any occasion on which a communication was sent to him . . . in which any useful purpose whatsoever was served. He was eventually proved to have used his Vice-Consul status to carry out currency smuggling operations.'[30] More effective in the latter stages of the war was a link to the American

Red Cross representatives in London and Geneva, the latter a 'real live wire' who was in daily contact with the ICRC in all its activities.[31] There were difficulties, too, at Lisbon, where the wife of the British ambassador, Mrs Ian Campbell, formed an organization to transmit relief to a limited number of POWs and attempted to raise money in Britain to do so, and Turkey, where the British Ambassador's wife did the same. These well-meaning but maladroit efforts appeared to have the tacit approval of the DPW, yet flew in the face of agreed government policy, which, mindful of the problems caused by misguided attempts to help small groups of POWs in the First World War that badly damaged the morale of others who received little or no assistance, deliberately placed the whole of the essential relief supply in the hands of the BRC & StJJ.

In tandem with the ICRC, the Protecting Power represented British interests, although the DPW and the Foreign Office's POW Department failed at times to appreciate their respective spheres of influence. In general, the Protecting Power dealt with prisoners' rights under the Geneva Convention of 1929, to which Britain and Germany were co-signatories, and the Hague Convention of 1907. Until December 1941, the United States acted for British interests via its embassy in Berlin. Between the outbreak of war and September of that year, the British government paid out to the US authorities $2,635,000 in connection with their work on British interests in enemy-occupied territories – the bulk of it on civilian internees. But in the first nine months of 1941, the Americans transmitted forty-four protests to the German government on behalf of the British alleging ill-treatment of POWs or failure to observe articles of the Geneva Convention, and received twenty replies deemed 'satisfactory'.[32] Not that this headed off genuine dissatisfaction amongst some sections of the general public, as when the Rochdale and District POW Committee, having evidence that some British POWs were forced to labour in salt and coal mines, demanded 'that German prisoners in this country be made to carry out similar work instead of being kept in idleness as appears to be the case at present'.[33] In fact, significant numbers of German POWs could not be put to work before the summer of 1944, because there were no guards to supervise them and, in any case, the great majority were transferred rapidly from the United Kingdom to Canadian camps.[34]

When Germany declared war on America, Britain had urgently to reorganize its international lines of communication, and the Swiss were asked by the British Ambassador in Berne on 13 December to take over her interests in Germany, Italy and occupied Europe. 'The Americans clearly did their utmost for us and in my view achieved surprisingly good results', commented Sir Harold Satow. 'I only hope the Swiss will be as successful.'[35] This desire was eminently fulfilled as a result of the sterling work carried out by the Swiss on behalf of the co-belligerents and in safeguarding directly the interests of British prisoners. In a telegram to Berne late in 1943, the Foreign Office forwarded the War Office's deep appreciation of the 'very valuable work being done by the Swiss in Germany and the great thoroughness and zeal shown by the inspectors of the Swiss Legation who by visiting many work camps not easily accessible are markedly contributing to the welfare of our men'.[36] Their reports after tours of inspection, strictly reciprocal in that they also visited Axis POWs in Allied hands, formed the basis of confidential reports that were sent to London and Berlin respectively.

Access to POWs whose governments were co-signatories to the Geneva Convention was also afforded to ICRC delegates.[37] However, because copies of their reports were sent to both belligerents, and unveiled criticism would undoubtedly have led to their exclusion from German camps, such reports were generally couched in anodyne terms that made it necessary to read between the lines. Nevertheless, the opportunity to keep in touch with its own prisoners was greatly valued by the British government, although, curiously, it was only comp-aratively late in the war that an opportunity was taken to ask the Protecting Power how best communications with the enemy might be phrased, the kind of matters on which some success might be expected and the nature of the action that Berlin took on Britain's formal com-munications.

With rather more forethought the British government might have avoided the difficulties into which it blundered over mass reprisals against POWs, which led, in turn, to a dangerous split in Allied relations. The inter-governmental POW Committee, set up in 1941 – the name was subsequently changed to the Imperial POW Committee – and chaired by the Secretary of State for War, was intended to create a united front of British and dominion governments in negotiations with the Axis authorities. However, the chaining of prisoners in 1942–3 laid great strain on this common unity, threatening to tear it apart, besides causing considerable misery and hardships for the POWs involved.

The problem began in October 1942, after the *Oberkommando der Wehrmacht* (*OKW*) alleged that German prisoners taken during the bloody assault at Dieppe and the British commando raid on Sark, on 3 October, had been bound by the hands. In retaliation, Hitler ordered the manacling of Allied POWs and, at noon on 8 October, British officers, NCOs and other ranks were among those tied up after German orders had been read to them. Only protected personnel together with the sick and wounded were spared this indignity.[38]

In Stalag VIIIB about 1,500 British and Canadian POWs were roughly pinioned with strips of Red Cross parcel string, and another 800 unfortunates were soon added to this figure. Prisoners found by their guards with the string loosened, smoking in their barracks, or even sitting on their bunks, were kept for several hours with their wrists bound harshly together and drawn up tightly behind their back, nose and toes touching a wall. At Oflag VIIB, 107 officers and twenty other ranks were tied with rope about their wrists and kept in that state for twelve hours each day. The Kommandant explained at length that he was acting only on direct orders from the *OKW*, and his staff obviously disliked carrying them out; one POW officer noted in his diary that the Germans were 'quite sympathetic and a little disgusted about it all'.[39] Nevertheless, three days later, three times the original number were handcuffed. A medical officer was in constant attendance, but signs of distress were reported by a Swiss delegate who visited the camp and observed 'serious effects on mental and physical health.'[40]

When handcuffs were first produced in Oflag VII C/H, guards were posted outside each hut to prevent prisoners removing them, and, back at Stalag VIIIB, Sergeant Harcus found that attending *appell* in icy weather and trying to carry on any kind of life inside the RAF compound was far from easy: 'Wish these damned chains would come off', he wrote in his diary on the last day of January 1943, 'Wrists ache with constant wearing.'[41]

Unfortunately, the British government proceeded to dig a deep hole for itself, from which extrication was going to prove formidably difficult. Earlier, after reading a Report on Reprisals against British and German POWs in the First World War, Churchill had warned against instituting such measures 'if they can be avoided', for, as he noted, 'we have today to deal with a German Government infinitely more ruthless and ferocious whose counter-reprisals are likely to exceed anything that the public conscience in this country would allow us to do in return'.[42]

This sensible advice seems to have been completely ignored by the Prime Minister himself, who was the author of reprisal measures taken against German POWs in Britain and Canada as a result of the manacling of British and Canadian prisoners. On 10 October 1942, the British government announced that all fit German POWs in its hands (240), including *Generalleutnant* Ludwig Crüwell, would be chained immediately after being read a 'suitable statement'. At the same time the Dominions Office requested the Canadian government to manacle 2,000 German POWs if the German military authorities carried out their threat of putting in chains three times as many British prisoners as the number similarly dealt with by the British.[43]

Thus, Churchill embarked on a policy that could never attain the single objective for which it was fashioned – the breaking of Hitler's will and his consequent submission over the issue of maltreating POWs.

Nor was there any indication that the dominion governments, especially Canada, could be kept in line behind this foolhardy policy. The day before British reprisals were due to take effect, the Canadians warned the Dominions Office in London that, while ready to take the desired action against German prisoners there, they had reached the decision 'with reluctance. We feel we have been committed without proper consultation to a course of doubtful wisdom', and that, in particular, 'a futile contest may follow . . . [which] the Germans are certain to win'. It was only to avoid an 'open difference with the United Kingdom government, who had already announced the measures to be taken even though their execution required Canadian co-operation' that the Canadians decided 'with regret' to take the necessary punitive measures.[44]

Churchill attempted to sound reassuring: 'Earnestly hope that you will stand by us in this anxious business in which we both have much at stake', he urged the Canadian government, 'I am sure it will be of short duration.'[45] In this he was wrong, and Sir Robert Menzies was soon writing personally to the Prime Minister to record the Australians' obvious reluctance and urging him to accept the offer of mediation by the Protecting Power and the ICRC. But Churchill remained obdurate in the face of a further personal intervention by the Canadian High Commissioner in London, hostile comment in the British press and discontent among his own colleagues.[46]

'For us to invite, at German dictation, a neutral state to examine the conduct of our troops in the field would be to accept humiliation which I am certain will arouse the deepest anger in Britain and also in Russia', he explained to Attlee. 'I must warn my [Cabinet] colleagues against these dangers in the face of a faithless and merciless enemy.' Arguing somewhat disingenuously that the punishment inflicted by the Germans reduced their use of POW labour in agriculture and mines – which conveniently overlooked the fact that the measures were visited largely against other ranks in permanent camps and officers, who could not be required to work – he added that if neutral enquiries were to be made into 'all our methods of waging war', which was not exactly the point at issue, then the Germans would be able to exert blackmail by threatening at any time to maltreat Allied prisoners. This would be the inevitable result, argued Churchill, 'if we were to accept the pusillanimous line suggested by the Canadian government. We have far more at stake than all the Dominions together. I hope, therefore, that the Cabinet will on no account weaken.'[47]

Despite a restive Cabinet meeting on 12 October, at which a statement on shackling prepared by Cripps was amended there and then by the Prime Minister and subsequently used by him in a statement to the House of Commons the next day, followed by another tense meeting on

22 October, Churchill stuck tenaciously to his deeply flawed conduct on this issue. By then, he had evidence of very considerable resistance to reprisals. At Bowmanville Camp, Ontario, both guards and prisoners were injured when German POWs forcibly resisted chaining, while the Archbishop of York informed the Prime Minister that the Bishops of the Upper House of Convocation had condemned the manacling of prisoners and reprisals on innocent POWs *wherever* they were carried out – to which the Archbishop of Canterbury added his own censure. Members of the British POW Relatives' Association registered their anxieties: 'We have often been told and I quite agree', wrote one, 'that the German Nazi is a pig of the first water. Are we going to lower ourselves to the same level and belittle ourselves in the whole nation's eyes? Surely, this is flying in Goebbel's [*sic*] hands.'[48]

By late autumn, public criticism had been damped down in Britain, where debate in the press had been stifled by employing a D-Notice; but the director of the DPW indicated privately and at length his belief that reprisals should be abandoned as soon as a justified or 'manufactured' occasion presented itself.[49] The most obvious way out was to ask the Swiss to mediate; but Churchill had by now turned the affair into a matter of personal prestige. Against a background of continued Allied concern, with the Canadians threatening to take unilateral action to break the deadlock, he told dominion heads of government that he strongly believed that the original order for tying up POWs came from the Führer and that he was 'very reluctant to give Hitler a triumph and admit ourselves wrong . . . The idea of giving up all hope of getting our men released is very painful to me', he confessed. 'It is a terrible thing to have one's will-power broken by the enemy. It reacts on every form and every phase of the struggle.'[50] Of course, Churchill was right, but he had chosen poor ground on which to conduct a trial of strength, and in the nature of this affair some means had to be found for getting the British government off the hook on which the Prime Minister had so neatly impaled it. The opportunity came when the German authorities announced that all Allied POWs would be unshackled for Christmas week. Without waiting for the Protecting Power to intervene, a War Cabinet on 7 December decided to seize the opportunity and announce through the press and the BBC that German POWs would be unshackled 'forthwith'.[51]

Such reprisals were never instituted again, though the War Cabinet and Chief of the Imperial General Staff agreed on 4 January 1943 that no assurance could be given forbidding shackling of prisoners in any circumstances whatsoever, since in certain limited situations on the field of battle this might be necessary. Dissatisfied by this, the German authorities again tied and manacled Allied POWs, and this practice was carried on long into 1943. It became, however, merely symbolic, as was freely admitted by the *Wehrmacht* in March. By then, there were still over 4,000 British and Canadian POWs in chains; but at Oflag VIIB in April a Swiss delegate reported that, though POWs were handcuffed for thirteen hours a day, they enjoyed 'some liberty of movement'. The selected prisoners, kept apart from their colleagues, were always shackled; but he noticed that many were without handcuffs and chains much of the time, and maintained an alarm system to warn of approaching guards. Even when prisoners were found without their shackles and punished with seven days' arrest, the ropes knotted about their wrists were so loose that they were able to slip out of them. His distinct impression was that 'without actually shutting their eyes to evasions of regulations camp authorities are in general indulgent as regards shackling'.[52] This was also true at Stalag VIIIB, where a delegate reported that the camp authorities 'appear to connive at prisoners removing their handcuffs and walking with their unshackled comrades'.[53] The general consensus of opinion among all POWs still manacled in August 1943 was that things could be worse, and might be made so by too many protests from home, and that their present treatment was 'quite bearable'.[54]

Still determined to pursue the issue, Churchill suggested to his colleagues that a public statement be issued to the effect that a record would be kept of the total number of man-days in which British and Canadian POWs were manacled, and that the officer corps of the German army would be required to serve double this number in chains after the defeat of the Axis Powers. His cabinet colleagues, including Eden and Grigg, were appalled, as was the Australian High Commissioner in London, Stanley Bruce, who thought the Canadian and Australian governments would strongly oppose this extraordinary idea. The Prime Minister decided he would not press his suggestion 'at the present time', and events soon overtook such considerations, because there were reports from the Swiss Foreign Minister that both Ribbentrop and Keitel were in favour of abolishing shackling and were considering approaching Hitler about the matter. On 22 November 1943, the German authorities notified the Swiss government that shackling had ceased, though the order was never publicly rescinded. No announcement was made on the radio or in the press either in the United Kingdom or the dominions, because the Führer's reaction could not be predicted.

This broke the log-jam that had built up in the negotiations surrounding the joint repatriation of sick and wounded POWs; even some of Churchill's strongest supporters had pointed out the damage that the impasse on reprisals had inflicted on British policy.[55] And in the immensely complex problems surrounding repatriation, the good offices of both Protecting Power and ICRC were essential, despite the fact that the War Office had stiffly repulsed an offer to mediate by the latter in the recently-concluded dispute, complaining that 'this is another example of the desire of the International Red Cross Committee [*sic*] to seek the limelight . . . It is clearly outside their normal function.'[56]

During earlier negotiations, the Foreign Office had been critical of the War Office's dilatory approach to the repatriation of sick and wounded prisoners under Article 68 of the Geneva Convention.[57] After much delay, occasioned by the government's insistence that it could not exchange equal numbers of members of the armed forces because this would imply that a bargain was being struck with the Germans and so negate the basis of the Convention, and on the need to bring all the dominions into complex discussions, an exchange was planned for October 1941. Much comment in the British press stoked up expectations, so that when Berlin tried to wring last-minute concessions out of the British government, which stood firm, the whole scheme collapsed.

Immediately after this near-débâcle, the question was again raised by the German government and, uncertain how to respond, the British procrastinated, despite Duncan Sandys's warning that 'Any suggestions of delay or indifference by Whitehall . . . are only too readily believed by the prisoners' relatives.'[58] However, it was not until May 1943, after several successful exchanges of prisoners between Italy and Britain, that delicate negotiations, carried on in the utmost secrecy via Swiss intermediaries, resulted in the British abandoning their opposition to numerical equality, so opening the way to 'AVANT PROJET'.[59]

A sensible news blackout on the progress of this repatriation scheme, in order to prevent another bout of false optimism, brought an unexpected result. So well did the War Office enforce censorship about the exchange of prisoners that even relatives had no idea what was happening until, one day in October 1943, they suddenly discovered a missing husband, brother or son at their front door. Special arrangements were to have been made for men to communicate directly with their next of kin; but they were never properly established, so there was what the chairman of the BRC & StJJ called 'a certain amount of criticism because the repatriated prisoners of war arrived at their homes from hospitals and dispersal centres unannounced'.[60]

For many in this first group of repatriates their first taste of freedom was soured by civic pomposity, lengthy speeches at the ports of arrival and full exposure to newspaper publicity, which they greatly resented. As one soldier remarked, 'The prisoner does not want speeches by people who have no personal interest in him. I was irritated by the propaganda efforts on board ship in Leith which delayed our landing. The newsreel people tried to make us appear what we are not . . .'.[61] And their insensitive handling brought out a deep hostility toward desk-bound officials, as a private who volunteered to stay behind at Dunkirk in 1940 'because I felt it was my duty', discovered when confronted by an ungrateful War Office quibbling about his small allowance: 'This makes a man a little bitter', he commented with admirable self-restraint.[62]

While the War Office managed to bring the first repatriation to an untidy conclusion, having managed to get most things wrong, it turned down an offer by the British Red Cross to mount a series of lectures throughout the United Kingdom on returned ex-POWs and their care, but was more circumspect in allowing it to set up bureaux at all hospitals and dispersal centres where arrangements could be made to notify relatives of the 943 British and Commonwealth ex-prisoners who arrived at Liverpool on 28 May 1944.

This more intelligent policy was accompanied by a strong over-reaction when the War Office received secret intelligence that embarkation of repatriates had been very loosely controlled, and unauthorized persons had possibly acquired British battledress. In consequence, the dock area at Belfast was cordoned off by 200 military police, special passes were issued and no reporters were allowed into the restricted area; nor were they allowed within range of individual ex-POWs. Not that this stopped the press from trying 'every underhand method to evade the restrictions ordered by the War Office', reported the GOC, Northern Ireland, while British and American reporters were furious at what they termed the 'drastic restrictions' imposed on them. Even a BBC van was unable to get close enough to record Churchill's speech of welcome.[63]

At least the men involved received a smoother passage than those in the first repatriation, and the lessons learned then ensured an expeditious conclusion to two more exchanges. Plans for a fifth fell through owing to an increasingly fluid tactical situation in April 1945, lack of hospital ships and delay in receiving replies from the German legation at Berne. Meanwhile, delegates of the Protecting Power were reported in numerous prison camps as the Nazi Reich disintegrated. Despite obvious dangers the Foreign Office did nothing to dissuade them, since it was considered, rightly, that the presence of a neutral observer 'will be a safeguard to our men in the critical period when German resistance collapses'.[64]

While we have examined some of the more conspicuous limitations in the British government's arrangements for safeguarding its prisoners in German hands, it should be remembered that, by adapting and patching, a system was created that did work. Of course major mistakes were made, especially when the British government instituted counter-reprisals against German POWs in 1942 which, whatever the provocation, ran counter to the letter and spirit of the Geneva Convention. As Sir Harold Satow observed: 'They were in any case a very double-edged weapon. To put it shortly reprisals and counter-reprisals simply "do not pay".'[65] Nor were lines of communication between home and POWs, who felt at times abandoned to their fate, always very clear. 'The existence of D.P.W. and the intimacy of contact between War Office, Protecting Power and the Red Cross is almost completely unknown to men in Germany, even to those in authority in the Camps', an army psychologist noted in March 1944.[66] Yet it was largely through the efforts of this somewhat unstable but workable triumvirate that every British POW stood a decent chance of survival while at the mercy of an unpredictable and often pitiless enemy. This, at least, was a not inconsiderable triumph for the spirit of improvisation over bureaucracy.

Notes

1. Asquith in *Hansard*, House of Commons, fifth series (1916), vol. 86, col. 1291, 26 Oct. 1916. See PRO, Foreign Office Papers (hereafter FO), FO 916/14, 'Work in Connection with POWs from August 1914 to January 1919'; Robert Jackson, *The Prisoners*, London, 1989, pp. 138–9; John A. Fairlie, *British War Administration*, New York, 1919; N. B. Dearle, *Dictionary of Official War-Time Organisations*, London, 1928.
2. Sir Harold Satow and M. J. Sée, *The Work of the Prisoners of War Department during the Second World War*, London, 1950, p. 5. I am indebted to Dr Moore for a copy of this report.
3. PRO, FO 916/14, memo. by Sir F. M. Shepherd, head of Foreign Office POW Department (Oct. 1939–May 1940), 16 Feb. 1940. Very few copies of Sir Herbert Belfield's report were ever produced, but one can be seen attached to this file.
4. See Hilary St George Saunders, *The Red Cross and the White*, London, 1949.
5. Major-General Sir Alan Hunter was a member of the Home Defence (Security) Executive (known to MPs as the Swinton Committee),

which, in all likelihood, instigated the mass internment of Austrians and Germans in Britain. See Peter and Leni Gillman, *Collar the Lot!: How Britain Interned and Expelled its Wartime Refugees*, London, 1980, pp. 142–5.

6. A massive archive was developed by the Comité International de la Croix Rouge and housed in the *Bâtiment Electoral* at Geneva, in which information on each POW was kept, from the original 'capture card' onwards. Although information could be delayed, sometimes for years, cross-references to this material (a concordance) could be made by the British authorities seeking information about any individual. This service was open also to the Germans, but was not used with reference to their Russian POWs, who were killed with impunity – as were Germans in Russian hands. See Hilary St George Saunders, *Red Cross* (see Note 4 above), p. 62.

7. On the ICRC, see *Report of the International Committee of the Red Cross on Its Activities during the Second World War (September 1, 1939 – June 30, 1947)*, vol. 1, *General Activities*, Geneva, 1948.

8. PRO, FO 916/2, Hunter to Satow, 9 Jan. 1941.

9. Private H. S. Bowers, answers to author's questionnaire. Manuscript now in Imperial War Museum, London.

10. PRO, FO 916/2, War Office memo. to Army Council secretariat, 3 Nov. 1941.

11. Ibid., Hunter to W. St C. H. Roberts, head of Foreign Office Prisoners of War Department (Mar. 1941 – July 1945), 26 June 1941.

12. Public dissatisfaction with the Red Cross and government arrangements for British POWs was 'likely to find expression in due course', noted Shepherd. See PRO, FO 916/14, memo., 16 Feb. 1940.

13. PRO, Prime Minister's Office Papers (hereafter PREM), PREM 4/98/1, Mrs W. Coombe Tennant to Mrs Churchill, 20 Nov. 1940. Captain Coombe Tennant eventually escaped from Oflag VIB, and, even more remarkably, reached home.

14. Ibid., note by P. J. Grigg, 26 Nov. 1940.

15. Ibid., J. H. Peck to C.S.C., 2 Jan. and reply, 3 Jan. 1941.

16. *Hansard*, House of Commons, fifth series (1939–40), vol. 365, cols 1183–7 and 1863–4, 5 and 19 Nov. and (1940–1), vol. 367, col. 132, 26 Nov. 1940.

17. Sir Edward Grigg was Parliamentary Under-Secretary of State (Civil) at the War Office (May 1940 – Mar. 1942).

18. PRO, WO 32/14423, Chetwode to Margesson, 27 Jan. 1942.

19. Ibid., Grigg to Cripps, 29 Apr. 1942.

20. Ibid., Chetwode to Duncan Sandys, 16 Mar. 1942.

21. PRO, WO 32/14423, Chetwode to P. J. Grigg, 22 Apr. 1942.
22. Ibid., Grigg hand-written note, 22 May and memo. 10 July 1942.
23. Ibid., Chetwode to P. J. Grigg and Duncan Sandys, 17 Apr. 1942. See also P. G. Cambray and G. G. B. Briggs, *Red Cross & St John: The Official Record of the Humanitarian Services of the War Organisation of the British Red Cross Society and Order of St John of Jerusalem 1939–1947*, London, British Red Cross Society & St John of Jerusalem, 1949, pp. 242–4.
24. PRO, WO 32/14423, Chetwode to P. J. Grigg, 5 Aug. 1942.
25. PRO, FO 916/15, internal Foreign Office memo. by Roberts, 13 June 1941.
26. Ibid., note in margin of copy letter R. A. Butler to Richard Law, Financial Secretary to the War Office (May 1940 – July 1941), 18 June 1941.
27. PRO, FO 916/14, internal Foreign Office memo., 7 Apr. 1941. See also WO 165/59, War Office DPW war diary first report (1–30 Apr. 1941).
28. Colonel H. J. Phillimore, historical monograph: 'Prisoners of War,' TS, War Office (1949). Copy seen at the Ministry of Defence. Heavily amended by W. H. Gardiner, an appended note explains that it is 'really an apologia for the Prisoners of War Directorate and not a full story of the War Office dealing with prisoners of war', and was written by 'an officer with no War Office experience outside D.P.W. and without experience in D.P.W. of the formative period at the beginning of the war'. Thus a decision was taken not to publish the manuscript in the official series of war histories. Also see PRO, WO 32/9906, N. Coates to Roberts, 30 Apr. 1941.
29. Phillimore, 'Prisoners of War' (see Note 28 above).
30. Gardiner's emandation in Phillimore, 'Prisoners of War' (see Note 28 above).
31. Ibid.
32. PRO, FO 916/15, Satow to DPW, 6 Nov. and DPW internal memo., 17 Sept. 1941.
33. PRO, FO 916/34, resolution from Rochdale and District POW Committee to Harold Sutcliffe MP and transmitted to Anthony Eden, 30 July 1941; Roberts to Law, 13 Aug. 1941.
34. See Helmut Wolff, *Die deutschen Kriegsgefangenen in britischer Hand: Ein Überblick*, Munich, 1974, Ch.1, *passim*, esp. table 1, p. 10.
35. PRO, FO 916/15, Satow to Major Walton, DPW, 23 Dec. 1941. See also WO 32/10712, Foreign Office to British Ambassador, Berne, 13 Dec. 1941.
36. PRO, WO 32/10712, Foreign Office to Berne, 20 Oct. 1943.

37. Marcel Junod, *Warrior without Weapons*, London, 1951, pp. 219–20.
38. PRO, PREM 3/363/2, German communiqué, 9 Oct. 1942.
39. See W. Wynne Mason, *Prisoners of War. Official History of New Zealand in the Second World War 1939–1945*, Wellington, 1954, p. 239; E. G. C. Beckwith (ed.), *The Mansel Diaries: The Diaries of Captain John Mansel, Prisoner-of-War – and Camp Forger – in Germany 1940–45*, privately printed, 1977, entry for 8 Oct. 1942, p. 85.
40. Beckwith, *Mansel Diaries* (see Note 39 above).
41. Imperial War Museum (hereafter IWM), IWM 80/2/1, Sergeant L.H. Harcus, diaries, TS transcript. Harcus, from 115 Squadron, was shot down over Hamburg, 26 July 1942.
42. PRO, FO 916/15, memo. by Churchill to Roberts, 3 June 1941. While First Lord of the Admiralty in 1915, Churchill had ordered captured German submariners to be confined in the Naval Detention Barracks at Chatham and Devonport, although at this time the Germans were not waging unrestricted submarine warfare. The German Admiralty retaliated by placing thirty-nine British officer POWs in 'arrest barracks'. The matter was only resolved when Balfour succeeded Churchill in May and treated the U-boat captives as ordinary POWs.
43. *Generalleutnant* Crüwell was taken prisoner by 50th (British) Division when his Fieseler Storch was shot down over the Gazala Line on 29 May 1942. He was repatriated in 1944 suffering from asthma. See J. A. I. Agar-Hamilton and L. C. F. Turner, *Crisis in the Desert: May–July, 1942*, London, 1952, p. 35.
44. PRO, PREM 3/363/2, Canadian government to Dominions Office, 9 Oct. 1942.
45. Ibid., Churchill to Canadian government, 10 Oct. 1942.
46. Ibid., Vincent Massey, Canadian High Commissioner in London, to Clement Attlee, 10 Oct. 1942; *The Times*, 10 and 12 Oct. 1943.
47. Ibid., Churchill to Attlee, personal minute, 11 Oct. 1942.
48. Ibid., Canadian Department of External Affairs to Canadian High Commissioner in London, 22 Oct. 1942. PREM 4/98/2, Archbishop of York to Churchill, 15 Oct. 1942; Archbishop of Canterbury to Churchill, 12 Oct. and Churchill's reply, 14 Oct. 1942; J. Craig Harvey, chairman, British POW Relatives' Association, to Anthony Bevir, private secretary, 10 Downing Street, 22 Oct. 1942.
49. PRO, WO 32/11107, memo. by Major-General E. C. Gepp, 25 Oct. 1942.
50. PRO, PREM 3/363/2, Dominions Office to dominion governments, 10 July 1943; Attlee to Churchill, 30 Oct. 1942 and reply same day.

There is some evidence from the Swiss Minister in Berlin that the order for shackling did indeed emanate from Hitler, and that he was supported in this by Ribbentrop.

51. Ibid., extract from War Cabinet minutes, 7 Dec. 1942.
52. Ibid., Dominions Office to dominion governments, 10 May 1943.
53. Ibid., 6 Aug. 1943.
54. Ibid., 10 Aug. 1943.
55. Ibid., Richard Law, now Parliamentary Under-Secretary of State, Foreign Office, to Churchill, 19 Mar. 1943.
56. PRO, WO 32/11107, War Office internal minute, 11 Jan. 1943.
57. PRO, FO 916/14, memo. by Satow, 24 Mar. 1941.
58. PRO, WO 32/10742, memo. by Duncan Sandys, 29 Jan. 1942. Sandys was Financial Secretary to the Treasury (July 1941 – Feb. 1943) and, more importantly perhaps, Churchill's son-in-law.
59. There are a few details of exchanges of British and German POWs by Count Folke Bernadotte, *Instead of Arms*, London, 1949.
60. PRO, WO 32/11136, Field Marshal Chetwode to DPW, 2 May 1944.
61. PRO, WO 32/10757, appendix to interim report by Lieutenant-Colonel Wilson, Directorate of Army Psychiatry, on returned Prisoners of War, 29 Aug. 1945. The appendix contained studies made on the first set of repatriates from Germany in Dec. 1943.
62. Ibid.
63. PRO, WO 32/11136, see secret cipher telegram from AFHQ, Algiers, to War Office, 22 May 1944; minutes of meeting of DPW, 24 May 1944; Lieutenant-General Cunningham to DPW, 1 June 1944.
64. PRO, WO 32/10712, Admiralty, Military Branch memo., Mar. 1945.
65. Satow and Sée, *Work of the POW Department* (see Note 2 above), p. 12.
66. PRO, WO 32/10757, War Office minute, 10 Mar. 1944.

−3−

The Trouble with Allies: Canada and the Negotiation of Prisoner of War Exchanges
Jonathan F. Vance

For the prisoner of war who felt he lacked the physical or mental strength to attempt escape, repatriation on medical grounds offered the only hope, faint though it may have been, for release from captivity before the war's end. The long-awaited exchange became something of a talisman, clung to as much out of desperation as anything, and POWs went to great lengths to present their cases in the most favourable light to the medical commissions that ultimately decided their fates. The process was protracted and complicated, and the outcome was never a certainty, even for the most seriously wounded prisoner. For all but about 250 of the roughly 10,000 Canadian POWs in German, Italian and Japanese hands, it ended only in disappointment and frustration.

The Canadian politicians and bureaucrats who monitored the negotiation of those exchanges shared in this frustration, though obviously not to the same degree; they were most bedevilled by the inability of Canada's two ranking Allies to agree on principles. As a result, Britain and the United States often put forward separate and even conflicting proposals. This placed the Canadian government in a difficult position. Despite its long-cherished role as linchpin between the two major Western Allies, the government was forced to choose between them by weighing the pros and cons of associating itself with either Commonwealth or American arrangements. The choices, based largely on self-interest, were not always wisely made, and created problems both for Canada and for the negotiations.

I

During the First World War, negotiations for the exchange of prisoners began in late 1914, when the Swiss government raised the possibility of a mutual release of seriously wounded POWs by Germany and France. There was no immediate agreement, but in February 1915, after Pope Benedict XV had lent his support to the plan, France and Germany came to terms, with the first exchange occurring on 2 March 1915; by November 1916, over 18,000 prisoners had been exchanged. Later agreements provided for the internment of less severely wounded prisoners in Switzerland and, eventually, for the release to the Netherlands of prisoners afflicted by a range of ailments, from tuberculosis to gout, as well as officers and NCOs who had been imprisoned for at least eighteen months. By the end of the war, tens of thousands of sick, wounded, and long-term prisoners had benefited from a series of exchanges that allowed them to recuperate either at home or in the more congenial surroundings of neutral Switzerland or Holland.[1]

The repatriation picture during the Second World War was far less rosy. The process began in May 1940, when Britain and Germany agreed upon the appointment of Mixed Medical Commissions to examine prospective repatriates; but the first attempt at reaching an accord ended in failure. There were certainly enough deserving POWs (by the spring of 1941, over 1,200 POWs on both sides had passed for repatriation),[2] and initial discussions gave every hope for a speedy release of at least some of these prisoners. In October 1941, however, the German government suddenly announced that it would only accept an exchange on the basis of numerical equality. Unfortunately, the talks collapsed while a group of Commonwealth prisoners were on their way towards the exchange port of Dieppe with high hopes of returning home; when they learned that the repatriation had been cancelled, the news came as a bitter blow.[3]

In the wake of this débâcle, the British government made changes to its mechanism for negotiating and administering exchanges. Most significantly, the War Office's Directorate of POWs (DPW) proposed the formation of two Repatriation Committees, one to formulate policy and liaise with the Foreign Office, and the other to handle the administrative work of carrying out the exchanges. The consensus in London was that the dominion governments should not be represented on either committee. The War Office felt that the committees should act as forums for ironing out disagreements between British government departments, and that dominion representatives should not be invited into the process until accord had been reached. It also believed that 'as negotiations proceed and the need for quick decisions increases, the presence on this Committee of representatives of the Dominions may act as a drag'.[4] The Dominions Office, however, took a different view. Realizing that his ministry would have to face the ire of High Commissioners excluded from the process, Clement Attlee pressed for their admission to the committees. He pointed out that they sat as members of the Imperial POW Committee and, furthermore, had attended the first three meetings of Repatriation Committee #2; to exclude them at this stage would provoke considerable anger.[5] Eventually, the War Office capitulated, and the dominions were invited to sit as members of Repatriation Committee #2, and to attend meetings of the other committee when necessary.

Despite attending these meetings, Ottawa had no input into the negotiations; once an agreement with Germany had been reached, the War Office would merely inform Canada's High Commission in London if Canadians were to be included in the exchange.[6] There is no indication that Ottawa wished to play a more active role at this early stage, for a number of reasons. In the first place, there were very few Canadian POWs in Germany, and all but one of them, at least until 1941, were members of the British forces. The government also admitted that exchanges should be negotiated on a Commonwealth-wide basis, simply because Germany normally treated the Commonwealth as a single political unit, unless there were specific goals to be achieved by doing otherwise.[7] In addition, there was no significant will, either in the government or the civil service, to push for the repatriation of Canadian POWs; most of the effort went towards repatriating Canadian civilians from continental Europe, which seemed to offer the best hope of success in the early years of the war. Only when military repatriations actually began did the government take a serious interest in the subject, and even then much of the motivation lay in forestalling feared criticism from a number of large and powerful philanthropic organizations if Canadian POWs did not return home at the same time as other Allied repatriates.[8] Finally, the Canadian government had no available alternative if it was unhappy with Britain's conduct of exchange negotiations. When the United States entered the war, however, this changed.

The Canadian government had long cultivated a special relationship with the United States, and Prime Minister Mackenzie King in particular was immensely proud of his close relations with President Franklin D. Roosevelt. Before the attack on Pearl Harbor, King's government had gone to great lengths to establish meaningful links with the most powerful neutral nation in the world, and King himself viewed Canada as a kind of Commonwealth conduit into the halls of power in Washington. When the United States entered the war, Canada's POW bureaucrats suddenly sensed an opportunity to take advantage of this preferred position. They saw two possibilities: of associating Canada either with Commonwealth repatriation schemes, for which there were strong emotional, historical, and practical reasons, or with American plans, for which there were also strong motives, not simply of geography but also in the light of the closer military and economic integration of the two countries that had been signalled by the Ogdensburg and Hyde Park agreements of 1940 and 1941. Self-interest could now play a major role in determining which scheme to support; Ottawa could make its choice largely on the basis of the anticipated benefits of any given proposal for Canada. Apparently absent from the equation was any consideration of the impact this conduct could have on the negotiation process.

It did not take long for the consequences of Canada's action to become evident. In December 1941, the Dominions Office circulated a German proposal for the exchange of up to 15,000 POWs and civilians, and advised that no reply would be sent to Berlin until each Commonwealth government had had the opportunity to consider the proposal. The Cabinet War Committee in Ottawa, however, was reluctant to assent to a united Commonwealth response. Canadian policy, thought the committee, should favour parallel instead of unified action, to retain the maximum freedom of movement.[9] In practical terms, this implied a realization that, with America now in the war, Canada might do better to participate in exchange schemes worked out by Washington.

This belief was stated explicitly in June 1942, when Ottawa learned the terms of a tentative agreement reached by Germany and Britain. The accord allowed for the repatriation of all seriously wounded POWs, all surplus medical personnel, and all civilians who wished to leave, whether or not they were interned, with the exception of those serving penal sentences or deemed to be dangerous to the Detaining Power. His Majesty's Government was keen to secure the concurrence of the dominions as promptly as possible; but some officials in the Department of External Affairs in Ottawa questioned the wisdom of tying Canada to Commonwealth exchange policy. On the contrary, as the Under-Secretary of State for External Affairs, Norman Robertson, wrote, 'there is a great deal to be said for our pursuing the same general policy in this field as the United States and the other American belligerents'.[10] The department warned its High Commissioner in London, Vincent Massey, that 'it may prove to be more convenient to tie the Canadian arrangements in with those made by the United States', and Massey made it clear to the Imperial POW Committee that Ottawa had not yet decided on its response to the tentative Anglo-German agreement.[11]

When a representative of the High Commission presented this opinion to the DPW Repatriation Committee, alarmed British authorities pointed out that the negotiations could be 'vitally prejudiced' if the German government learned that a member of the Commonwealth was attempting to make separate arrangements.[12] They also maintained that it might be 'embarrassing' to the rest of the Commonwealth if Canada secured the repatriation of its own nationals separately from other British subjects. To this, Canadian officials responded that geography had to be taken into account, and that it would be just as embarrassing if Canada were the only North American nation that did not bring prisoners home on the MS *Drottningholm*, the neutral ship that the Americans hoped to use on their exchange operation. Even when the German government cancelled the safe-conduct pass for the ship, External Affairs believed that Canadian interest in future American schemes should not be renounced 'unless there are definite developments in [a] British Empire scheme which would be of distinct advantage'.[13] It appreciated the Foreign Office's desire to inform Berlin that it had the full support of all Commonwealth governments, but insisted on preserving Canada's freedom of action *vis-à-vis* any exchange plan that the Americans might formulate; for this reason, Britain's response to Germany must include the reservation that Canadian participation in the Commonwealth scheme did not signify Ottawa's disavowal of any scheme negotiated by the United States.[14]

As it turned out, Canada's view had precisely the effect on negotiations that British authorities feared: the German Legation in Switzerland declined to forward Britain's telegram to Berlin while the reservation stood. That reservation, according to the Legation, implied that '[the] Canadian Government would not be bound by the agreement under negotiation'. This was unacceptable to Berlin; in light of the number of German POWs transferred to Canada and the belief that plans were in train to make Canada the detention site of all POWs captured by Commonwealth forces, Germany refused to consider any accord that did not have the full and unqualified support of Ottawa.[15] Officials in the Foreign Office realized that the Canadian government 'evidently mean[t] to keep a back and a front door open for repatriation', but found it difficult to argue with the position taken by the German Legation. Although W. St. C. H. Roberts of the Foreign Office POW Department thought the Legation's reply 'high-handed', the general consensus within the Foreign Office was that Germany's attitude was understandable and not unreasonable, given that, of the roughly 18,000 German POWs captured thus far, over 16,000 were detained in Canada.[16]

Indeed, it was the Canadian government that seemed to be acting unreasonably. British officials believed that Ottawa was quick to act on any request from Washington, but grew uncooperative when dealing with a request from London. For example, when the United States was close to securing an agreement with Berlin for an exchange of diplomats, Ottawa promptly acceded to an American request for a small number of sick and wounded POWs to return to Germany as a goodwill measure. The Foreign Office was disturbed by this development, partly out of a belief that the American plan could jeopardize a larger exchange scheme under negotiation, but mostly out of irritation that Canada had responded promptly to American entreaties yet still had not approved Britain's general plan for periodic exchanges negotiated separately.[17] In practical terms, this meant that the next exchange proposal could go to Germany with the approval of every Commonwealth government except Canada's. Foreign Office officials can surely be forgiven for envisioning a repetition of the July 1942 situation, when the German authorities had refused to consider a proposal that included a Canadian reservation.

At the same time, External Affairs took another decision that could easily be considered obstructionist. In the autumn of 1943, the International Committee of the Red Cross had raised the possibility of arranging an exchange of long-term prisoners of the sort that had been so successful in the First World War. British officials canvassed the dominion governments, most of which expressed support for the plan. The only dissenting voice came from Ottawa. External Affairs informed its High Commission in London that Canada could not support the scheme, as only one Canadian POW met the requirements for release. Vincent Massey, anxious to save the government from the embarrassment this decision would inevitably cause, dashed off a sharp rejoinder to External Affairs: 'This attitude was purely selfish as in [the] plan then proposed virtually no Canadians would be returned. [The] Canadian refusal would perhaps keep 3000 Commonwealth prisoners from Sweden and if such grounds were suspected would be resented by other Commonwealth countries.'[18] Fortunately, Massey's rebuke was sufficient to convince External Affairs to change its mind, and Canada was rescued from the possibility of being blamed for the failure of a promising exchange scheme.

By this time, the consequences of Canada's insistence on working independently of the Commonwealth were becoming evident. With the creation of Anglo-American repatriation committees in London and Washington (on which Canada was not represented), the two DPW repatriation committees met less frequently; furthermore British officials, perhaps tiring of the obstacles Canada had raised to exchange negotiations, grew increasingly lax about keeping Ottawa informed of the progress of POW planning in general. By the spring of 1944, the practical effects of being slowly elbowed out of the decision-making network were evident in the process for raising a Canadian request in Allied circles: 'External [Affairs] should cable to Canada House asking them to request Foreign Office to instruct British Embassy, Washington, to approach State Department in support of the Canadian request.'[19] The days of the linchpin were past. Thanks in part to an insistence on keeping a foot in both the American and Commonwealth camps, the government in Ottawa was in danger of becoming little more than an observer to negotiations for the exchange of POWs with Germany.

II

The difficulties experienced in securing the repatriation of prisoners from the European theatre were considerable, but they were multiplied tenfold in the Pacific. Allied governments knew at the outset that the prospects of negotiating an exchange with Tokyo were slim, partly because they had few prisoners to offer (in October 1944 the Allies held only 6,400 Japanese POWs, against over 100,000 Allied combatants in Japanese captivity),[20] but also because the Imperial Japanese Army showed little desire to secure the return of soldiers who had disgraced themselves by surrender. As an intercepted diplomatic transmission from Tokyo to the Imperial minister in Switzerland revealed, 'our Army maintains the position that Japanese prisoners of war do not exist'. A year later, the Foreign Office made a similar observation, noting that 'as the Japanese take no interest in their own prisoners of war', there was little chance of Tokyo's responding favourably to any exchange proposals.[21] Despite this discouraging intelligence, Allied officials refused to turn their backs on the possibility of a negotiated repatriation of Far East POWs, and laboured hard to formulate a scheme that might appeal to the Japanese government. Just as they had in the European theatre, Canadian officials expended as much effort on the specifics of the schemes as on warily treading the path between Ottawa's two ranking allies.

Much of Canada's conduct with respect to repatriation negotiations in the Pacific theatre was determined by the first exchange of civilian internees, which had occurred in the summer of 1942.[22] At that time, Ottawa had decided 'on grounds of practicable convenience' to link itself with a scheme being worked out by the American government, instead of the plan under consideration in the Commonwealth.[23] A number of factors probably entered into this decision. The King government certainly feared a public backlash if Canadians did not return with other North American repatriates; as National Defence Headquarters in Ottawa noted on another occasion, the Canadian government was keen to avoid the 'invidious public comparison should US personnel get home before Canadians'.[24] There was also the suggestion, never explicitly admitted but underlying much official correspondence, that the United States government might be able to achieve a result much quicker than Britain. In short, Canadian officials believed they would do better with Washington than with Whitehall.

That the decision regarding civilian exchanges would carry over into negotiations for POW exchanges was evident as soon as the latter were seriously discussed. In March 1944, when the State Department transmitted to the American Legation in Berne details of a proposal it intended to submit to Japan (for the exchange of 100 sick and wounded

POWs and surplus protected personnel, and about 1,400 civilians), it intimated its assumption that 'if this proposal is accepted by the Japanese government, nationals of the other American Republics and of Canada will be admissible to the resultant exchanges'.[25] However, External Affairs was not hopeful that the American proposal would lead anywhere. A similar British proposal to Japan had already been rejected, and, even if the American plan came to fruition, only about a hundred repatriates could be returned because of a severe shortage of shipping space. Of this group, no more than fifteen or twenty would be Canadian.[26]

Because of this gloomy forecast, External Affairs toyed with the idea of going it alone. Margaret Meagher, an assistant in the department, began to consider the possibility of reaching a bilateral agreement with Japan. Mindful of the relative care with which Canada had treated Japanese nationals and Japanese-Canadians evacuated from British Columbia, Meagher believed that Tokyo could find no reason to refuse a direct exchange with Canada and that Canadian officials should begin searching for a suitable vessel for an exchange at a Soviet port.[27] Alfred Rive, the head of External's POW section, was keen on the idea (he was drawn by the opportunity to get rid of 'unwanted Japanese' from Canada), but other members of the department were less enthusiastic. George Magann, who represented Canada on a number of exchange voyages, thought it impolitic to attempt a strictly Canadian operation, especially as the government had defended the pooling principle in the shipment of relief supplies; Magann believed that Canada would have to offer space on the exchange to all nations that had also supported the pooling principle.[28] Morley Scott, another External Affairs POW administrator, had doubts about the scheme too, and did not think that Canada would gain much from the effort: 'A lot of our folk don't want to come back, nor do we much care if we get them back; one of our chief aims is to get rid of a boatload of Japanese.' Like Magann, Scott believed that the plan would raise problems with Britain and the United States, both of which had included Canada in their previous exchange schemes; he believed they would not take kindly to being left out of a Canadian plan.[29] Seeing the force of the arguments raised by Magann and Scott, Norman Robertson too declared against a separate Canadian proposal, and it was never carried through.[30]

By this time, Allied officials had arrived at a common repatriation policy: a series of continuing exchanges at Bikini until all military repatriables were exchanged, after which civilians would be turned over. To make the plan more appealing, the Allies agreed to release all Japanese nationals in custody who wished to return to Japan.[31] However, this common front was soon breached. In June 1944, the United

States announced its intention to offer Japan the opportunity to evacuate the isolated garrisons on Wake, Wotje, Mili, Maloelap, Jaluit, Ocean, and Nauru islands in exchange for the release of American POWs from Bataan, Corregidor, Guam, Wake, and Tientsin (Tianjin). It was to be a strictly bilateral agreement, but the State Department moved to head off criticism by pointing out that the deal could set a precedent for similar arrangements between Japan and the Commonwealth.[32] In September, the United States unveiled another bilateral proposal: the exchange of 10,000 Japanese civilians captured on Saipan for an equal number of American, Latin American and Canadian POWs and civilians.[33]

The reaction of Britain and the dominions to these proposals was, not surprisingly, uniformly negative. His Majesty's Government regretted the American action, expressing concerns that if most American POWs were released under the garrison exchange plan, Washington might be less interested in assisting with continuing efforts to ship Red Cross relief supplies to prison camps in the Far East. The Foreign Office also feared a public backlash if the United States freed its POWs and Britain was unable to do the same. One official, J. H. Lambert, questioned the American contention that the proposal might open the way for the Commonwealth to try a similar plan, and pointed out that by including the isolated Japanese troops in their garrison exchange proposal, 'the Americans had in fact "scooped" all the useless Japanese military for the purpose of a purely American exchange with no advantage to their Allies at all'.[34]

The Australian government, too, was very doubtful that the proposal had any chance of success, given that it would presume a Japanese admission of defeat with respect to the isolated garrisons. Furthermore, the government pointed out that Australians captured in the Dutch East Indies, Singapore, and Thailand had been in captivity longer than the Americans involved, and so had a greater claim on repatriation. Finally, Australia noted that there were Japanese garrisons in the south-west Pacific, at Rabaul, Wewak, and the Solomon Islands, that were equally isolated and could be used for a similar proposal.[35] The governments of Canada and New Zealand added their voices in disapproval of the American action, suggesting that it could cause dissent among the Allies and lead to public resentment in those nations that were left out of the plan.[36] The India Office had a different problem. It was, of course, concerned that Indian POWs benefit from any exchange proposal, but admitted that their position was anomalous because Tokyo regarded them not only as prisoners, but as nationals of a country within the Greater East Asia Co-Prosperity Sphere.[37]

Few Commonwealth observers, however, had any illusions about the likelihood of convincing the United States to change its mind. One official in the Foreign Office pointed out that the Americans viewed their soldiers captured on Bataan as special heroes; in their eyes, the resistance of those troops had saved Australia from invasion, so the Commonwealth owed them a certain debt.[38] For its part, the War Cabinet acknowledged that Washington had always maintained its right to deal bilaterally with enemy states; it predicted the proposal would raise hackles in the Commonwealth and Dutch governments, but admitted that it might be difficult to dissuade the United States from forwarding it. Instead, the War Cabinet intended to ask the Americans to expand the proposal to include all Allied POWs on a proportionate basis. If that failed, the Commonwealth would devise a similar plan to present to Tokyo, involving the exchange of 140,000 surrounded Japanese troops in the New Guinea area for an equal number of Commonwealth and Dutch POWs.[39] To match the Saipan exchange, the Commonwealth would offer 3,000 Japanese civilians in India and Australia for an equal number of sick and wounded Commonwealth prisoners; if this was accepted, the Canadian government would provide more Japanese civilians for a further exchange.[40]

External Affairs must have regarded these developments with considerable interest. When the first American proposal was broached, the department had expressed its hope that the United States would back away from bilateral negotiations and return to the joint Allied proposal that had been agreed upon earlier. Nevertheless, the department again saw the opportunity to throw Canada's lot in with either the Americans or the British.[41] The pitfalls of this approach, if they were not evident to External Affairs, were certainly apparent to Vincent Massey. When the British government raised the possibility of a united Commonwealth protest against the garrison exchange proposal, Massey was at a loss how to respond: 'I may be invited to reconcile our action in joining other Commonwealth countries in protesting to the United States against their presenting a proposal from which the Commonwealth was excluded with our inclusion in another and very similar proposal from which all parts of the Commonwealth, except Canada, are excluded.'[42] In Massey's view, the government in Ottawa was in danger of painting itself into a very awkward corner.

Canada did indeed join Britain's protest that exchanges should be negotiated collectively by all the Allies; but another hurdle appeared when the Foreign Office announced that the time was ripe for putting forward its own scheme, either the New Guinea plan or the offer of a fixed number of Japanese civilians for an equal number of Commonwealth sick and wounded POWs.[43] With this prospect, Canada was again caught in the middle. Massey wondered if it was politic to take part in both the Commonwealth and American plans, or if Canada should ask to be excluded from the US proposals in favour of the Commonwealth scheme. External Affairs, however, took a different view and again endeavoured to keep both a back and a front door open in terms of repatriation. External decided that Canada could safely associate itself with both proposals, in order to have two chances of getting some Canadian POWs out of Japanese camps.[44]

As it happened, Canada was deprived of the opportunity to see if the double game would work. In November, the Americans rejected the Commonwealth's idea of an exchange of POWs for the garrisons around New Guinea, stating that such a plan would free up some of the best Japanese troops in the Pacific. To soothe Commonwealth feelings, the Americans agreed to include other Allied prisoners in its original scheme, but not on a proportionate basis, for the very good reason that specifying numbers to be repatriated from each country would complicate matters and make Tokyo less likely to accede to the agreement.[45] It transmitted this proposal to the Swiss government, appending it with an extraordinary concession: if Tokyo raised the matter, the United States government was willing to waive Article 74 of the Geneva Convention, which stipulated that repatriates could not be used for further military service. This would mean that, if the scheme went ahead, tens of thousands of Japanese troops currently in isolated garrisons would be freed under guarantees of safe conduct, and could then return immediately to combat duties elsewhere in the Pacific theatre. It is difficult to say whether this was a desperate attempt to make the plan appealing to Tokyo or an admission that, having ignored the rest of the Geneva Convention's articles in its dealings with POWs, Japan would almost certainly ignore this one as well. Whatever the reason, the State Department was obviously not keen that the offer become widely known, and the Canadian Embassy in Washington only learned of it, after some prodding, in January 1945.[46]

In London, the specifics of the proposal provoked less debate than the Commonwealth's response to it. The War Office proposed a lengthy reply to Washington that acknowledged the American concession, but reiterated the demand for exchanges on a proportionate basis, raised again the alternative Commonwealth exchange proposals, and expressed strong disapproval of the way the government in Washington had acted. Australia, New Zealand, and India all agreed to this reply, but Morley Scott of Canada House said that it was pointless to protest further, and advised instead the transmission of a simple note acknowledging the American concession and reaffirming the Commonwealth desire for exchanges on a proportionate basis.[47] Scott's opinion led Foreign Office officials to raise the matter again with the dominions. The representative of the Australian High Commission agreed with

Scott, and believed that there was no point in further protest because the American proposal had already gone to the Protecting Power; in any case, he saw not the slightest chance of Tokyo's accepting the plan. British Foreign Minister Anthony Eden, however, was evidently growing weary of the Canadian tail wagging the Commonwealth dog, and responded rather less calmly. He wondered why the matter had dragged on so long, and strongly criticized the way it had been handled: 'Why couldn't we stick to our guns . . . I don't see why we should all bow to Canada, nor do I agree with Canada.'[48]

Even Japan's rejection of the American proposal did not mark the last word on repatriation. In the summer of 1945, the United States formulated another proposal for transmission to Tokyo. The Allies would release all Japanese nationals who wished to return home, regardless of number; these would be taken, in the first instance, from Europe, Turkey, India, and Australia. In return, Japan would be asked to free any civilians who wished to leave, as well as all POWs captured before 1 June 1942.[49] The British government demurred. It believed there was little chance of the American scheme's being accepted by Japan, and proposed instead the mutual release of all POWs eligible for repatriation on medical grounds under the Geneva Convention. Once again, Canadian officials threw their support behind the United States. The examination of POWs by Mixed Medical Commissions, as proposed in the British scheme, would be a time-consuming process, and it was not certain that a large number of Canadians would be passed for repatriation. On the other hand, eligibility based on duration of captivity (as the United States proposed) promised to free virtually all Canadian POWs in the Far East, the vast majority of whom had been captured at Hong Kong in December 1941. In short order, both External Affairs and the Department of National Defence declared their preference for the American scheme. This decision, however, is less significant than External's final word on the subject. The department acknowledged that both Britain and the United States had far larger stakes in the matter than Canada and concluded that, if the two could reach a compromise, the government would probably support it.[50] At last, at this late stage of the war, Ottawa admitted that its interests in repatriation were really quite small and, by inference, that Canada should be a little more flexible for the benefit of Allies with more at stake.

III

In both the European and Pacific theatres, the Canadian government's practice of using considerations of self-interest to choose between British and American repatriation schemes was fraught with difficulties. In the first place, there was little account taken of how enemy governments viewed Canada's status as an independent nation. It should have been obvious that Germany treated the Commonwealth as a single political unit, and was not willing to deal with any one dominion unless it furthered the aim of sowing dissent among the Allies. External Affairs admitted this fact in December 1941, when exchange negotiations were in their infancy; yet for the rest of the war it was either ignored or forgotten. Regardless of domestic political imperatives, External Affairs should have realized that insisting upon independent action played directly into the hands of the Germans by allowing them to blame Canada for the collapse of talks. There was little point in insisting upon freedom of action in repatriation negotiations if enemy governments would happily seize upon that insistence to score a propaganda victory.

More importantly, there was no admission until very late in the war that Canada's stake in POW matters, however important it was in Ottawa, was really quite small compared to those of Britain, the United States, and the rest of the Commonwealth. Canada lost about 10,000 soldiers, sailors and airmen as prisoners during the Second World War, fewer, in both relative and absolute terms, than any of the other major Allies. By comparison, over 190,000 members of the British forces and over 110,000 American servicemen were held captive during the war. Roughly 30,000 Australians were captured, and even South Africa, with over 12,000 prisoners in enemy hands, had a bigger stake in POW matters than Canada.[51] Despite this fact, External Affairs complained, with increasing frequency as the war progressed, that Canada was not accorded a sufficient role in the decision-making process.

As the locus of POW planning shifted from London to Washington, Canada's role did wane; but this was largely Ottawa's own fault, for the process of weighing the desirability of British and American plans was often protracted. It was clearly easier for British officials to avoid consulting Canada than to wait for Ottawa to reach a decision, which might be distinctly unhelpful in any case. But even though Canada's part in the decision-making process was limited, the government in Ottawa took full advantage of any opportunity it had to voice an opinion and, in this way, exerted an influence in Allied POW circles that was out of all proportion to the number of Canadians in enemy captivity. Various factors contributed to this, including Canada's role in the provision of Red Cross food parcels to Allied POWs and the number of Axis prisoners detained in Canada. These were compelling reasons to be sure; but they were not enough to justify the government in Ottawa playing, as it did on more than one occasion, the role of spoiler in repatriation negotiations. Vincent Massey was quite justified in pointing out that Canada, with comparatively few POWs, had little right to throw up roadblocks to a possible exchange of long-term prisoners for the sole reason that few Canadians would benefit. Such attempts to weigh the desirability of any scheme on the basis of self-interest meant that Canadian officials often took a position that, as Massey recognized, was far too parochial.

Notes

The author would like to extend thanks to the Social Sciences and Humanities Research Council of Canada for financial support that made this chapter possible.

1. For the full story, see Richard B. Speed, *Prisoners, Diplomats and the Great War: A Study in the Diplomacy of Captivity*, New York, 1990.
2. National Archives of Canada (hereafter NAC), Department of National Defence Records, Record Group 24, vol. 48, f. HQ 240–1–73, Caldecote to External Affairs, 23 May 1940; W. Wynne Mason, *Prisoners of War. Official History of New Zealand in the Second World War 1939–1945*, Wellington, 1954, p. 93.
3. *The Times*, 8 Oct. 1941; Mason, *Prisoners of War* (see Note 2 above), p. 93. For descriptions of successful repatriations, see International Committee of the Red Cross, *Report of the ICRC on Its Activities during the Second World War (September 1, 1939 – June 30, 1947)*, vol. 1, *General Activities*, Geneva, 1948, pp. 378–82.
4. Public Record Office, (hereafter PRO), Foreign Office Papers (hereafter FO), FO 916/264, minutes by W. St. C. H. Roberts, 9 May and 9 July 1942.
5. Ibid., Dominions Office to War Office, 25 July and 13 Aug. 1942.
6. NAC, Department of External Affairs Records, RG 25, series A6, vol. 428, f. Cas 1/6/1, pt. 1, memo., 29 Sept. 1941.
7. Ibid., vol. 2944, f. 3033–A–40, External Affairs to High Commission, 23 Dec. 1941.
8. One of these groups, the Canadian POW Relatives Association, was a thorn in the side of the government for much of the war and was frequently rebuked by civil servants for ignoring government instructions. See Jonathan F. Vance, 'Canadian Relief Agencies and Prisoners of War, 1939–1945,' in *Journal of Canadian Studies*, forthcoming.

9. NAC, RG 25, vol. 2943, f. 3033–40–1, High Commission to External Affairs, 23 Dec. 1941; Privy Council Office Records, RG 2, series 7c, vol. 8, Cabinet War Committee Document #53, 'Exchange of British and German POWs and Civilian Internees', 6 Jan. 1942.

10. NAC, RG 25, vol. 2943, f. 3033–40–1, High Commission to External Affairs, 18 June 1942; unsigned memo. [June 1942]; memo. by Robertson, 17 June 1942.

11. Ibid., External Affairs to High Commission, 19 June 1942; series A6, vol. 428, f. Cas 1/6/1, pt. 1, High Commission to External Affairs, 23 June 1942.

12. NAC, RG 25, vol. 2943, f. 3033–40–1, minutes of #1 Repatriation Committee (first meeting), 24 June 1942; High Commission to External Affairs, 30 June 1942.

13. Ibid., vol. 2943, f. 3033–40–1, undated memo [June 1942]; telephone transcript, 15 July 1942.

14. Ibid., External Affairs to Canadian Minister, Washington, 25 June, 13 July and 23 July 1942.

15. Ibid., External Affairs to Canadian Minister, Washington, 30 July 1942; Mills Library Microform Collection, McMaster University (hereafter MLMC), Akten der Partei-Kanzlei der NSDAP, teil 1, band 1, fiche 119, report by German consulate in Geneva, 20 July 1942.

16. PRO, FO 916/262, minutes by Roberts, 21 and 29 July 1942; CAB 79/24, Joint Intelligence Sub-committee report on POW reprisals, JIC(42)434(Final), 10 Nov. 1942.

17. NAC, RG 25, series A6, vol. 430, f. Cas 1/6/2, pt. 1, Scott to Foreign Office, 14 Feb. 1944; Massey to External Affairs, 15 Feb. 1944; External Affairs to Dominions Office, 15 Feb. 1944.

18. Ibid., vol. 2783, f. 621–HX–40, Massey to External Affairs, 11 Mar. 1944.

19. Ibid., series A6, vol. 431, f. Cas 1/6/2, pt. 3, minutes of interdepartmental meeting on repatriation arrangements, 24 Apr. 1944.

20. André Durand, *From Sarajevo to Hiroshima: History of the ICRC*, Geneva, 1984, p. 524.

21. MLMC, Magic Documents, reel 5, SRS–955 (summary of 4 May 1943), p. 404, Tokyo to Japanese Minister, Berne, undated; PRO, FO 916/1076, minute by Davidson, 25 Feb. 1944.

22. For an examination of these exchanges, see P. Scott Corbett, *Quiet Passages: The Exchange of Civilians between the United States and Japan during the Second World War*, Kent, OH, 1987.

23. NAC, RG 25, vol. 3342, f. 4464–40, pt. 6, memo. entitled 'Exchange of Civilians with Japan', 1 Feb. 1945.

24. NAC, RG 24, reel C–5330, f. HQS 9050–4, pt. 5, NDHQ to CMHQ, 2 Mar. 1944.
25. MLMC, Records of the Joints Chiefs of Staff, pt. 1 (1942–45) Strategic Issues, reel 12, State Department to American Legation, Berne, 30 Mar. 1944, p. 0781. Earlier in the war, the American government had invited twelve Latin American countries to send their German and Japanese internees to the United States to ensure their continued internment and in the hopes that they could be used for exchange purposes. See Edward N. Barnhart, 'Japanese Internees from Peru', *Pacific Historical Review*, vol. 31, 1962, pp. 169–78.
26. NAC, RG 24, reel C–5337, f. HQS 9050–14–7, pt. 2, Rive to Deputy-Minister of National Defence, 11 Apr. 1944.
27. NAC, RG 25, vol. 3342, f. 4464–40, pt. 6, Meagher to Rive, 11 Apr. 1944.
28. Ibid., Magann to Rive, 21 Apr. 1944.
29. Ibid., Scott to Rive, 25 Apr. 1944. Scott was referring to the fact that many Canadian missionaries in the Far East did not wish to desert their charges before, during or after the war. Patricia Roy, J. L. Granatstein, Masako Iino, and Hiroko Takamura, *Mutual Hostages: Canadians and Japanese during the Second World War*, Toronto, 1990, pp. 57–61, 208.
30. NAC, RG 25, vol. 3343, f. 4464–40, pt. 6, note by Robertson, 20 June 1944.
31. NAC, RG 24, reel C–5337, f. HQS 9050–14–7, pt. 2, Rive to Deputy-Minister of National Defence, Army, 11 Apr. 1944; Canadian Minister, Washington, to External Affairs, 27 May 1944.
32. PRO, CAB 66/53, WP(44)404, US Embassy, London, to Foreign Office, 14 June 1944; NAC, RG 24, reel C–5337, f. HQS 9050–14–7, pt. 2, High Commission to External Affairs, 3 July 1944.
33. *Foreign Relations of the United States, Diplomatic Papers, 1944*, vol. 5, *The Near East, South Asia and Africa, The Far East*, Washington, 1965 (hereafter *FRUS*), Secretary of State to US Minister, Washington, 4 Sept. 1944, p. 1090.
34. PRO, FO 916/1096, minute, 16 June 1944; minute by Lambert, 5 July 1944.
35. W. J. Hudson and N. J. W. Stokes (eds), *Documents on Australian Foreign Policy*, vol. 7, Canberra, 1983, doc. #218, Commonwealth Government to High Commissioner, London, 10 July 1944, p. 444.
36. NAC, RG 24, reel C–5337, f. HQS 9050–14–7, pt. 2, External Affairs to High Commission, 3 July 1944; Scott to External Affairs, undated [July 1944].
37. PRO, FO 916/1096, India Office to Eden, 28 July 1944.
38. Ibid., minute by Butler, 11 July 1944.

39. PRO, CAB 66/53, WP(44)404, 23 July 1944; CAB 65/43, WM98(44)4, 28 July 1944.
40. PRO, FO 916/1096, minute by Davidson, 9 Sept. 1944.
41. NAC, RG 24, reel C–5337, f. HQS 9050–14–7, pt. 2, External Affairs to High Commission, 3 July 1944.
42. NAC, RG 25, vol. 3342, f. 4464–40, pt. 6, High Commission to External Affairs, 25 Sept. 1944.
43. Ibid., External Affairs to High Commission, 28 Sept. 1944; High Commission to External Affairs, 18 Oct. 1944.
44. NAC, RG 24, reel C–5337, f. HQS 9050–14–7, pt. 2, High Commission to External Affairs, 18 Oct. 1944; RG 25, vol. 3342, f. 4464–40, pt. 6, External Affairs to High Commission, 24 Oct. 1944 (two cables).
45. PRO, CAB 66/57, WP(44)650, 15 Nov. 1944, containing letter from American Embassy, London, to Foreign Office, dated 9 Nov. 1944; CAB 65/44, WM151(44)3, 16 Nov. 1944; *FRUS*, vol. 5, Secretary of State to chargé d'affaires, Switzerland, 1 Dec. 1944, p. 1097.
46. PRO, FO 916/1389, British Embassy, Washington to Foreign Office POW Department, 19 Jan. 1945.
47. Ibid., minutes by Davidson, 13 Nov. and 22 Dec. 1944, 2 Jan. 1945.
48. Ibid., Wheeler to Foreign Office, 3 Jan. 1945; minute by Eden, 20 Jan. 1945.
49. NAC, RG 25, vol. 3342, f. 4464–40, pt. 6, Dominions Office to External Affairs, 5 June 1945.
50. Ibid., memo. entitled, 'Proposed Exchange of POWs and Civilians with Japan', 20 June 1945; External Affairs to Canadian Embassy, Washington, 23 June 1945.
51. W. Franklin Mellor (ed.), *Casualties and Medical Statistics*, London, 1972, p. 837; R. J. Pritchard and Sonia Zaide (eds), *The Tokyo War Crimes Trials*, New York, 1981, p. 14909; John Ellis, *The Sharp End of War: The Fighting Man in World War 2*, Newton Abbot, 1980, appendix.

Captives of their Countrymen: Free French and Vichy French POWs in Africa and the Middle East, 1940–3

Martin Thomas

Before General Charles de Gaulle's triumphal arrival in Paris in August 1944, one of the many divisive issues across France was that of prisoners of war (POWs). Between the armistice in June 1940 and Germany's occupation of southern France in November 1942 the return of French POWs evoked similar passions within Vichy France and the *zone occupée* to the north. French historians have understandably been drawn to the fate of the 1,850,000 prisoners held captive in Germany following the French collapse. The release of these men was intimately linked to Premier Pierre Laval's introduction of the hated *Relève* and the subsequent *Service du Travail Obligatoire* (STO) which sent hundreds of thousands more Frenchmen to work in German industry from 1942 to 1944. The work on prisoner exchanges has been complemented by analyses of the treatment and indoctrination of French POWs within German camps.[1] The return of POWs from Germany was a key litmus test of the justifications for the collaborationism of Vichy France. French prisoners held by the Germans were central to political debate inside France, their projected release always an issue of the utmost popular concern.

There were, however, other French prisoners detained outside Europe, not by the Axis powers, but by French colonial governments. In Vichyite colonies, those sympathetic to the Free French cause were detained. From August 1940, the reverse applied in the colonies that rallied to the Free French cause. Unlike their brethren in Germany, these men were France's forgotten POWs: prisoners held captive by their countrymen. Historians have neglected the fate of French POWs in the hands of other Frenchmen. There has been little study of the Vichy and Free French servicemen and administrative personnel imprisoned by their compatriots. These prisoners deserve closer attention. Just as the

Frenchmen held inside Germany became pawns in Germany's manipulation of Vichy, so the POWs detained across the divided French empire were instruments within the shifting balance of power between Marshal Philippe Pétain's regime and General Charles de Gaulle's Free French movement. Indeed, these prisoners became part of a wider diplomatic game as Britain and later the United States moved towards open confrontation with Vichy France.

Once de Gaulle issued his appeal calling for continued French resistance on 18 June 1940, a Free French movement quickly took shape. The resultant Free French administration was officially sanctioned and financed by the British authorities. It operated as a quasi-government-in-exile from its headquarters in Carlton Gardens until the establishment of a Gaullist-led committee of national liberation (FCNL) in Algiers in June 1943. From the first *ralliements* in June 1940 there was thus a possibility for French citizens to take one another prisoner on the grounds either of treason to the Vichy state or, conversely, of a craven submission to the Axis.

Why then has the fate of these Frenchmen attracted so little interest? After all, their problematic legal status as POWs sets them apart from the regular forces captured during the battle for France. So too does the bitterness that was evident between French captors and captives, men caught on opposing sides in an undeclared imperial civil war. There are perhaps two principal explanations for the lack of historical attention paid to these POWs to date. The first is that these prisoners were rarely held captive for more than two years. Allied and Free French operations against the Vichy empire spread slowly to French Africa after the British-directed seizure of Syria and Lebanon in July 1941. With the conversion of French North Africa to the Allied cause after the American-led 'Torch' landings in November 1942, it was only a matter of time before the remaining Gaullist and Vichyite prisoners were released by their respective French guardians.

The second explanation is that, unlike either the regular forces captured during the battle for France or the POWs of the principal combatant nations, Free French and Vichy French POWs were numbered in thousands, not hundreds of thousands. Individual disputes over prisoners between the French national committee and its patron, the British government, on the one hand, and the Vichy government and its chaperons, the German and Italian armistice commissions, on the other, rarely involved groups of more than two hundred detainees. As will be seen, the bulk of these POWs, whether service personnel or interned civilians, were taken prisoner far from metropolitan France in Africa and the Syrian Levant.[2]

The unique status of Free French prisoners – recognized as the legitimate servants of France by the British but derided as traitors by Vichy – raised particular problems for both sides. It was always doubtful whether the Vichy authorities would grant Free French POWs recognition as such. These prisoners were disloyal to the regime in their homeland, so why should they be accorded the status of 'serving forces' at all? Equally, how could the Free French authorities hope to bargain for the release of their personnel when the French national committee, the executive arm of the movement, was not recognized by the Vichy state or by the Axis governments?

What of Pétainist prisoners in Allied hands? Most of the Vichyite POWs were not captured by Free French but by British empire forces. But who was best qualified to administer them? How would the treatment of prisoners loyal to Pétain's regime affect Vichy's attitude to Britain? Were these prisoners the only leverage available to the Free French to secure the release or fair treatment of their own personnel? In short, the issues affecting POWs raised by the conflict between Vichy France and Free France were as complex as they were bitterly contested; an acute reflection of the trauma of French defeat.

Three additional aspects of the Vichy French–Free French POW question must be borne in mind. Firstly, as has been suggested above, neither the French national committee nor the Vichy authorities were free operators. There was a simple inverse ratio at work here as the war progressed. After it decamped to North Africa in 1943, the Free French movement was recast as a French committee of national liberation following its amalgamation with General Henri Giraud's Algiers administration. In consequence, it acquired greater independence from its erstwhile British protector.[3] Conversely, after the American landings in French North Africa in November 1942, the German High Command quickly swept southwards into Unoccupied France and the quasi-independence of the Vichy state was gone. Before this operation, the Free French and their most effective advocate in London, Major-General Edward Spears, were at pains to stress that the armistice commissions were the real power behind the Vichy throne in the matter of POWs. In February 1941 Spears reminded the Foreign Office of this, 'To rub shoulders with Vichy, moreover, is to be in contact with Wiesbaden [the German armistice commission office]. Every favour granted to Vichy is a favour granted to Germany.'[4]

The second point to remember is that French POWs held by both sides were overwhelmingly composed of forces serving in the French empire. As there was no fighting between regular French armed forces within mainland France, the manner in which that empire divided in 1940 is fundamental to an understanding of how and why prisoners came to be taken during the subsequent three years. The far greater number of French POWs taken by the German invading army in 1940 became bargaining chips in relations between Vichy and Berlin. This was a matter beyond Free French control, except in so far as Gaullist propaganda fastened upon this issue in order to pour scorn upon the alleged independence of the Pétainist regime.[5] As those prisoners taken during the battle for France did not feature in the POW exchanges contemplated between the Free French movement and the Vichy government, they fall outside the scope of this chapter.

The final oddity in the Free French–Vichy French POW situation arose naturally from the preceding two. As the war slowly turned the Allies' way, so recruitment of volunteers from among the Vichy POWs for de Gaulle's *France combattante* increased. To the Free French, the Vichy POWs taken in Africa and the Middle East were always seen as a pool of potential military manpower. In addition, they provided a powerful political weapon to a movement striving for recognition as a full Allied Power.[6]

I

French prisoners were taken by both the Vichy and Free French forces during the intermittent fighting between the two sides before the effective collapse of the Vichy empire in the wake of Operation Torch in November 1942. By February 1943 only Indo-China maintained a nominal allegiance to Vichy. A clutch of French West Indian territories and a powerful naval squadron dormant in Alexandria also opted for a continued *de facto* neutrality.[7] After Admiral François Darlan's crucial North African deal with the Allies in the first days of the Torch landings, the more protracted negotiations between Anglo-American represent-atives and General Pierre Boisson, Vichy Governor of French West Africa, eventually brought over the most significant remaining Franco-phone territory in June 1943.[8] The French empire's civil war – and with it, the disputes over POWs – was all but over by the time the Anglo-American land offensive in southern Europe began with the Sicily landings in July. The remaining active units of what had been Vichy's army in Africa, limited under the terms of the 1940 armistices with Germany and Italy to 120,000 poorly equipped troops, were by then incorporated within Fighting French forces under the military authority of General Giraud. The General was in turn subordinate to Eisen-hower's Supreme Allied Command.[9]

Governor Pierre Boisson had always exercised jurisdiction over the majority of Free French prisoners in Vichy hands since the most bitter fratricidal engagements occurred in West Africa. Nevertheless, the fighting was neither protracted nor did it increase over time. The apogee occurred early with Operation Menace on 24–25 September 1940. This was the abortive Anglo-Free French effort to seize Dakar, capital of Senegal and administrative heart of French West Africa.[10] Thereafter, Boisson added to his tally of prisoners by the occasional capture of airmen and the crews of detained merchant vessels, the incarceration of Free French agents and the internment of those colonial officials whose loyalty to Pétain was deemed questionable. Following a tour of French North and West Africa in October 1940, General Maxime Weygand, Pétain's appointee as *Délégué Général* in Vichy Africa, concluded that the majority of serving civil and military personnel remained danger-ously Anglophile. Venting his prejudices against Freemasons, Jews and civilian administrators in general, Weygand pressed for the detention of any French personnel whose sympathies for Vichy were less than exemplary.[11] Over subsequent months many of those placed in detention in French West Africa were former colonial civil servants held on sus-picion of Free French bias. After the failure of Menace, neither the British nor the Free French attempted any further forced landings against Dakar, although German U-Boats gained limited access to French West African port facilities from May 1941.[12]

While the first significant Free French military defeat took place in Africa, so too did the initial successes. By November 1940, Gabon was added to the Equatorial African territories that, like Chad, had either voluntarily rallied to de Gaulle in August, or had been captured with minimal resistance, as was the case in the French Cameroons and the French Congo. All of these *ralliements* produced few casualties and small collections of POWs; typically, Vichy officials and the local colonial garrisons. The defending forces were usually composed of black African conscripts officered by white French career soldiers. The capture of Libreville, the principal port of Gabon, brought the richest bounty. Its garrison had been hastily reinforced from French West Africa with aircraft, a submarine and a new commander, General Têtu, Vichy's nominee as Governor of Equatorial Africa.[13] As one would expect, the civilian personnel, often with their families alongside them, were interned, rather than being held under the same terms as captured servicemen. Where the Free French take-over began with operations against a port, as at Douala in the Cameroons and Port Gentil in Gabon, naval personnel were also taken, most notably the crews of the submarines *Ajax* and *Poncelet*, captured at Dakar and Libreville res-pectively.[14] By Christmas 1940, both Vichy Africa and Free French Africa had thus acquired a broadly equivalent stock of POW bargaining chips. During 1941 and 1942 the Vichy empire suffered a series of mil-itary defeats without any compensatory victories. Although Admiral Decoux's capitulation to Japanese–Thai demands between July 1940 and July 1941 effectively ended undisputed French sovereignty across the Indo-Chinese peninsula, neither was there a protracted campaign nor were substantial numbers of French troops kept prisoner during the 'co-existence' period. Some 2,500 troops were captured following bitter fighting with the Japanese around Langson on the north Vietnam–China border in September 1940. A further 200 were held captive by Thai forces pending Decoux's signature of an armistice with the Thais on 28 January 1941.[15] From May 1942, the Japanese army began housing British and Australian POWs in four camps across Indo-China, without the consent or active co-operation of the French colonial authorities. Decoux's inability to prevent the operation of the camps, or even to secure International Red Cross access to them, illustrated that there was little the Vichy government, let alone the French national committee, could do to influence the lives of POWs in south-east Asia.[16]

By contrast, General Dentz's Levant army resisted a joint British empire and Free French invasion for six weeks before Syria and Lebanon fell in July 1941. In the following year, British empire forces completed a two-stage invasion of Vichy-controlled Madagascar between May and November 1942. Administration of the island was then transferred to de Gaulle's appointee, General Paul Legentilhomme, in December. In the same month, the isolated and blockaded Vichy enclave of French Somaliland caved in as soon as a British-led invasion was launched, Djibouti being taken without loss of life.[17]

In the Syria, Madagascar and Somaliland operations Vichy prisoners were taken. As before, the French passport-holders among them were either civilian officials and their families, professional army officers, or naval personnel. Once again, the bulk of those captured were black African conscripts, whose personal loyalty to Vichy's national revolution or to *Pétainisme* was understandably slight. Another of the largest homogeneous groups of Vichy troops captured was some 1,700 Annamite soldiers, who were kept in detention centres in South Africa during 1941.[18] The key difference between the 1940 actions in West and Equatorial Africa and the more lengthy campaigns in 1941 and 1942 lay in the involvement of British land forces. To be precise, Free France's share in these later victories was more political than military.

This was ironic, since de Gaulle devoted much effort to the construction of *Forces Françaises Libres* (FFL) army divisions capable of front-line operations alongside Allied forces. Syria was captured after fighting directed by General Archibald Wavell's Middle East command, in which Australian and Indian troops played the greater part. Madagascar fell to a combination of British, South African and Indian troops, the British cabinet and Chiefs of Staff having endorsed Churchill's decision to exclude Free French forces altogether. Finally, French

Somaliland fell to troops from General Platt's East African command in December 1942. In anticipation of this, several months earlier, the War Office Directorate of POWs had laid plans to exchange any prisoners taken at Djibouti for British servicemen held in French North Africa. In January 1943 the most senior French officers detained in French Somaliland, Generals Truffert and Dupont, were offered the chance to serve with General Giraud's reconstituted French forces.[19]

As the Djibouti example suggests, although the Vichy empire contracted and Free French overseas administration correspondingly increased, General de Gaulle did not find himself in charge of appreciably larger numbers of Vichyite POWs. By the time the Syrian campaign began in June 1941, the British government was determined to keep control of Vichy personnel in order to arrange prisoner exchanges directly with both the metropolitan Vichy authorities and individual Vichy colonial governments. This applied particularly to Pierre Boisson's French West Africa, where a number of British servicemen and merchant seamen were incarcerated in addition to Free French detainees.[20] Paradoxically, as the British enjoyed greater success in liberating Vichy colonial territory and introducing the French national committee to a share in its administration, jurisdiction over Vichy POWs became one of the many open wounds in relations between Whitehall and de Gaulle's headquarters in Carlton Gardens.

II

In the matter of POWs, the British government was more conciliatory towards the Vichy government and its colonial administrations than were the Free French. This reflected British strategic thinking. Churchill and his operational planners in all three Service Ministries did not want to fight a general war against the Vichy empire. After the failure to capture Dakar in September 1940, they preferred to pick off territories one by one as opportunity allowed. Typically, this involved waiting for sufficient manpower and shipping to embark on offensive operations that held less strategic importance than actions against German and Italian forces. The notable exception was the Levant campaign, driven as it was by the threat of Axis penetration to the Middle East inherent in Germany's use of Syrian air-bases and strategic facilities.

Between October 1940 and July 1941 the usual British practice was to repatriate pro-Vichy prisoners and merchant crews as soon as possible, either by the use of neutral – often Portuguese – shipping, or by putting detainees across a land frontier into a Vichy colony. This procedure was directed primarily by the cabinet committee on foreign resistance, chaired by Churchill's private secretary Major Desmond Morton. The Foreign Office POW Department, containing a number of senior French Department personnel, also played a key role in the process. Other ministries, such as the Ministry of War Transport and the Colonial Office, became involved in prisoner exchanges, depending upon the location of the detainees and the method of repatriation adopted.[21]

The surprisingly fierce resistance put up by General Dentz's troops in the Syrian campaign confirmed the British resolve to 'localize hostilities' against Vichy forces. This infuriated de Gaulle. According to the Free French diplomatic *direction des affaires politiques*, captured Vichyite soldiers were 'genuinely astonished' to learn of the presence of Free French troops in the Levant, their commanders having told them they were fighting only British empire forces.[22] Whatever the truth of this, British treatment of Vichy POWs became subsumed within this policy of successive localized campaigns, the paramount consideration being to avoid any unnecessary exacerbation of friction with the Pétain or Laval governments. In practice this meant that the British authorities were willing to negotiate the repatriation of French military and administrative personnel, and the demobilization and return home of black African forces, usually to Senegal, the Ivory Coast or Madagascar. The pre-requisite to this was reciprocity.[23]

The feeling that neither Pétain nor Boisson were playing fair over exchanges did lead to a firmer British attitude after July 1941. The nub of the uncooperative attitude of Vichy officialdom was its insistence that the 1940 armistice terms precluded the return to British territory of British and Allied personnel – including Free Frenchmen – of military age.[24] Desmond Morton's inclination was to respond in kind. He suggested to the committee on foreign resistance on 16 December 1941 that, in view of British hostility to the Pétain regime, no person 'of potential military value' should be repatriated to Vichy territory. Greater British firmness was also nurtured by increasing evidence of the occasional ill-treatment of British personnel in French North Africa in reprisal for alleged South African and Free French maltreatment of the Vichy POWs under their control.[25]

Once the Syrian campaign was completed, British policy on prisoner exchanges with Vichy territories became inconsistent. Practice varied according to the territory and the category of prisoners in question. Furthermore, by September 1942, as several hundred Vichyites captured in Madagascar were detained in South Africa, Jan Smuts's Pretoria government was introduced to policy discussions on an *ad hoc* basis.[26] By December 1941, the Gold Coast administration was preparing to release Vichy merchant seamen in Freetown who had made it plain that they would not serve de Gaulle. Yet merchant crews were detained indefinitely in Durban, although pro-Vichy servicemen held alongside them were repatriated.[27] Conversely, the Annamite prisoners held in South Africa could not be safely returned to Indo-China after Japan's entry to the war. In July 1942 the Foreign Office's POW Department agreed that the 1,700 troops in question should be shipped north to Syria to undertake manual labour on various public works projects for General Georges Catroux's Fighting French command. Such inconsistencies nourished de Gaulle's criticism of British handling of Vichy POWs. But these anomalies remained a limited problem within Whitehall; the numbers involved never exceeded the Syrian total of 3,716.[28]

The British were also able to remain the chief arbiters in the handling of Vichy POWs in Africa, as the United States government showed little interest in wresting control of the matter from London. Immediately after the Torch landings in November 1942, the urgent redeployment of troop-ships and the continued intensity of the U-Boat war undermined tentative plans to transfer Vichyite loyalists captured in North Africa to the United States. Darlan's change of loyalties effectively nullified the need for such a scheme. The spaces allotted to Vichy prisoners were reallocated to Italian POWs taken in Tunisia during 1943.[29]

Although no formal diplomatic links existed between London and Vichy after the British recognition of de Gaulle in June 1940, dialogue was relatively simple. It normally took place through one of three channels. The British government could make use of Admiral William Leahy, American ambassador to Vichy. In view of Churchill and Eden's abiding disdain for Roosevelt's conciliatory attitude to Pétain, the former foreign secretary, Madrid ambassador Sir Samuel Hoare, was frequently preferred as an intermediary. Just as Hoare was able to talk direct to his Vichy French counterpart, so Sir Bernard Bourdillon, Governor of Nigeria and chairman of the British West African Governors' conference, gradually established unofficial communications with Governor Boisson in Dakar.[30] These channels to Vichy naturally put the British in a commanding position relative to the Free French movement whenever POW questions of joint interest arose.

The status of the Free French movement as equivalent to a recognized government-in-exile was also crucial here. Although Churchill had publicly acknowledged de Gaulle as the legitimate voice of France since June 1940, the Carlton Gardens administration did not claim to be a provisional government in waiting. America's continued diplomatic relations with Vichy, while often useful to Britain, illustrated that the Anglo-Saxon powers did not see eye to eye over the constitutional position of Free France. Washington's ties with Vichy implied a recognition that Pétain had taken office legally, since the Third Republic had effectively voted itself out of existence in 1940. De Gaulle's claim to authority rested on the premiss that defeat and the armistice had undermined the legitimacy of government within France.[31]

This bore directly upon Free French rights to exercise jurisdiction over POWs in the colonial territories under their control. The Foreign Office maintained that recognition of de Gaulle entitled the Free French movement to the privileges accorded to lawful belligerents under international law. This implied that Gaullist forces could take and keep prisoners for themselves. But even de Gaulle's protagonists within the Foreign Office French Department conceded that the French national committee could not be construed as a combatant 'power' as the term was understood within the Geneva Convention. Furthermore, as the movement was so heavily dependent upon British funding, British logistical support and British shipping for the detention of POWs, the enemy powers might argue convincingly that the Free French were wholly *libre* in name only. There was thus the danger of reprisals against British empire prisoners in response to alleged ill-treatment of POWs by de Gaulle's forces.[32]

Finally, another powerful argument levelled against the detention of prisoners in Gaullist territory was that few countries had established any diplomatic representation in the outposts of the Free French empire. This would leave any Vichy or Axis POWs held there without the impartial supervision of a 'protecting power', usually a neutral state whose representatives had rights of access to prisoners under the terms of the Geneva Convention.[33] In August 1942 the Foreign Office's POW Department used this objection to reject the possibility of any detention of German *Afrika Korps* in Free French Chad, despite the fact that the territory was contiguous to Libya, where the fighting in North Africa was concentrated. One outcome of this legal uncertainty was that the British frequently exercised indirect control over prisoners theoretically in Fighting French hands, most notably in Syria, in order to prevent any accusations of neglect of the Geneva Convention.

What then of the Free French response? After the September 1940 humiliation at Dakar, Carlton Gardens and de Gaulle's commanders in the field regarded British eagerness for prisoner exchanges as at once cavalier and militarily unsound. Ironically, before this, the first Vichy soldiers and officials taken by the Free French when Chad, the Cameroons and the French Congo rallied to de Gaulle had not been treated as POWs. Labelled as 'political prisoners', the handful of colonial administrators and troops taken were dealt with as 'evacuees' in the weeks prior to the launch of Operation Menace.[34]

At this early stage of the French war in Africa, de Gaulle shared the British Colonial Office view that those detained should be promptly returned to France or to French West Africa in order to proclaim both

British fair play and the Free French credo.[35] In mid-August the Ministry of National Defence at Vichy had approved a more rapid turnover of young French officers within the colonial commands. This would give the maximum number of armistice army personnel direct exposure to active service and life in the empire.[36] If captured by British or Free French forces, the rapid release of these junior officers was expected to undermine their loyalty to Pétain. This thinking was easily explicable in the light of the recent British attack on the French fleet at Mersel-Kébir on 3 July. For several weeks, Churchill's cabinet feared a more active Vichy collaboration with the Axis. The bombardment also brought recruitment to the Free French cause to a virtual standstill in July.[37]

From the perspective of the Free French, the die was cast by the assault on Dakar. While sailing for West Africa with the British naval task force, on 6 September, de Gaulle instructed his senior officers to do all possible by word and deed to prove to the Dakar garrison that Free France was a noble cause. This high-mindedness extended to the planned treatment of prisoners, who were to be treated less as captives than as guests pending their anticipated conversion to the Free French banner.[38] This naïve idealism was buried by the failure of the Dakar operation. There remained little prospect of any further colonial territories' rallying to Free France without some use of force.[39]

There were echoes of this change of sentiment in the German POW camps for French officers captured during the battle for France. Unbeknown to de Gaulle, official Nazi propaganda acquired a new respectability among the officer POWs precisely because it directed its fire against British and Free French treachery across the French empire. These views were disseminated to prisoners through the Berlin government's French-language weekly *Le Trait d'Union*. Tapping a deep vein of Anglophobia, this propaganda compounded the Pétainist sympathies of the 29,000 or so officers in detention inside Germany. As Jean-Marie d'Hoop has shown, the Nazi argument appeared seductive: '. . . after Dakar, there was nothing left to prove regarding Perfidious Albion: from the Middle Ages, to Joan of Arc, Fashoda and soon the Syrian campaign, Britain always opposed French aggrandizement and was France's real enemy'.[40]

De Gaulle's attitude to captured Vichyites hardened correspondingly. In theory, any British or Allied prisoners released by Vichy would then be able to resume their front-line service. In practice, the majority of personnel exchanged were merchant seamen. De Gaulle insisted that the British government was prepared to exchange Vichy prisoners without adequate recompense. Had these Vichyite POWs been retained, they might have converted to Free France. More importantly, a pool of prisoners was essential as a means to bargain for the release of Free French POWs. In de Gaulle's eyes, by virtue of their comparative scarcity, these serving Free Frenchmen were a more valuable resource than a sundry collection of British merchant sailors. Furthermore, any Vichy personnel who rallied to de Gaulle were a vital propaganda weapon. Again, to de Gaulle, this was a factor more important to the Allied war effort than for the British to obtain some temporary gratitude from Vichy for the prompt repatriation of Vichyite POWs.

With hindsight, de Gaulle's arguments seem persuasive. By 1942 the Vichy French High Command was disconcerted by the creeping demoralization of the armistice army under its control. In March there remained over 100,000 troops across French North and West Africa who appeared increasingly restive, if not rebellious. Prior to the German take-over of unoccupied France, dissatisfaction stemmed primarily from boredom. Lacking modern equipment and any strategic purpose beyond the preservation of colonial order, the soldiers of French North Africa were increasingly receptive to Gaullist propaganda. It is reasonable to deduce that this same demoralization might have affected any Vichy prisoners kept by the British. As de Gaulle argued, these POWs might indeed have converted to Fighting France as the allies achieved wider military success.[41]

At the outset of British operations in Madagascar in May 1942, General Leclerc, then Governor in Free French Chad, requested that any surrender terms avoid a repetition of the Syrian armistice, which had allowed not only Vichy personnel but also war *matériel* to be returned to Vichy-controlled territory.[42] On 16 July 1941 most of the air force squadrons sent to reinforce Dentz's command had slipped back to French North Africa without challenge, although the Syria armistice had been signed two days earlier.[43] Though Leclerc's complaints were valid, such criticism was counter-productive. It added to the British military conviction, espoused most insistently by Major-General Edward Spears, head of the British liaison mission to Carlton Gardens and later the *de facto* joint administrator of Syria and Lebanon, that Free French thinking on POWs was animated by visions of new recruits. This in turn increased British reluctance to cede to the Free French any autonomous control over military government in colonial territories. Were this to be done, it was expected that de Gaulle's representatives would immediately levy black African conscripts in order to increase their regional political leverage with the British.[44]

III

Those prisoners held captive in either Free French or Vichy black African territory faced three principal dangers. The first was disease, malaria above all. This threat ebbed and flowed depending upon the season and the proximity of camps to stagnant water or marshy rivers. The second problem was poor diet. No prisoners were kept deliberately under-nourished, but, in the Vichy territories especially, the provision of a 'European' diet, including meat, bread and root vegetables, became near impossible as the pressures of the British naval blockade of French North and West Africa intensified in 1941.[45] The final problem was the general paucity of camp medical supplies, applicable in both Vichy and Free French territory. One British prisoner gave an informative account of his experience at Vichy's Koulikoro internment camp in French Sudan,

> The treatment of British internees . . . in French West Africa was, on the whole, reasonably satisfactory. The principal defects at the Camp were the unnecessarily close confinement in which we were kept, lack of facilities for exercise, poor medical attention, flies, dirt and discomfort. These short-comings were due not so much to the attitude of those immediately in charge of us . . . as to the extraordinary inefficiency and muddle-headedness of the authorities and to the less extent to shortage of supplies.[46]

In often tropical conditions, relatively minor ailments, wounds and abrasions frequently developed into serious illness in the absence of antiseptic treatment. Both the British and Vichy colonial authorities tended to treat such exceptional problems sympathetically, expediting prisoner exchanges and repatriation where possible. The Free French colonial authorities, though more reluctant to release prisoners without compensation, were occasionally prepared to secure better medical provision for sick prisoners by transfer to British territory.[47]

British sensitivity to accusations of flouting the Geneva Convention led the Foreign Office's POW Department to look unfavourably upon any transfers of Vichy or Italian POWs to Gaullist territory in tropical Africa. In December 1941 and again in May 1942, the French national committee lodged a request for the shipment to Brazzaville, first of 230, and then of 150, skilled Italian POWs from South Africa. These prisoners would then work as builders, fitters and road-menders. On each occasion the Foreign Office argued that the harshness of the Brazzaville climate would be cited in order to allege ill-treatment. This hardly squared with the wholesale British shipment of Italians to camps in India. The French national committee response was to suggest that only those who volunteered for transfer would be accepted. This proposition was intended to satisfy British insistence that no POWs should be transferred against their will to Free French territory. Although this met the principal objection of the POW department, the transfer of these Italian tradesmen stalled. The Foreign Office and War Office feared that the Free French authorities would offer to pay higher wage rates to those prisoners willing to transfer. This was a precedent bound to have adverse consequences upon British policy regarding the use of POW labour.[48]

The Free French authorities in Equatorial Africa and Chad did control some Italian prisoners and internees of their own, since 110 Italians were interned in these colonies immediately Mussolini entered the war in June 1940.[49] Unlike their more fortunate compatriots in Vichy territories, these internees were not freed upon French signature of the armistice with Italy on 24 June 1940. But it was during 1941 that Free French forces first captured significant numbers of Italian troops during the Libyan campaign. This led to the first Free French codification of the procedures to be followed in the detention of Italian POWs. Colonel Edgard de Larminat, recently appointed high commissioner in French Equatorial Africa, issued a six-chapter report specifying that the Italians were to be treated according to the requirements of the Hague and Geneva Conventions. The immediate spur to this was the capture of 327 troops at Koufra in March 1941. Among these prisoners, 273 were askaris. This left only 54 Italians in total. As the drive through Libya progressed, additional POWs joined those held in Free French camps across the frontier in Chad. Most were put to work in public work projects in Fort Lamy (now N'Djamena) in Chad. They performed tasks akin to those planned for the POWs requested by the French national committee in May 1942.[50]

During the Syrian campaign in June and July 1941, lists of prisoners held by both sides were swiftly exchanged via the American consulate in Beirut. The medical treatment of wounded was also fully documented. British troops in Beirut hospitals received comparable standards of care to the 200 or so Vichy personnel moved to hospitals in Jerusalem.[51] The War Office decision to place all POWs in a 'common pot', regardless of whether they were taken by British or Fighting French troops, denied either de Gaulle or his regional commander, General Georges Catroux, any role in the subsequent negotiation of prisoner exchanges, particularly since the Vichy captives were held in Palestine pending repatriation. Instead, this task fell to a sub-committee of the Commission of Control created to administer implementation of the armistice.[52] As soon as Dentz's forces surrendered following the capture of Beirut on 15 July, the retention of 3,716 prisoners in Palestine Camp #321 was simply an unwanted headache for the Middle

East command. General Wavell had displayed little enthusiasm for the Syrian venture from its outset. Colonel Philibert Collet, Free French liaison officer with the Middle East command, complained to de Gaulle over British complacency in refusing to allow Gaullist personnel early access to the holding camps. This had enabled Vichyite officers to continue intimidating those POWs who appeared ready to change sides. Several hundred potential recruits had been lost.[53]

Hence the largest single group of Vichy POWs were kept out of de Gaulle's hands. As a sop to the General, a Free French representative, Captain Tredez, sat on the Jerusalem-based sub-committee administering the return of the Levant army prisoners. By 12 September 1941 all those Vichy prisoners who requested repatriation had been embarked. The sole exception was a group of ten French officers. These men were kept as hostages pending the return of an equivalent number of British officers who had been removed to France soon after their capture in Syria. In sum, 1,098 of Dentz's troops chose to remain in the Middle East under Catroux's Fighting French command. But virtually all of Dentz's officers and NCOs remained faithful to Vichy.[54] In November the German armistice commission approved the transfer to French North Africa of the remaining units of the Levant army that had been in metropolitan France since the Syria campaign, including certain officers repatriated from Beirut. Following requests from Vichy's Minister of Colonies, Admiral Charles Platon, to the Wiesbaden commission, additional reinforcements were also approved for French West Africa.[55]

While the British were gratified at the conversion of so many of Dentz's troops to the Free French cause, it irritated Carlton Gardens that the entire process had been conducted on British terms. Originally, the Syria armistice offered Vichy troops a free choice between repatriation or enlistment with Fighting French forces at British rates of service pay. In early August 1941 the British and Free French representatives on the armistice commission of control denounced this agreement on the grounds that the Vichy government had contravened it.[56]

Soldiers contemplating a conversion to Fighting France were threatened with loss of French citizenship, state confiscation of their property and judgement *in absentia* by Vichy military tribunal. This raised a ticklish point of international law. If troops changed sides under terms previously sanctioned by armistice, these men could not be classified as deserters, provided that their transfer was supervised by the British forces signatory to that armistice. But if Vichy repudiated the armistice and appealed to the higher legal authority of the French military code, then any soldiers rallying to de Gaulle faced a more uncertain future. In a further bid to discourage senior personnel from changing sides, Vichy ordered the transfer of the personal belongings of Levant army officers to Beirut in readiness for repatriation.[57] Just as rallying troops to Fighting France was central to the credibility of de Gaulle's movement, so the discouragement of such conversions was essential to the national self-image of the Vichy armed forces. If a large proportion of troops and, above all, officers, joined the Free French then the characterization of Darlan, Boisson and Dentz as true patriots would collapse.[58]

In retaliation for Vichy's acts of bad faith over the Syria armistice the War Office belatedly permitted Gaullist recruiters unrestricted access to the remaining POWs in Palestine. Although the British authorities had taken responsibility for the care and lodgement of the Vichy prisoners without encouraging significant Free French involvement, Catroux's representatives were thus allowed to assist War Office personnel in attempting to rally as many prisoners as possible.[59] Prospects for recruitment improved once it was made plain to prisoners that any future combat would be against German or Italian forces, and not against other Vichy troops. Held under Jewish guard, the eleven hundred Vichy POWs in Palestine that eventually rallied to Fighting France were composed of broadly equivalent numbers of French and colonial troops. Many of these served in the Tunisian campaign in 1943.[60]

Relative to the proportion of Vichy POWs that rallied to the Free French in Syria in 1941, few of the prisoners taken in Madagascar in the following year followed suit. This was easily explained. The majority of Frenchmen detained were either professional colonial army officers, very few of whom counted themselves republican, or naval personnel for whom the recollection of British treachery at Mers-el-Kébir and Dakar was a vivid memory. Reporting on preliminary interrogations of the French prisoners taken in the attack on Diego Suarez, Captain R. D. Jeune of the army intelligence corps, noted:

> There is unfortunately no denying that the regrettable conflicts at ORAN [Mers-el-Kébir], DAKAR [Operation Menace] and in Syria have made an indelible impression on the minds of nearly all the officers interrogated and in many cases this has become, as a result of brooding, low morale and possible enemy propaganda, a kind of masochistic cult, which they have no wish to give up.[61]

A key difference in the minds of these POWs was that Laval, Darlan and the Governor of Madagascar, Paul Annet, had all given repeated assurances that use of the island's port facilities would never be conceded to the Japanese. It was fear of this eventuality that prompted the British-led invasion, much as the appearance of the *Luftwaffe* in Syria had catalysed operations there. Dentz, though, had been 'caught in the act' whereas the Vichy Ministry of National Defence had issued formal instructions to Annet to resist any Japanese incursion into Madagascar.[62]

The rest of the Madagascar garrison taken prisoner by British and South African forces was dominated by Malagasy and Senegalese troops. They were most anxious to be allowed home. Prime Minister Smuts certainly had no wish to detain more black Africans in South Africa, their most likely destination had they been detained for long. It was thus a matter of holding prisoners temporarily pending the arrangement of exchanges or the availability of shipping to take prisoners to West Africa, whichever came the sooner. General Platt, head of East Africa command in Kenya, which had directed the Madagascar operation, did not intend to leave Vichyite POWs in the hands of General Legentilhomme, the Fighting French Governor of Madagascar. To do so would have invited an energetic Gaullist recruitment drive. This was bound to cause friction with the British political and military missions on the island.[63]

IV

Article four of Darlan's 10 November 1942 proclamation to French commanders in North Africa ordered the immediate exchange of any Allied POWs still in the hands of the armistice army. Free French captives were not specifically referred to.[64] Admiral Jean-Pierre Esteva and General Georges Barré, supreme commanders in Tunisia, did not comply. Their ability to do so was curtailed by the landings of Axis forces within the country. It was not until the final defeat of Axis forces in Tunisia in May 1943 that the remaining Allied POWs in French North Africa were freed.

This process of emptying the Vichy camps was complicated by two additional factors. The first was the inevitable confusion inherent in dealing with rival French authorities all now claiming adherence to the Allied cause. The profound mutual animosity between Darlan's North African administration and the Fighting French movement prohibited any swift establishment of a unified French administrative and military hierarchy in French North Africa. The territory was, of course, composed of three countries, Morocco, Algeria and Tunisia. Each of these was directed by separate French colonial governments, pursuing fundamentally different methods of administration. Before the war Algeria had been constitutionally a part of France. Between January and June 1943 it was governed by former Vichy Interior Minister, Marcel Peyrouton. General Charles Nogues ruled Morocco from his Rabat residency almost as a personal fiefdom, encouraged by the strategic imperative of preventing any Spanish or Axis sweep southwards from the coastal enclave of Spanish Morocco. Finally, General Barré and Admirals Esteva and Darrien in Tunisia operated under the direct gaze of Axis forces.

Personal jealousies among these military governors, and their suspicion of their erstwhile Free French opponents, were gradually overcome during 1943. This was assisted by the replacement of the unfortunate Darlan by General Giraud, a figure-head whose captivity at Koenigstein in Germany during 1940–1941 left him untainted by close association with either Vichy or Carlton Gardens.[65] Despite Giraud's political incompetence, the eventual replacement of Noguès and Peyrouton confirmed the pro-Ally spirit in the French North African leadership. So too did the liberation of Tunisia.[66] But the power struggle between Giraud and de Gaulle for control of the Algiers administration perpetuated the problems of dealing with prisoners still in French hands until the creation of the French committee of national liberation on 3 June 1943.

The second complicating issue regarding the detainees across French North Africa was that the great majority of those held captive were not POWs at all, but civilian internees. Approximately 43 per cent of these were Spanish republican refugees and diverse members of the International Brigades that had fled into exile in France upon Franco's victory in the spring of 1939.[67] Some 39 per cent were allegedly French communists, including twenty-seven parliamentary deputies of the Parti Communiste Français. All had been hastily shipped to North Africa by the Vichy authorities in 1940.

Between December 1942 and February 1943, Resident Minister Harold Macmillan's staff at his Algiers headquarters worked with British and American consuls across Morocco and Algeria to establish the numbers held in camps under French control. In January a joint Anglo-American-French investigative team began a roving commission to visit all camps. This commission gathered details of the prisoners and the reasons for their detention. Although it proved difficult to arrive at a verifiable figure, the picture that emerged was surprising. Early estimates suggested that 7,435 internees were held in nine camps across the region.[68] By 9 February Macmillan was able to advise the Foreign Office that there were 3,562 detainees held in Morocco, of whom 1,217 were Spaniards. In Algeria the figure was 5,956, of whom 1,991 were Spanish. By this point, 903 internees had been freed in Morocco. The majority of these were International Brigaders of various nationalities, as well as Gaullists, most of whom had been arrested on the grounds of pro-Ally sentiments or actions on the eve of Operation Torch.[69] Soviet International Brigaders were promptly repatriated. Most of the rest came from countries under German control. Hence, as with the Spanish internees, the chief problem regarding Czech, Polish and Belgian International Brigaders was less to secure their release than to determine what to do with them next.[70]

The American ambassador to Madrid warned his British colleague, Sir Samuel Hoare, that any arming of the Spanish refugees or their employment on Allied public works projects would provoke Spanish governmental protests and a fresh wave of Axis propaganda within Spain.[71] Most of these refugees were unfit, poorly clothed and effectively stateless. Only the Mexican government's willingness to accept them offered hope of a solution. As was often the case in POW matters, the shortage of shipping meant that the Spaniards faced further months in North Africa living on handouts and menial employment offered by Eisenhower's supreme command.

The Spanish refugees were the most numerous category of detainee in French North Africa in early 1943. But French communists and Gaullist sympathizers yet to be released caused more disturbance to relations between the British, the Fighting French and the Giraudists. Disagreements between Giraud in Algiers and de Gaulle in London over the liberation of these detainees illustrated the political cleavage between the two. Giraud's right-wing outlook surfaced in his reluctance to accelerate the release of individuals who, whether communist or not, now saw themselves as Fighting French republicans.

Speaking to a press conference on 29 January 1943, Giraud made the following statement:

> I have liberated some prisoners. I expect to liberate others in increasing numbers. However, I must know for what reason they were arrested and I must be the judge of the decision to be taken. I shall quickly set free all those who have taken part in warlike deeds against Germany or Italy. I do not want dissension and I shall not worry anybody on account of the quality of his political opinions.[72]

These ambiguous remarks were unhelpful. Giraud only agreed to speak on the subject of detainees at the prompting of his close associate General Jean Bergeret, a reactionary figure who had applauded the General's willingness to keep in custody those considered subversive by Darlan's regime.[73] Giraud's sluggishness in pressing ahead with the repeal of Vichy ordinances across North Africa, above all the discriminatory legislation restricting the rights of Jews, added to British, American and Gaullist alarm over the remaining political prisoners in his charge.[74]

René Pleven, the French national committee member with responsibility for colonial affairs, was also anxious over the continued detention of Gaullist sympathizers by General Boisson's Dakar administration. Although he did not expressly request their assistance, Pleven relied upon the British Resident Minister in West Africa, Lord Swinton, and the newly appointed British consul to Dakar, E. W. Meiklereid, to verify the numbers of Frenchmen still in Boisson's hands. As in North Africa, a wave of arrests took place on the eve of the Torch landings. Eighty-four of those detained had been tried by a Vichy military tribunal. They received sentences ranging from two years' imprisonment to twenty years' hard labour. Many more had been convicted and then transferred to metropolitan France in the aftermath of the Dakar assault in late 1940. Such practice clearly ignored the Geneva Convention. Boisson's premiss was that these personnel had been found guilty of treasonous acts, and were certainly not entitled to recognition as Allied POWs.[75]

This naturally added to Free French interest in a rapid Allied achievement of a *modus vivendi* with the Dakar government. As in North Africa, this was tempered by concern lest Boisson and his immediate entourage be retained in office in return for a swifter agreement.[76] There were at least two hundred Vichy troops and administrators still in custody in Gaullist African territories. To the British it seemed feasible to exchange these men for the French prisoners in Boisson's hands. Here again, the French national committee was reluctant to enter any such bargain. The Dakar administration was expected to rally anyway after a few weeks of negotiation. De Gaulle's Vichy POWs would have been surrendered for little profit. The result was a stand-off, in which Swinton, Meiklereid and the American consulate in Dakar together monitored the treatment of Boisson's prisoners.[77]

Boisson knew that the majority of the military personnel held captive by the Fighting French in Equatorial Africa were originally members of his own staff. This compounded his reluctance to give ground in the talks over POW swaps.[78] Urged on by Meiklereid, in late February Boisson conceded a preliminary transfer of Gaullist detainees to Equatorial Africa. But the Governor indicated his enduring contempt for Free France by continuing the transfer or demotion of officials known to support de Gaulle.[79] Furthermore, Boisson claimed that a definitive agreement on French detainees was conditional upon a comprehensive settlement between Giraud and de Gaulle in Algiers.[80]

By contrast, the British were keen to divest themselves of the remaining Vichy POWs on Crown territory. The Foreign Office was encouraged by the conversion of Morocco and Algeria, the likelihood of military victory in Tunisia, and the expectation that Boisson would resign in order to make way for a *ralliement* in French West Africa. In late January the bulk of the French service personnel captured in

Madagascar and since detained on the Isle of Man, some 443 POWs in all, were embarked for North Africa. A week earlier Eisenhower wrote to Boisson on behalf of the British government to assure him that the Foreign Office would work for the early release of Vichy personnel from Free French Equatorial Africa, provided that reciprocity was assured.[81] Since early December the American commander had repeatedly urged the British government to pressure de Gaulle into the release of these POWs. Eisenhower feared that de Gaulle's refusal to comply would compromise the chances of reaching an early agreement in Dakar. This added to the American conviction that de Gaulle failed to place Allied strategic interests above all else.[82]

By the time Boisson finally quit French West Africa in early July there remained few Free French supporters, whether military or civilian, in detention outside France. The one exception was Indo-China, where several civilians had been arrested on suspicion of anti-Vichy sympathies in 1940. As Decoux's territory was unable to maintain communications with Vichy and was closed to Allied representatives, it was difficult to put a figure on those detained. Elsewhere, after being subjected to increasingly coercive attempts at recruitment, the majority of low-ranking Vichy personnel in Fighting French hands accepted the authority of the Algiers administration. This was made easier because de Gaulle's paramountcy within the FCNL was briefly concealed over the summer of 1943 by the fiction of power-sharing with Giraud. Nevertheless, the Algiers committee detained several former leading Vichy military and civilian officials, having agreed in September that all ex-Vichy Ministers should stand trial in France after the Liberation. Much to American and British annoyance, in November 1943 the FCNL arrested Boisson, Peyrouton and Pierre-Etienne Flandin, all former Vichy administrators with whom the Allies had negotiated at some point in the preceding twelve months.[83]

Despite the detention of this senior trio late in the year, the image presented by the Vichy–Free French prisoner situation in 1943 was one of diminishing numbers, steady improvements in treatment and the first tentative steps towards reconciliation. Ironically, one of the few pressing threats still posed by Pétain loyalists in 1943 was not even in Vichy territory, but in Alexandria. In this vital British imperial port Admiral René Godfroy's naval squadron refused to recognize Giraud's North African administration until the Allies achieved victory in Tunisia.[84] Under two agreements reached with the British naval commanders in the Mediterranean in July 1941 and November 1942, Godfroy's squadron had maintained an uneasy neutrality. While Godfroy's guns were trained on Alexandria, his men were fed with British supplies. His ships only moved anchorage with British consent.[85]

In Martinique, Godfroy's colleague, Admiral Georges Robert, had also kept his naval squadron neutral but theoretically loyal to Vichy. Robert also maintained two detention camps, one on Martinique, the other on Guadeloupe. These housed over a thousand Gaullist sympathizers, many under heavy sentences of penal servitude. When the French Guyanese-born Governor of Chad, Félix Eboué, protested to the American State Department about the fate of these political detainees, his complaints were dismissed on the grounds that 'the great majority of the islanders were illiterate negroes who had no views one way or the other'. Ignoring Eboué's pleas, from November 1942 the Americans preferred to deal with Robert direct. Faced with a disintegration of support among his ships' crews, Robert eventually caved in to US envoys in July 1943.[86] Like Robert, Godfroy's ridiculous loyalism to Pétain was hardened by the fact that several of his sailors either rallied or found themselves in custody as POWs whenever they took shore leave in Alexandria. When the Torch landings began in Morocco, Alexandria was on maximum alert. Godfroy's seamen were effectively besieged. The situation was resolved peacefully by Godfroy's belated change of allegiance in May 1943.[87] These French naval squadrons provide a fitting epitaph to the many twists, turns and outright contradictions evident in the treatment of the personnel of the Vichy and Free French empires between 1940 and 1943.

V

In some senses the fate of Vichy and Free French prisoners held outside metropolitan France was not as grave as those of POWs in numerous other theatres of war. Being a prisoner within the French empire was likely to be memorable more for the daily rigours of climate than because of the cruelty of one's captors or the presence of an active front nearby. This is not to minimize the unpleasantness of captivity. Camps within Vichy West Africa, where the majority of Free French and British service personnel captured by the Vichy military were held, were beset with disease. This was compounded by acute supply problems as the British naval blockade intensified. Numerous Free French volunteers captured in 1940 were tried by Vichy military courts. These meted out harsh terms and frequently punished the families of detainees.[88] Anyone treated as a 'political prisoner' was liable to the full rigours of the Vichy penal code rather than to the privileges of the Geneva Convention.

Prisoners in Free French hands were not subjected to the same Draconian legal penalties. But the French national committee's continual quest for authority and new recruits meant that the Free French colonial authorities tended to guard their prisoners jealously. This was born of the hope of converting Vichyite POWs, and of using them as a means to add to Free French standing. It was questionable whether the French national committee was entitled to any of the privileges of an Allied power before the creation of the FCNL in June 1943. This doubt meant that guardianship over POWs, although cited as evidence of Free French authority, sometimes worsened de Gaulle's sense of inferiority in his dealings with London and Washington.

It was primarily to avoid accusations of neglect or ill-treatment by proxy that the British grew more unwilling to pass Vichy POWs over to the Free French. This reluctance was also shaped by a dislike for de Gaulle's manoeuvring. All POWs were inevitably pawns in a war involving so many combatants over so many parts of the globe. Whitehall reasoning in the light of this was that it served Britain's interests best if the pawns were not given away too liberally, even to friends.

The acrimony between Frenchmen generated by the fall of France and the subsequent division of the French empire naturally affected the attitudes of the custodial French authority to their compatriot captives. Detainees were too often cast as traitors, a tendency that was in part sustained by the bitter propaganda campaign fought between Carlton Gardens, Vichy and Algiers. This was a war of words that did not lend itself to lengthy, sympathetic consideration of the multiplicity of factors that actually determined the loyalties of individual French citizens.[89] In January 1943, Eisenhower commented on the realities of co-operation with people of a divided nation:

> We did not find the ideal Frenchmen which our critics see from the heights of their Ivory Towers. We found Frenchmen who had been defeated by Germany and who had undergone two years of German pressure and propaganda. We found Frenchmen who have changed and who do not think as Clemenceau thought. We worked with them making one condition, that is, that they wanted to fight Germany. . . . Our critics are apparently primarily interested not in the military operation but [in] an ideological return to the France which they see in their memory. That simply cannot be done in the Colonial Area.[90]

This brings us to a final point: the British view of the Free French as guardians of POWs. British governmental reluctance to surrender control of Vichy prisoners to the Free French did not reflect any desire to keep large numbers of Vichyite POWs *per se*. Whitehall's POW agencies were acutely conscious that British POWs in enemy hands might be the innocent victims of reprisal against any maltreatment of detainees held by the Gaullist authorities. Hence the British unwillingness to hand over Vichy personnel to de Gaulle's forces and the general rejection of several Free French requests to take charge of German or Italian captives.

Although the pace of British prisoner exchanges with the Vichy authorities slowed in 1941, the lack of shipping was always as much an impediment to the transfer of detainees as the periodic recalcitrance of the Vichy regime or its colonial administrations. In this respect, the speed with which the officers of the Levant army were repatriated to France between July and September 1941 was at variance with the fate of French naval personnel who had languished in West Africa for want of ships to carry them to Vichy territory. Perhaps the lasting image of French prisoners held captive in Africa and the Middle East is one of the tedium of long waits between countries and camps on the slow march home.[91]

Notes

1. The figures for prisoners captured in the battle for France are from Jean-Pierre Azéma, *From Munich to the Liberation*, English trans., Cambridge, 1984, pp. 107–10. Azéma gives a broad figure of 650,000 workers affected by the STO. Under the terms of the *Relève* negotiated in June 1942, French workers were to be traded for POWs on a 3:1 ratio. Laval made the scheme conscriptive in September, and widened it still further under the STO introduced in February 1943. For the legislative background see H. R. Kedward, *In Search of the Maquis. Rural Resistance in Southern France, 1942–1944*, Oxford, 1993, pp. 3–19. Among the recent works on the French POW experience in Germany, two stand out: Yves Durand, *La captivité: histoire des prisonniers de guerre français 1939–1945*, Paris, 1980 and Christophe Lewin, *Le Retour des prisonniers de guerre français*, Paris, 1986. Durand sets the overall total of 1940 POWs at 1,900,000. Lewin traces the development of the POW Fédération Nationale and gives a figure of 1,850,000 captured in summer 1940, 1,575,000 of whom passed through German camps. For an outstanding insight into the French POW situation and life in France, see Sarah Fishman, *We Will Wait. Wives of French Prisoners of War, 1940–1945*, New Haven, 1991. Fishman gives a figure of 1.58 million prisoners captured in 1940. Regarding indoctrination, see Jean-Marie d'Hoop, 'Propagande et Attitudes Politiques dans les Camps de Prisonniers: Le Cas des Oflags', *Revue d'Histoire de la Deuxième Guerre Mondiale*, vol. 122, 1981, pp. 3–26 and S. Fishman, 'Grand Delusions: The Unintended Consequences of Vichy France's Pris-

oner of War Propaganda', *Journal of Contemporary History*, vol. 26, 1991, pp. 229–54.

2. The most detailed treatments on the political divisions in Africa and the Syrian Levant are John Kent, *The Internationalization of Colonialism: Britain, France and Black Africa, 1939–1956*, Oxford, 1992; Aviel Roshwald, *Estranged Bedfellows. Britain and France in the Middle East during the Second World War*, Oxford, 1990; and Desmond Dinan, *The Politics of Persuasion: British Policy and French African Neutrality, 1940–42*, New York, 1988. The armistice commissions also supervised the release and eventual repatriation of Germans and Italians interned in the Vichy Empire before the French defeat, see Colette Dubois, 'Internés et prisonniers de guerre Italiens dans les camps de l'empire français de 1940 à 1945', *Guerres mondiales et conflits contemporains*, vol. 39, 1989, pp. 56–63.

3. The French committee of national liberation was founded in Algiers on 3 June 1943 under the co-presidency of Generals Henri Giraud and Charles de Gaulle. Throughout this article the terms 'Free French' and 'Fighting French' will be used interchangeably. By 1942 the French national committee in Carlton Gardens favoured the latter appellation. The acronym FFL (*Forces Françaises Libres*) refers to the Free French military.

4. Public Record Office (hereafter PRO), Foreign Office Papers (hereafter FO) FO 892/65, memo. by E. L. Spears, 'Vichy', 21 Feb. 1941.

5. PRO, FO 898/126, Rex Leeper to Anthony Eden, 'Propaganda in French Africa', 6 Oct. 1940 and PWE memo., 'Propaganda – Algeria', 13 Oct. 1940.

6. Jean-Noël Vincent, *Les Forces Françaises dans la lutte contre l'Axe en Afrique*, Paris, 1983, p. 50. Vincent provides a useful illustration of this Free French quest for authority by highlighting French national committee arguments with the British War Office over the first Free French 'Division', which British military officials insisted was only of independent brigade strength. During 1941 de Gaulle insisted upon the term Division to emphasize Free French capability for the conduct of offensive operations.

7. PRO, Admiralty Papers (hereafter ADM), ADM 199/1279, British policy towards movements of Vichy French warships, 1940–2: this file contains numerous documents relating to French naval vessels in Vichy French colonial ports. Until the battle-cruiser *Dunkerque* slipped into Toulon on 19 Feb. 1942, three of the four battleships of the French navy were in Vichy colonial ports; *Dunkerque* in Oran, *Jean Bart* in Casablanca and the damaged *Richelieu* in Dakar. There were squadrons of vessels that were effectively *hors de combat* in Alexandria, Guadeloupe and Martinique.

8. Regarding Darlan's arrangements with the Allies, see Arthur L. Funk, 'Negotiating the "Deal with Darlan"', *Journal of Contemporary History*, vol. 8, no. 2, 1973, pp. 81–117. See also Hervé Coutau-Bégarie and Claude Huan, *Darlan*, Paris, 1989, pp. 624–83. Regarding the negotiations with Boisson in Dakar, see PRO, FO 892/173, report for Eden by E. W. Meiklereid on the political situation in French West Africa, 10 May 1943.

9. Service Historique de l'Armée de Terre, Vincennes, Paris (hereafter SHAT), Carton 1P137/D1, 'Organisation du commandement en A.F.N.', General Colson to Charles Noguès, 30 July 1940. Also D5, 'A.F.N. – Armement, Matériel, Munitions', General Huntziger to Maxime Weygand, 11 Sept. 1941. Under the terms of the 1940 armistices, the French army maintained in North Africa was kept at a little over 111,000 men, but heavy artillery and mechanized armour were prohibited.

10. Regarding the Dakar assault, see Arthur J. Marder, *Operation Menace*, London, 1976 and M. Thomas, 'The Anglo-French divorce over West Africa and the limitations of strategic planning', *Diplomacy and Statecraft*, vol. 6, no. 1, 1995, pp. 252–78.

11. SHAT, 1P89/D2, 'Organisation et Attribution du commandement', Weygand report to Pétain on his tour of French North and West Africa, 10 Nov. 1940.

12. SHAT, 2P12/D1, 'Questions "Marine" relatives à la Défense de l'A.F.N. et de l'A.O.F.', 12 Oct. 1941. From May 1941, in return for the use of Dakar's port facilities, the German armistice commission allowed additional Vichy reinforcement of French West Africa against a possible Anglo-Free French attack.

13. SHAT, 4P12/D1, 'Afrique Française Libre – Situation militaire', Free French communiqué, 10 Nov. 1940.

14. PRO, Colonial Office Papers (hereafter CO), CO 968/30/3, Committee on Foreign [allied] Resistance (hereafter CFR), CFR (41) 24th meeting, 23 Mar. 1941, also copy of Foreign Office to Halifax, 22 Mar. 1941.

15. SHAT, 1P34/D7, Réunion interministérielle à l'Amirauté Française – procès-verbal, 'Résistance aux prétentions du Thai-land en Indochine', 5 Oct. 1940. See also Yves Gras, 'L'intrusion japonais en Indochine 1940–1945', *Revue Historique des Armées*, vol. 4, 1983, pp. 86–102 and John E. Dreifort, 'Japan's Advance into Indochina, 1940: The French Response', *Journal of South East Asian Studies*, vol. 13, no. 2, 1982, pp. 279–95. Regarding British policy towards Thailand's incursion into Indo-China, see Richard J. Aldrich, *The Key to the South: Britain, the United States and Thailand during*

the Approach of the Pacific War, 1929–1942, Oxford, 1993, pp. 273–95.

16. PRO, FO 916/493, report by Saigon Consulate, 8 Sept. 1942.

17. Regarding the Syrian campaign, see Roshwald, *Estranged Bedfellows*, and A. B. Gaunson, *The Anglo-French Clash in Lebanon and Syria, 1940–1945*, London, 1987. Regarding events in Madagascar, see M. Thomas, 'Imperial Backwater or Strategic Outpost? The British Takeover of Vichy Madagascar in 1942', *Historical Journal*, vol. 39, no. 4 (1996), forthcoming. Regarding the Djibouti operations see Ministère des Affaires Etrangères, Paris (hereafter MAE), Guerre 1939–1945, Comité National Français Londres (hereafter CFN), cartons 88 & 89 supplement, dossier général, 1941–1943.

18. PRO, FO 916/387, meeting of the Directorate of Prisoners of War, 1 July 1942. Black African POWs suffered disproportionately, whether among the estimated 15,000 captured by German forces during the battle for France, or among those detained following engagements in Africa: see Myron Echenberg, '"Morts pour la France": The African Soldier in France During the Second World War', *Journal of African History*, vol. 26, 1985, pp. 363–80.

19. Regarding the FFL, see Vincent, *Forces Françaises* (see Note 6 above), pp. 44–50. For campaign reports on Syria, Madagascar and Djibouti respectively, see PRO, War Office Papers (hereafter WO), WO 32/10168, report by General Maitland Wilson on the Syria Campaign, 8 June – 11 July 1941; ADM 199/937, flag officer commanding Force F, war diary for 3 June 1942 – 9 July 1942; ADM 199/1293, 'Operation Streamline Jane', undated, Oct. 1942; CO 968/3/12, report by General Platt, 'Operations of East Africa Command', 31 Mar. 1943. Regarding the arrangement of exchanges for Djibouti prisoners, see CO 968/30/4, CFR (41) 191st meeting, 12 Nov. 1941; CO 968/86/4, Platt to War Office, 3 and 4 Jan. 1943.

20. PRO, CO 968/30/4, CFR (41) 191st meeting, 12 Nov. 1941.

21. Ibid., CFR (41) 206th meeting, 14 Dec. 1941.

22. PRO, ADM 199/1277, memorandum by Admiralty directorate of plans, 'Réunion island and Madagascar-Policy', 22 June 1941; MAE, Guerre 1939–1945, CNF Londres, vol. 39, Politique Extérieure Syrie–Liban, CNF Direction des Affaires Politiques, 'Note sur l'intervention alliée en Syrie', 2 July 1941.

23. PRO, WO 193/884, War Office to force commander, 121 Force, 19 May 1942.

24. PRO, FO 371/32025, CFR (42) 1st meeting, 14 Jan. 1942, and CFR (42) 12th meeting, 11 June 1942.

25. PRO, CO 968/30/4, CFR (41) 66th meeting, 16 Dec. 1941.

26. PRO, ADM 199/1284, Admiralty minutes by C. H. M. Waldeck, 21 May 1942 and memo. by Waldeck, 8 June 1942.
27. PRO, CO 968/30/4, CFR (41) 206th meeting, 14 Dec. 1941.
28. PRO, FO 916/387, R. L. Speaight to Major H. J. Phillimore, 4 July 1942. Also see WO 201/904, commission of control, sub-committee #8, final report, n.d., Sept. 1941.
29. PRO, Treasury Papers (hereafter T), T 160/1146/17006/3, Lord Moyne to East African Governors' conference, 23 Nov. 1942.
30. Robert D. Pearce, *Sir Bernard Bourdillon. The Biography of a Twentieth Century Colonialist*, Oxford, 1987, pp. 283–306.
31. For a discussion of the organizational structure of the French national committee as a proto-government, see Andrew Shennan, *Rethinking France. Plans for Renewal, 1940–1946*, Oxford, 1989, pp. 53–6; regarding United States views of Free France, see Kim Munholland, 'The United States and the Free French', in Robert O. Paxton and Nicholas Wahl (eds), *De Gaulle and the United States*, Oxford, 1994, pp. 68–94.
32. PRO, FO 916/387, minutes by P. Dean, 4 June 1942, and W. St. C. H. Roberts, 5 June 1942.
33. Ibid.
34. PRO, CO 323/1791/39, Lord Lloyd to Bourdillon, 29 Aug. 1940, and Lord Lloyd to West African Governors, relays message from de Gaulle to Leclerc, 3 Sept. 1940.
35. SHAT, 4P12/D5, 'Situation militaire des territoires ralliés', Rapport du Gouverneur des colonies de Saint-Mart, 15 Aug. 1940.
36. SHAT, 1P55/D5, Ministère de la Défense Nationale, Note au sujet de l'organisation des troupes coloniales, 19 Aug. 1940.
37. PRO, CO 323/1791/57, COS(40)53, 'Implications of French hostility', 16 July 1940. See also François Kersaudy, *Churchill and De Gaulle*, London, 1981, p. 81.
38. SHAT, 4P16/D2, E.M.A., troisième bureau, memo. by de Gaulle, annexe 1, 6 Sept. 1940.
39. SHAT, 1P34/D4, Boisson Rapport, 'Attaque Dakar du 23 au 25 Septembre', 30 Sept. 1940.
40. D'Hoop, 'Propagande', p. 7. Jean-Marie D'Hoop was himself a POW officer in a German Oflag.
41. SHAT, 1P89/D3, Commandement en chef des forces en Afrique du Nord, 'Note sur le moral de la troupe et des cadrés en A.F.N.', 29 Mar. 1942. De Gaulle was especially bitter at the exclusion of Free French recruiters from the Vichyite POWs taken in Syria: see papers of Major-General E. L. Spears, St Antony's College, Middle East Centre, Oxford (hereafter Spears papers), Spears IA/Pre-armistice telegrams, de Gaulle to Catroux, 15 July 1941.

42. PRO, ADM 199/1277, Parr, Brazzaville, to Foreign Office, 7 May 1942. Also Foreign Office to Washington, 'Free French protest about Madagascar', 14 May 1942. De Gaulle reiterated Leclerc's warning in more forceful terms. See also WO 193/884, 121 Force command to War Office, 21 May 1942.

43. SHAT, 1P89/D1, Délégation Générale du Gouvernement en Afrique Française, 'Journal de marche', n.d., 1940–1942; Spears papers, I/B, file I5, Oliver Lyttelton to Eden, 14 Aug. 1941.

44. PRO, T 160/1146/17006/3, W. H. B. Mack to Sir R. Campbell, Washington, 10 June 1942.

45. PRO, T 160/1100/F17006/03, Ministry of Economic Warfare memo., n.d., Aug. 1941; FO 892/117, Ministry of Economic Warfare to Washington, 12 Nov. 1941.

46. PRO, CO 968/30/3, 'Notes on Koulikoro Internment Camp' by Hugh Ashton, 5 June 1941.

47. Ibid., Foreign Office to Hoare, Madrid, 21 July 1941. As part of one of these exchanges agreed with Boisson, the crew of the vessel *Poitiers* were released into French Guinea in July 1941. For their part, in May 1943 the French national committee agreed to repatriate from Douala General Têtu, a former administrator of Hué, and two senior Vichyite officers, Colonel Claveau and Commandant Morru, all on grounds of ill health. See MAE, Guerre 1939–1945, CNF Londres, vol. 132, Politique Extérieure du CNF, no. 486, Catroux to CNF, 5 May 1943.

48. PRO, FO 916/387, Foreign Office POW Department, meeting of 1 July 1942, and minute by Dean, 4 Aug. 1942.

49. Dubois, 'Internés' (see Note 2 above), p. 58.

50. Ibid., pp. 65–7.

51. PRO, FO 916/215, Cordell Hull to US embassy, London, 21 June 1941; Spears papers, I/B, file I5, Lyttelton to Eden, 5 Jan. 1942.

52. PRO, FO 916/215, War Office to Wavell, 16 June 1941; WO 201/904, commission of control, sub-committee #8, final report, n.d., Sept. 1941.

53. PRO, WO 32/11434, War Office directorate of military operations report, 'Syria: Planning and operations', 20 Oct. 1944; MAE, Guerre 1939–1945, CNF Londres, vol. 39, Politique Extérieure, Syrie-Liban, note by Collet, 'Note de la situation actuelle en Syrie', 27 July 1941.

54. PRO, WO 201/931, committee #8 to commission of control, 5 Aug. 1941; WO 201/904, committee #8 final report, n.d., Sept. 1941. Pending the repatriation of British officer POWs captured in the early stages of the Syria campaign, the British commission of control temporarily held General Dentz and over fifty senior French

officers hostage in Aug. 1941: see WO 201/908, Major-General Chrystall to General de Verdilhac, 5 Aug. 1941.

55. SHAT, 1P14/D2, lettre 662, Darlan aux Secrétaires d'état à la guerre/marine, 27 Nov. 1941.

56. PRO, WO 201/950, commission of control, progress return of 9 Aug. 1941; WO 201/918, Major-General Chrystall to General de Verdilhac, 2 Aug. 1941.

57. Ibid.; Spears papers, I/B, file K2, Lyttelton to de Gaulle, 1 Aug. 1941.

58. SHAT, 1P89/D2, 'Organisation et attribution du commandement', Weygand note for Pétain, 29 Sept. 1940.

59. PRO, WO 201/904, committee #8, final report, n.d., Sept. 1941.

60. PRO, WO 201/931, committee #8 'Report of a visit to Palestine in connection with POWs', 16 Aug. 1941. Regarding French forces in Tunisia, see Vincent, *Forces Françaises* (see Note 6 above), pp. 52–3.

61. PRO, ADM 199/1278, Intelligence corps report by Captain R. D. Jeune, 'Diego Suarez Prisoners', 15 July 1942.

62. SHAT, 1P34/D6, Etat-Major d'Armée, 'Etude sur la défense de Madagascar', n.d., Mar. 1941. Also PRO, WO 208/1518, intelligence report, B.J.102203, Vichy Ministry of Marine cypher, 14 Mar. 1942.

63. PRO, FO 371/36138/Z 8719, Consul Grafftey-Smith to Eden, 10 Aug. 1943.

64. SHAT, 5P49/D1, 2444/EM/S/3, pièce 8, Darlan communication à Général Barré, 10 Nov. 1942.

65. PRO, FO 371/32082/Z 3625, Charles Peake memorandum on Giraud's escape, 30 April 1942. Immediately after his escape, the Foreign Office was much influenced by the French national committee's apprehension about Giraud's potential to supplant de Gaulle. See also Azéma, *From Munich* (see Note 1 above), p. 261, n. 293. Azéma points out that Giraud was not well received in North Africa either, Juin telling him upon his arrival, 'You are nothing here.'

66. MAE, PA-AP 288, Papiers Maurice Dejean, v. 25, memo. by Dejean, 'La situation politique en Afrique du Nord', 6 May 1943. In June 1943 Noguès was replaced by Gabriel Puaux, Peyrouton was replaced by Catroux.

67. PRO, Papers of the Special Operations Executive, North Africa files, HS 3/47, SOE report on meeting with Count Mohl, 21 June 1941. There are two outstanding studies of the fate of Spain's Republican refugees during the Second World War: Louis Stein, *Beyond Death and Exile: The Spanish Republicans in France,*

1939–1955, Cambridge, MA, 1979 and David Wingeate Pike, *In the Service of Stalin. The Spanish Communists in Exile, 1939–1945*, Oxford, 1993.

68. PRO, FO 660/64, W. Makins, Algiers, to Foreign Office, 20 Jan. 1943, and minutes of the joint [Anglo-American] commission on political prisoners and refugees in French North and West Africa, 11 Jan. 1943.
69. Ibid., Macmillan to Foreign Office, 3 and 9 Feb. 1943; regarding detention of Gaullists see HS 3/47, Sir Charles Hambro to Desmond Morton, 28 Nov. 1942.
70. PRO, FO 660/64, Foreign Office to Makins, 21 Jan. 1943.
71. Ibid., Halifax to Foreign Office, 17 Jan. 1943.
72. Ibid., Foreign Office memo., 'Gaullists and Giraudists', 28 Dec. 1942.
73. Ibid., Macmillan to Foreign Office, 30 Jan. 1943; Azéma, *From Munich* (see Note 1 above), p. 169. See also Harold Macmillan, *War Diaries: Politics and War in the Mediterranean, January 1943 – May 1945*, London, 1984, pp. 42–6.
74. PRO, FO 660/64, Macmillan to Foreign Office, 4 and 21 Feb. 1943; Jean Monnet, *Memoirs*, London, 1978, pp. 187–91.
75. PRO, FO 660/64, Richard Speaight to P. J. Dixon, Algiers, 13 Jan. 1943. Pleven had confided his fears to Speaight at the Foreign Office the previous day.
76. PRO, FO 892/173/Z 6137, Meiklereid to Eden, 10 May 1943.
77. PRO, FO 660/68, Eden to Macmillan, 16 Jan. 1943.
78. PRO, WO 193/843, Eisenhower to Combined Chiefs of Staff, 3 Dec. 1942.
79. PRO, FO 892/173/Z 3752, Meiklereid to Eden, 25 Feb. 1943.
80. Ibid., Viscount Swinton report to Colonial Office, 18 Jan. 1943; FO 660/31, W. E. Houstoun-Boswell, Accra, to C. Stirling, 17 Jan. 1943.
81. Regarding the transfer of the French POWs from Britain, see PRO, WO 165/59, monthly directorate letter, #15, 11 Feb. 1943. Regarding Eisenhower's statement, see FO 660/68, Eden to Macmillan, 16 Jan. 1943.
82. PRO, WO 193/843, joint staff mission, Washington, to British Chiefs of Staff, 4 Dec. 1942, and Chiefs of Staff committee memorandum, 'West Africa – Negotiations with the French', 5 Dec. 1942.
83. PRO, FO 371/42132/Z 72, Macmillan to French department, 3 Jan. 1944 and /Z 690, Duff Cooper to Foreign Office, 18 Jan. 1944; Robert Murphy, *Diplomat among Warriors*, New York, 1964, pp. 183–4. Churchill took up the matter of these three arrests in a

meeting with de Gaulle at Marrakesh on 14 January 1944. See also Kersaudy, *Churchill and de Gaulle*, pp. 303–5.

84. PRO, WO 106/2287, C.-in-C. Mediterranean to Admiralty, 21 Jan. 1943.

85. PRO, FO 371/31892, WP(42)185, copy of Admiralty paper, 'The Vichy Squadron at Alexandria', 2 May 1942. Also WO 106/2287, C.-in-C. Mediterranean to Admiralty, 4 Nov. 1942.

86. PRO, CO 968/8/6, Parr to Foreign Office, 4 June 1942; Halifax to Foreign Office, 1 and 15 May 1943.

87. PRO, WO 106/2287, C.-in-C. Mediterranean to Admiralty, 4 and 8 Nov. 1942.

88. At various points in July and August 1941, for example, the Vichy government made thinly veiled threats of reprisal against the families of men who rallied to Catroux in Syria. See PRO, WO 201/918, Chrystall to de Verdilhac, 2 Aug. 1941.

89. As examples of this characterization of Vichy officials, see PRO, FO 898/126, Political Warfare Executive (hereafter PWE) memo., 'Propaganda – Algeria', 13 Oct. 1940. Also FO 898/129, PWE memo., 'Joint American–British Plan of Psychological Warfare for France and the French Empire', 23 Sept. 1942. Drawn up following consultation with Carlton Gardens, this plan stressed the treachery involved in continued loyalty to Vichy.

90. PRO, WO 193/844, Murphy to Cordell Hull and Combined Chiefs of Staff, relayed message from Eisenhower, 23 Jan. 1943.

91. The same point has been made regarding French POWs in German hands. D'Hoop, 'Propagande' (see Note 1 above), p. 4, and Fishman, *We Will Wait* (see Note 1 above), pp. 148–9. Both authors illustrate the seemingly endless wait for release endured by French POWs in Germany and by their wives in France respectively. D'Hoop has also charted the changing morale of French POWs in Germany as the Allies neared victory: see his article, 'Prisonniers de guerre français témoins de la défaite allemande (1945)', *Guerres mondiales et conflits contemporains*, vol. 38, 1988, pp. 77–98.

5

Propaganda and Political Warfare: The Foreign Office, Italian POWs and the Free Italy Movement, 1940–3

Kent Fedorowich

The comprehensive victories over the Italians by British and Common-wealth forces during the initial stages of the North African campaign in late 1940 – early 1941 surprised military commanders and their political masters. A major consequence of these impressive victories was the capture by early February 1941 of 133,000 Italian prisoners of war (POWs). However, these military successes introduced a myriad of logistical problems. Egypt was far from secure as a place for the long-term incarceration of these Italian captives, and the feeding, processing, guarding and relocation of such huge numbers put a severe strain on the already overstretched resources available to Middle Eastern Command. Equally spectacular victories in Abyssinia throughout 1941 swelled Italian POW numbers and further aggravated an already critical situation. In May, the War Office was informed by its Directorate of Prisoners of War (DPW) that, apart from the prosecution of the war and the protection of Britain's strategic interests in Egypt, the disposal and transfer of prisoners captured in the Middle East, the Balkans and East Africa had 'continued to be the most urgent matter requiring attention'.[1] During the course of the war, tens of thousands of Italian prisoners were eventually transported to the United Kingdom or relocated throughout the British empire. Indeed, their utilization as a source of military and civilian labour in Africa and overseas proved a most attractive and practical option for wartime policy-makers.[2]

From the outset of war POWs were considered important sources of political and military intelligence, although it was not until 1942 that the various British military intelligence branches classified POW interrogations as among the more reliable sources of information.[3] Another idea, which was broached in early 1941 by officials who worked in SO1 (the secret propaganda branch of the Special Operations Executive established by Prime Minister Winston Churchill in June 1940),[4] was to use Italian POWs in the propaganda war that was being waged against Fascist Italy. It was mooted that, if large numbers of POWs proved receptive to the political warfare being orchestrated in the camps by the Allies, not only would this provide grist to the propaganda mill, but it could also provide the foundation of a more ambitious policy whereby POW volunteers would be recruited to fight against their former Fascist leaders in a Free Italy force and serve in anti-Fascist pioneer or combatant units that might be employed during the Allied liberation of Italy. As a wartime tool, therefore, POWs were deemed invaluable in the all-important psychological battle to win Italian hearts and minds, and as a potential anti-Fascist fighting force.

However, there was more at stake than just winning the war. Questions were raised in the Foreign Office and SOE about the utility of Italian POWs in reshaping a new Italy after the war; an integral component of which was their political 're-education' during the war. In other words, could these prisoners be persuaded that Fascism was evil, that Britain was their friend and that democracy was the key to international peace and post-war harmony? Could these POWs be moulded into a political vanguard that would provide the basis of a pro-British element within a new and democratic post-war Italy? This was a long-term strategy that would take careful wartime planning and execution. It was also something that officials at the Foreign Office and in SOE believed should not be underestimated, for in the uncertainties of the post-war world it was considered essential that Italy become an ally of the Western democracies.

While historians have written extensively about the de-Nazification of Germany and its armed forces after the Second World War, the 'de-Fascisation' of Italy's armed forces has been relatively neglected.[5] Indeed, the work involving the 're-education' of these Italian POWs pre-dates those schemes subsequently directed by the Allies at their German captives later in the war. As a contribution to rectifying this neglect this chapter examines British attempts to conduct a systematic campaign of political segregation and indoctrination amongst its Italian POWs during the Second World War. It analyses the competing interests within the higher echelons of the British government, in particular those of the War Office and the Foreign Office. In addition, it examines the tensions that arose at the grass-roots level between the political and military agencies responsible for the drafting and implementation of propaganda, intelligence gathering and political warfare such as, SOE, the Political Warfare Executive (PWE) and the military, especially the Directorate of Military Intelligence (DMI). The geographical focus for this study is India, for it was on the subcontinent that the first concerted but largely unsuccessful effort was made to segregate and indoctrinate Italian POWs, the main objective of which was the creation of a Free Italy movement.

I

In April 1940 plans were initiated by the Anglo-French Enemy Propaganda Committee to establish a shadow organization that would conduct a propaganda offensive against Italy if and when it joined the war on Germany's side. One of the tasks of this joint venture was to create the necessary propaganda machinery and direct it against Italian garrisons in Libya and Abyssinia.[6] Little, if anything, had been accomplished when Italy declared war on 10 June 1940. Major-General Dallas Brooks, a key individual in SO1 who was later appointed deputy Director-General of the PWE in August 1941, refrained from commenting on the propaganda operations that were being directed against Italy except to say that 'I am unable to find either a policy or an object!'[7]

Nevertheless, over the summer of 1940 and well before the stunning victories in Libya, British intelligence officers began formulating plans to conduct a political warfare campaign against the Italians. The Military Liaison Officer for SO1 at General Headquarters, Cairo, Colonel C. J. M. Thornhill, was responsible for the dissemination of subversive propaganda, both overt and covert, in Libya and Italian East Africa. In addition, his department was assigned to convert the 45,000 Italian civilians resident in Egypt from a Fascist into an anti-Fascist community. Finally, perhaps the most important, as well as the most challenging, task of his mandate was to spread anti-Fascist feeling throughout Italy and its empire.[8] Success, however, would depend upon the co-operation and co-ordination between Thornhill's department, local civilian authorities, the British Army, the Royal Air Force, the Foreign Office and the British Broadcasting Corporation (BBC).

In August 1940 a detailed memorandum was tabled at GHQ Cairo that set out the measures to be adopted, including the conversion, segregation and organization of Italian POWs 'into anti-Fascist instruments'. Thornhill admitted that this programme would take time to produce results; but he argued that the potential long-term benefits would far outweigh the 'trouble' involved. 'In the event – not improbable – of Italy's making a separate peace', he continued, 'it would be very useful to be able to flood her with some thousands of pro-British Italians.' Moreover, it was not enough to have them 'vaguely friendly', for Thornhill insisted that they be carefully trained to 'say what will be most useful to our purpose. We should, in fact, be training a "Fifth Column" of our own.'[9] The basis of a Free Italy movement had been tentatively laid. In October 1940 these embryonic ideas were taken one step further when the Foreign Office initiated discussions on the creation of a Free Italian committee and embarked upon a search for a potential leader of a Free Italy movement.[10]

By late January 1941, Thornhill had become convinced that it was essential to solve, before a Free Italy movement could be established, two key problems. The first problem was to educate the POWs to reject Fascist doctrine, and become not only 'trustworthy' anti-Fascists but also decidedly pro-British. The second problem, the teaching of 'revolutionary methods and tactics', naturally depended on the solution of the first, and this involved the selection of an equal number of POW officers and men whom the British would employ as agents for covert military and political work within Italy itself. Recruits from the internee population would be chosen from all parts of Italy and from all social classes, in order to facilitate the development of a comprehensive anti-Fascist underground network. It was intended that this vanguard would provide the channel through which British propaganda would infiltrate the Italian mainland, help spread revolutionary ideas throughout Italy, and bring about the overthrow of Mussolini's Fascist government.[11]

The capture of huge numbers of Italians during the first four months of 1941 prompted a great deal of discussion on the potential propaganda windfall the British had been given and how best to conduct a political warfare campaign amongst Italian POWs; and it was Thornhill's memorandum that may have been the catalyst in stimulating discussions at a higher level. For instance, one idea that attracted growing attention from high-ranking British military and civilian authorities alike was the raising of a 'Garibaldi' Legion or Free Italian force from amongst the Italian captives. The Foreign Office was aware that from a political point of view the formation of such a force held potential, not least of which was its usefulness for propaganda purposes. More importantly, however, its formation might provide a nucleus round which anti-Fascists in Italy could identify themselves. Indeed, initial intelligence reports from the Middle East indicated that there were some Italian captives who suggested the creation of just such a force.[12] Churchill added his endorsement. He informed the War Cabinet in February 1941 that he saw no reason why the raising of an anti-Mussolini or Free Italian force in Cyrenaica should not be considered.

> Volunteers might be called for from the . . . prisoners we have taken. There must be a great many who hate Fascism . . . Can we not make [Cyrenaica] a base for starting a real split in Italy and the source of anti-Mussolini propaganda? We might make it a model of British rule, hold it in trust for the Italian people and have 4,000 or 5,000 Italian troops sworn to the liberation of Italy from the German and Mussolini yoke.[13]

The War Office did not share either the prime minister's or the Foreign Office's optimism. The Director of Military Intelligence, Major-General F. H. N. Davidson, acknowledged that it was true that some captured officers had expressed a willingness to fight against their former Fascist masters, but 'Italian words [were] usually better than their deeds', and it was doubtful if a Free Italian force would have much combatant value. On the other hand, Davidson saw some benefit in using Italian POWs as civilian or military labour. If units composed of technically skilled personnel such as motor drivers and mechanics could be raised they would be of immense value, especially in the Middle East, where there was an acute shortage.[14] Despite War Office reservations, and doubts amongst some of its own officials about the value and loyalty of such combat units, the Foreign Office thought the idea of creating a Free Italian force was still worth pursuing.[15]

General Sir Archibald Wavell, Commander-in-Chief Middle Eastern forces, advised caution. Although in principle not against the idea of raising a Free Italian force, he recognized that in practice there were a number of obstacles that had to be overcome. For instance, it took time for intelligence officers to assess the quality and value of all military and political information gleaned from POW interrogations. Moreover, even if it was possible to raise such a force, Egypt was far from secure. He suggested Eritrea would be a safer base for such operations once it was wrested from the Italians. For Wavell the essential point was the need to choose a leader of sufficient calibre 'to command respect and avoid jealousies'.[16] Concomitant with this, was the proper screening and segregation of potential recruits. Initial indications were that it was going to be a slow and painstaking task. One intelligence officer, Lieutenant-Colonel John de Salis, warned that most Italian POWs interviewed at Geneifa Camp #3 were quite prepared to say that they were non-Fascists if they thought they would obtain better food or privileged conditions. Unable to 'trust a single one of them', de Salis firmly believed that 'a good many pretend to be Non- or Anti-Fascist in order to find out what we want and so warn the others, who are in collusion with them'.[17]

Senior military authorities in London realized very soon after the North African victories the need to separate Fascists from non-Fascists if British propaganda and political warfare were to have any chance of success amongst their Italian POWs. In late January 1941, the War Office also canvassed the Commander-in-Chief India, General Sir Robert A. Cassels, about his views on the segregation of Italian regulars from the specially recruited Fascist or Blackshirt battalions. This initiative, argued the War Office, offered 'considerable political advantages' for Britain in the conduct of its propaganda war against the Axis.

Indeed, if 'de-Fascisation (sic)' was to have any chance of success segregation had to be applied to both officers and other ranks in both categories and made effective as soon as possible after capture. The strategy was twofold. First, it would break the authority and discipline that existed between the Italian officers and their men. Secondly, and more importantly, the resultant segregation of Fascists from non-Fascists would eliminate the influence of hardline Fascism. This would allow the British to conduct almost unhindered their own political warfare campaign amongst the non- and anti-Fascist POWs.[18] However, this was easier said than done. Continued military successes increased dramatically the tally of Italian POWs, which by March 1941 had mushroomed to 160,000.[19] Wavell demanded that for strategic and political reasons as many as possible be evacuated immediately from Egypt to destinations such as India and Australia. Such urgency therefore precluded the careful sorting that was vital if a Free Italian force was to be recruited.

By June 1941 very little had been accomplished. The POW camps in Egypt were overcrowded and prisoners were constantly being moved about, mainly to embarkation ports, which made it extremely difficult for Thornhill and his staff to segregate friendly elements from die-hard Fascists. Furthermore, morale amongst the Italian POWs was high, for the military situation in North Africa had swung in favour of the Axis Powers. In January the prisoners had been demoralized by their defeats in Cyrenaica, with the result that prospects for British propaganda looked encouraging. However, the successful counter-attack launched in April 1941 by the newly-arrived German commander, General (later Field Marshal) Erwin Rommel, rejuvenated hopes amongst the Italian POWs that their release was imminent, which in turn hardened their will to resist the blandishments of British propaganda.

External factors aside, intelligence officers complained that the spartan conditions in the compounds combined with the indifferent, unenthusiastic and at times obstructionist attitude of the military authorities, especially some camp commandants, made it exceedingly difficult to conduct a systematic propaganda campaign. The 'best propaganda among prisoners is good food, comfortable quarters and facilities for recreation', wrote one political warfare officer, Lieutenant-Commander G. A. Martelli. However, Egypt was simply unsuitable, not only because it was vulnerable to attack, but also because POW facilities lacked space and adequate amenities. In other words, it was far from an ideal environment for a concerted political propaganda campaign. If Egypt was deemed infertile for propaganda work, then this raised the question of where within the British empire could a selected team of experts 'conduct an experimental campaign of propaganda' and recruit a Free Italian force amongst the thousands of Italian POWs. Martelli recommended that efforts be concentrated in India, not only because the bulk of the Italian prisoners would eventually be transported there, but also because it was thought by political warfare officers such as he that India possessed the conditions necessary to conduct this sensitive work.[20] The War Office and Foreign Office agreed. Lieutenant-General Sir Claude Auchinleck, Wavell's successor as C.-in-C. Middle East, was informed that upon review of the situation and owing to the persistence of 'adverse conditions' in Egypt all propaganda aimed at raising a Free Italian force or the enlistment of Italian POWs to fight for the Allied cause would cease immediately.[21] Efforts for such a mission were redirected towards India.

II

The Indian government had been quick to respond to Wavell's desperate appeal to evacuate and accommodate Italian POWs. In early January 1941 it had agreed to accept 16,000; but the quota was quickly raised to 68,000 in mid-March. Shortages of shipping dictated the rate at which the captives arrived in India, but by the end of May there were 4,867 officers and 26,993 other ranks distributed in six (later five) POW groups or cantonments throughout the subcontinent. Officers, including most of the general staff, were billeted in four camps at Dehra Dun, designated Group #4, which was nestled in the spectacular scenery of the Himalayan foothills. At Yol in the Punjab, Group #5 was being prepared. Here, four camps were under construction, which were suppose to house half the estimated 24,000 Italian officers assigned for removal to India. Non-commissioned officers and other ranks were incarcerated at Bangalore, Bhopal and Ramgarh, that is, Groups #1–3 respectively; a total capacity of 60,000. POW numbers increased steadily over the summer, and were expected to climb to 84,000 by the autumn, including one camp (probably Yol) that would house at least 9,500 officers. However, by November 1941 shipping constraints had interrupted the steady flow of Italian POW traffic to India; by then the numbers had reached 45,676 officers and men.[22]

Meanwhile, as the Italian POWs were being processed in India, the British government was undertaking a major review of its propaganda machinery and political warfare strategy. A key issue was ministerial jurisdiction. Even before the establishment of SOE in July 1940, fierce battles had already been fought between the Foreign Office and the ministries of Information and Economic Warfare for control of both overt and covert – white and black – propaganda activities. The infighting intensified with the creation of SOE, as ministers jockeyed for the political and operational high ground. Indeed, more energy was probably expended between Hugh Dalton, the dynamic and forceful Minister of Economic Warfare and head of SOE, and his colleagues at the Ministry of Information and the Foreign Office than was directed against the Axis during the first two years of the war. This unnecessary internecine warfare was thankfully halted during the summer of 1941, when the War Cabinet decided to restructure the political warfare machinery.

In July 1941, the Joint Intelligence Committee had decided that SOE would be responsible for all propaganda amongst POWs. However, it was decided to create a new agency – the Political Warfare Executive – that would be under the joint ministerial control of the heads of the Foreign Office, Ministry of Information and Ministry of Economic Warfare. Dalton lost his coveted SO1 to the new agency, and the more amenable Brendan Bracken, Duff Cooper's successor as Minister of Information, agreed to relinquish his control of the BBC's European Service to the PWE.[23] The PWE was now solely responsible for waging the propaganda war against the Axis.

As we have seen, the conduct of political warfare in the Middle East had been assigned to Colonel Thornhill, who, after the reorganization of SOE, was now transferred to the PWE. Before the restructuring in August 1941, and in addition to his Middle Eastern responsibilities, Thornhill had co-ordinated propaganda work amongst the Italian POWs in India from Cairo through the Directorate of Military Intelligence (DMI), India. This had proved highly unsatisfactory. Wavell, now C.-in-C. India (and one of the few military commanders who saw the real potential of political warfare),[24] recognized this, believing that it was extremely difficult to conduct propaganda work in India from the Middle East, where POW conditions were totally different. He recommended that SOE (later the PWE) should have direct representation in India, for this 'would ensure [that the] political condition and attitude of [the] prisoners of war [was] being correctly gauged and propaganda suitably applied'.[25] The request was sanctioned, and two officers, Major F. L. Stevens and Major I. S. Munro, were ordered to India by the PWE. They arrived at GHQ New Delhi on 20 November 1941. It was none too soon.

Three days before, the military authorities in India had despatched an urgent telegram demanding policy guidelines on the conduct of political propaganda in their POW camps. Without it, they argued, the reorganization of the POW administration in India could not be completed, as the propaganda programme had a direct bearing on the restructuring being undertaken.[26] Growing impatient, the DMI India asked what was the basis of British propaganda in the POW camps.

Is it [the] creation of [an] impression of our strength and invincibility and that it will pay them to support [the] winning side[?] Or that we are essentially liberal and peace-loving and [that] Anglo-Italian interests could be coincident[?] Or that they are in their present position because of misgovernment and misdirection of their nation by [the] Fascist regime[?][27]

Answers were forthcoming. Earlier that month, the PWE's plan of action towards Italian POWs was tabled and approved by a high-ranking ministerial committee consisting of the Foreign Secretary, Anthony Eden, Brendan Bracken, Hugh Dalton and the Chiefs of Staff. Its strategy was based on the over-arching principle 'that the treatment of prisoners is a powerful means of influencing Italian morale'.[28] The objects of the policy were twofold. First, it was necessary to exploit the treatment of Italian captives in British hands in order to influence Italian domestic opinion. Secondly, the prisoners themselves had to be imbued with 'friendly sentiments' towards Britain, so that upon their return home at the end of the war they would become pro-British propagandists. In addition, the POWs might be persuaded, if circumstances presented themselves, to perform a combatant role for the Allies against their former Fascist masters during the remainder of hostilities. Short of this, they could give 'valuable assistance to our war effort by their willing labour as agricultural workers [and] road-makers'.[29]

In order to fulfil these objectives, the PWE's policy depended upon the careful implementation of a six-stage programme. The sympathetic and humane treatment of the prisoners was essential for success, because such treatment implied not only decent living conditions but also a level of understanding towards the prisoners on the part of their captors. 'Italian prisoners who are contented morally as well as materially are usually willing workers and not unresponsive to propaganda. On the other hand, if they are treated with contempt or indifference, they will rapidly turn sour and become useless for our purpose.'[30] A key factor in ensuring that the prisoners remained contented was to prevent boredom. Recreation was the answer, be it through games, concerts or theatrical performances; or by arranging other occupations during their leisure time, such as workshops in carpentry, carving or basket-weaving. Another highly recommended 'pastime' was education, especially the teaching of basic English.

Equally important was their segregation from 'incurably hostile elements'. The PWE believed that the majority of Italian POWs had no strong political opinions. In other words they were non-Fascist, but were 'often terrorised by the presence of a small number of ardent Fascists, some of whom are police agents, belonging either to the O.V.R.A. (the Italian secret police) or the Carabinieri'. For this reason it was deemed essential that these small but disruptive elements were removed to a separate camp whenever possible. Under no circumstances were ardent Fascists to occupy positions, such as camp leaders, where they could exercise influence or authority over their fellow inmates. Furthermore, camp intelligence officers were warned to monitor the camp chaplains and doctors, who, by abusing their status as protected personnel, might operate unmolested as Fascist agents in the camps.[31]

Only when the above two conditions had been fulfilled would it be possible for the four remaining objectives to have any prospect of success. These included the initiation of propaganda among the prisoners, the publication of a prisoners' newspaper in Italian, the raising of a Free Italian force, and the use of POWs as propaganda material in the war for hearts and minds. It was recognized that the process of 'defascisation' or political re-education would be a gradual one, involving careful planning and forethought. For years the prisoners had been brought up in a Fascist atmosphere in which they had been taught that Britain and the other democracies were their enemies. Therefore, direct attacks on Fascism had to be avoided, because many prisoners would equate these with attacks on Italy itself. The need therefore was to concentrate on attacking the Fascist political ideology and leadership, but not the Italian nation. A more subtle approach was recommended, which concentrated on explaining the disastrous consequences for Italy if she continued the alliance with Nazi Germany.

> We should constantly keep before them the picture of what the German New Order means for Italy and the individual Italian, and thus lead them to realise for themselves the terrible position in which their country has been placed by Mussolini and the men around him, and make them see that these men are serving the German and not the Italian interest.

The ideal aim was not to classify the POWs as Fascists and anti-Fascists, but 'to unite them all spiritually as anti-Germans'.[32]

The best medium for such propaganda was an Italian language newspaper, whose staff should be recruited if possible from among the POWs themselves. At first, the weekly *Il Corriere del Campo* was introduced to the POWs from Cairo, before printing facilities were organized in India. As well as publishing leading articles, this paper not only printed the communiqués of all the belligerents, but also supplied POWs with puzzles, chess problems, English lessons, and, eventually, the serialization of Rudyard Kipling's *Kim*. In mid-1942, *La Diana*, the Italian edition of a Government of India monthly publication known as *The Bugle*, was also circulated to provide more of a focus on Indian events and issues.[33]

Newspapers were supplemented by radio broadcasts, lectures and open discussions. For example, prisoners were allowed to listen to the BBC, Vatican Radio and Radio *Roma*, so that they could make up their own minds about the 'veracity' of British and Italian propaganda. Guidelines were laid down as to the best approach to use in the implementation of these policies; the central tenet being that the various media, especially the newspapers, should not be seen as propaganda tools. For instance, the newspapers were to confine themselves to 'objective news about the war [*sic*], . . . world events, the situation in Italy and life in the prisoners' camps'. Correspondence and suggestions from the POWs were to be encouraged, and from this would 'emerge currents of opinions, which should help in formulating editorial policy and facilitate its gradual development on lines favourable to our cause, without provoking too violent reactions'.[34] Eventually, it might be possible to recruit a Free Italian force or labour corps. In fact, the first step towards raising a combat force amongst the anti-Fascist POWs would be the establishment of a pioneer corps under British command to work in the rear echelons. Finally, there was no doubt as to the immediate propaganda value provided by the indulgent treatment of these men. Descriptions of camp life, and sound recordings of typical scenes or amusing incidents, supplemented by broadcasts of personal messages from prisoners to their families and sweethearts in Italy, provided first-rate material for the British propaganda campaign to Italy.[35]

The basic outline of these principles was telegraphed to GHQ India two days after Stevens and Munro had arrived in New Delhi.[36] The PWE were confident, on the basis of their experience with Italian captives in the Middle East and the United Kingdom, that their policy directive was sound. However, they clearly recognized that its execution would have to be carried out chiefly by the military authorities, 'who alone can judge what is practicable' in the camps under their charge.[37] Herein lay the source for future conflict between the PWE and the military authorities in India. The PWE mission relied on the goodwill and whole-hearted co-operation of all levels of command of the British military in India, in particular the DMI. Without it, the PWE mission was helpless, if not stillborn.

III

The immediate task that Munro and Stevens had to tackle upon their arrival in India was the establishment of clear lines of communication and responsibility between themselves and the various military agencies involved with POW administration. In this, they were firmly supported by Wavell. At a conference of POW group commanders held at GHQ New Delhi between 2 and 4 December 1941, Wavell circulated a secret directive that stressed that uniformity and centralized control were essential conditions if the ultimate aims of the PWE's policy amongst the Italian POWs was to succeed. Thus, the Chief of the General Staff (CGS), India, would be responsible through the DMI, India, for the execution of the political policy. The Adjutant-General, working through the Director of Prisoners of War, India, would ensure that the provisions of the 1929 Geneva Convention were observed, and that the administration of POW affairs was kept as far as possible in accordance with the political policy. This meant that group commanders and their camp commandants would be restricted to the housing, clothing and feeding of POWs. Orders regarding the treatment, discipline and security within the camps would be issued directly from GHQ alone through the group commanders. The co-ordination of both the administrative and political policies was the sole responsibility of the CGS, India.[38]

The overall structure and demarcation of responsibilities seemed clear enough; but the mechanisms by which this policy was to operate were not. Matters arising out of the political aspects of the directive were to be forwarded by the group commanders to the DPW at GHQ. To facilitate the co-ordination and execution of both the political and administrative policies, a military intelligence section under the control of the DMI was installed in the DPW. It was this branch of military intelligence that was the all-important linchpin between the military authorities in India and the PWE mission, which was ultimately responsible to the Foreign Office in London. Although Stevens and Munro were attached to the DMI, they were not part of the intelligence section that was attached to the DPW, which meant they had no direct line of communications with the POW authorities in India.[39]

There was a real danger, therefore, that vital intelligence material of a political nature would not necessarily reach these officers, whose primary responsibility was to gauge political opinion in the camps and advise accordingly. In addition, the PWE mission did not have direct communication with London. In theory, the PWE had to process all its correspondence through the General Staff at GHQ. In practice, the DMI saw all reports and messages before their dispatch, and had the right to refer them to the DPW and Adjutant-General for comment.[40] In other words, not only could the military authorities monitor the PWE's communications with London, but they could also defer or delay the implementation of PWE policy. The lack of a direct channel to London, compounded by the exploratory nature of its work, was later to prove a serious bone of contention between PWE personnel in India and their military superiors at GHQ New Delhi. For, as the PWE staff argued, it delayed unnecessarily the implementation of policy objectives and subsequently limited their effectiveness in the camps.

One of the fundamental requirements for the successful operation of the PWE mission in India was the active support of the camp authorities. Thornhill, writing shortly after Munro's departure for India in October 1941, informed him that the camp commandants would be instructed to offer assistance, but that it was vital for him to meet them individually and

> endeavour to interest them in the work and open their eyes to the importance of the task in which they are asked to cooperate. Few commandants have any knowledge of the political situation in Italy, or of the value of the long term propaganda policy of converting as many prisoners as possible into friendly emissaries working for understanding and cooperation with England in post-war Europe.[41]

This was sound, practical advice; but the job of proselytization was fraught with many pitfalls.

Discussions held at the group commanders' conference in early December and subsequent visits to their facilities by Stevens made it abundantly clear that drastic alterations in attitudes, camp conditions and policy were needed. A trip to Group #2 at Bairagarh near Bhopal, which comprised eight POW camps and housed just over 15,000 captives, revealed that nothing had been done to 'de-root Fascist activities'. It was 'utterly impossible' to initiate any PWE policy, wrote Stevens, and unless segregation was carried out 'thoroughly and completely' it would prove an absolute waste of time for the PWE to initiate its political warfare campaign.[42]

Equally worrying for the British was the fact that morale and Fascist discipline had improved markedly among the POWs since their capture and relocation to India. At one POW facility, Fascist membership cards had been fashioned from cigarette cartons, and a nominal roll of all members and their activities within the camp was kept, as well as a record of the movements of Fascists between camps. 'The Fascists have made it known that they are keeping a tally of each prisoner for report back to Rome', reported Stevens. As a result, the POWs were

> consequently more in awe of the secret Fascist cells than of the British authorities. Collective bravado and love of heroics without danger is a contributory factor to this state of mind. Men who in Italy joined with everyone else in feeling bored when *Giovanezza* was sung now join in its choral chanting with the utmost fervour Fascism has become identified in their minds with patriotism.[43]

The distribution of *La Diana* also met with widespread and organized opposition. One senior Italian officer went so far 'as to buy up all the copies allotted to his wing and have them publicly burnt. Any P.O.W. found reading literature published by us became a marked man, and went in danger of being beaten up.'[44]

Meanwhile, some commandants tolerated Fascism in their camps because it was the Fascists who maintained order and discipline. To ignore or turn a blind eye to these political activities in order to ensure a quiet or cosy billet was self-defeating, argued the PWE. Vigorous action was needed to suppress these manifestations if the Italian POW was to be turned against Fascism. Firm discipline had to be imposed in all camps and any undue dependence upon Fascist POWs for the maintenance of order was to be deprecated.[45] In addition, Munro recommended that the status and powers of intelligence officers and interpreters in the camps be increased. This was supported by the DMI, India, which admitted that the quality of many of its camp commandants and interpreters was poor. The main stumbling-block, however, remained the inability of the military authorities to segregate and sieve the officers and the known Fascists from the remainder. Until segregation had been completed it was deemed unwise by the PWE to enforce political discipline among the Italian POWs.[46]

Why were the military authorities apparently dragging their feet over this matter? Part of the problem was organizational, while another was operational. The sudden influx of Italian prisoners from North Africa during the winters of 1940–1 and 1941–2, coupled with the fact that Egypt was threatened on both occasions by an Axis invasion shortly after each campaign, had made it imperative that as many enemy POWs as possible should be evacuated from the Middle East. Given this state of flux, it was not possible to carry out any but the most rudimentary classification of captives. Once in India, there were the logistical challenges of housing, feeding and guarding the Italian POWs. Delays ensued, in particular the construction of the POW compounds. Men were shunted from place to place while the camps were built and expanded. Prisoners were 'herded into camps', wrote one officer, and, 'provided they did not attempt to escape, they were allowed to organise themselves as they liked' without interference from their captors. By apparent good behaviour and the maintenance of discipline, the Fascists gained the confidence of the camp staffs and took control.[47] The pressures generated by the initial administrative chaos therefore made it extremely difficult for the Indian military authorities to establish a systematic segregation policy. The Director of Military Intelligence, India, Major-General W. J. Cawthorn, claimed that 'the delay in the arrival of the Mission and in the issue by the P.W.E. of a definition of policy [had] been an adverse factor'.[48]

The latter point is debatable and, in part, could be interpreted as sour grapes on the part of the DMI. Nevertheless, the PWE agreed that under the circumstances the segregation of hostile elements into separate camps had to be sacrificed to the need to evacuate enemy POWs from operational areas.[49] The entry of the Japanese into the war in December 1941 and their subsequent conquest of Burma in the first four months of 1942 compounded the problem. Intensive troop movements necessitated by the defence of India's eastern frontier had absorbed all available rolling-stock at the very moment orders for the concentration of officers at Yol in the Punjab were about to be enacted; an essential pre-requisite of the segregation strategy. Nonetheless, General Brooks stressed in an *aide mémoire* that unless some measure of segregation was undertaken, however dire the operational situation or however overstretched the military authorities were in India, the task of the PWE mission would be rendered impossible. It was imperative, he continued, not to lose sight of the far-reaching political repercussions the creation of a Free Italian force, however insignificant militarily, would have not only in Italy, but also amongst her Axis partners and the neutral countries and, especially, in the United States.[50]

The strength of Fascist opposition in the camps must not to be underestimated. The number of known Fascists, or 'blacks', which included most of the Italian officers, was put at 12,000 by Munro in January 1942. The DMI, India, believed that this was an exaggerated figure and that Munro was overstressing the point,[51] perhaps to give further credence to his continual demands for segregation. However, Munro countered that an orderly camp was not necessarily a 'politically healthy' camp, because the discipline that prevailed was more than likely being imposed by Fascist cells rather than British administrators.[52] 'From the top to the bottom of the group organisation the attitude was', observed another PWE officer in January 1943, 'that trouble must be avoided at all costs, [one] which had as its source the indifference of the [DPW] to the possibilities of turning this mass of P.O.W. from a liability into an asset'.[53]

The central factor that lay at the heart of the tensions between the PWE officials and certain powerful elements within the military bureaucracy in India was control. The mission's independent authority must have rankled with some senior officers, who, as a result, were unprepared or unwilling to extend their full co-operation. Similarly, political warfare was no doubt a strange and unfamiliar concept to many Indian Army officers. To them 'the methods of fighting a war began and ended on the battle-field, and they were unable to fit propaganda [and]

POW[s] into the larger strategic picture'.[54] It was a learning process for all who dealt with POWs, and there were bound to be misunderstandings, petty jealousies and jurisdictional disputes between departments and individuals during the first stages of implementation.

The confusion and delay that plagued the implementation of the mission's policy during the winter of 1941–2 were eventually overcome. The policy of educating group commanders and their staffs as to the aims and objectives of the PWE's strategy, although painstakingly slow, began to pay dividends. At a second group commanders' conference held in May 1942 problems were identified, recommendations were made and steps were taken to rectify many of the organizational and administrative problems that had led to inefficiencies and misunderstandings in the past. Indeed, the conferences provided an excellent forum to air concerns and settle disagreements. The greatest achievement was recognition of the fact that group intelligence staffs could communicate directly with the PWE mission and the DPW on intelligence matters. The appointment of PWE liaison officers to each POW group was another major improvement, for under the old system, this material went first to the DMI, which was supposed to, but did not always, forward it to other departments.[55] Furthermore, the upgrading in status of camp intelligence officers and interpreters was a marked step forward in improving intelligence-gathering and the waging of a political warfare campaign.

IV

These were indeed trying times for the beleaguered band of PWE officials in India. Despite scoring some successes, especially the promise of closer co-operation with the military authorities, there were moments when enthusiasm for the mission seemed to be wavering. Confidence among some of the mission's personnel was fragile. Most of the pessimism stemmed from the lack of progress made in segregating the POWs. Moreover, as Colonel Stevens remarked, doubts had arisen concerning the usefulness and scope of the mission because of the unfavourable military developments in Burma. The question arose, would the Government of India continue to support a venture that was experimental in design, keeping in mind that the obstacles to a vigorous segregation of prisoners seemed insurmountable.[56] As far as the Foreign Office was concerned nothing had arisen to make them want to abandon the project. Reassured, the PWE sanctioned funds for the establishment of a 'rallying centre' at Jaipur in Rajasthan, where anti-Fascists could be removed from existing camps 'with a view to exploring the possibility of inducing them to form a Free Italian Force'.[57]

Thornhill, who had arrived in India in February 1942 to become head of the mission, informed his superiors in London that Stevens had compiled a list of 3,000 anti-Fascist Italian POWs. The Jaipur proposal also had the enthusiastic support of the DMI, India.

> All other heads of departments have given [their] approval and [have] prom-
> ised assistance. I and the senior officers of my Mission consider it to be the
> only way of putting to a practical test the possibility of success of the task
> entrusted to us. It is not possible to assess the prospects one way or the other
> unless and until we have a camp apart such as Jaipur will provide.[58]

The plan was to send the first instalment of 1,000 POWs to a special facility at Jaipur. The balance would remain in their present camps until additional accommodation was built.

Construction began in late August 1942. However, difficulties in finding building materials, further delays in segregation work and the inability of the Quartermaster's branch to supply rations meant that by December the camp, which was still unfinished, had billets for only 400 of the proposed complement of 1,000 'white' (anti-Fascist) POWs. It was not until the end of January 1943 that accommodation for 200 officers and 1,000 other ranks was completed. Despite these annoying hold-ups, Stevens was convinced that, given more resources, the Jaipur facility could be expanded. A further 3,000 'whites' were earmarked for transfer as soon as accommodation became available. Given the right conditions, Stevens assured his superiors in London that up to 10,000 could be relocated to Jaipur in just five months.[59]

At long last a nucleus of POWs who were willing to assist the Allied war effort had been formed. Jaipur would be the base of operations for specially formed Italian POW labour battalions, which would be employed in technical support in India or to provide guides for Allied landing parties in the forthcoming invasions of Sicily and mainland Italy. They would be led by their own officers, and it was proposed that they wore a uniform of British design with *Italia Redenta* (Italy redeemed) embroidered on the right sleeve. These men would also provide the core of 'something more ambitious', that is, the basis of fighting units for a Free Italian force. 'To take full advantage of the potentialities of this scheme there must be no delay in the provision of special accommodation and improved living conditions for those who wish to declare themselves anti-Fascists' reported the Indian mission to Sir R. H. Bruce Lockhart, Director-General of the PWE, in January 1943. 'We are gaining the confidence of the POW, and to lose it at this juncture will endanger the whole scheme.'[60] However, only the War Cabinet in London could sanction expansion, and time was of the essence.

The idea of the *Italia Redenta* received Eden's fullest support and his approval for the expansion of the Jaipur experiment. There were three advantages in the formation of these anti-Fascist labour battalions. In light of the shortage of manpower they possessed a utilitarian value. In addition, they were useful weapons in the propaganda war and, finally, as pioneer battalions they could be quickly converted into military units and deployed during the forthcoming liberation of Italy. This was an attractive idea, and one which the PWE and Foreign Office had continually supported. There was an additional reason for pushing the PWE's argument forward, according to one senior Foreign Office official, P. Dixon. The Americans might well raise their own anti-Fascist units in North Africa, and it was therefore advisable for the British to have a body of anti-Fascist Italians under their control so that, for example, if 'they were ever needed in connexion with an invasion of Italy, we should not be dependent on the Americans'.[61] Indeed, such military potential could hardly be ignored, as the number of Italian POWs in British hands was approximately 274,000 in February 1943, 68,000 of whom were located in India. The question now posed by Eden to his cabinet colleagues was, how desirable was it to extend this scheme to the 98,000 Italian POWs in East Africa and the United Kingdom?[62]

The War Cabinet endorsed Eden's proposal four days later; but refused to extend the labour battalion scheme to the United Kingdom because, argued the Ministry of Agriculture and Fisheries, Italian POWs were already engaged in work of national importance, namely agriculture. Therefore, it did not see the advantage of creating special, anti-Fascist labour battalions in the British Isles. The War Cabinet were also unwilling to sanction the creation of armed anti-Fascist units.[63] As officials grappled with the possibility of expanding the labour battalion scheme, there were indications that Thornhill's men in India were winning the propaganda war in the camps and turning the tide against the hardline Fascists. The yardstick that measured the change in attitude was information gleaned by the censors from POW correspondence. Accustomed to grumble about food, the POWs were finding themselves impressed by the more disturbing home news and the worsening situation within Italy. 'I am alright and the treatment meted out to us . . . is excellent', wrote Captain Antonio Lombardi. However, when he contemplated what his children ate, which he claimed was not even a third of what he was rationed, 'I feel very sad.'[64] An extract from a letter sent to India from a loved one in Italy revealed the severity of the situation that ordinary citizens faced on a daily basis. 'We suffer famine here. The farmers have enough, but the country is in a plight. The Axis fares badly and the tide of war is turning against us.'[65]

Morale within most of the Italian POW facilities in India was adjudged to be 'precariously balanced'. This prompted Munro to suggest that the propaganda directed from London should now encourage the flow of correspondence with Italians abroad; 'that all broadcasts, open and covert, make as much as possible of Free Italy Movements, and that every emphasis be laid on any scraps of information which indicate bad feeling between Italians and Germans'.[66] The PWE mission was adamant that the opportunities now being presented should not be squandered as they had been in the past. One long-standing complaint lodged by PWE liaison officers was that British propaganda concerning the Italian POW had always been negative. A more positive approach was required. It was not enough, argued Thornhill, 'to rub in that Mussolini has bartered the Italian people to the Germans. The [POWs] want a constructive vision of the future of Italy' after the war. If the Foreign Office failed to confront this issue then the POWs would be looking to Washington or Moscow for solace.[67] This was why it was vital for the Foreign Office to expand the facilities at Jaipur and give those POWs who had openly committed themselves to helping the Allies an opportunity to contribute to the war effort. Failure to enlarge Jaipur or a delay through lack of funds might jeopardize the entire project. As one field officer noted: 'We have already lost prestige among the P.O.W.[s] on account of our inability to house those Whites who have openly declared themselves for us, . . . a repetition of this might have serious consequences.'[68]

For the moment it looked as if the PWE mission had finally secured the proper environment and support that it had demanded for such a long time. Unfortunately for Thornhill and his hardworking team, old problems resurfaced, and several new obstacles were introduced that by July 1943 effectively stymied the mission and led to its recall from India. At the War Office, some officials were still at a loss as to the objects of Thornhill's activities.[69] The real difficulties, however, remained with elements within GHQ, India, especially the Adjutant-General's branch. PWE officers commented repeatedly that the co-operation given them by GHQ was marred and overshadowed by the Indian military's lack of interest and understanding of political warfare. It was a new idea, and was inclined to be viewed as a 'waste of time'. The Adjutant-General's branch were singled out as the chief offenders. 'Full co-operation is continually promised, but our projects are apt to be hindered by administrative difficulties, which, by the use of a little imagination, could be overcome. The Adjutant-General's Branch do not like doing anything which will disturb the even tempo of the life of the camp staffs.' The PWE were adamant that the amount of co-operation their mission had received and was still receiving from the military authorities in India left much to be desired.[70]

The death knell came with the Australian request in May 1943 for the removal of 10,000 anti-Fascist Italian POWs from India for agricultural work in the dominion.[71] This, argued the PWE, rendered the formation of the Labour Corps units 'well-nigh impossible'. The entire programme depended upon the combing out of 'white' and 'grey' (anti-, non- or slightly Fascist) personnel from the camps. Eden was informed by one disgruntled official that

> if all converts and likely converts are now to be removed to Australia, the retention of our Mission will not . . . be worth while. Clearly, so far as [the] P.W.E. is concerned, nothing can be gained by attempting to re-educate prisoners who, as soon as they are reaching a standard which would enable us to make use of them for the purposes of political warfare, are removed.[72]

The same official bemoaned the fact that after two trying years the labour corps scheme, which was now in its opening stages and which had been 'carried out in the teeth of very considerable difficulties', was being terminated.[73]

When the news reached Lieutenant-Colonel A. C. Johnston, who had replaced Thornhill in March 1943 as head of the Indian mission, it came as a 'complete bombshell'. Shocked and angry, Johnston raised the all-important point that it was those POWs who had openly declared their support for the Allied cause who would suffer the bitterest disappointment. They and their families had taken great risks in whole-heartedly assisting the PWE in the formation of the *Italia Redenta*. Men had been intimidated and beaten up by 'blacks' in the camps, and there were several unconfirmed cases where the families of several co-operators had been made to suffer as well.[74] One senior PWE official in London, Air Commodore P. R. C. Groves, complained that there were no mechanisms through which these 'whites' could be compensated for the risk that they and their families had undertaken by volunteering to fight against their Fascist masters. The Jaipur camp was now a dead end; 'the prisoners find themselves treated precisely as they were before the transfer with no hope of preferment'.[75]

When Brooks notified the War Office of the decision to recall the mission from India it came as something of a surprise. According to R. Evelyn-Smith, Deputy Director of the War Office's DPW, both Wavell and his successor as C.-in-C. India, General Sir Claude Auchinleck, had not been consulted. Furthermore, the suggestion that the mission's work had been vitiated by the decision to transfer 10,000 anti-Fascist POWs to Australia was based on a misapprehension. Thus, the premiss on which the PWE had decided to withdraw the mission was inaccurate, and moreover, the decision had been taken without reference to the War Office.[76] Similarly, GHQ India vigorously denied that the transfer of Italian POWs to Australia precluded the continuance of the PWE recruitment policy for the *Italia Redenta*. They also stated that they were not transferring any of those already enrolled or earmarked for the labour corps.[77] Besides, the availability of shipping would dictate the flow of prisoners to Australia. The damage, however, had been done.

Throughout July, discussions took place between officials from the PWE, the India Office and the War Office on the future conduct of political warfare in the Italian POW camps in India. It was unanimously agreed that recruitment to the *Italia Redenta* be maintained. The PWE would continue to finance *La Diana* on condition that GHQ India undertook guidance as provided by the PWE's weekly directives. Acknowledging the importance of the radio broadcasts, GHQ India also agreed to take full operational and financial responsibility for them. All wireless apparatus on charge to the PWE was handed over to GHQ India, again on the stipulation that the PWE would waive demands for reimbursement provided that GHQ continued to use its weekly directives for the broadcasts. Finally, English would still be taught in the camps, but on a much reduced scale. With the exception of the clerical staff and those personnel who would be redeployed to GHQ India to assist in the continuation of the propaganda work, all members of the mission were withdrawn to the United Kingdom or the Middle East.[78]

V

It was ironic that, when the decision to withdraw the PWE mission in India was being made, the Allies were scoring successive victories against the Axis in the Mediterranean theatre. On 13 May 1943 Axis forces surrendered in Tunisia. Two months later the Allies invaded Sicily, which was conquered on 17 August. Meanwhile, Mussolini had resigned on 25 July. The Allied invasion of mainland Italy was launched on 3 September, and five days later Italy surrendered. Shortly afterwards, on 13 October, Italy declared war on Germany and became an Allied co-belligerent. The sudden and dramatic turn of events during the summer of 1943 seemed to preclude the need for a Free Italy movement.

However, the collapse of Italy introduced new and perplexing problems for the Allies *vis-à-vis* Italy, one of which was the status of Italian POWs in Allied hands. This is beyond the scope of this essay. Suffice it to say, attempts to negotiate a formal agreement between the Allies and the new Italian government, under the leadership of Marshal Pietro Badoglio, on the future status and utilization of Italian POWs by the Allies were unproductive. As a result, even though Italy was an ally of sorts, the British and Americans were able to administer and employ their Italian charges much as they had before the surrender.[79]

This irritated a large number of Italian POWs, who grew increasingly restless as the war progressed. They could simply not understand why they had not been released now that Italy had changed sides. Were the Italians not allies? If so, why had their status as POWs been maintained? The initial euphoria was soon replaced by frustration, which in some cases was translated into acts of disobedience, including strikes, ill-discipline and an increase in anti-British feeling in the camps. Many POWs who had willingly volunteered to assist the Allies by enrolling in the pioneer or 'co-operator' units began to question their original decision to do so. The Allies countered by improving their rations, pay and privileges. The results were mixed.[80]

The central question remains, however. Did the Italian surrender mean that the PWE's political warfare campaign was unnecessary or wasted? The answer must be an unqualified no, even though there was no apparent need for an armed *Italia Redenta* after July 1943. Admittedly, the Italian surrender in September meant that the importance of propaganda directed to the Italian POWs had diminished.[81] However, it did not mean that the knowledge and expertise gained during this entire process was lost, as some of the techniques and personnel were incorporated into those 're-education' programmes later undertaken amongst the growing number of German POWs. Meanwhile, the return in terms of the numbers of 'white' Italian POWs recruited and actively engaged for political purposes with the Allies was small, although the number of 'co-operators' employed as labourers was indeed significant.[82] However, the dramatic turn of political and military events that took place in 1943 should not be overestimated. While the changed circumstances had a great impact on the PWE's policies, the challenge now was to adapt to these new conditions in order to reap some post-war political dividends, however small.

More specifically, what of India and the work that the PWE had initiated amongst the Italian POWs there? Once the mission had been recalled, the idea of transforming the *Italia Redenta* from a pioneer unit to a fighting force was quickly and predictably shelved by the military authorities. They had strongly deprecated the formation and employment of armed POW units in India. Instead, GHQ India welcomed the formation of unarmed labour units, which could be deployed anywhere in India on vital military projects, such as road-building and airfield construction. The preferred option involved the release of the 'white' prisoners and their formation into small units of 250 men each. This, argued GHQ India, was the most effective use of surplus Italian POWs.

As 1943 progressed the military authorities in India took a harder line. A severe famine was ravaging India, and threatened the internal security of the country. Stocks of military food supplies were already being diverted for famine relief, and those designated for the POWs had been the subject of 'acid comment' by members of the Legislative Assembly. The War Department of the Government of India welcomed their removal from India altogether.[83] Over the next few months many thousands were in fact relocated to Australia, the Middle East and the United Kingdom. In turn, PWE staff were transferred to the Middle East and the United Kingdom to carry on work amongst the growing number of prisoners in those two theatres.

The failure of the PWE mission to move beyond the exploratory stage of its work was due, in part, to the fact that it had no executive authority over the Italian POWs in India. This was firmly in the hands of the Adjutant-General. As the mission was limited in scope to an advisory capacity, it had neither the executive power nor the resources to implement an effective or large-scale propaganda campaign. Segregation had been piecemeal. Therefore, despite the initial interest and support of Wavell, the effectiveness of the small cadre of PWE officials in India was constrained from the very beginning, because of their dependence on the goodwill and co-operation of the Indian military authorities. As we have seen, this was not always forthcoming. The shortage of trained personnel, in particular Italian-speaking intelligence officers, hampered further the mission's efforts. In the end, the immediate demands and manpower requirements of the military were to triumph over the long-term political aims of the PWE. The Free Italy movement, although an interesting experiment, was not to be.

Notes

1. Public Records Office (hereafter PRO), War Office Papers (hereafter WO), WO 165/59, 'Summary for Army Council 1–30 April 1941' by General Sir Alan Hunter, DPW, 6 May 1941.
2. Kent Fedorowich, '"Mopping up the Wops in Africa": Italian POWs and their British Captors, 1940–5', unpublished conference paper.
3. F H Hinsley, *British Intelligence in the Second World War*, vol. 2, London, 1981, p. 33.

4. For the SOE's involvement in political warfare see Charles Cruick-shank, *The Fourth Arm: Psychological Warfare 1938–45*, London, 1977 and Michael Balfour, *Propaganda in War 1939–1945: Organisation, Policies and Publics in Britain and Germany*, London, 1979.

5. See for example, M. B. Sullivan, *Thresholds of Peace: Four Hundred Thousand German Prisoners and the People of Britain 1944–48*, London, 1979; C. Fitzgibbon, *Denazification*, London, 1969; A. Hearnden (ed.), *The British in Germany: Educational Reconstruction after 1945*, London, 1984; Kurt Jürgensen, 'British Occupation Policy after 1945 and the Problem of "Re-educating Germany"', *History*, vol. 68, 1983, pp. 225–44; and more recently, Arthur L. Smith, Jr, *The War for the German Mind: Re-educating Hitler's Soldiers*, Oxford, 1996.

6. PRO, Foreign Office Papers (hereafter FO), FO 898/161, secret memo., 14 Apr. 1940.

7. Ibid., secret and personal, Brooks to R. J. H. Shaw, Department EH, 11 June 1940.

8. PRO, SOE Papers for the Near and Middle East, HS 3/146, Dalton to Oliver Lyttleton, Minister of State, 9 July 1941; FO 898/110, 'Memorandum on Anti-Fascist Propaganda in the Middle East', by Thornhill and Miss Freya Stark, Assistant Information Officer, Ministry of Information, Aden, 15 Aug. 1940.

9. Ibid.

10. PRO, FO 898/161 possesses fleeting references to these initial discussions and FO 371/29936 contains a great deal of material concerning the suitability of Carlos Petrone as a potential leader of the Free Italy movement.

11. PRO, FO 898/110, 'Memorandum on the Use of Italian Prisoners of War for Anti-Fascist Political Work', by Thornhill and Stark, 30 Jan. 1941.

12. PRO, FO 371/29920/R 23, C.-in-C. Middle East to War Office, 30 Jan. 1941; minute by Sir P. Dixon, 4 Feb. 1941.

13. PRO, Cabinet Office Papers (hereafter CAB), CAB 66/15, WP(41)51, minute by Churchill, 11 Feb. 1941.

14. PRO, FO 371/29935/R 1376, Davidson to P. Nichols, Foreign Office, Feb. 1941.

15. PRO, CAB 65/11, WM19(41)12, 20 Feb. 1941; CAB 66/15, WP(41)51, 'The Formation of a Free Italian Movement in the Italian Colonies', 6 Mar. 1941; FO 371/29936/R 3055, minute by Sir M. Lampson, British Ambassador, Cairo, 3 Apr. 1941.

16. PRO, CAB 66/15, WP(41)51, 6 Mar. 1941; WO 193/352, Wavell to War Office, 21 Mar. 1941.

17. PRO, FO 371/29947/R 5913, report by de Salis on Geneifa POW Camp #3, Apr. 1941.
18. PRO, Colonial Office Papers (hereafter CO), CO 968/45/1, War Office to C.-in-C. India, 23 Jan. 1941.
19. PRO, WO 165/59, 'Summary', 6 May 1941.
20. PRO, FO 898/111, draft letter to Sir Orme Sargent, 30 June 1941; FO 371/29947/R 5913, minute by Martelli, 7 June 1941.
21. PRO, FO 371/29936/R 5642, War Office to Auchinleck, 16 July 1941 and Foreign Office to Lampson, 26 July 1941.
22. PRO, CO 968/45/1, C.-in-C. Middle East to War Office, 7 Jan. 1941 and C.-in-C. India to War Office, 14 Mar. 1941; WO 193/344, Middle East POW location table as of 31 May 1941, n.d. (probably June 1941); FO 898/110, C.-in-C. India to War Office, 30 July 1941; WO 193/352, C.-in-C. India to War Office, 14 June and 23 July 1941; CO 968/45/2, return of enemy POWs as on 1 Nov. 1941; WO 222/ 1360, medical quarterly report on POW camps in India, Dec. 1941. Ramgarh was eventually closed in August 1942 and its POWs redistributed. See PRO, FO 939/370, Thornhill to Sir R. H. Bruce Lockhart, Director-General of Political Warfare Executive, mission report for August 1942, 2 Sept. 1942. Useful tables are produced from Italian archival sources by Flavio Giovanni Conti, *I prigionieri di guerra italiani 1940–1945*, Bologna, 1986, pp. 452–3. However, they largely deal with the 1943–5 period. Also see Carlo Felici, 'I prigionieri nella seconda guerra mondiale', *Revista Militare*, 1 (1988), pp. 132–8, and Romain H. Rainero, 'I prigionieri italiani in mani alleate', in Romain H. Rainero and Renato Sicurezza (eds), *L'italia nella 2^{a} guerra mondiale: aspetti e problemi (1944–1994)*, Milan, 1995, pp. 383–401.
23. Cruickshank, *Fourth Arm* (see Note 4 above), pp. 28–43; Balfour, *Propaganda in War* (see Note 4 above), pp. 93–102; FO 898/286, contains PWE directives on the reorganization of the SOE and the establishment of the PWE.
24. Cruickshank, *Fourth Arm* (see Note 4 above), p. 57.
25. PRO, FO 898/110, Wavell to War Office, 30 July 1941.
26. Ibid., telegram from DMI India to PWE, 17 Nov. 1941.
27. Ibid.
28. PRO, WO 163/583, Imperial POW Committee, sub-committee A, Paper PWCA/P(42)15, 25 Feb. 1942, appendix A, PWE memo. entitled, 'Policy towards Italian Prisoners of War', 14 Nov. 1941.
29. Ibid.
30. Ibid.
31. Ibid.; FO 898/111, Stevens to Munro, 27 Nov. 1941.
32. PRO, WO 163/583, appendix A, 14 Nov. 1941. The concentration

on the Italian leadership as opposed to the Italian people is empha-sized by a former POW, Alberto Rovighi, in his piece entitled, 'Obiettivi, metodi e resultati dell'azione politica condotta dalla Gran Bretagna nei riguardi dei prigionieri di guerra italiani', in Romain H. Rainero (ed.), *I prigionieri militari italani durante la seconda guerra mondiale: aspetti e problemi storici,* Milan, 1984, pp. 249–54.

33. PRO, FO 898/112, Thornhill to Lockhart, mission report for July 1942, 6 Aug. 1942; FO 939/402, Thornhill to Lockhart, 28 Nov. 1942; FO 939/370, 'Scheme for the Employment of Italian P.O.W.', 1 Feb. 1943.

34. PRO, WO 163/583, appendix A, 14 Nov. 1941. For the develop-ment of white propaganda and the importance of the BBC's remaining 'objective' in its news coverage and programming see Cruickshank, *Fourth Arm* (see Note 4 above), pp. 69–86 and Bal-four, *Propaganda in War* (see Note 4 above), pp. 80–91.

35. Ibid.

36. PRO, FO 898/111, War Office to C.-in-C. India, 22 Nov. 1941.

37. PRO, FO 898/321, secret memo. on treatment of Italian POWs in United Kingdom, 9 Oct. 1941; WO 163/583, PWE directive, 14 Nov. 1941.

38. PRO, FO 898/110, secret policy directive concerning Italian POWs in India, 1 Dec. 1941.

39. Ibid., circular from GHQ, 2 Dec. 1941.

40. Ibid., memo. by DMI, India, 3 Mar. 1942.

41. Ibid., Thornhill to Munro, 27 Oct. 1941.

42. PRO, FO 898/112, PWE report by Munro as to progress up to 19 Jan. 1942; Stevens to Munro, 8 Jan. 1942.

43. Ibid., PWE report by Munro as to progress up to 19 Jan. 1942.

44. Ibid., 'Report of the Work of the P.W.E. Mission in India', by Lieu-tenant A. Trower, submitted to Lockhart, Jan. 1943.

45. Ibid.; FO 898/110, Adjutant-General, India, to Headquarters, POW camps, India, 24 Apr. 1942.

46. PRO, FO 898/112, PWE report by Munro as to progress up to 19 Jan. 1942.

47. Ibid., Trower report, Jan. 1943.

48. Ibid., Cawthorn to DMI, London, 21 Jan. 1942.

49. PRO, FO 898/111, Brooks to Lieutenant-Colonel A. R. Rawlinson, War Office, 10 Feb. 1942.

50. Ibid., Brooks *aide mémoire*, 15 Apr. 1942; Brooks to Rawlinson, 10 Feb. 1942.

51. RO, FO 898/112, Cawthorn to DMI, London, 21 Jan. 1942.

52. Ibid., written report no. 2 by Munro despatched to Brooks, 19 Jan. 1942.
53. Ibid., Trower report, Jan. 1943.
54. Ibid.
55. PRO, FO 898/110, notes supplied to Thornhill by Munro for group commanders' conference, 11 May 1942; FO 898/112, Thornhill to Lockhart, mission report for August 1942, 21 Sept. 1942.
56. PRO, FO 898/111, Stevens to Air Commodore Groves, PWE, 21 Apr. 1942.
57. Ibid., David Stephens to Air Commodore Groves, 4 Mar. 1942; Brooks to Lockhart, 22 Apr. 1942.
58. Ibid., Thornhill to Brooks despatched to War Office via C.-in-C. India, 8 May 1942.
59. PRO, FO 898/112, Thornhill to Lockhart, mission report for August 1942, 2 Sept. 1942; WO 208/841, E. L. Philip to Dixon, 17 Nov. 1942; FO 939/402, Thornhill to Lockhart, 28 Nov. 1942 and Thornhill summary of reports on PWE mission India, 6 Jan. 1943.
60. PRO, FO 898/112, report by Trower submitted to Lockhart, c. Jan. 1943; FO 939/402, 'Summary of reports on PWE mission India', 6 Jan. 1943.
61. PRO, FO 371/37274/R 1057/G22, minute by Dixon, 9 Feb. 1943.
62. PRO, CAB 66/34, WP(43)73, memo. by Eden, 18 Feb. 1943.
63. PRO, FO 939/370, PWE briefs, 2 and 28 Apr. 1943; FO 939/404, War Office to C.-in-C. India, 6 Feb. 1943.
64. PRO, FO 898/112, propaganda notes for London compiled by Thornhill, 25 Feb. 1943; FO 939/403, extract from a letter sent to PWE mission, 27 Apr. 1943.
65. PRO, FO 939/403, extract from a censored letter, 10 Dec. 1942.
66. PRO, FO 898/112, Munro note to Thornhill, Feb. 1943.
67. Ibid., extracts from PWE Indian mission propaganda notes, 6 Oct. 1942; FO 939/402, summary of reports on PWE mission India, 6 Jan. 1943.
68. PRO, FO 939/363, Trower to Thornhill, 19 Jan. 1943.
69. PRO, WO 208/841, War Office to D. F. Howard, southern department, Foreign Office, 1 Dec. 1942.
70. PRO, FO 939/363, PWE mission progress report, 28 Apr. 1943; Air Commodore Groves to Brooks, 22 May 1943.
71. PRO, FO 371/37274/R 5404, ministerial meeting of PWE, 10 June 1943; Australian Archives, CRS A373, item 6221, War Cabinet Agendum submitted by F. M. Forde, Minister for the Army, outlining employment of POWs in Australia, Sept. 1944.
72. PRO, FO 939/370, minute to Eden, 3 June 1943.
73. Ibid.

74. PRO, FO 939/398, Johnston to Brooks, 7 July 1943.
75. PRO, FO 939/363, Groves to Brooks, 21 June 1943.
76. PRO, 939/398, Evelyn-Smith to Brooks, 7 July 1943 and Brooks to Lockhart, 29 June 1943; FO 939/370, Wavell to Eden, 28 June 1943.
77. PRO, FO 371/37274/ R 5404, C.-in-C. India to War Office, 12 July 1943.
78. PRO, FO 939/398, minutes of meeting to discuss questions relating to the recall of POW mission to India, 16 July 1943; minutes of meeting between PWE, India Office and War Office, 22 July 1943; War Office to GHQ India, 24 July 1943.
79. Kent Fedorowich and Bob Moore, 'Co-Belligerency and Prisoners of War: Britain and Italy, 1943–45', *International History Review*, vol. 18, no. 1, 1996, pp. 28–47.
80. PRO, Ministry of Information Papers, INF 1/905, PWE memo. on Italian POWs, 8 Sept. 1944.
81. Ibid., Brooks to Bracken, 18 Oct. 1943.
82. At the end of the war the Americans had enlisted 31,000 co-operators into Italian Service Units, 1,000 of whom were shipped overseas to serve as support troops behind American forces fighting in Europe. The British scored an even more marked success. In early 1944, in anticipation of serious labour shortfalls in part created by the extensive preparations required for the forthcoming Normandy invasion, the War Office transported 30,000 co-operators to England from the Middle East, East Africa and India. Moreover, Italian POWs were used extensively in North Africa and Sicily and on the Italian mainland. In Sicily in January 1944 there were 2,051 unskilled and 768 skilled Italian POWs employed in pioneer units on the island. In North Africa, the numbers were much higher. Divided into the categories of unskilled, skilled and POWs used within the war establishment of British units, there were 25,798, 5,289 and 4,793 respectively. In April 1944 two pioneer units with a compliment of 283 men each and commanded by British officers were transferred to Italy. By the end of June 1945, 5,179 Italian co-operators were retained in North Africa, while 21,702 were employed in the Central Mediterranean Force on a variety of non-combatant duties. According to Foreign Office statistics there were 114,400 co-operators out of a total of 154,728 Italian POWs in the United Kingdom in April 1945. George C. Lewis and John Mewha, *History of Prisoner of War Utilization by the United States Army 1776–1945*, Washington, 1955, pp. 93–100 and 175–205; Louis E. Keefer, *Italian Prisoners of War in America 1942–1946*, New York, 1992, pp. 73–101; PRO, CAB 106/453,

'Employment of Co-operators in the Italian Campaign', n.d., fos. 69–70; FO 898/324, memo., 24 Apr. 1945.
83. PRO, FO 939/370, minute for Brooks, 3 June 1943; WO 193/352, minute for Director of Military Operations, 12 Feb. 1943; PRO, Prime Ministers' Papers, PREM 3/364/2, War Deparment, Government of India, to Secretary of State for India, 16 Nov. 1943, circulated to the War Cabinet.

−6−

Human Vivisection: The Intoxication of Limitless Power in Wartime

Charles G. Roland

26 September [1942] – Discovered and captured the two prisoners who escaped last night in the jungle . . . To prevent their escaping a second time, pistols were fired at their feet, but it was difficult to hit them. The two prisoners were dissected while still alive by Medical Officer YAMAJI and their livers were taken out, and for the first time I saw the internal organs of a human being. It was very informative.[1]

One of the earliest reports of human vivisection in the Far East during the Second World War, this account was translated from a diary captured on Guadalcanal. It never became a war-crimes case, presumably because the medical officer concerned did not survive the fierce fighting on the island. But the entry certainly alerted Allied officials to the likelihood that such cases might have to be dealt with after the war.[2]

When Allied Intelligence and Legal Officers began interrogating released prisoners-of-war (POWs) in the Far East in 1945, they soon realized that the volume and apparent severity of the war crimes alleged by these men suggested a massive scope to the contemplated proceedings against suspected war criminals. Trials began late in 1945, and went on throughout the Pacific area into 1948 and, in the case of the Australian courts, in some instances into 1951.

Examining the extensive documentation of these trials, one becomes aware that many of the war crimes were medical in nature; that is they were cases in which one or more of the following behaviours was alleged: withholding medical and related supplies; forcing ill men to work; maltreating medical personnel; maltreating patients; preventing the ill from obtaining medical care; conducting illegal or unethical experimentation; withholding food; functioning in a medically incompetent manner; wilfully neglecting the welfare of the sick and injured; interfering with International Red Cross supplies; and finally, performing euthanasia. This survey will be limited to illegal or unethical medical experimentation, which was charged in a substantial number of the trials conducted by the United States, Great Britain, Australia, and Canada. The Dutch trials have not been examined.

In this chapter, the word vivisection is used as a synonym for the conduct of illegal or unethical experimentation on unwilling human beings, particularly though not exclusively prisoners of war held by Imperial Japanese forces. Some mention of crimes against civilians is included for comparative purposes. In assessing the evidence, answers to a number of questions will be sought. Is there evidence of systematic experimentation in the Far East, comparable, for example, to that conducted by the Nazis in certain concentration camps? Was the vivisection directed towards explicit scientific purposes, was it primarily a form of aggression against defenceless men, or can other explanations be found? Can one arrive at any measure of the competence of Japanese medical officers from examining these war crimes transcripts and other documentation? Is there evidence of reluctance to participate in vivisection?

Human vivisection by the Japanese during the Second World War can be seen as either official or freelance. The official variety was known, sanctioned, and funded from Tokyo; freelance experimentation was undertaken by individuals or groups of individuals on their own initiative, without central support and in most or all cases without the knowledge of Tokyo. Only one instance of official vivisection is as yet known: the infamous work of General Ishii Shirō[3] and his colleagues in Unit 731 and related 'water purification' establishments.

Freelance experimentation is known to have been carried out in fewer than a dozen cases, both in the Home Islands and, more commonly, on the outlying frontiers of wartime empire. These occurred in sites as disparate as university medical schools and platoon jurisdictions on islands in the South Pacific. The experimenters were medical school professors, Imperial Japanese Army officers or NCOs, and personnel of the Japanese secret police or *Kempeitai*.

The recent revelations about the bacteriological experiments carried out by Unit 731 and related units in Manchuria not only describe a particularly heinous example of illegal experimentation, but also point up one weakness in relying on war crimes trial transcripts for information: there may be none. No Unit 731 official has ever been tried on charges related to the operation of that vast bacteriological warfare complex. The reason is straightforward. The Japanese-engendered information was the sole source of data from scientifically controlled experiments on the effects of bacteriological warfare agents on man. United States officials bargained away immunity from prosecution for the Japanese researchers in return for full access to this mass of unique data.[4]

The central figure in this extensive bacteriological warfare experimentation programme is Ishii Shirō (1892–1959). Early in his career Ishii became famous by inventing a highly effective water filter, which he once demonstrated by urinating into it and then drinking from its output.[5] But his major professional interest was bacteriological warfare.

In 1933 Ishii began his researches in this field, the importance of which he advocated tirelessly. He created the first laboratory in Harbin, Manchuria, in a former soy sauce factory. The secret code-name he gave it was *Togo*, and Ishii often travelled under the pseudonym of Captain Tōgō Hajime.[6] Presumably both names honour the great Japanese admiral of the Russo-Japanese War of 1904–5. The widespread experimental enterprise eventually comprised many divisions, including the Ishii Unit, Tōgō Unit, Kamo Unit, Unit 731, Unit 100, Unit Ei 1644, Manchuria Unit 25202, and the Kwantung Army Epidemic Prevention and Water Supply Unit.[7] Massive funds supported these extensive activities, money that the Japanese government supplied generously, if indirectly, through army funds. We can only speculate as to how much government officials or the monarchy actually knew about Ishii's work, because there was no trial nor any official investigation.

Experimentation was conducted into ways of infecting humans with the organisms that cause a remarkably wide range of diseases. These included particularly anthrax, plague, typhus, and dysentery, though the full list is a long one.[8] Ishii considered anthrax the most effective bacterial agent. It could be produced in quantity, was resistant to destruction over time, retained its virulence, and was 80 to 90 per cent fatal. The 'best' epidemic disease for warfare he considered to be plague, and the most reliable vector-borne disease, epidemic encephalitis.[9]

One of the chief Manchurian research sites was in a village called Pingfan. At least 3,000 people, mostly Chinese and Manchurian, died here as a result of the experiments of Ishii and his associates.[10] Experimental subjects were referred to as *maruta*, or 'logs'. A recent book suggests that the total number of victims killed in these types of experiments at all locations between 1933 and 1945 may be as high as 30,000, but can never be measured accurately.[11] Because of the dearth of documentation, the proportions of POWs and of civilians used as test subjects also cannot be determined. The POWs were largely Chinese, though some western ex-POWs claim to have been among this group; most would not have survived. Ishii exhorted his workers with patriotic speeches; in one he was quoted as saying:

[T]he research upon which we are now about to embark . . . may cause us some anguish as doctors. Nevertheless, I beseech you to pursue this research based on the double medical thrill; one, as a scientist to exert effort to probing for the truth in natural science and research into, and discovery of, the unknown world, and two, as a military person, to successfully build a powerful military weapon against the enemy.[12]

We have information about some of Ishii's plans for field applications. For example, to deny the Allies the use of the Saipan airstrip the Japanese devised a plan for sprinkling the runway with billions of plague-infected fleas. But before reaching its destination the ship carrying the team was sunk by a submarine.[13]

One might have anticipated an analogy between the Unit 731 case and 'The Doctors' Trial' held at Nuremberg after the war. The German trial resulted in one concrete moral accomplishment, quite aside from its juridical conclusions. That was the canon of ethics that came to be called the Nuremberg Code, which laid down reasonably rigid and specific guidelines to provide limits and protections to future experimental subjects. Nothing similar came from the Unit 731 trial, for the obvious reason that there was no trial. Nor was any other Far East case analogous to the 'Doctors' Trial', since, as will be seen, the various Japanese experiments that came to trial were limited in scope and usually scientifically frivolous in design, despite their lethal effects on many American, British, Australian, Indian, Dutch and Canadian prisoners.

Many of the cases to be described seem unequivocally to be vivisection; but others raise considerable doubt as to whether this is the correct designation. Some of the instances cited did not come to trial, the information about them deriving from a variety of sources. The cases are organized by the site of the experimentation, beginning with the Home Islands and proceeding to more distant locations.

The first to be examined is Shinagawa POW Hospital, Tokyo. Shinagawa is a district in the south-western part of Tokyo where that city spreads along the edge of Tokyo Bay towards Yokohama. The Shinagawa facility began as an ordinary work camp on 12 September 1942. Eleven months later it was transformed into the chief POW hospital in the Tokyo area. Located on an island in the general area now occupied by Haneda airport, the wooden structures were built originally for Korean labourers or Japanese unemployed, and included an administrative block and five or six barrack buildings, each capable of housing up to eighty patients.[14]

During 1943 it became apparent to Japanese POW officials, as it was painfully clear to the prisoners and their medical officers, that they must create some new arrangement for handling sick and injured POWs in the Tokyo area. A delegation from the International Committee of the Red Cross (ICRC) visiting Tokyo-area camps noted that while theoretically the seriously ill prisoners were admitted to the Red Cross hospital in Tokyo, in practice this military hospital was overfilled by Japanese army patients. Consequently, it had become impossible to get POW patients admitted, even those with severe injuries. Effectively the POWs were without proper hospital care, and had to be looked after in the quite inadequate sick bays in individual camps, some of which lacked medical officers.[15] It was to correct this problem that Shinagawa was transformed into a hospital exclusively for POW patients, who therefore would not have to compete for accommodation with Japanese soldiers, a competition they almost always lost.

The hospital passed through two distinct phases, before and after the assumption of absolute control of a portion of the patients by the chief Japanese medical officer, Captain Tokuda Hisakichi,[16] in March 1945. From August 1943, when it became a hospital, until March 1945, Shinagawa functioned in a straightforward though often medically unsatisfactory manner. The medical staff consisted of Allied POW medical officers and orderlies, with a Japanese administrative staff. Patients were sent there from POW camps in the Tokyo administrative area, which extended as far north as Niigata. Supplies and accommodation were consistently sub-standard.

As everywhere throughout the Far East, the Japanese supplied few drugs and in small amounts – the quantities were described by one ex-POW as being 'on a homeopathic scale'.[17] Fortunately, drugs were available in reasonably satisfactory amounts from the International Red Cross. For surgery, spinal anaesthesia and intravenous pentothal were used, and the POW surgeons reported excellent results with abdominal surgery. Sulfa drugs were used extensively.[18]

Tokuda and his staff had a curious way of welcoming the patients to their new medical institution. On 10 August 1943, ten days after it opened, he organized and led a mass beating of 250 POW patients. Tokuda forced the POWs to stand in front of him and the interpreter; the two men beat each of the prisoners 'four cracks with wooden shoes and section leaders were given eight cracks with wooden shoes'.[19]

Tokuda, the central figure in this venture into vivisection, is an enigma. Loathed by most of the surviving medical staff, he nevertheless had a supporter in one American pathologist-prisoner. Supposedly he had arrived at Shinagawa as a master sergeant 'and worked his way up to Captain and began to call himself doctor',[20] though this probably represents a misunderstanding of Japanese ranks. Despite voluminous testimony to the medical incompetence of this man, especially as a surgeon, his American apologist, Major Harold Keschner, stated that in comparison with other Japanese physicians he had contacted medically, Dr Tokuda 'stood out head and shoulders above them'. He seemed to have good medical knowledge, was an avid reader, well informed on current literature, had an extensive medical library and 'as far as Japanese standards were concerned was an able practitioner'.[21] Keschner seems to have been the only POW to hold this favourable opinion. We do not have any information to explain the difference between Keschner's assessment and that of the other medical officers in the camp. Perhaps, since late in the war Keschner was the only POW medical officer permitted full access to the patients, he believed he had to justify this role by emphasizing Tokuda's competence and thus, by association, his own.

Dr Tokuda, wrote Dr Alfred Weinstein, a former POW medical officer in the camp,

> was a young man of twenty-eight, son of wealthy parents in the moving-picture industry, a recent graduate of a Tokyo university and medical school. He had not yet submitted a medical thesis and was not licensed to practice medicine other than in the Army. He was short, slight, with shaven head, sloping forehead, and receding chin. His shifty eyes never focused on your face. He waddled about in glittering riding boots and baggy britches, the crotch of which almost reached the back of his knees. We called him 'Dung in Britches'. His bowlegged gait and beetle head also earned him the pseudonym [*sic*] of the 'Spider'.[22]

Weinstein observed sarcastically that Tokuda was not only a physician and surgeon, 'but also a great research man, a second Noguchi'. He wrote papers on malnutrition among the starving prisoners, and did blood studies, gastric analyses, and clinical observations on beriberi. These studies were poorly planned and incorrectly analysed. Once, he studied blood pressure, systolic and diastolic, among the patients with beriberi. His figures suggested that the average blood pressure of the patients was 112/28. The diastolic pressure (the second figure) is normally about 80. The POWs pointed out that the figure for average diastolic pressure cited by Tokuda was actually the average age of the patients in camp. Tokuda had confused two sets of figures: the list of blood pressures and the list of ages.[23]

Lieutenant-Commander James Davis, USN, not a medical officer, functioned as liaison between the POWs and the Japanese, a thankless task. He noted that Tokuda was studious, and spent hours, day after day, in his room surrounded by books. When shipments of books from the YMCA arrived at Christmas, 1944, and again in 1945, he appropriated the medical books for his own use. Tokuda appeared to Davis to be a highly nervous individual, awkward, confused, and hesitant in his relations with the prisoners.[24] But Tokuda did some good, as when he conducted a systematic study of body weights and calories, resulting in increased food supplies. Davis knew the details of this because Tokuda, unable to handle the mathematics of the study, drafted his assistance as an engineer. Davis constructed a logarithmic nomogram from which thousands of readings were taken.[25]

Unfortunately, it was this very area of Tokuda's research ambition that led to the problems between March and August 1945. In March 1945, the Japanese commandant decided to take over complete control of all tuberculous and other serious medical cases. These were isolated in one barrack, out of bounds to all other prisoners except two medical orderlies, retained for nursing duties,[26] and Keschner, the pathologist. While Tokuda did his experiments, all other medical personnel in the Shinagawa POW hospital laboured with pick and shovel from 7.30 a.m. to 7.00 p.m.[27]

What exactly was Tokuda doing that was claimed to constitute vivisection? Allegedly, he administered to some POWs a milky soy-bean material, intravenously, as part of an experimental programme as a possible cure for beriberi. One of the men died three days later 'after suffering a painful case of diarrhoea'. His diarrhoea and death were a direct result of Tokuda's experiment, according to one of the POW medical officers.[28]

During July–August 1945, Keschner saw Tokuda inject three men, Saxida (Italian), and Holland and Hampson (British), with a solution of soy-bean milk. He was certain that this was what was injected; on occasions he had heard Tokuda instruct the English orderly to bring the soy-bean-milk solution, Tokuda speaking in English. Sometimes the solutions were in wide-mouthed flasks and 'I smelt the contents and therefore know that it was soy bean milk solution.'[29] One of the cooks reported that he had seen the soy beans used for this test being ground in the cook-house.[30]

Holland died eleven hours after receiving the injection of soy-bean-milk solution, Hampson about five hours after the injection, and Saxida between eight and ten hours after receiving his injection. Keschner believed that if the material injected had caused the deaths, at post-mortem there would have been evidence in the lungs, brains, and kidneys of the presence of fat globules. But he had no microscopic and staining facilities to make these determinations. Autopsies at Shinagawa were confined to gross anatomical findings. At autopsy, he found that Holland had primary cancer of the stomach with metastases, Saxida had cirrhosis of the liver, and Hampson had far advanced pulmonary tuberculosis.[31] At Tokuda's trial, the experiments on these three men were specified individually in the charges against him, and he was found guilty on all three counts.

Tokuda conducted other experiments as well. In some he administered caprylic acid to patients in an attempt to arrest tuberculosis.[32]

Keschner was questioned about these experiments with caprylic acid. He hypothesized that since the tuberculosis organism is acid-fast, as is the organism that causes leprosy, and since caprylic acid is somewhat allied chemically to the active principle of chaulmoogra oil[33] (which is known to have some curative effect on leprosy), Tokuda probably felt that the tuberculosis organism would be affected favourably by caprylic acid.[34] No clinical improvement was seen.

Why did Tokuda exclude the POW medical officers from these wards? One opinion was that he thought he was going to make some great discovery and he did not want anyone else in on it. Keschner concluded that Tokuda, except for his scientific curiosity, which 'did not cause any deaths, but which may have caused some discomfort to some of the patients, really was sincere in his work and made the best of a bad situation'.[35] Ultimately, the war crimes court disagreed.

So did Captain Alex Mohnac, DDS, anaesthetist at all surgical operations at Shinagawa. He pointed out that anyone with medical training knows, or should know, that soy-bean milk contains much protein, and, if injected intravenously, will invariably cause severe pain and possibly death. 'Another thing I saw Dr Tokuda do was this: after sterilizing a needle preparatory to a spinal injection, he blew his breath on the needle to cool it off.'[36]

Tokuda was tried in 1947–8. The trial was adjourned repeatedly so that his mental status could be determined. His behaviour became increasingly irrational: he requested solitary confinement in Sugamo prison, became convinced that his counsel had given up his case as hopeless, appeared to have lost his decisiveness, and was evasive and moody.[37] Nevertheless his trial continued. He was found guilty on several specifications, particularly the soy-bean milk injections, and was sentenced to death by hanging early in 1948. Three years later his sentence was commuted to life imprisonment because of his continued mental deterioration. On 2 January 1951 a Board of American medical officers examined Tokuda and found him to be a catatonic schizophrenic – mute, apathetic, and refusing to eat – and concluded that he 'did not possess sufficient mental capacity to understand the nature of the proceedings against him and intelligently to conduct or cooperate in his defense'.[38] What happened to Tokuda after the transfer of administrative power from the USA to Japan is not known.

Several of the war crimes trials created great interest after the war, perhaps none more so than the one involving Kyūshū Imperial University Faculty of Medicine. On 5 May 1945, an American B-29 was shot down over the island of Kyūshū. Eleven parachutes were seen to open, but, after the war ended, no record was found of the fate of any of these men. Careful investigation finally convinced US authorities that the eight men who died after vivisection at Kyūshū Imperial University, and who could not be identified by name, were part of the missing group of eleven.[39] The crime charged against almost three dozen Japanese nationals (including fourteen physicians and one woman, a nurse) seemed peculiarly unpleasant: vivisection and cannibalism. The Japanese also have shown some interest in the case: Endō Shūsaku wrote a challenging novel based on this episode, entitled in translation *The Sea and Poison.*[40]

Kyūshū Imperial University is located in the city of Fukuoka on Kyūshū, the westernmost of the Japanese main islands. Kyūshū Imperial University's Faculty of Medicine was considered first-rank in 1945, among the best outside the environs of Tokyo. One of the potential defendants, Dr Ishiyama Fukujirō (who committed suicide before trial), was Chief of the First Surgery Clinic; another, Dr Hirako Goichi, was Director of the Anatomy Section; Miss Tsutsui Shizuko was Chief Nurse in Ishiyama's clinic.[41]

The doomed flyers were first placed in a so-called detention barracks; according to Japanese policy they were considered 'captured enemy flyers' rather than POWs until they could be investigated on the blanket charge of indiscriminate bombing. If found innocent, the men would then be transferred to a POW camp. One defendant, Komori, persuaded Satō, the officer in charge of the detention barracks, to release the flyers for medical experimentation. Satō alleged that he did so on the understanding that the release had been approved by higher authority. Komori contacted Ishiyama at the surgical clinic, offering him use of the men 'for the advancement of medicine'. (Physicians at another hospital rejected the offer.) On approximately 15, 23, and 26 May and 3 June 1945, operations were performed. None of the POWs had any injury requiring surgical treatment.

On the first date, a lung was removed from each of two POWs. While the first victim was still alive, Ishiyama removed the ligatures on the pulmonary arteries, and Komori 'scooped blood out of the chest cavity with a cup'.[42] In the second series, operations were done on the stomach, heart, and liver of two victims. Ishiyama at one point returned to the first prisoner in this group, still alive, opened his chest, incised the heart, sutured it, then had two associates do the same to demonstrate that a puncture of the heart is not always fatal.

On the third date in May only one flyer was operated on. The purported object of the surgery was to reach the trigeminal nerve 'from the top of the brain'. This flyer died from haemorrhage and brain damage. A professional colleague of Ishiyama, observing, did not exude confidence in Ishiyama's competence: 'I was asked by Dr. Ishiyama as to what was the quickest way to locate the "Trigeminus" nerve. My answer was that it was impossible to locate the "Trigeminus" nerve because they had opened the skull at the wrong place.'[43] The final three American flyers all had surgery on 3 June. One man had his stomach removed, another was exsanguinated and infused with sea water, while the third had several operations affecting gall bladder, liver and heart. Yakumaru Katsuya, Chief of the National Defence Guard, went with Satō to see an operation on a POW. They arrived in the autopsy room while the surgeons performed a liver operation.

> I thought the POW must have had a liver ailment but as the operation progressed I noticed the surgeons removed the liver so I thought this to be a funny operation. I saw the surgeon tie the liver vein. At this point I left the room and went home because I felt sick . . . after the liver was removed Komori turned his head and said to me, 'this is a removal of the liver and we are going to see how long the man would live without his liver.'[44]

All eight flyers died before leaving the operating room, which was a poorly-equipped dissecting room in the anatomy department. No records were kept of these 'experimental' operations at the time or later. Ishiyama and Komori were present at all eight operations and acted as principal and first assistant in their performance.[45] These two men seem, from the evidence, clearly to have played the most significant roles. Ishiyama committed suicide; the trial records state that Komori was 'allegedly deceased', a remarkable coincidence that engenders suspicion. According to a statement by Ishiyama, Komori was wounded during an air raid on 19 June 1945; his leg was amputated but he developed tetanus and died.[46]

After the death of the eight flyers the heads were severed and the bodies were dissected. Various parts were removed by members of the anatomy department. Komori took one POW's liver to his base at Kaikōsha Hospital, and he also took away pails full of blood. There was an allegation of cannibalism regarding ingestion of human liver by some of the accused, but this charge was not sustained. Nevertheless, there is testimony in affidavits about a social event at which cooked human liver supposedly was served to the guests.

All eight bodies, minus the removed portions, were cremated by staff members of the anatomy department. The ashes were discarded, in some instances hurriedly when the case began to be investigated.[47] False records were prepared to indicate that the flyers had all died during a later bombing of Fukuoka. This report ultimately was replaced by one alleging that the flyers were transferred to Hiroshima, where they were purportedly destroyed when the atomic bomb exploded on 6 August 1945.

Clearly science was no factor in carrying out the vivisections. The so-called research was nothing more than pointless cruelties culminating in murder, with no genuine attempt to learn anything. The fact that no notes were made is proof that no benefit to human knowledge was anticipated. A genuinely scientific approach would not have mitigated the crimes significantly, had it existed; it did not.

Ishiyama escaped justice by killing himself. In his suicide note he seemed unrepentant: 'I have devoted my heart and soul in giving medical treatment to the American soldiers. However, I regret that they did not understand me. My children have nothing to be ashamed of.' He then invoked research as an honourable activity, though he refrained from claiming that his crime exemplified such research. 'To the fellow doctors and persons concerned at the hospital: Please forgive this ignorant doctor with one death for his crimes which are equivalent to 10,000 deaths. Continue research to the end. To all the professors: I do not know how to apologise. I bow and pray for the Emperor.'[48]

These two cases, involving Shinagawa Hospital and Kyūshū University, are the only two that have been identified to date as occurring in Japan proper. The remaining instances of vivisection took place much farther afield. For example, at Tanoura, New Britain, two Japanese medical officers were charged with vivisection in connection with treating tropical ulcers. In contrast to the preceding case, this one is equivocal in the alleged offences and in the outcome. Tropical ulcers were a serious problem in the Far East during the Second World War. POWs were more likely than fighting men to suffer this incapacitating disease, because of poorer nutrition, working conditions, and medical facilities; but these ulcers also afflicted the rank and file in the Imperial Japanese Army.

Two medical officers, Numata Kimio and Nakagawa Kōichi, attached to 67th Field Commissary Hospital at Tanoura, New Britain, were charged with experimentation on Indian POWs in 1943. Explicitly, the claim of Captain Daw, Indian Medical Service, in charge of medical affairs at the camp, was that these two medical officers had removed inguinal lymph nodes surgically from several Indian POW patients who had tropical ulcers. Moreover, they were alleged to have injected the patients with Salvarsan or insulin or both.

The Japanese medical officers testified that they had incised infected lymph nodes to release pus, but had not removed any tissue; they stated unequivocally that such removal would be inappropriate treatment for tropical ulcers. They claimed that the use of Salvarsan was warranted where there was any possibility of syphilis being present. This claim and their use of insulin were supported by an Allied expert medical witness from Singapore. The Japanese medical officers were both acquitted. The other defendants were found guilty of various offences, but were sentenced to extremely short periods of imprisonment, indicating that none was seen to have been guilty of serious misconduct.[49] Perhaps the most telling evidence was Daw's admission that he had not seen any of the operations. He was going by hearsay evidence: some of the patients thought that 'something' might have been removed.

This case points to a common difficulty in any criminal trial, perhaps even more so in those involving wartime experiences. Inevitably, evidence given is coloured strongly by the fact that witnesses were themselves involved in the events. Justice Pal, in his dissenting opinion after the conclusion of the trial of major Japanese suspects, commented on: 'the special difficulty that the events occurring then [during wartime] are likely to be witnessed only by excited or prejudiced observers'.[50] The affidavits produced as evidence in this case seem clearly to show the efforts of this group of POWs to see oppressors punished; but equally clearly, some of the charges seem exaggerated or spurious.

In another case, later in the war, approximately sixty-seven Allied POWs were incarcerated in the 6th Field *Kempeitai* POW camp, Tunnel Hill Camp at Rabaul on the northern tip of New Britain. On 16 April 1945, Dr Hirano Einosuke came to the camp; he took blood samples from one Australian and nine American prisoners, the first phase in his experiments into supposed malarial immunity. Purportedly, Dr Hirano conducted his experiments on the POWs at the invitation of Medical Captain Fushita Shigeo.[51] The officer in charge claimed that he had orders from headquarters to permit Hirano to proceed with his experiments at will.[52]

About 19 July 1945, Hirano returned. Five of the prisoners whose blood had been sampled were ordered to report to some buildings on a hill across the road from Tunnel Hill Camp where Hirano carried out his experimental injections. Four of the POWs were given an injection, an action they protested against; the fifth, Captain José Holquin, could speak Japanese, and he questioned the doctor about the experiment. When Hirano had visited in April 1945, the prisoners of war were tested for the presence of malarial organisms in their blood; he had found that these five POWs did not have malaria or any evidence that they were harbouring the disease.

Hirano contended that there was such a thing as immunity against malaria, contrary to the findings of modern medicine. But before he could prove that this immunity existed he needed to expose the five prisoners to malaria. Presumably his rationale was that men who had survived in that area and who did not have signs of malarial infestation in their blood *must* have some sort of immunity – a commentary on the ubiquity of malaria in the South Pacific. He told Holquin that if he could prove that immunity existed, he would go to the New York Mayo Clinic [*sic*], saying, 'I may be a very famous man.'[53]

Hirano was accompanied by five Japanese soldiers who had severe malaria; his plan was to inject some of their blood into the supposedly immune prisoners. Holquin protested, but he was given no choice. At his urging, Hirano promised that if Holquin developed malaria, he, Hirano, would give him medicine: 'you have my word for it'.[54] Holquin was injected with about 10 cc of what he was told was blood from one of the Japanese soldiers ill with malaria.[55]

Two days later, the five men began to suffer painful headaches and severe shivering, and unquestionably had contracted malaria. They were not immune. Holquin and another POW did not have malaria as severely as did the other three men, whose illnesses worsened day by day. They had constant fever, lost their appetites, and grew weaker. An orderly took temperatures, pulses, and samples of blood, but they received no treatment. 'At about 10:00 o'clock on the night of 29 July 1945, Gunners Mate Lanigan died and about three o'clock in the morning on 30 July 1945, Ensign Atkins died. No medical assistance or aid was provided by the Japanese. . .'.[56]

In response to a specific question, Holquin stated that he had no knowledge of sheep's blood being used in the experiments conducted by Hirano. But Captain John Murphy was injected with sheep's blood, or was told that he was. In an affidavit, Murphy explained that he and another prisoner had had 'positive results' from the original blood tests, apparently meaning that they had malarial organisms in their bodies. Thus, unlike Holquin and the other men who were negative and who were given the blood of malarial Japanese, they were treated quite differently. On two occasions they were injected with a serum that Hirano said came from sheep. He hoped to immunize Murphy and his comrades against malaria. 'Speaking for myself', Murphy stated, 'I was willing for the experiment to be conducted.'[57] But nothing was changed by the injections.

No evidence has been located to suggest that Hirano came to trial in connection with these experiments. Since the crimes were serious and well documented, with at least three deaths, we may speculate that he died before he could be tried or, as with so many war criminals, he managed to disappear.

Unnecessary surgery was the charge made in a case originating on Dublon Island, Truk. This sorry tale relates the fate of two anonymous American flyers who had the misfortune to be shot down over Dublon Island, part of the Truk Atoll, in June 1944. The men were executed without trial by Japanese members of 41st Naval Guard Unit. Defendants in the subsequent trial were six Japanese naval officers, one of them a physician, Surgeon Lieutenant Ueno Chisato, and one a dentist, Ensign Eriguchi Takeshi.

One of the captured flyers had been injured or wounded. His fate was particularly cruel: he was put in Ueno's hands for what can only be called a practice session in various surgical techniques. He was anaesthetized and had a toenail removed, his scrotum was incised and – perhaps – one testicle removed, his femoral artery was exposed, his abdomen opened and the appendix removed, and finally an incision was made in his chest.[58] Then he was carried by stretcher to the execution site, placed on a board, and beheaded.[59] The execution was done by Eriguchi, under orders from Ueno to 'put him at ease', though Eriguchi was a dentist with no skills in swordsmanship.[60]

When the trial began, defence lawyers immediately protested the absence of physicians from the Trial Commission; they requested that one member be replaced by a US Navy medical officer so that the medical content would be fully understood. This request was not acted upon. At the trial the events were not questioned, except for whether a testicle had been removed or not. (Surgeon Lieutenant Kinoshita testified that he saw Ueno remove the testicle while lecturing his audience on how to sterilize a patient; the testicle was put on a porringer and placed on a table.)[61] The defence tried to show that Ueno was ill at the time, physically and mentally, and that there were genuine medical indications for all the operations performed. Ueno, a graduate of Jiheikai Medical College in 1932, attempted to justify himself on the grounds of medical necessity. His statement deserves quotation at some length:

> The first thing I had to do was an incision in the abdomen for diagnosing purposes. Next I searched closely but I could feel only one testicle on this prisoner. My feeling at this time was that this prisoner had been exposed to a bomb blast or else due to the pressure released outside or inside the body the one testicle may have become ruptured or the testicle had been blown into the body and I thought to discover where it had gone. The big toe of his right foot was black and blue and the area around it was inflamed. This was clearly a result of the bombing and showed symptoms of paronychia. In such cases the most simple and best treatment is to remove the nail. In cases of infection in the lower parts of the leg the newest and most effective way of treatment was to inject sulfa drugs into the femoral artery so I determined to reveal the femoral artery. Above the sixth rib on the right part of the chest there was a swelling and the colour of the skin was changed. Because of this I thought there was something wrong with the bone or symptoms of something wrong in the breast. Because I was afraid something may be wrong, to determine this I made a small incision of two centimetres in that portion of the chest.[62]

That is, he performed two operations for what seems to have been a mildly infected toenail (paronychia), one of these an incision so that he might perform the medically dramatic and rare procedure of giving sulfas intra-arterially (though he did not actually make the injection), plus castrating the prisoner, plus doing an abdominal incision for a bowel survey, plus a chest operation, all of them in response to medical indications. The most obvious weakness in this testimony, among many, is the suggestion that it was necessary to inject sulfa drugs into the femoral artery in order to treat an essentially trivial toe-nail infection in a man who was to be executed within the hour. His professors at Jiheikai would not have been proud of their student's naïve defence, though no one can fault him for attempting to save his own life. After the war, witnesses were ordered to say, if questioned, that the prisoners came to the sick bay but were treated and returned to their cells. The bones of the victims were dug up and disposed of.[63] Ueno, Eriguchi, and two others were sentenced to death, though Eriguchi had his sentence commuted to life imprisonment. Ueno was hanged.

Dublon Island, Truk, was also the site of a case involving murder by bacteria and shock. This especially gruesome case centred on the activities of Surgeon Captain Iwanami Hiroshi and two other medical colleagues, Surgeon Commander Okuyama and Surgeon Lieutenant Nabetani, these two not coming to trial because both were dead. In addition, eighteen other members of the Imperial Japanese Navy were arraigned, charged with participating in illegal medical experiments on prisoners of war. The first charge specified that Iwanami, at Dublon Island, Truk, did: 'assault, strike, injure, infect and kill, by experimenting, with injections of virulent bacteria, with exposures to shock and with other methods . . . six (6) American Prisoners of War'. It was a long and complicated case.

In July 1944, Iwanami asked the medical officers in the mess if they wished to do medical experiments on some American POWs. Most declined, but Okuyama and Nabetani agreed.[64] Eight prisoners were experimented upon, four by Okuyama and four by Nabetani and Iwanami together. Okuyama tied tourniquets on the arms and legs of his four prisoners. The tourniquets were tied so tightly that they arrested blood flow into the extremities completely. Two of these men had the tourniquets left on for between seven and eight hours. Then the tourniquets were released and, within a few minutes, the two prisoners were dead from shock 'induced by the application of the tourniquets for that great length of time'.[65]

The two POWs who died after the torture of the tourniquets were dissected. Some portions of the viscera were removed and Iwanami decided to keep the skulls as curios to be sent to the Naval Medical

School in Japan. He personally severed the heads and ordered one of the corpsmen to boil them in order that the skin, hair, and interior contents of the heads would be removed. Iwanami admitted removing the heads and shipping the skulls to Japan. His disingenuous explanation was that 'the Americans were a great people and he wished the Japanese medical authorities to have a chance to study the skulls of Americans'.[66]

The two other prisoners from the Okuyama group did not die when the tourniquets were removed. The Japanese then subjected them to a peculiarly bizarre ordeal. They were taken into an open space and tied. A hole was dug just in front of each prisoner and a charge of dynamite was planted in each hole. Iwanami gave a speech. It was just after the fall of Saipan and in his harangue Iwanami was furious over this disaster. 'He talked in angry tones about the bombing of the hospital in the end of June or the beginning of July in the daylight by enemy aircraft and he also stated that today he was going to test our spirit.'[67]

Then the dynamite was exploded, mangling the feet of the two men but not killing them. Okuyama sent Surgeon Lieutenant Nakamura Kiyoshi for morphine, which was injected into the two prisoners. While the intent seemingly was to alleviate their pain, Okuyama nevertheless did not wait for the morphine to take effect. After about ten minutes he ordered Sakagami, another defendant, to 'put the prisoners out of their misery'. Sakagami strangled them with his bare hands.[68]

The other four flyers fell into the hands of Nabetani and Iwanami, who injected virulent *Streptococcus* bacteria into their veins. The prisoners developed high fevers and great pain until, within two or three days, they died. Once the bacteria had been injected, no medications were given.[69] As was the case in so many of these instances of vivisection, the so-called experimentation was spurious in that there was no real attempt to pose a research problem and seek its solution.

Headquarters staff of the Japanese Fourth Fleet at Truk elaborated a remarkably detailed plan for concealing these war crimes. The plan included meticulous but false POW reports; key members of the navy received explicit directions about cover stories in case they were questioned. There was developed 'an intricate strategy of deception . . . with primary and secondary retreat plans for concealment and limitation of information'.[70] Nevertheless, several Japanese perpetrators were convicted after the war, including Iwanami. Nakamura Kiyoshi testified against Iwanami and afterwards committed suicide.[71]

In April 1943 a group of about 2,000 POWs embarked from Java in two badly overcrowded freighters. About half the men were sent to the small island of Haruku, just east of Ambon and south of Ceram, surrounded by the Banda Sea in what is now called Maluku. When they reached Haruku they were already hard-hit with dysentery; they landed in torrential rain to find an unfinished camp, and in five days were forced to stop camp-building and go to work constructing an airstrip near the village of Pelauw. Through the next few months mortality and morbidity waxed to horrendous levels, sufficiently so that the Japanese themselves became concerned (more, it seems certain, for the airstrip than for the prisoners). This concern may explain the one brief attempt at experimental medicine that the captors conducted. It took place between 5 and 11 October 1943. There were eighteen experimental subjects, all British.[72]

According to one of the British POW medical officers at Haruku, Flight Lieutenant Forbes, the subjects (of whom he was one) were injected on the inner side of the thigh with a colourless fluid. He was told that it was vitamin B1, but it did not have the characteristic odour. 'Later I had reason to believe the fluid was sterile Cocoanut milk.'[73]

The fluid was indeed coconut milk, and there is no secret about this in the Japanese report.[74] Injections of coconut milk were made, subjects receiving various doses over the experimental period. For example, five of the eighteen subjects had a course of four injections each, on 7, 8, 9, and 11 October, the total dosage being 30 ml.[75] The unidentified Japanese medical officers used both sterilized and unsterilized milk.

If the translated file is complete, the actual investigations were meagre indeed. In addition to the standard Name, Rank, and Nationality, there was also a column for Present Symptoms; cited here were pulse rates and terse diagnostic labels such as 'Malnutrition', 'Ambulatory difficulty', or 'Vitamin B deficiency'. The date of injection, amount, and type also were recorded ('type' meaning hypodermic, 14 subjects, intramuscular, 2, and intravenous, 2).[76]

The final two columns on the chart record symptoms at the time of injection, and 'Progress'. According to the Japanese, all subjects had slight prickling pain when injected, and little else. However, Forbes described the pain caused by the injections as 'considerable'.[77] He also noted that the POW medical officers gave the injections under Japanese direction, '. . . and we gave them as small a quantity as possible'.[78]

With regard to 'Progress', perhaps not surprisingly there was little to tell. Even if coconut milk were a panacea for beriberi it would scarcely have produced discernible results in only one week when given in such small amounts to men whose disease had already existed for many months. In seven subjects, slight headache was reported. 'Satisfactory breathing', 'satisfactory sleep' and 'satisfactory progress' characterized the course of several of the men. In those instances where the pulse rate was noted beforehand and after, no particular change was seen. What comes through clearly in examining the meagre results is the evident uselessness of the experiments. Granted the best will in the world, the Japanese investigators could not have discovered much of a positive nature from these grossly inadequate studies. The experiments purportedly were conducted to see if coconut milk could replace Ringer's solution in the prevention of beriberi. However, Ringer's solution, an electrolyte fluid used to offset the effects of dehydration, contains no vitamins and has no preventive or curative effect on beriberi.

Of course, the fundamental problem causing beriberi was the grossly insufficient diet coupled with enforced hard labour. Beriberi and other deficiency diseases were inevitable. The Japanese medical officers knew this just as well as did the British and Dutch, but there was scant likelihood of the rations' being increased. One of the interpreters at Haruku, known universally to the POWs as 'Slime', has described the pertinent regulation: 'Japanese army regulations specified that we were to feed the Japanese first, then the locals, and what was left was for the prisoners.'[79]

In yet another case, two captured airmen, an Australian and one from the Netherlands East Indies, were murdered at Kilwick Island, in the South Pacific, in the autumn of 1944. After their planes were shot down the men were condemned to death by a Japanese court martial on 19 October 1944. One of the defendants, Lieutenant-Colonel Kondō Hideo, ordered another, Major Ōtsuka Yasumasa, to execute the POWs as well as some Indonesians held at the same place, and to report their deaths as due to illness. The third defendant, Lieutenant Iwasaki Yoshiho, the gas officer, was ordered to carry out the executions by testing 5th Division's hydrocyanic-acid frangible grenades.

Chemical Warfare Officer Akiyama Kanemasa testified that in 1941 a gas grenade, commonly referred to as the HCN frangible grenade and known officially by the code name of 'Chibidan', was issued. The grenades were intended for use against enemy tanks and pillboxes, but had not been used. The grenade was a spherical glass flask about 10cm in diameter, with a short neck, and filled with about 250gm hydrocyanic acid solution. He noted that the glass flask was quite thick, so it was necessary to throw the grenade with force in order to cause it to break.[80] There was doubt that the grenades would be effective after such a long time, so it was decided to test them in what one Japanese medical officer identified as 'a prussic acid grenade experiment'.[81]

Medical Captain Ōshiba Yoshifumi, Regimental Medical Officer, 5th Artillery Regiment, was present at the executions. 'Because of the danger, Kambara and I stayed in the rear to one side. Those in the front were creating quite a commotion and later started to insult us by saying, "What weaklings the medical officers are! Why don't they watch?"'[82] After this badinage the messy execution began.

The grenades were thrown from a distance of seven or eight metres. Only after the fifth or sixth attempt did one of the bombs strike the target and explode. The POWs fell over in a few seconds and, two or three minutes later, their breathing stopped and they died. Three Javanese prisoners were executed in the same manner. Iwasaki was able to report to Kondō: 'The frangible grenades are effective.'[83]

There was at least one instance of experimental medicine in a POW camp, organized by the Japanese, that seems to have been well reasoned and sensibly carried out. This is not an example of vivisection, but is included here to make the point that proper (though in this case essentially unsuccessful) research could be carried out by the Japanese using POWs as subjects. The setting was Cabanatuan Camp in the Philippines. There, beriberi ravaged the American POWs. Dr Ralph Hibbs was one of the imprisoned medical officers there, and he published a detailed analysis of the disease after the war.[84]

Of the 8,000 men in the camp essentially all had beriberi by 1943, but fewer than 100 were adequately treated. These few were the group of ninety-six patients selected by an unnamed Japanese medical officer for the study. Seven American POW medical officers conducted the actual work, under Japanese supervision. The patients were chosen from the severest cases of painful feet, all of them showing the gait termed locally the 'Cabanatuan shuffle'. Any patient showing signs or symptoms of other serious disease was excluded from the study group.[85] The men all ate the same diet, with a caloric value estimated at 1600 daily; as Hibbs drily commented, the patients were needlessly advised to eat all the ration 'and nothing else'.[86] There was nothing else.

They were divided into eight clusters of twelve men. Each group was treated with a selected course of treatment. The men received various vitamins and combinations of vitamins and vitamin-containing materials such as cod liver oil; emulating good experimental design, one control group received only a placebo. The experimental period lasted for five months, with daily examination and questioning of every subject for the first month, weekly thereafter.

The results were not impressive. Three of the groups had received vitamin B1 in some form, and these men fared appreciably better than did the others. The changes were general: less insomnia, less irritability, and improved appetite. The pulse rate, which had been rapid, dropped substantially. The group that received vitamin B1 alone showed no more change than the control group. It took four months before the completely treated group showed slightly greater improvement. As the American doctors understood all too well, as long as the men remained on a sub-standard diet there could be no major improvement in their beriberi.

However, the Japanese did not limit their illegal vivisections to POWs, a fact already established in the case of Unit 731. Two of these civilian cases occurred in Malaya, one involving anatomical dissection of a living man, Pak Taroeng, a Javanese employee of the Imperial Japanese Army who was to be executed for theft when he came to the attention of IJA Medical Captain Komoi Yoshirō. This is a classic instance of undeniable guilt readily admitted. Komoi asked his superior officer to permit him to carry out an anatomical dissection of a human body; Pak Taroeng was selected as the healthiest among a group of prisoners awaiting execution.

Komoi went to the execution site, had the victim tied to a stretcher after removing his only piece of clothing, and injected him with an 'anaesthetic' which he stated was hydrochloric acid; a second injection was made, purportedly of iodine in alcohol.[87] He then made incisions into the thigh, abdomen, and chest of the patient. The avowed purpose of this display was to give a lesson in first-aid to several medical orderlies, present on his order. At trial, Komoi admitted that any knowledge that he may have imparted to the orderlies could have been better given by means of a lecture with diagrams on a blackboard.[88]

Experiments into the effects of so-called Ipoh Poison were also carried out in Malaya.[89] A Chinese man, Chan Pak, detained in Taiping Prison and condemned to death as a communist, was either, according to the prosecution, done to death by the defendants in the course of experimentation into the effects of Ipoh poison, commonly used by the Sakai natives of that region, or, according to the defence, experimented on after he had been hanged judicially. The prosecution presented a powerful case based on non-Japanese employees in the Taiping Gaol at the time, some of whom heard the condemned man groaning for hours after being taken into the execution chamber by the Japanese officers. In this instance the first accused, a medical colonel, was acquitted; the other three medical officers received sentences of life imprisonment.

Finally, experiments to devise a vaccine against tetanus were performed at Lombok in the Netherlands East Indies.[90] By the spring of 1945 a group of seventeen inhabitants of Lombok were in the Japanese jail on the island under sentence of death. At the time the war was going badly for the Japanese. Army and navy personnel were being abandoned on the periphery of empire, there being insufficient material to supply them and inadequate transportation to remove them. The medical units were no better supplied than combatant formations. The medical officer on Lombok who figures most prominently in this case was Surgeon Captain Nakamura Hirosato.

Vaccines and serums for prevention of various diseases and for treatment were in short supply. This failure was of particular concern because of the likelihood, during the heavy fighting anticipated in the immediate future, of a high incidence of tetanus. Also known as lock-jaw, this disease, if untreated, usually kills the patient.

Anti-tetanus serum was unavailable at Lombok. But Nakamura thought that an anatoxin or toxoid could be made, using toxin destroyed by heat but still containing the proteins that will cause the body to produce antibodies and thus combat the disease. The method, using modern techniques, is effective with several diseases, so Nakamura's approach was not illogical. Nevertheless, he ended up on trial for his life in 1951.[91]

Nakamura manufactured a tetanus anatoxin and informed the officer in charge of the seventeen Lombokese that he wished to experiment on them. Each was injected with anatoxin. The men were not informed of the nature of the injections, nor given any opportunity to refuse to be inoculated.[92]

The experiment was carried out in three stages. First, a small amount of anatoxin was injected; two weeks later a second dose of anatoxin was given; finally, several weeks after the second injection, tetanus toxin was injected.[93] Before long, fifteen of the prisoners were admitted to hospital, where they died in less than three weeks. Nakamura testified that the direct cause of their death was the effects of the toxin that was injected into them in order to prove the efficacy of anatoxin.[94] For whatever reason, the anatoxin was a lethal clinical failure. Nakamura was sentenced to only four years at hard labour, Tatsuzaki to three years. Perhaps considerable weight was given to the plausible scientific rationale of the experiments; but one must ask whether the sentence would have differed had the victims been American or Australian.

These are harrowing cases replete with graphic details of serious crimes. Nevertheless, the number of instances of vivisection is not large. Always excepting the bacteriological warfare work done in Manchuria by Ishii and his colleagues, both the number of known victims and the number of known perpetrators is small. Naturally, the only satisfactory number would be zero. But the Second World War was a brutal war characterized by much cruelty on all sides.

Of the instances of vivisection described, several came to trial. Of these, the case involving the supposed removal of inguinal lymph glands in Indian prisoners with tropical ulcers was seen by the Court, and appears in retrospect, to have been highly questionable, and the defendants were acquitted. The execution by prussic acid grenades certainly took place, and the defendants were punished appropriately; but the case is only marginally vivisection. So we are left with only a handful of cases that came to trial and that could be categorized as true cases of human vivisection. Clearly this category was a minor one in terms of overall war crimes trials, which numbered almost 1,000 in the Far East. The Allies prosecuted 5,570 minor war criminals (Class B and C crimes), convicted over 4,000, and executed about 1,000.[95]

Examination of these trials distinguishes more or less genuine attempts at experimentation to achieve a nominally scientific answer (no matter how inept the performance), from what can only be characterized as flagrant torture of defenceless human beings. Tokuda at Shinagawa Hospital, Hirano and his malaria immunization experiments, the experiment on Chan Pak and Ipoh poison, and Nakamura's attempt to create a tetanus anatoxin seem to fit the first category. On the basis of non-evidence we might include as well the bacteriological warfare experiments and the Haruku coconut-milk studies.

The crude brutalities of Dr Ishiyama and colleagues at Kyūshū University, and of Dr Ueno and Dr Iwanami at Truk, and Dr Komoi's dissection of Pak Taroeng at Taiping represent blatant cruelty. These members of the medical profession totally abandoned their humane mission and ethical heritage. These standards may not be universal; in numerous trials, Japanese physicians were asked whether in medical school or on graduation they had subscribed to the Hippocratic Oath or to any analogous prescription of ethical behaviour. The response was uniformly negative. This question requires further study. Ishii's work, ignoring for the moment its grossly unethical and illegal background, seems to have met reasonable standards for the mechanics of scientific experimentation. We cannot be sure, since this material never has been made public; but it convinced a substantial number of American scientists that the results were valid and worth bartering for. The problem here, in addition to the atrocity, is that science must not exist in an ethical vacuum. Many scientists, ethicists, and historians today believe strongly that, for example, the results of Nazi cold-weather experiments on prisoners, which cost many lives, should not be cited in the scientific literature.[96] Apparently in the underworld of government secret weapons research no such distinction is made, or at least was not made in the 1940s, when the US gladly acquired the Manchurian evidence. Justice in the name of the dead thousands carried no weight when balanced against obtaining data. As Harris has pointed out:

> In the course of nearly three years of probing Japanese experts for biological warfare data, not one American scientist privy to the negotiations raised issues of morality or ethics. No one accused these men of being war criminals who had committed crimes against humanity or said the U.S. should not be dealing with them.[97]

Even the 'best' of these vivisections were notably ascientific. Experimentation usually was done on small numbers of subjects for short periods and without apparent use of controls. As a consequence, even if results had been obtained, they would have been inconclusive. But consideration of these cases in terms of their scientific content is irrelevant, and inappropriately dignifies what was done. Crimes of this nature cannot be excused no matter how 'scientific' they may seem.

The Japanese attitude towards being taken prisoner themselves played a significant role in conditioning them to feel not only indifference but even contempt for men of other races and nationalities who allowed themselves to become POWs. The impression one gets from examining the voluminous documentation is that POWs in Japanese hands were considerably more likely to be viewed with contempt than with either pity or sympathy. Certainly, the principle that no Japanese fighting man should permit himself to be taken captive, and that he should commit suicide should he be captured after being wounded,[98] was a fixed part of the Japanese attitudes in the 1930s and 1940s. Tōjō Hideki testified to this point during his trial as a war criminal: 'The Japanese idea about being taken prisoner is different from that in Europe and America. In Japan, it is regarded as a disgrace. Under Japanese criminal law, anyone who becomes a prisoner while still able to resist has committed a criminal offense, the maximum punishment for which is the death penalty.'[99] If the Minister of War held this opinion it seems safe to conclude that it was one that permeated the armed forces. The effect was profound, and impacted on both the Japanese soldier and the Allied POW.

This attitude was seen as being part of the spirit of Bushidō. If a Japanese was taken prisoner, he was considered to be dishonoured, and his relatives were expected to look upon him as being dishonourably dead. Given that, there was little likelihood that opposing POWs would be seen with sympathy. This Japanese assumption of dishonour being intimately related to surrender was displayed dramatically as recently as 1971, when the distinguished Japanese novelist, Ōoka Shōhei, refused to accept a prestigious literary award because of the shame he felt over having been a prisoner of war.[100]

What can we discern of the motivation of the individual Japanese doctors mentioned? Personal ambition drove several of the men. Ishii certainly sought to accelerate his rise up the promotion ladder, and succeeded. Hirano yearned for fame and an invitation to the Mayo Clinic. Tokuda excluded Allied medical officers from the wards so that he would be assured of receiving full credit for his elusive discoveries.

Nakamura, seeking a tetanus anatoxin, stands out in the group as perhaps having the most altruistic approach. Nevertheless, it cost fifteen men their lives. But he contrasts strongly with the butchers who carved up living humans for no apparent reason. Some of these men, notably Iwanami at Truk, appear to have been fuelled by a desire for revenge on their opponents because of personal or national injury. These were classic examples of power abused. But unlike the situation in Nazi Germany, this abuse was sporadic, isolated, and directed largely by individual ambition or initiative or by a desire for revenge. Ishii's work apparently was unique. There is, to date, no other evidence of systematic human vivisection.

Notes

1. International Military Tribunal for the Far East, IMTFE Exhibit No. 1850, Extracts from Interrogation of Japanese POWs and Material from Captured Diaries, 1942, p. 2 of anonymous captured diary.
2. A similar case purportedly took place at Khandok, allegedly involving a healthy unwounded African POW: 'The man was tied to a tree outside the Hikari Kikan office. A Japanese doctor and four Japanese medical students stood around him. They first removed the finger nails, then cutting open his chest, removed his heart, on which the doctor gave a practical demonstration' (Suitland, National Archives and Records Administration (hereafter, NARA), Records of the Office of the Judge Advocate General (Army), War Crimes Section, RG 153, File 51–54, Atrocities by the Japanese Medical Department).
3. Names of Japanese nationals are cited throughout in the Japanese manner, surname first followed by given name.
4. Peter Williams and David Wallace, *Unit 731: The Japanese Army's Secret of Secrets*, London, 1989, p. 209.
5. Williams and Wallace, *Unit 731* (see Note 4 above), pp. 10–11.
6. Ibid., p. 15.
7. See Sheldon Harris, *Factories of Death: Japanese Biological Warfare 1932–45 and the American Cover-up*, London, 1994; Williams and Wallace, *Unit 731* (see Note 4 above).
8. Harris, *Factories of Death* (see Note 7 above), p. 30, lists, among others, smallpox, yellow fever, tularaemia, hepatitis, gas gangrene, tetanus, diphtheria, cholera, glanders, scarlet fever, undulant fever, tick encephalitis, epidemic haemorrhagic fever (songo fever), whooping cough, pneumonia, typhoid fever, epidemic cerebrospinal meningitis, tuberculosis, salmonellosis, gonorrhoea, and syphilis.

9. Williams and Wallace, *Unit 731* (see Note 4 above), p. 197.
10. Ibid., p. 35.
11. Harris, *Factories of Death* (see Note 7 above), pp. 66–7 and 110.
12. Williams and Wallace, *Unit 731* (see Note 4 above), p. 38.
13. Ibid., p. 81.
14. A. J. N. Warrack, 'Conditions experienced as a Japanese prisoner of war from a medical point of view', *Journal of the Royal Army Medical Corps*, vol. 87, 1946, pp. 209–30 especially pp. 219–20.
15. Public Record Office (hereafter, PRO), War Office Papers (hereafter WO), WO 224/192, Reports of International Red Cross and Protecting Powers, Far East: Tokyo Group, p. 3.
16. Variously spelled Tokuda, Takuda, Tokeda, Takuta, Toheda, Dakuda, Tukada, Takoda, Takida, Takeda, and others. Tokuda seems to be correct.
17. PRO, WO 222/22, report on POW Camps in Hong Kong and Japan by Captain A. J. N. Warrack, RAMC, 23 Jan. 1946, p. 39.
18. This paragraph is derived from Mack L. Gottlieb, 'Impressions of a POW medical officer in Japanese concentration camps', *US Navy Medical Bulletin*, vol. 46, 1946, pp. 663–75.
19. NARA, RG 153, Box 5, entry 139, file 35–9, Shinagawa Hospital.
20. NARA, RG 153, File 35–9, deposition of CRM David Goodman, 22 Mar. 1946, p. 2.
21. Ibid., deposition of Major Harold Keschner, 21 Dec. 1945, p. 4.
22. Alfred A. Weinstein, *Barbed-Wire Surgeon*, New York, 1948, pp. 194–5.
23. Ibid., p. 211.
24. NARA, RG 153, File 35–9, deposition of Lieutenant-Commander James Robert Davis, USN, 22 Jan. 1946, p. 4.
25. Ibid., p. 5.
26. PRO, WO 222/22, Warrack memo., p. 44.
27. Gottlieb, 'Impressions of a POW medical officer' (see Note 18 above), p. 664.
28. NARA, RG 153, File 35–102, 'Deposition of John A. Conner in the Matter of the Death of Lance Corporal Gerald Dawson, British POW, Caused by Lieutenant Takuda, Officer in Charge of Shinagawa Hospital, Tokyo, while Conducting a Medical Experiment on or about 10 July 1944', p. 3.
29. NARA, RG 153, File 35–9, Keschner deposition, 23 Sept. 1947, p. 2.
30. Ibid., Davis deposition, p. 8.
31. Ibid., Keschner deposition, 23 Sept. 1947, p. 4.
32. Caprylic acid is also known as octanoic acid, and is a saturated fatty acid that occurs in butter fat after hydrolysis.

33. But caprylic acid is a straight-chain fatty acid and chaulmoogric acid is a cyclic fatty acid; there is some chemical resemblance, but it is not close.
34. NARA, RG 153, File 35–9, Keschner deposition, 23 Sept. 1947, p. 2.
35. Ibid.
36. Ibid., deposition of Captain Alex M. Mohnac, DDS, 25 July 1946, p. 2.
37. NARA, Office of the Judge Advocate General (Army), RG 338, Records of the US Eighth Army, Sugamo Prison Records, 1945–1952. 8132nd Army Unit, Sugamo Sup. Det., Box 231, File: Tokuda Hisakichi; letter from his defence counsel to Officer Commanding, Sugamo Prison, 27 Aug. 1947.
38. Ibid., Box 231, File: Tokuda Hisakichi; findings of medical board conducted at 361st Station Hospital, Tokyo, 24 Dec. 1950, report dated 2 Jan. 1951, p. 2.
39. NARA, RG 153, File 36–286, memo., GHQ SCAP, 21 Oct. 1946, requesting photographs of eight US flyers who survived a crash in Japan 5 May 1945, seven of whom '. . . were killed at Kyushu Imperial University Hospital by illegal experimental operations'.
40. Endo Shusaku, *The Sea and Poison*, trans. Michael Gallagher, Tokyo, 1972, p. 167.
41. NARA, RG 153, File 36–527, trial of Captain Aihara Kajurō, Colonel Akita Hiroshi, Major-General Fukushima Kyūsaku, Lieutenant Goiyama Shinju, Goshima Shirō, MD, Hirako Goichi, MD, Hirao Kenichi, MD, Major-General Horiuchi Kiyoma, MD, Lieutenant-General Inada Nasazumi, Ishiyama Fukujirō, MD, Major-General Itō Shōshin [Akinobu], Lieutenant-Colonel Jin Iichirō, Komori Taku, MD, Kubo Toshiyuki, MD, Makinō Reiichiro, MD, Mori Yoshio, MD, Norimoto Kenji, MD, Nogawa Nobuyoshi, MD, Ryi Miki, MD, Colonel Satō Yoshinao, Senba [Semba] Yoshitaka, MD, Tashiro Jirō, MD, Tashiro Tomoki, MD, Torisu Tarō, MD, Tsutsui [Tsutsue] Shizuko RN, Lieutenant-General Yokoyama Isamu, and others, on numerous charges, especially illegal medical experimentation, vivisection, and related charges; tried at Yokohama, 11 Mar. to 27 Aug. 1948.
42. Ibid., trial of Captain Aihara Kajurō; opinion of the Board of Review, Smoak, Murray, and Sewell, Judge Advocates, 25 Mar. 1950, p. 4.
43. NARA, RG 331, Allied Operational and Occupation Headquarters, World War II. Supreme Commander for the Allied Powers (SCAP), Legal Section, Administrative Division, "Area" Case File, 1945–48, Box No. 927, Fukuoka POW Camps #19 to #256. Folder 21,

FU-256. Statement of Hirako Goichi, MD, 15 July 1946, p. 2.
44. Ibid., Fukuoka POW Camps #19 to #256. Folder 21, FU-256. Statement by Yakumaru Katsuya, 18–19 July 1946, p. 1.
45. NARA, RG 153, File 36–527, trial of Captain Aihara Kajurō and others; opinion of the Board of Review, p. 5.
46. NARA, RG 331, Box No. 927, Folder 21, FU-256, Doc. 21297B, translation of undated statement signed by Ishiyama Fukujirō.
47. 'The ashes of the first four were brought to my office. There were no records, so I numbered the paper bags that they were in from one to four. I was told by ISHIYAMA about March 1946 to throw the ashes away. I then emptied the bags on an ash pile in back of the crematory. I wanted to make a grave for the ashes but ISHIYAMA had told me not to leave any proof, so I threw the ashes away' (NARA, RG 331, Box No. 927, Folder 21, FU-256).
48. NARA, RG 153, File 36–527, trial of Captain Aihara Kajurō, Pros. Exh. 70: suicide note of Ishiyama Fukujirō, 17 July 1946.
49. PRO, WO 235/1035, trial of Colonel Suwabe Masato, Captain Shimotsura Hiroshi, Medical Captain Numata Kimio, Medical Captain Nakagawa Kōichi, Sergeant Noto Tomizō, and Corporal Ogura Seijirō, IJA, for war crimes allegedly committed at Tanoura, New Britain, between 1 Mar. 1943 and 31 Mar. 1944; tried at Singapore, 6–24 Jan. 1947.
50. R. John Pritchard and Sonia Magbanua Zaide (eds), *The Tokyo War Crimes Trial*, vol. 21, *Separate Opinions*, New York, 1981, see p. 1061.
51. NARA, RG 153, File 51–88, Combined Report on Circumstances of Imprisonment of 67 Allied POWs in the Tunnel Hill Camp, Rabaul, New Guinea, p. 1.
52. Melbourne, Australian Archives, MP 742/1, Department of Defence (III), Army Headquarters, correspondence files, Multiple Number Series, 1943–1951, File No. 336/1/1955, Box 108, Attachment 4, correspondence and affidavits by Captain José Holquin, undated, p. 22.
53. Ibid., correspondence and affidavits by Holquin, p. 21.
54. NARA, RG 153, File 51–88, deposition of Captain José Holquin, pp. 15–16.
55. Ibid., p. 16.
56. Ibid., pp. 16–17.
57. AA, MP 375/14, War Crimes Investigation Files, Dec. 1945 – Aug. 1949. WC 48, Affidavit of Captain John Joseph Murphy *re* capture at Gasmata, 1 Nov. 1943 and his treatment as a POW of the Japanese, undated.
58. NARA, RG 153, File 48–36–1, trial of Captain Asano Shimpei,

Surgeon Lieutenant Ueno Chisato, Lieutenant Commander Nakase Shōhichi, Ensign Eriguchi Takeshi, Warrant Officer Kobayashi Kazumi, and L/S Tanaka Sueta, all IJN, charged with a number of alleged violations of the laws and usages of war in connection with American Prisoners of War at Dublon Island, Truk Atoll, Caroline Islands, in 1944; tried at Guam, Sept.–Oct. 1947.

59. The formal Charge relating to vivisection is worded as follows: Charge II, Specification 1: the accused did 'willfully, unlawfully, inhumanely, and without justifiable cause, assault, strike, mistreat, torture, and abuse, an American prisoner of war, name to the relator unknown, then and there held captive by the armed forces of Japan, by conducting, before a group of Japanese nationals, surgical explorations in and upon the live body of the said American prisoner of war, consisting of subcutaneous cuts on the breast, abdomen, scrotum, right thigh, and right foot of the said American prisoner of war, this in violation of the law and custom of war'. NARA, RG 153, File 48–36–1, trial of Captain Asano *et al.*

60. Ibid., testimony of Eriguchi, p. 270.

61. Ibid., testimony of Kinoshita Hiroshi, p. 52.

62. Ibid., testimony of Ueno, pp. 285–6.

63. Ibid., testimony of Petty Officer Kodama Akira, pp. 18–20.

64. Ibid., trial of Surgeon Captain Iwanami Hiroshi, Surgeon Lieutenant Kamikawa Hidehiro, Surgeon Lieutenant Ōishi Tetsuo, Ensign Asamura Shunpei, Chief Petty Officer (hereafter CPO) Yoshizawa Kensaburō, CPO Homma Hachirō, CPO Watanabe Mitsuo, CPO Tanabe Namo, CPO Mukai Yoshihisa, PO/l (Petty Officer, First Class) Kawashima Tatsusaburō, PO/l Sawada Tsuneo, PO/l Tanaka Tokonusuke, PO/2 (Petty Officer, Second Class) Namatame Kazuo, PO/l Takaishi Susumu, PO/2 Akabori Toichirō, PO/2 Kuwabara Hiroyuki, PO/2 Tsutsui Kisaburō, and PO/2 Mitsuhashi Kichigorō, Imperial Japanese Navy. Testimony of Surgeon Commander Okamura Takeo, p. 134.

65. Ibid., trial of Iwanami *et al.*, opening statement by Prosecution, pp. 1–2.

66. Ibid., p. 3.

67. Ibid., testimony of Surgeon Commander Okamura Takeo, p. 134.

68. Ibid., trial of Iwanami, statement by Prosecution, p. 2.

69. Ibid.

70. William H. Stewart, *Ghost Fleet of the Truk Lagoon*, Missoula, Montana, 1985, p. 101.

71. Ibid., p. 106.

72. NARA, RG 153, File 52–18, Documentation of Experimentation by Japanese on 18 POWs at Haruku, Dutch East Indies.

73. Flight Lieutenant F. Alastair Forbes, RAFVR, *Medical Report on Certain Prisoners of War Camps in Java and the Ambon Group, with Special Reference to Diseases Encountered and Treatments Thereof: April 1942 – August 1945*, London, mimeographed report, 1945. This was Forbes's official war-end report, a copy of which he gave the author in 1985; see p. 36.

74. One wonders if the identification of the fluid as vitamin B1 may have been yet another in the myriad of linguistic confusions that helped to make POW life so hard for prisoners of the Japanese. Perhaps the interpreter was told that it was thought or hoped that the milk contained vitamin B1, but the translation was that it *was* vitamin B1.

75. NARA, RG 153, File 52–18, Experimentation by Japanese on 18 POWs at Haruku, Dutch East Indies, 11 p.; see Chart No. 2, Clinical Experiment Chart.

76. Ibid.

77. Forbes, *Medical Report* (see Note 73 above), p. 36.

78. Transcript of interview with F. Alastair Forbes by author held in the Oral History Archive, McMaster University, HCM 78–85, 24 Sept. 1985, p. 14.

79. Haruko Taya Cook and Theodore F. Cook, *Japan at War: An Oral History*, New York, 1992, p. 116.

80. Canberra, Australian War Memorial, AWM 54, File 1010/5/1, trial of Lieutenant-Colonel Kondō Hideo, Major Ōtsuka Yasumasa, and Lieutenant Iwasaki Yoshiho: Charge – Murder of Flight Lieutenant A. D. Nelson, RAAF, and Sgt. F. Engelsman, RNEIAF, on Kilwick Island, Oct.–Nov. 1944; testimony of Chemical Warfare Officer Akeyama Kanemasa, pp. 1–2.

81. Ibid., trial of Kondō, Ōtsuka, and Iwasaki; affidavit of Kambara Hideo, 7 Feb. 1947.

82. Ibid., trial of Kondō, Ōtsuka, and Iwanami; p. 2 of statement by Medical Captain Ōshiha.

83. Ibid., statement of Iwasaki, 17 Apr. 1947.

84. Ralph E. Hibbs, 'Beriberi in Japanese prison camp', *Annals of Internal Medicine*, vol. 25, 1946, pp. 270–82.

85. Ibid., p. 280.

86. Ibid.

87. It must be pointed out that translations of scientific terms are especially unreliable in these war crimes transcripts. Though most of the translators seem to have been competent in conversational Japanese, few had any scientific training. Consequently Komoi may have said something other than hydrochloric acid and iodine in alcohol, neither of which is known to have any anaesthetic

properties. On the other hand, he may have meant exactly these terms, perhaps because he was administering a lethal substance, not an anaesthetic.

88. PRO, WO 235/951, trial of Major Yotori Kichizō, Lieutenant Watanabe Kasumasu, and Medical Captain Komoi Yoshirō, for war crimes allegedly committed in connection with the killing of Pak Taroeng, a native of Java, at Oudong, French Indo-China, July 1945; tried at Singapore, 30 July to 7 Aug. 1946; Case no. 139, testimony of Komoi, p. 43.

89. Ibid., WO 235/1101, Trial of Medical Colonel Ōtsubo Minoru, Medical Major Honjō Hiroshi, Medical Captain Utsunomiya Daiten, and Medical Captain Hakamada Toshihiko, IJA, for war crimes allegedly committed in connection with the unlawful killing of Chan Pak, a civilian resident of Malaya, 23 Mar. 1945; tried at Taiping, 3–27 Nov. 1947; Case no. 289, testimony of William Pillay, p. 80.

90. AA, CRS A471/1, item 81968, Record of Military Court (Japanese War Criminals), Trial of Vice Admiral Shibata Yaichirō, Surgeon Captain Nakamura Hirosato, and Lieutenant-Commander Tatsuzaki Ei, IJN, for murder of 15 natives of Lombok, NEI, by administering to them a substance alleged to be a tetanus anti-toxin; tried at Manus Island, 20 Mar. – 2 Apr. 1951; see pp. 4–5.

91. The actual charges were: 'COMMITTING A WAR CRIME, that is to say, MURDER in that they, at SOERABAJA, JAVA, about April, 1945, murdered 15 natives at LOMBOK in the Netherlands East Indies. SECOND CHARGE (alternative to the first charge) COMMITTING A WAR CRIME, that is to say, UNLAWFUL KILLING in that they, at SOERABAJA, JAVA, about April, 1945, unlawfully killed fifteen natives of LOMBOK in the Netherlands East Indies by the injection of a deleterious substance. . .'.

92. AA, CRS A471/1, item 81968, trial of Shibata, Nakamura, and Tatsuzaki.

93. Ibid., trial of Shibata, Nakamura, and Tatsuzaki; testimony of Nakamura, p. 44.

94. Ibid., testimony of Nakamura, p. 42.

95. R. John Pritchard, 'An overview of the historical importance of the Tokyo War Trial', in C. Hosoya, N. Andō, Y. Ōnuma, and R. Ninear (eds), *The Tokyo War Crimes Trial: An International Symposium*, Tokyo, 1986, p. 95.

96. Several chapters in a recent book address this debate. A section of five papers under the rubric, 'The Use of Information from Nazi "Experiments": The Case of Hypothermia', are particularly

germane. See Arthur L. Caplan (ed.), *When Medicine Went Mad: Bioethics and the Holocaust*, Totowa, NJ, 1992.

97. Sheldon Harris, 'Japanese Biological Warfare Research on Humans: A Case Study of Microbiology and Ethics', in Raymond A. Zilinskas (ed.), 'The Microbiologist and Biological Defense Research: Ethics, Politics, and International Security', *Annals of the New York Academy of Sciences*, vol. 666, 1992, p. 41.

98. In a novel about a Japanese officer captured by the Russians in 1945, the author describes the collective suicide of a group of tank crewmen, who wire their tanks together and detonate a massive explosion. The protagonist attempts to persuade them not to kill themselves; but it is significant that his appeal depends on the fact that the Emperor *ordered* them all to surrender, thus obviating the need for feeling disgrace – not that they should ignore the code itself. Tokoyo Yamasaki, *The Barren Zone*, trans. James T. Araki, Tokyo, 1985, pp. 29–30 and 34.

99. IMTFE, Exhibits, Document 1981A, Interrogation of Hideki Tōjō, 26 Mar. 1946.

100. Agatha Dillard Hahn, 'Commentary on Ōoka Shōhei's Prisoner of War Memoirs (Furyoki)', unpublished Ph.D thesis, Stanford University, 1983, p. 33.

7

Africans and African Americans in Enemy Hands

David Killingray

When France went to war in September 1939 her European borders were defended by 80 divisions. Of these ten were colonial divisions, of which seven were African. At the armistice with Germany, in the summer of 1940, West African troops formed approximately one-tenth of the French army in Europe, some 100,000 men. Colonial casualties were extremely high, with as many as 48,000 men of the *tirailleurs sénégalais* declared missing; 15,000–16,000 became prisoners of war (POWs), of whom only half survived captivity.[1] That high death rate for African POWs gives poignant notice as to why non-European and black captives during the Second World War should be singled out for separate attention in this volume of essays.

All the major European combatants, excluding Germany, employed colonial troops in the Second World War. African Americans constituted approximately 12 per cent of the total United States forces mobilized for home defence and for use in the Pacific and European campaigns. Wars tend to intensify ethnic hostilities, and the presence of non-European and black soldiers as opponents only made a harsh scene even harsher. In all colonial armies, African soldiers formed separate corps, although there was some integration for certain combatant roles, as with the French *régiments mixtes*. Colonial troops were used for imperial wars, and in some cases for war in Europe, but they were treated differently from metropolitan troops in respect of conditions of service, pay, pensions, and leave. Invariably all, or most, officers were white. Colonialism was based, in part, on notions of white racial superiority, and thus African soldiers were regarded as both different from and inferior to European soldiers and, at times, more readily expendable in battle than white troops. The colonial wars of the late nineteenth and early twentieth centuries were termed 'savage wars', to be distinguished from the 'civilized wars' fought between European armies. 'Savage wars' had their own distinctive morality; dum-dum bullets that inflicted ghastly gaping wounds were developed for such campaigns, but declared illegal for 'civilized' warfare; the wounded were often killed or left to die of their wounds on the battlefield, while selected POWs might be incorporated into the victorious colonial army.[2]

In the South African War, 1899–1902, Africans and Coloureds captured under arms were at risk of summary execution, although more usually from Boers than from Britons.[3] During that hard-fought war over 14,000 Africans, including a few combatants, died in concentration camps as the British sought to defeat the Boer guerrillas.[4] Many of Britain's African troops in the Second World War were labourers in uniform, used in pioneer roles, while the South Africans refused to arm any non-European soldiers and confined them to support and labouring tasks. Even in the United States forces, the majority of blacks served in non-combatant corps and belonged to segregated units. Racial discrimination in the armed forces reflected many of the white social attitudes towards black people then to be found over a large part of the United States.[5] If African and African American soldiers were treated differently or discriminated against within their own armies, then as military opponents they were certainly viewed as both different and inferior by their German, Italian, and Japanese enemies and captors. German Nazi and Italian Fascist ideology portrayed black troops, especially French West Africans, as both inferior and barbaric. German propaganda replayed the 'horrors of the Rhineland', when, at the end of the First World War, the French had used *tirailleurs* as occupation troops in Germany.[6] As POWs African and black troops generally received harsher treatment from their captors than did white troops; if they reached prison camps their diet was poorer, and the conditions of captivity more severe, and as a result they were less likely to survive incarceration. Most of the available evidence seems to indicate that in Burma the Japanese killed African captives out of hand; in one case an eyewitness said they were castrated and tortured to death.[7]

Black Soldiers

During the Second World War there were three main categories of black POWs: those in uniform as combatants and non-combatants; merchant seamen; and a small number of civilian internees. This chapter is concerned mainly with Africans and African Americans in uniform who were captured by one side or the other, but mainly with those made prisoner by the Germans and Italians and, in one rare case, by the Japanese. The United States forces had the largest number of black personnel, altogether 1.15 million by the end of the war in 1945. Segregated units existed for most of the war, particularly in the army, even to the extent of the Red Cross's having 'white blood' and 'black blood' for transfusions. Black officers were carefully placed so that they would not be in positions of seniority over their white counterparts, or be able to give orders to white servicemen. In comparison with the First World War many more African Americans served in combat units, although the breakdown of this discriminatory schedule, which tried to confine blacks to labour and stevedore units, was only achieved after 1948. African American men and women served in all branches of the service, including the Army Air Force, and participated in the Pacific, North African and European campaigns.

South Africa recruited 125,000 non-whites for the Union Defence Force, and 45,350 for the Coloured Cape Corps, and enlisted 76,000 blacks in the Native Military Corps (NMC), all organized in what was termed the Non-European Army Services (NEAS). In the First World War coloured troops had been combatants; in the 1939–45 conflict Smuts's government refused to entertain the idea of non-Europeans being armed, and both the Cape Corps and African troops acted in non-combatant roles. The Non-European Army Services saw action throughout Africa, in Madagascar, in the Middle East, and also in the Italian campaign. In the First World War few, if any, black and coloured South African soldiers were captured; as supply line troops and pioneers in East Africa, the Middle East and Europe, they invariably operated behind and in support of their own lines, and rarely met the enemy. It was different in the Second World War, particularly in North Africa, where the military reverses of 1941–42 exposed unarmed troops on the line of supply to capture by the Italian and German forces.[8]

The British, French and Canadian home armed forces contained a few black people. Canada had a small indigenous black population, mainly in the Maritime provinces, and other black recruits came from the United States and the Caribbean. Compared with the British Empire, the French colonial system was less colour-conscious. Black men could gain commissions in the French colonial army; in the First World War about one in ten officers in the colonial army in Africa were either from the African or the Caribbean colonies. The British armed forces operated a colour bar for commissioned rank until October 1939, when it was dropped for the duration. Although black people were not banned from the forces, many found it difficult to enter, and encountered a good deal of prejudice when they succeeded. Nevertheless, black Britons and immigrants from the Caribbean and West Africa did enlist, several thousand serving in the Royal Air Force, with 70 or more becoming officers. Several pilots and crew from the West Indies and Africa were shot down and made POWs in Germany, as were a number of black seamen and soldiers serving in British ships and military units.[9]

All the European colonial powers in Africa had locally recruited armed forces for internal security and guarding frontiers. The largest armies were those of the French and Italians, with the Belgian *Force Publique* next in order of size, and the smallest armies those of the British. When Italy entered the war in June 1940 her colonial army in East Africa numbered 92,000 Italian troops, supported by 250,000 mainly locally enlisted *askaris*. Eritrea was the principal recruiting ground, but pre-war conscription of African troops for use against the British in East Africa had provided an unreliable and unwieldy army. In battle against the Allies the Italian colonial army performed lamentably, and by November 1941 all of Mussolini's East African empire had been captured, along with large numbers of prisoners. In the north the small Gideon Force, operating from the Sudan, alone captured over 15,000 Italian prisoners within three months.

Since the mid-nineteenth century the French colonial army had been used in imperial wars and also in Europe.[10] In the decade before the First World War the French, faced with the prospect of conflict with Germany on the eastern border, turned to West Africa for military man-power. *La Force noire,* designed by General Mangin to relieve French troops in North Africa for European service if the country found itself at war with Germany, in the event was actually used on the Western Front in late 1914. By 1939 African divisions from North and West Africa were stationed in and committed to the defence of metropolitan France. With the collapse in June 1940 a large part of what remained of the colonial army still deployed in France went into captivity. A handful of French African troops were evacuated from Dunkirk. When De Gaulle raised his Free French standard in London the majority of the troops that supported him were in central Africa, and African. By the terms of the armistice French forces overseas were reduced, but under the Vichy regime those in West Africa were increased in response to the British threat and the attack on Dakar in September 1940. British and South African forces invaded Vichy-held Madagascar in May 1942, and after a brief campaign captured the island and took several hundred prisoners, including *tirailleurs*, some of whom were sent to South Africa. De Gaulle's Free French *tirailleurs* served in the Levant and in North Africa, where they fought against African troops under Vichy command. Many of the Vichy prisoners taken in Syria were re-enlisted in the Free French forces. West and North African troops provided a substantial French presence in the invasion of southern France in August 1944, a few weeks after the D-day landings in the north. French African troops fought across Europe and served as garrison troops in defeated Germany.[11] The Belgian colonial army, the *Force Publique*, was deployed throughout the Belgian Congo and designed for use within the vast tropical colony. On Belgium's defeat in the summer of 1940, the *Force Publique*, then about 23,000 strong, assumed a new significance for Belgium, which wished to maintain a military presence in the war, and also as an Allied force for the defence of African territory. The *Force* was slightly increased in number; but the weak colonial economy served as a restraint on recruitment. Belgian colonial soldiers were used in a combatant role in Ethiopia, but thereafter mainly as garrison troops, for example guarding prisoners, supplies and munition dumps in Egypt.

Britain's African colonial armies in 1939 were small, and little better than lightly armed gendarmeries. They consisted of the 8,000-strong Royal West African Frontier Force, a quasi-federal body recruited from the four West African colonies, the King's African Rifles, numbering a few thousand men, drawn from and deployed in East Africa and Nyasaland, and small local forces such as the Somaliland Camel Corps and the Northern Rhodesia Regiment. In addition there was the Sudan Defence Force of 5,000 men. All of these forces were intended for use within the colonies from which they came, or in immediately neighbouring colonies, and not as Imperial forces for use outside Africa. That role was performed by the Indian Army, drawn from that 'dusky barracks in an oriental sea'. As an imperial fire-brigade, the Indian Army, at the expense of the Indian taxpayer, was used in Asia and Africa. By the early winter of 1914 Indian troops had been deployed on the Western Front, and throughout the First World War they were used in East Africa, in the Mesopotamia campaign, and in the Mediterranean theatres. However, by 1939 pressure from the rising tide of Indian nationalism resulted in Indian troops' being largely confined to the defence of India. On several occasions, when faced with manpower shortages in times of crisis, the British thought of raising a large imperial African army for use outside the continent. This was resisted by military men and politicians; but eventually, in 1942–43, it was decided to use West African troops, and some East Africans, against the Japanese in the forests of Burma. By then a sizeable army drawn from all over British Africa, and mainly composed of labourers in uniform, was being deployed in North Africa, the Levant and, after mid-1943, in Italy.

By the terms of the Hague and Geneva Conventions, POWs were to be treated humanely, given adequate protection and food, and not placed in dangerous positions, or used in manufacturing, transporting or handling material intended for combatant use. The capture and control of prisoners in the heat of battle is invariably a time of tension and heightened anxiety. At such times in all armies, however close the discipline, it is inevitable that the finer points of the Geneva

Convention are in danger of being forgotten or disregarded. Rounding-up, disarming and providing for prisoners are tedious and sometimes time-consuming tasks for an army in the field, and some neglect is likely to occur. The lot of a POW is hardly a pleasant one. So most armies have their dark moments in the initial handling of captives. The German army had more than most, and its record for treatment of Soviet prisoners is an appalling one. Japan's inhumanity to military and civilian POWs is well known. In their handling of black POWs the Germans often showed a callous disregard for the rights of prisoners. This is not altogether surprising given Nazi racial ideology, and in particular Hitler's denunciation of French African colonial troops in the pages of *Mein Kampf*.[12] German propaganda also made great play with the brutality of African colonial troops both in battle and towards cap-tured and wounded Germans, although there was no evidence for this. For example, General Guderian's Chief-of-Staff, Nehring, instructed in May 1940 that because 'colonial soldiers have mutilated in bestial fashion our German wounded . . . all kindness would be an error. It is rigorously forbidden to send these prisoners towards the rear without a guard. They are to be treated with the greatest rigour.'[13] As French colonial troops were the first black soldiers to be captured by the Ger-mans, it is to their experience that we now turn.

French Colonial Captives

In May and June 1940 the French deployed eight divisions of North and West African troops in their front line facing the Germans; most *tirailleurs sénégalais* were in *régiments mixtes*. One French military historian wrote that the 'North African divisions were sacrificed to no gain whatever'.[14] They collapsed before German armoured columns. In some cases colonial troops fought long and fiercely, as shown by the proportionately higher casualties in *régiments mixtes*, fearful of the consequences if they fell into German hands. And the treatment of all colonial prisoners, but especially blacks, was more harsh than that given to French war captives. One French officer recorded of his capture:

> The Germans, young ones wearing the black uniforms, are very excited. They shoot in the air, on the ground, steady bursts of machine guns. The sight of the *Tirailleurs Sénégalais* exasperates them still more. I sense a massacre. Second Lieutenant Sauze beside me, receives a machine gun burst in the stomach and drops down, asking to be finished off. A few *Tirailleurs* are killed as well. We are searched. Pistols, wallets, pens, the lot are taken. It's over.[15]

The German capture and treatment of African soldiers varied greatly. Edmund N'Guetta, from Côte d'Ivoire, described how he and his companions hid and then decided to surrender: 'We left on the main road. Everyone was on it. Some Germans passed us and asked if we wanted to surrender. The soldier said to keep going towards Chartres. We left for Chartres with a German guard. A truck came by with other prisoners – other *tirailleurs*.'[16] But at the same time African prisoners were shot out of hand by the Germans. Captain Charles N'Tchoréré, a *tirailleur* veteran from the First World War, was captured at Airaines, in the Seine valley not far from Amiens. When he insisted on his officer status and refused to stand with the African rank-and-file, a German officer shot him dead.[17] On 10 June 1940, at Erquinvillers, near Lyons, a retreating and exhausted column of *tirailleurs* made a stand against the advancing Germans. Out of ammunition, they were soon forced to surrender. On the order of the German commander between 400 and 500 prisoners, including the wounded, were shot beside the road, and those that attempted to flee were picked off by riflemen.[18] At the village of Chasselay-Montluzin, some twenty kilometres north-west of Lyons, the 25th Regiment of *tirailleurs sénégalais* confronted the Germans in the battle for the main route to the city. After stiff resistance the French surrendered, including a convent which had been used as a defensive position. The Germans retaliated by lining up 212 wounded colonial soldiers and shooting them.[19] A similar fate almost befell Léopold Sédar Senghor, the future president of Senegal. In mid-1940, as a second-class private in a colonial regiment, he was captured at Charité-sur-Loire, where his unit was helping to defend a bridge. It was only the intervention of a French officer that prevented the German captors immediately shooting the African prisoners.[20]

German indifference to the rights and welfare of African POWs was also strongly marked in the first stages of captivity. The exigencies of war exacerbated a predetermined German racial hostility. Tuo Lielourou recalled that following his capture 'it took us three days to get there [the prisoner-of-war camp]. The Germans are not human. They gave us nothing to eat on the road. Many were dying and wounded.'[21] Another Ivorien soldier told how he and his fellow African captives were 'put in an enclosure for eight days. There was no food, the water tap was broken. On the ninth day they [the Germans] sent a truck with coffee, but no sugar or bread. When they had us in that house, they beat some of us.'[22] It seems clear that the Germans also shot a good number of the African prisoners. Tuo Lielourou, whose testimony has already been cited, says that in the camps 'there were lots of deaths. The Germans killed many prisoners. . . . So in camp, when morning came, they would pick a portion of the men – we were still in bed – and put them in a trench and shoot them.'[23] A similar story was told by Ehouman Adou: 'So every day for three or four days they did this. They just picked out men and shot them.'[24]

French African prisoners usually were put in segregated camps, most of which were located in north-eastern France; a few were in Brittany, and some also within Germany. One hundred and twenty North African prisoners were sent as forced labour to Jersey.[25] Separated from their officers, many African soldiers believed that they had been abandoned. Low morale matched the harsh conditions. Peleguitamnadio Yeo's account recalls the wretchedness of camp life and the constant sense of fear at how the Germans would behave towards the prisoners.

> We walked four days and nights before we got to the camps. At first we were just behind wire, later there were eleven houses in the camp – sixty persons in each house. They separated the French and the *Sénégalais*. We thought that meant they were going to just kill all of us. The whites were not in the same wire enclosure as we were. When we got to the houses, we saw the whites again. They were there, but in separate houses. The camp was in Mirecourt. I was there for nine months. After that we were sent to Reims. We did nothing. We had nothing to eat. We cooked leaves. When you eat nothing, you cannot work. . . . Many died of starvation. I was in good health at Mirecourt. At Reims I had a bad foot. Even if you cut my foot, there was no blood there. It was very cold at Reims, no snow but very cold.[26]

Some African soldiers spent four years in prison camps. Life was hard and exposure to the unfamiliar winters increased the discomfort and wretchedness. Under a regimen of poor diet and forced labour, inadequately clothed and housed, a large number of African prisoners sickened and died. Perhaps half of those imprisoned did not survive captivity. Many men suffered from various forms of pulmonary disease, and dysentery was endemic. Two of Nancy Lawler's informants described conditions:

> What did we do? We cut wood. I was there for four years. Yes, it was bad, we always had to line up by fives. If you were standing alone, they killed you. It was very cold. There was so much ice – if you put your foot in it, it would freeze. We ate a small piece of vegetable chopped up in hot water, a little bit of potato, and some grass. We would mix it all together and eat it.[27]

At Morasse camp, Daouda Tuo-Donatoho suffered from malnutrition, recalling that he and his comrades had 'a small piece of bread and they'd put a little vegetable in a pot of boiling water and give it to us. Many of the men were so hungry they cut weeds and grass outside and boiled them and ate them. They got very sick – distended stomachs.'[28]

To survive, the bolder or more desperate prisoners stole food whenever they could; some paid for this with their lives.

Colonial POWs, like other captives, suffered from all the psychological traumas of captivity. In the case of colonial troops this was compounded by the alien environment (some African troops had only been in Europe for a very short time before capture), the sense of loneliness, the strange language, and the great distance from home. To this was added the fear that they had been abandoned by their officers. Not that the prisoners were completely cut off from outside news. Information about the condition of France and the progress of the war percolated into the camps through transfers of prisoners, contact with civilians, and from those sent outside on work details. An indeterminate number of prisoners were moved from one camp to another. Senghor was incarcerated at Romilly-sur-Seine, Troyès, Amiens, and Poitiers. For him, the years of captivity, from mid-1940 to February 1942, were an important part of his intellectual pilgrimage to *négritude*: 'It is thus, I thought near the barbed wire of the camp, that our most incarnate voice, our most Negro works would be at the same time the most human.'[29] Senghor later said that 'after two years of captivity . . . two years of meditation, I came out cured. Cured of . . . racism.'[30] Along with his small library of Virgil, Pascal, Plato, and Goethe (he taught himself German while in captivity), Senghor recalled the 'literary evenings' in the camps, telling tales and reciting poetry and the music of a makeshift *kora*, the Senegalese lyre. *Stalag* 230 at Poitiers was also where Senghor, 'the humiliated soldier fed on rough millet', wrote many of his poems, including *Prère de Tirailleurs*, sent to Georges Pompidou through a friendly German guard. Of great significance was that captivity brought the intellectual lycée teacher into contact with the peasant soldiers of his own country. As Senghor says in one of his poems:

> In the evening, grouped shivering around the dish of amity . . .
> Make place for me around the stove, that I may take back my still warm seat
> Let our hands touch scooping in the steaming rice of friendship
> Let the old Serer words pass from mouth to mouth like a friendly pipe.[31]

Escape for *tirailleurs*, either in the chaos of rout or from the camps, was both difficult and unlikely. Their colour marked them out, and where could they go? As Torno Sokongo said: 'We didn't know France. We had black skin. The French could save themselves by changing into civilian clothes. They could escape . . . We had no contacts, so we were always there.' Another POW said that he had no thought of escape as he did not know either France or Germany: 'We didn't know how to start – most didn't try.'[32] Nevertheless, some *tirailleurs* did escape. Edmond N'Guetta and five companions, with the help of French people, made their way to the Loire, hid in woods, and then safely crossed the river into Vichy France.[33] Many of the *tirailleurs* who spent several years in prison camps adapted to their conditions, using their ingenuity to pilfer food, make tools and toys, and to organize a regime of control, education and entertainment to fill the long hours of tedium. Farm work, either in France or Germany, gave *tirailleurs* access to food; French farmers employed prison labour, but also fed them, so that despite the hard work a few captives lived fairly comfortably. In some cases Germans used colonial soldiers as domestic and personal servants, which ensured better treatment and improved food supplies. By late 1940 Red Cross food parcels, containing special items for colonial soldiers, supplemented the meagre food rations of the camp. Also the Vichy regime took an interest in the welfare of colonial prisoners held by the Germans. Vichy officials were allowed to visit the camps in northern France, and negotiations began to arrange the repatriation of some colonial soldiers. For example, in late 1940 some 16,000 *tirailleurs sénégalais* were released from POW camps and remobilized in Vichy-controlled North Africa. In West Africa organizations such as the *Comité pour le Ravitaillement des Prisonniers de Guerre* were established to collect money and goods for the relief of POWs. At the same time Vichy officials succeeded in gaining the release of many colonial prisoners who were sick; Senghor was one of these, and in early 1942 he moved to Paris and resumed teaching.

Senghor played a role in the Resistance, and so did a few other freed or escaped POWs. After D-day and the Allied landings in the south of France, the *maquis* became more active, and attempted to disrupt the German evacuation. In several incidents railways were destroyed, preventing the Germans from moving colonial POWs. At Salbris, in August 1944, a train carrying nearly 400 colonial prisoners was attacked, and the released soldiers were incorporated into the Resistance until the American forces arrived. The advancing Allies liberated the several thousand colonial troops held in camps in northern France. One man remembered that 'in the morning there were no guards. The Americans were in front of the camp. They did not speak French, so that is how we knew they were Americans.'[34] Colonial soldiers now became guards over their former German captors; revenge was sought and delivered, with Germans killed; but kindness was also shown. 'I had pity', said one ex-soldier, 'because I thought of my brother who was being submitted to the same kind of thing.'[35] Not all prisoners immediately gained their freedom with the defeat of Germany; a handful of *tirailleurs* in German camps were kept by the Soviet authorities as labourers, and treated more harshly than they had been by their former enemy. And a certain amount of resentment was felt by colonial soldiers towards the French, who released them from captivity only to put them in labour battalions. As the French camps emptied, many freed *tirailleurs* drifted to Paris, where 5,000 or more were estimated to be located in the latter half of 1944 and early 1945. A small number showed all the marks of psychological stress caused by years in captivity.

Repatriation of colonial ex-prisoners was a slow process – partly a question of logistics, but there were also political considerations. The French authorities feared that the experience of captivity and warfare had nurtured discontent among colonial troops. In late 1944, René Pleven, the colonial minister, wrote to the Governor-General of French West Africa that in the years of separation from Africa, *tirailleurs* 'have acquired European habits and a different mentality' and that 'this confused situation has been bad for morale'; later he said that 'prisoners of war may be a factor in stirring up discontent among the people, especially around Dakar where there are so many of them'.[36] Freed colonial POWs at times proved troublesome. *Tirailleurs, en route* from German camps to West Africa, were temporarily housed by the British at Monshire Camp, Huyton, near Liverpool in the autumn of 1944. The men were already angry at the slow process of repatriation, and when they were confronted by racist actions by British soldiers and curbs on their freedom to go into Liverpool, their indiscipline increased.[37] The most serious disturbance involving ex-POWs occurred in Senegal, at Thiaroye, near Dakar, on 1 December 1944. The immediate cause was the failure of the French military authorities to provide back pay and repatriation premiums. The mutiny of 1,200 ex-POWs, and French action to crush the protest at the cost of 35 lives, sent shock-waves through French West Africa. Thiaroye also became a symbol of national protest against French rule, commemorated in Senghor's poem *Tyaroye*, and over forty years later in a feature film, *Le Camp de Thiaroye*, directed by Ousmane Sembène.[38] Less serious protests by colonial ex-POWs occurred in southern France in August 1945. For the French colonial authorities in West Africa the events at Thiaroye meant that former POWs had to be treated with some care. Measures were taken to disperse returning prisoners to prevent pools of discontent, and to pay entitlements to those who had been injured and in captivity for more than six months. In the post-war politics of French West Africa former POWs played an active part, through their *ancien combattant* organizations and new political parties such as the *Rassemblement Démocratique Africain*.[39]

David Killingray

British and South African Prisoners

Unlike French colonial troops in 1940, the various Allied African forces involved in the East African campaign of 1940–1 suffered few POWs. On one occasion a soldier of the Gold Coast Regiment was captured by the Italians, and he was either released or escaped to arrive back at his unit wearing only boots![40] In the short Somaliland operation in which the British were defeated by the Italians, members of the small Somaliland Camel Corps discarded their uniforms and melted into the population. The large Italian colonial army in East Africa was little more than an army on paper, conscripts and mercenaries of very limited use to their colonial masters. One account describes the surprise of soldiers of the Gold Coast Regiment at being greeted in a northern vernacular of the colony by two Italian *askaris* with their hands held high. The men, from the northern Gold Coast, had gone on the *hajj* to Mecca, lost their way in the Sudan, and wandered into Italian territory, where they had been conscripted into the colonial army. They stripped off their Italian uniforms and were soon re-enlisted in the British forces alongside their compatriots. As the Allied forces advanced into Italian East Africa they captured few *askaris*. Many simply disappeared into the countryside to merge with the populace, and this included many of the Eritreans, who formed the more reliable part of the Italian colonial forces. Those who were captured were treated as the mercenaries they were and soon released. The British had no desire to tie down men and material guarding unnecessary POWs. In response to a War Office request for information on Italian POWs, including *askaris*, captured in East Africa in 1941, the C.-in-C. Middle East replied: 'Problems of Africans insignificant as all in Sudan and East Africa will be released retaining only undesirables and those required for labour.'[41]

In the North African campaign of 1941–3, British colonial and non-European South African troops served largely in non-combatant roles. For the most part these soldiers operated well behind the battle front, servicing the lines of supply. However, a small number of black and coloured South African troops were captured at Sidi Rezegh in November 1941, and many more in mid-1942, when Rommel's forces suddenly struck eastward. The rapid German and Italian advance overwhelmed the British and South Africans, and among the 35,000 Allied prisoners captured were *c*.2,000 African soldiers from South Africa and the High Commission Territories. The black prisoners were locked in compounds and used as labourers by their captors. Initially, in some of the camps black and white prisoners were housed together, much to the outrage of white South African captives.[42] German and Italian treatment fell far short of the standards demanded by the Geneva Convention.

According to Article 31 of the Convention, POWs were not permitted to handle munitions. Non-European prisoners were forced to unload munition ships at Mersa Metruh, Tobruk and Benghazi. During Allied air raids they were denied access to shelters.[43] The explanation of the Germans and Italians for this harsh treatment and indifference to the welfare of non-European troops was that 'natives' were 'irregulars' and did not come within the terms of the Geneva Convention.[44] Food was also poor, and with hard labour, often from early in the morning to late at night, men fell sick and some died. One South African officer kept a record of the hard conditions suffered by non-European troops:

> Homs (Tripolitania). 400 Natives (not necessarily all South Africans). 1 month no attention. Hygiene nil. Severe dysentery. Average daily sick 50. Men in moribund state. Sent 3 ambulance loads to hospital. Took 24 hours to obtain ambulance. Working party on roads. 6 days of 8 hours. Ration, 400 grammes bread, rice and greens. No meat. Calorific value 1400.

At Benghazi he noted that conditions were appalling, the hygienic standards very bad, the men infected with lice, suffering from scabies, and without bandages or dressings: 'S.A. natives, Free French, Mauritians and Indians singled out for bad treatment', he further noted, with 'rifle butts, whips and sticks by Italian officers and men. Several shot. Men who tried to escape manacled together or hands and feet. Free French and Mauritian Natives singled out for more severe treatment.'[45] Red Cross parcels helped supplement the meagre diet of the prisoners, but official discrimination touched even this part of the Union Defence Force; nine pence per day was spent on Red Cross organized allowances for non-European soldiers, compared to the 2 shillings per day for whites.

Several prisoners escaped from the North African camps by wriggling under barbed wire fences, avoiding guards, and making their way through minefields and desert to the Allied lines. Sergeant Reuben Moloi, a South African of the 15th Ambulance Unit who was captured at Tobruk, escaped from the camp at Mersa Metruh and after a 100 mile journey through the desert lasting 17 days reached the British side.[46] Several other escapes were made, although not all were successful; one or two men perished in the arid wastes and others were recaptured.[47] To supplement their meagre diet many prisoners pilfered whenever or whatever they could find. As forced labour they also worked slowly and clumsily. Lance Corporal Job Masego, of the South African 2nd Division, was part of a detail made to offload munition ships after the fall of Tobruk. He made a 'bomb' using cordite from old cartridges and found a length of fuse. With the help of five other POWs he exploded his device on a German freighter in Tobruk harbour and sent it to the bottom. Fearful that he might be suspected of sabotage, Masego made a successful escape a few days later.[48] A number of Military Medals were awarded to South Africans for their bravery and fortitude in captivity (to Reuben Moloi and Job Masego, for example); predictably, some prisoners were apathetic; but only one non-European member of the NEAS is known to have actively collaborated with the Germans while in captivity – Private Dhlamini, who had worked in Namibia and spoke German.[49]

As the British pushed the Germans back in North Africa they were able to release some of the African POWs. The Germans and Italians evacuated several hundred other captives, on a journey by ship across the Mediterranean and by train that proved to be fraught with danger; they were subjected to Allied bombing and one ship carrying prisoners was torpedoed. In Europe, non-European prisoners were scattered in camps as far afield as Italy, Greece, France, Germany, Poland and the western reaches of the Soviet Union. Treatment in these camps varied from the relatively humane to the brutal. Barber records meeting fifty men of an East African company, who had been captured at Tobruk and taken to Italy and then to Germany through France, who said that they had been relatively well-treated by their captors.[50] On the other hand it is clear that often there was a general indifference on the part of both the Germans and the Italians to the living conditions and welfare of black African prisoners. When the Italians asked for an armistice in the summer of 1943, the Allies attempted to keep POWs from falling into German hands. An Italian war office directive instructed camp commandants that if they were unable to defend their camps against the Germans they were to 'set at liberty all the white prisoners but keep the blacks in prison'.[51]

The German POW camps at Babenhausen and Chartres were notorious camps for members of the NEAS. Prisoners died of unattended illnesses and also of starvation. Nzamo Nogaga, who was eventually released by the Americans at Munich in April 1945, was imprisoned in Italy and then taken to southern Germany. Passing into German captivity in Italy, following the armistice, he was forced to work in stables. Taken from Florence to Munich in railway cattle trucks for three days he and his fellow-prisoners 'had no room to move or breathe'. Some of the prisoners, he recalls, 'pushed up the floors of the cattle trucks and dropped through, only to be killed in that way'. He was in several camps and suffered considerable privation, kept barely alive by irregular Red Cross parcels of food. 'Personally, the only dead meat I did not eat was dog's flesh. I ate horse, donkey, cat, anything to keep life in me. The reason I did not eat dog's meat was because no dog came my way!' Nogaga saw prisoners shot for infringing rules. He endured frostbite and was employed as a labourer on the railways, in demolishing bombed buildings, and in burying the victims of air raids.[52] Mathews Letuku, a private in the NMC, was a prisoner for three years; but his lot was a more fortunate one. He was employed as a batman by a German fighter pilot first in North Africa and then in Germany, eventually being moved to *Stalag* 17A in Austria, from where he was liberated.[53]

The Italian surrender in September 1943 provided the opportunity for some African prisoners to escape. A few joined up with partisans, for example Gunner William Loubser, who survived being torpedoed by the British, escaped twice from Italian camps and eventually made his way to the Allied lines. The harshest part of the war for non-white prisoners was in Germany in 1944–5. South African captives were part of a column forced to march from Sagan in eastern Germany to Babenhausen, as the Germans retreated before the Soviet advance. Half-starved, sick, beaten along the road, the prisoners were exposed to a hard winter. Those who fell beside the road were either left to die or shot by the Germans.[54] At the end of the war, South African prisoners freed from German prison camps were repatriated via Britain. Black South Africans were in a temporary camp near Horsham, Sussex, before being shipped home. The experience of being kept in an English camp, and the failure to receive expected compensation on return to South Africa, left bitter memories for many.[55] East African prisoners, who had been captured in North Africa, were liberated by the advancing Allies in Europe and repatriated via Britain. In camps at Buckinghamshire and then at Keele, in Staffordshire, the former POWs were screened, the sick were sent to hospital, and an effort was made to turn those that were fit 'into soldiers again'.[56]

Prisoners and Propaganda

Both the Germans and the Italians attempted to use captured African soldiers for propaganda purposes. Two months after the fall of France, Rommel was involved in directing a film of the German crossing of the Somme which was later released as *Victory in the West*. In Irving's account

> A battalion of French black troops was hauled out of the prison camps to stage the surrender of a village. Again, this time for the cameras, Rommel's tanks charged, guns blazing. He told the blacks to come out toward the tanks with their hands up and looking scared; but the men overacted, rolled the whites of their eyes and screamed with terror.[57]

Several Africans lost their lives in the making of this film, which was early evidence of the German disregard for the welfare of non-white POWs. The Italians also used black South African prisoners in films intended for propaganda purposes. Nzamo Nogaga described being shipped to Sicily and then going to Naples and Rome, where 'we were employed making bioscope [cinema] films. We did not like these stunts as we were made to go naked all the time . . .'.[58] One attempt by the Italians to demonstrate on film white superiority went disastrously wrong when they staged a boxing match between Primo Carnera, the former world heavyweight champion, and Kay Masaki, a Zulu of splendid physique who had been captured at Sidi Rezegh. Masaki had never been in the boxing ring before and, reputedly, had been denied food for three days before the contest. As the cameras rolled for the first round the African was floored by Carnera. Picking himself up from the floor Masaki delivered a heavy blow at the Italian and succeeded in knocking him out. The cameras stopped; the propaganda stunt was cancelled.[59]

There were casual attempts by the Germans to use African prisoners for racial scientific purposes, for example measuring their skulls. Also, with the expectation of regaining African colonies, some moves were made to cultivate the sympathies of their captives. To this end propaganda magazines proclaiming German good intentions towards Africans were produced and distributed among French African prisoners in an effort to win hearts and minds.[60] Such German propaganda may have had some effect on disillusioned colonial soldiers, as the French authorities claimed when 800 recently repatriated *tirailleurs algériens* mutinied in Algeria in January 1941.[61]

African American Prisoners of War

The United States entered the war in late 1941 with armed forces that were segregated. Racial discrimination ran throughout each arm; there were separate corps in the army, the navy only accepted African Americans as 'mess boys', and there were no black pilots in the air force. Most blacks served under white officers in labour battalions building roads and handling munitions and supplies, while a few served as medical orderlies. Experimental integration was tried with certain units of the army during the Battle of the Bulge in late 1944; but segregation only came to an end after the war was over. Indeed, German interrogators often asked captured black officers why they fought for a country that despised them.[62] Most African Americans were bitterly aware of the irony of segregated southern eating houses and railway dining cars serving paroled German POWs but refusing admission to blacks in US uniform.

For all the reasons given above there were very few African Americans serving with US units in the western Pacific in late 1941 and early 1942. It is not known whether there were any American blacks among the 25,000 prisoners taken by the Japanese when the Philippines fell.[63] Even by mid-1943, when over half-a-million blacks had been recruited for military service, 425,000 remained within the United States. This was due to official racial attitudes that questioned the morale and efficiency of black soldiers, and also to the opposition from foreign governments to the use of African American troops, and particularly to the stationing of them, on their territory. Nevertheless, by the end of the war over one million blacks had enlisted, and over half of them saw service overseas. For many African Americans their first foreign posting was to the United Kingdom; in October 1942 just over 12,000 black troops had arrived, and by May 1943 more than ten times that number. But US black soldiers served in all the campaigns from Operation Torch in North Africa, to the invasion of Italy, the assault on France, and the final push into Germany. The majority of African American prisoners were soldiers captured following D-day; others were pilots and crew flying with the US Air Forces shot down over Germany and central Europe.

German behaviour towards black captives was at times harsh, particularly towards soldiers. At the end of the war several cases of murder by German forces of black prisoners were investigated by the US War Crimes Commission. At Wereth, in Belgium, in December 1944, eleven African American soldiers of the 333rd Field Artillery Battalion were executed by soldiers of a Panzer division. On another occasion two SS guards testified that in September 1944 they saw, near Merzig in Germany, 'Negro American soldiers being executed after they were ordered to dig their own graves'. They also alleged that instructions had been given that 'Negroes are not to be taken prisoner'.[64] At Debrecen, in Hungary, two black airmen who baled out were clubbed to death. For most US black prisoners, the treatment they received at the hands of the Germans was probably more severe than that meted out to other captives who were white. As Germany steadily collapsed before the advancing Allied forces from east, west and south, conditions for prisoners became worse. Food was in short supply as production systems and transport were disrupted or broke down, and consequently the sufferings of prisoners increased.

Captured African American flyers were sent to *Stalag Luft* III at Sagan, a large camp that housed 10,000 prisoners. There the officers were housed in huts several to 'a room about 16 x 16 feet. We did our own cooking and made our own implements for cooking and eating. Most of the pots and pans were made from cans received in Red Cross parcels.'[65] The camp was evacuated in early 1945, and the prisoners endured a forced march in bitterly cold weather. At the end of an 85-kilometre march, air force officers, including African Americans, were put into cattle trucks and taken to *Stalag* 7-A at Moosburg. 'The conditions at *Stalag* 7-A were deplorable. We lived in tents about forty feet wide and one hundred feet long. We slept on the ground as comfortably as possible, but had one faucet [tap] for approximately four hundred men.'[66] The handful of West Africans and West Indians serving with the Royal Air Force who were shot down and fell into German hands had similar experiences. Flight Lieutenant Johnny Smythe, from Sierra Leone, who joined the RAF in 1941, was a navigator in a bomber brought down over Ludwigshafen-am-Rhein in November 1943. He was sent to *Stalag Luft* I at Bad Vogelsang. The treatment that he received was slightly better than that given to his fellow officers, as the Germans hoped, unsuccessfully, to use him for propaganda purposes.[67]

War with Japan

West and East African troops fought against the Japanese in Burma. The British authorities assumed that some West Africans reported missing in Burma 'may be made prisoners' of the Japanese;[68] but most indications are that the Japanese killed any Africans that they captured, and this author has no record of Blacks surviving as POWs. Japan's treatment of POWs, both military and civilian, between 1937 and 1945 was deplorable and has not yet been fully acknowledged as such by successive governments in Tokyo. There are numerous accounts of wartime experiences at the hands of the Japanese, but only one by a West African. This is an unpublished story by Isaac Fadoyebo, a Nigerian serving with the Royal West African Frontier Force. Fadoyebo joined up at the age of 18 and was sent to Burma, where he served as a non-combatant with a casualty clearing unit. In March 1944, his unit was ambushed while resting on the river bank along the Kaladan valley. Most of the soldiers were killed, and Fadoyebo was badly wounded in the leg and captured by a Japanese patrol. The surviving European officers were taken away, and Fadeyebo, and another African soldier who was mortally wounded, were left to die. Fadoyebo was in great pain and could hardly move. Fortunately, Sergeant David Kagbo from Sierra Leone, who had been with the unit, was only slightly wounded; he evaded the Japanese and escaped into the forest. When the Japanese patrol had gone, Kagbo found Fadoyebo and carried him to a more secure place. For the next nine months, with the help of local villagers, the two West Africans lived in enemy-held territory, survived appalling privations, and avoided Japanese patrols that came looking for them. Both men were rescued by a Gurkha advance patrol in December 1944.[69]

Conclusion

The Second World War was marked by harsh and brutal treatment of many POWs, particularly by Germany and Japan. The Japanese treated all POWs harshly, so it is not altogether surprising that they killed captured African soldiers; many white troops suffered a similar fate at their hands. The attitudes of the Germans, and to a lesser extent the Italians, were conditioned by Nazi and Fascist antipathy towards Africans and other 'inferior races'. African POWs certainly received harsher treatment than white troops at the hands of the Germans in the victorious onslaught on France in mid-1940. Nevertheless, physical and material conditions improved relatively quickly as soon as the Vichy authorities began to demand access to the camps and could monitor the day-to-day treatment of prisoners.

In North Africa, Africans captured by the Italians were forced to do work contrary to the Geneva Convention that would not have been demanded of white POWs. This appears to have been due to a mixture of contempt for black captives and the exigencies of front-line labour shortages. However, for much of the war period German and Italian treatment of colonial and black captives was probably conditioned by the knowledge that the Allies held large numbers of German and Italian prisoners. Thus the needs of reciprocity overrode racial antipathy, as was also the case with German attitudes towards captured Allied soldiers who were Jewish.[70] As the Germans increasingly faced defeat after mid-1944, with the accompanying shortages of food and materials and the steady destruction of the transport infrastructure, the conditions of all POWs held in German camps deteriorated.

African and black POWs were more vulnerable than their white comrades, especially at the time of capture and early incarceration. It appears that units that were solely colonial or black were much more likely to receive harsh treatment than individual black soldiers serving in mainly white units. There are numerous accounts by French colonial soldiers of brutality, neglect and indifference at the hands of the Germans in 1940. Thereafter, and for most of the war, black war captives were a relatively small proportion of total Allied prisoners, and this may also have helped save them from being singled out for harsh treatment.

Notes

1. Myron Echenberg, *Colonial Conscripts: The Tirailleurs Sénégalais in French West Africa, 1857–1960*, London, 1991, pp. 88 and 191 note 8. The statistics for POW deaths are from Hélène de Gobineau, *Noblesse d'Afrique*, Paris, 1946, p. 12. See also Yves Durand, *La captivité: histoire des prisonniers de guerre français, 1939–1945*, Paris, 1982.

2. The British and Egyptians shot wounded prisoners following the battle of Karari (Omdurman), 1898; Ismat Hasan Zulfo, *Karari. The Sudanese Account of the Battle of Omdurman*, London, 1980, pp. 233–4. Similar action took place in Northern Nigeria following the defeat of Sokoto in 1903; see F. P. Crozier, *Five Years Hard*, London, 1932, pp. 149–50 and illustration. There is frequent mention of prisoners being re-enlisted by their captors, which indicates the mercenary nature of much African military service: e.g. Chari Maigumeri, enlisted by the Germans in Kamerun and awarded the Iron Cross, was captured by the British in 1915 and enlisted in the West African Frontier Force. See A. Haywood and F. A. S. Clarke, *The History of the Royal West African Frontier Forces*, Aldershot, 1964, p. 502, appendix V. Also see Public Record Office (hereafter PRO), Colonial Office Papers (hereafter CO), CO 1012/1, registry entry 9422/4, 9 Feb. 1942, in which there is mention of a note from the War Office to G.O.C.-in-C., East Africa, on the enlistment of 'native prisoners' (i.e. Italian *askari*) in the African Colonial Forces.

3. Bill Nasson, *Abraham Esau's War. A Black South African War in the Cape, 1899–1902*, Cambridge, 1991.

4. Peter Warwick, *Black People and the South African War 1899–1902*, Cambridge, 1983, Ch. 8.

5. John Hope Franklin, *From Slavery to Freedom. A History of Negro Americans*, 3rd edn, New York, 1969, Ch. 29; Ulysses Lee, *United States Army in World War II. Special Studies. The Employment of Negro Troops*, Washington DC, 1966, which does not mention African American prisoners of war. Most official histories of the Second World War, from all belligerents, ignore POWs other than making brief mention of enemy captives. An exception is the New Zealand history, which has a separate volume: W. Wyne Mason, *Prisoners of War. Official History of New Zealand in the Second World War 1939–1945*, Wellington, 1954.

6. German propaganda in the First World War had also been directed against African soldiers; see mention of the special leaflet dropped to black South African troops on the Western Front warning them that they would be singled out for special treatment if captured:

Brian Willan, 'The South African Native Labour Contingent, 1916–18', *Journal of African History*, vol. 19, no. 1, 1978, p. 73. Also the fears of Norman Manley, a black Jamaican serving with the British Army, at the prospect of being captured by the Germans: Norman Manley, 'The autobiography of Norman Washington Manley', *Jamaica Journal*, vol. 7, no. 1, 1973, p. 12.

7. Information from Major F. Bailey, interviewed by Dr Anthony Clayton, Sandhurst, 17 Sept. 1978.

8. See S. Horowitz, 'The Non-European War Record in South Africa', in Ellen Hellman and Leah Abraham (eds), *Handbook on Race Relations in South Africa*, Cape Town, 1949, Ch. 12; L. W. F. Grundlingh, 'The Participation of South Africa Blacks in the Second World War', unpub. D.Litt. thesis, Rand Afrikaans University, 1986; Ian Gleeson, *The Unknown Force. Black, Indian and Coloured Soldiers through Two World Wars*, Rivonia, 1994.

9. Roger Lambo, 'Achtung! The Black Prince: West Africans in the Royal Air Force, 1939–46', in David Killingray (ed.), *Africans in Britain*, London, 1994, pp. 145–63. An account of a West African seaman, Ransford Boi from Ghana, in German captivity is in *West Africa*, vol. 22, 8 May 1995, p. 778.

10. See the drawing of the 'African prisoner of war in Germany, 1870', by Ludwig Knaus, in H. W. Debrunner, *Presence and Prestige. Africans in Europe*, Basle, 1979, plate 27.

11. For a detailed account see Anthony Clayton, *France, Soldiers and Africa*, London, 1988.

12. Adolf Hitler, *Mein Kampf*, English trans., London, 1939, pp. 524–5.

13. Echenberg, *Colonial Conscripts* (see Note 1 above), p. 94.

14. Clayton, *France, Soldiers and Africa* (see Note 11 above), p. 126.

15. Quoted by Echenberg, *Colonial Conscripts* (see Note 1 above), p. 94.

16. Nancy Lawler, *Soldiers of Misfortune: Ivoirien Tirailleurs of World War II*, Athens, OH, p. 95.

17. Echenberg, *Colonial Conscripts* (see Note 1 above), pp. 166–7.

18. Lawler, *Soldiers of Misfortune* (see Note 16 above), pp. 95–6.

19. Echenberg, *Colonial Conscripts* (see Note 1 above), pp. 167–8.

20. Janet G. Vaillant, *Black, French, and African. A Life of Léopold Sédar Senghor*, Cambridge, MA, 1990, pp. 166–7.

21. Lawler, *Soldiers of Misfortune* (see Note 16 above), p. 98.

22. Ibid., p. 101.

23. Ibid., p. 98.

24. Ibid., p. 99.

25. Margaret Ginns, 'French North African Prisoners of War in Jersey', *Channel Islands Occupation Review*, 1985, pp. 50–70.

26. Lawler, *Soldiers of Misfortune* (see Note 16 above), pp. 101–2.
27. Kone Farnan, quoted ibid., p. 102.
28. Ibid., p. 112.
29. Jacques Hymans, *Léopold Sédar Senghor: An Intellectual Biography*, Edinburgh, 1971, p. 111.
30. Vaillant, *Black, French, and African* (see Note 20 above), p. 175.
31. Hymans, *Léopold Sédar Senghor* (see Note 29 above), p. 112.
32. Lawler, *Soldiers of Misfortune* (see Note 16 above), pp. 109 and 111.
33. Ibid., p. 111.
34. Ibid., p. 183.
35. Ibid., p. 187.
36. Ibid., pp. 188 and 194.
37. Echenberg, *Colonial Conscripts* (see Note 1 above), p. 100.
38. Myron Echenberg, 'Tragedy at Thiaroye: the Senegalese soldiers' uprising of 1944', in Peter Gutkind, Robin Cohen and Jean Copans (eds), *African Labor History*, Beverley Hills, 1978, pp. 109–28.
39. See Echenberg, *Colonial Conscripts* (see Note 1 above), pp. 129–33, 157–8. Also 'Entretien avec Monsieur Doudou Diallo, Président de l'Association de Anciens Combattants et Prisonniers de Guerre du Sénégal 1939–1945', in János Riesz and Joachim Schultz (eds), *Tirailleurs Sénégalais*, Frankfurt am Main, 1989, pp. 260–4.
40. PRO, CAB 106/554, East Africa, 53 Field Company, Gold Coast Regiment, 1943.
41. PRO, Foreign Office Papers, FO 371/27561/J 1633, and FO 371/27563/J 1944, dd., 16 June 1941.
42. Joel Bolnick, 'Sefela Sa Letsamayanaha – the wartime experience of Potlako Kitchener Leballo', *Wits History Workshop*, 6–10 Feb. 1990, p. 18.
43. Gleeson, *The Unknown Force* (see Note 8 above), p. 196.
44. Grundlingh, 'Participation of South African Blacks' (see Note 8 above), p. 217.
45. Quoted from the South African Defence Force Archives by Gleeson, *The Unknown Force* (see Note 8 above), p. 196.
46. Ibid., pp. 188–90. Escape from the enemy did not necessarily bring any reward for African POWs. For example, escaped Mauritian POWs were returned to their units, whereas escaped British POWs were invariably given leave. This was probably due more to the availability of shipping than to racial attitudes, but it was a keenly felt grievance; see PRO, CO 968/131/3, 'Notes on Mauritian Pioneers and Artisans', by Major D. G. Pirie, 1 Jan. 1944.

47. Nzamo Nogaga, 'An African Soldier's Experiences as a Prisoner of War', *The South African Outlook*, 1 Oct. 1945, p. 151; Gleeson, *The Unknown Force* (see Note 8 above), pp. 191–3; Grundlingh, 'Participation of South African Blacks' (see Note 8 above), pp. 219–20.
48. *Cape Times*, 8 Mar. 1976, retold by Donald Woods; Maxwell Leigh, *Captives Courageous. South African Prisoners of War. World War II*, Johannesburg, 1992, pp. 159–60; Grundlingh, 'Participation of South African Blacks' (see Note 8 above), pp. 220–1.
49. Grundlingh, 'Participation of South African Blacks' (see Note 8 above), p. 221. Dhlamini was subsequently sentenced to seven years imprisonment and discharged with ignominy.
50. D. H. Barber, *Africans in Khaki*, London, 1948, p. 96. On 9 Dec. 1941 the British submarine HMS *Porpoise* torpedoed and sank the Italian cargo ship *Sebastian Venier*, which was carrying 2,000 British and Commonwealth POWs from North Africa to Italy. Approximately 500 were killed, including a number of Africans. Thanks to Jane Flower for the reference.
51. Richard Lamb, *War in Italy 1943–1945*, London, 1995 (Penguin edn), p. 163.
52. Nogaga, 'An African Soldier's Experiences' (see Note 47 above), p. 151.
53. Gleeson, *The Unknown War* (see Note 8 above), pp. 203–6.
54. Grundlingh, 'Participation of South African Blacks' (see Note 8 above), p. 218.
55. Ibid., pp. 222–3.
56. Bildad Kaggia, from Kenya, was one of the twelve East African soldiers from the Middle East sent to Britain to help with repatriating East African POWs at 201 Holding and Transit Camp; see his *Roots of Freedom, 1921–1963. The Autobiography of Bildad Kaggia*, Nairobi, 1975, pp. 43–4.
57. David Irving, *The Trail of the Fox*, London, 1976, p. 72.
58. Nogaga, 'An African Soldier's Experiences' (see Note 47 above), p. 151.
59. *Springbok* (South African war veterans' journal), vol. 71, Mar.–Apr. 1988.
60. Echenberg, *Colonial Conscripts* (see Note 1 above), p. 110.
61. Clayton, *France, Soldiers and Africa* (see Note 11 above), pp. 255–6.
62. Charles E. Francis, *The Tuskegee Airmen. The Story of the U.S. Negro in the U.S. Air Force*, Boston, 1955, Ch. 20.

63. E. Bartlett Kerr, *Surrender and Survival. The experience of American POWs in the Pacific 1941–1945*, New York, 1985, does not mention any African American prisoners. Only *c*.10,000 of the US captives survived the harsh conditions of imprisonment by the Japanese.

64. Robert W. Kesting, 'Forgotten Victims: Blacks in the Holocaust', *Journal of Negro History*, vol. 78, no. 1, 1992, pp. 33–4.

65. Francis, *Tuskegee Airmen*, p. 152, recollections of Lieutenant Alexander Jefferson.

66. Francis, *Tuskegee Airmen*, p. 153.

67. Lambo, 'West Africans in the Royal Air Force', p. 154; 'To Hell and Back', *West Africa*, 8–14 May 1995, pp. 704–5; *The Times*, 13 May 1995.

68. PRO, CO 980/153, 'British Red Cross Society – West Africa', 1944.

69. Isaac Fadoyebo, 'A Stroke of Unbelievable Luck', a 53 pp. TS. in possession of the author. See also Rhodes House Library, Oxford, MSS. Afr. s. 1734, Box 10, Captain R. R. Ryder, copy of a report by two soldiers of nine months in hiding from the Japanese in Burma.

70. Mitchell G. Bard, *Forgotten Victims: The Abandonment of Americans in Hitler's Camps*, Boulder, 1994, pp. 36–7 and 71–5.

8

Italian Prisoners of War in Great Britain, 1943–6

Lucio Sponza

On 10 July 1943 *The Times* reported that: 'An Italian prisoner of war escaped from a camp in the Home Counties last night and made a dash for freedom after killing one of the guards with a bill-hook.' Two days later he was himself killed by a Home Guard, into whose farmhouse he had broken.[1] Escape attempts by Italian POWs were not infrequent – as will be mentioned later – but were never normally accompanied by violence, and had always ended up with apprehension within a few days. They were the result of blind frustration, rather than rational design. What happened on that July evening resulted from an individual case of demented desperation, but also indicated that the mental condition of some prisoners had begun to waver. Most of them had been captured two and a half years earlier, and the long imprisonment was taking its toll in terms of apathy and general malaise, if not mental imbalance.

By coincidence, on the very day of the fatal escape the Allies launched their invasion of Sicily, thus precipitating the fall of Mussolini and his replacement as the head of the Italian government by Marshal Pietro Badoglio. The Italian prisoners received the news with a mixture of incredulity and bewilderment. Six weeks were barely enough for that shock to sink in when they were told that Italy had unconditionally surrendered and that an armistice had been signed on 8 September 1943. The distinct hope that the worst was over and that the day of their repatriation was not far away was soon confounded, as they learned that Mussolini had been 'rescued' by the Germans and that he had established a new fascist, republican government over northern and central Italy, including Rome, on 23 September. As a result, Italy was split in two, as were the loyalties of the Italian people and POWs. Obviously, every occasion was used to impress upon the prisoners that Mussolini was now a mere puppet in the hands of the Germans and that the real and royal Italy was fighting with the Allies against the Germans and the latter-day fascists.

This chapter will look into the attitudes of, and towards, the Italian POWs. Firstly, and briefly, the early years of captivity in Britain will be considered, from the arrival of about 3,000 in the summer of 1941 to the climactic summer of 1943, when their numbers had increased to nearly 75,000. Secondly, and more extensively, the prisoners' position *vis-à-vis* the opportunity to co-operate in the war effort will be discussed from mid-1944 to the end of the war. Finally, a concluding section will deal with the full year between the end of the war in Europe and the prisoners' repatriation, which curiously took place while the British government was arranging for Italians to come over to Britain as immigrant workers.

The attitude of the POWs towards their condition and their captors was very complex, as it was affected by such factors as their individual cultural, political and social background; the prevailing sentiments in the camp; the way men related to each other, and to the more influential personalities amongst them; the unfolding of world events and the way the prisoners came to know about them; changing personal circumstances; the type and frequency of the news they received from their kin in Italy; and – last but not least – the duration of their captivity and the expectation of its coming to an end.[2] We can only provide a few observations here; but a general point needs first to be made. Contrary to what appears to be the norm with prisoners, the Italians did not show any intransigent opposition at first, which would gradually grow weaker as adaptation and resignation crept in. On the contrary, on their arrival and for a more or less long subsequent period they manifested a great willingness to work and co-operate (before the technical 'co-operation' was introduced to divide them). It is not difficult to understand why, as the prisoners brought over to Britain had been carefully selected for the purpose, by the weeding out those who notoriously expressed fascist and anti-British sentiments (the two did not necessarily coincide) and chronic malcontents.

An interesting report on the early Italian prisoners in Britain was written by Colonel Harold Stevens, who knew Italian people and their language well.[3] He noted at first that 'the very great majority of the prisoners are peasants who are particularly suitable for employment on farms and on land reclamation work', and that when he visited a squad at work and addressed them in their own language, 'they stopped and gathered round me with smiling faces. Very soon there was a general conversation.' He then added:

> Here, they are quite pleased with the general conditions and agreed that though they didn't get much pay it was nice to be able to buy cigarettes with the money: anyhow, it was a great thing to be out at work in the open air

rather than to be cooped up in camp . . . Farming operations as far as the prisoners have seen them bore no great difference to those in their own country. They liked the look of the land and one man said that after the war he would come back and settle down here with his wife . . . The farmer who is employing the second squad I visited . . . told me that two of these lads are worth ten of the men he could get as casual labour. The only fault he had to find with them was that they were so keen to get on with the work that he had to be sure to have a job ready for them as soon as another was done; otherwise they rather tended to try and work four men where there was only room for two.

As for the men's attitude to the war, Stevens noted that 'the theme of the duration of the war lies very close to the hearts of all these prisoners. They didn't say so in so many words, but I believe they don't mind really much who wins or loses, so long as they can get back to the peaceful, laborious life to which they are accustomed.'[4]

A contemporary informative letter by an interpreter who had visited another camp confirms the good spirits of the prisoners, while also conveying some mild complaints. After noting that they were crowded into tents, waiting for the huts to be completed, the interpreter wrote: 'The Italians are good-natured and cheery and very clean, and turn themselves out well. They complain only about . . . not getting anything like enough bread, absence of sufficient soap, sugar, absence of means of writing home . . . They are called "Wops" incessantly. I wonder if it strikes our fellows what their feeling would be if "Wop" or "Dego" was a synonym for Englishman.'[5]

Although some prisoners also asked for books and Italian–English dictionaries, it is unlikely that they were too curious to discover what those unintelligible forms of address meant. In fact, an early report by a camp-visiting officer of the International Committee of the Red Cross (ICRC), while reiterating the point that the prisoners would have liked to have had more bread (even at the expense of meat), stated that 'no classes for study [had] been organized . . . and the desire to do so was not expressed'; instead, the prisoners asked for 'musical instruments (violins, mandolins, guitars, saxophones, etc.); balls for the game of "Boccia", a football and a volley-ball'.[6]

In numerous subsequent reports by ICRC officers from various camp visits, it was pointed out that classes of Italian grammar and reading were organized by some Italians for the benefit of their illiterate fellow-prisoners. The better-educated members of the captive community also provided theatrical shows (for which they made the costumes out of any spare material, and a lot of imagination) and musical performances. These exhibitions were normally held in the canteen, where an altar was also improvised for the celebration of Sunday Mass, celebrated either by an Italian Padre (also captured with his countrymen), or by any Roman Catholic priest who might be found in the area. Often, real chapels were built and profusely decorated; the most famous case is that of the chapel erected in Camp #60, on the island of Lamb Holm (Orkney), which is still there, and is included as an attraction in the tourist guides for Scotland.[7]

Few views on the Italian POWs from the public are recorded for 1941 and 1942, when they were still in small numbers. Nor were the national papers interested (or briefed) to dedicate much space to them. The first arrival of Italians at the end of July 1941 was laconically announced in *The Times*: 'Two thousand Italian prisoners of war have arrived in this country for ditching, draining, land reclamation, and general work under the Ministry of Agriculture.'[8] The first relevant letter to the editor that appeared in that august daily in November 1941 was by a woman who praised the prisoners 'in a small camp somewhere in England' (the address of the correspondent was accordingly expunged) because they had offered the value of their week's earning (paid to them in token money) to the poor of the local village, 'especially to any poor families who have lost men in the present war'. The collection amounted to £2 14s 3d. Most prisoners in that camp, it was also noted, were peasants from southern Italy.[9]

Tender attitudes by the Italians towards children were also observed when comments on their presence became later more frequent. But an affectionate recollection of furtive encounters with early POWs was kindly sent to the author by a woman who had been evacuated as an eleven year-old child to Northampton:

> The winter of 1941–42 was very cold and snowy ... One day we were wandering through the field of 'our' estate when we saw a lot of men moving in, building huts and erecting wire fences. It was to be an Italian POW Camp – 'Eye-ties' – I'd no idea what an 'Eye-ty' was or indeed where Italy was. After a few short weeks there were olive skinned, dark-haired men in dark brown ill-fitting outfits with either big pink or blue round patches on their backs and knees. [They called] to us through the wire fence. We'd been told not to go near the wire, but of course we did [and] they threw rings made from aluminium and 'stones' from tooth brush handles. I still have one somewhere, wouldn't you know! They had to complete the camp themselves and dig the drainage, which was the only occasion they were allowed outside the wire.[10]

Yet, when the Italians began to be billeted in farms or placed in hostels at some distance from their parent-camps, some people found reasons to complain. One such case was reported in *The Times* in April 1943. It was stated that while the British workers were having difficulty in obtaining bicycles, 'Italian POWs in the rural areas were seen without an escort riding almost new machines to farm work in the district.' The complaint had reached the War Office, which replied in the following terms:

> After careful consideration, approval was recently given to a proposal that selected prisoners should be allowed to cycle up to seven miles to their work without escort . . . There have been no complaints about the prisoners' behaviour when cycling to work, and they are allowed to go unescorted because the man-power situation makes it impossible to spare soldiers to go with individuals or small parties . . . Cycles for the prisoners are provided either by the farmer or by the Ministry of Agriculture through their County War Executive Committees.[11]

As for the discipline of the prisoners who were confined to camps, in the first phase of their stay in Britain, only rarely did disturbances take place that worried the authorities. One notable instance occurred in December 1942 at Camp #155 (Penrith, Cumberland – as that county was then called), when no prolonged punishment could break striking prisoners. One hundred and thirteen men refused to work below ground in lead mines, and when 'the Ministry of Supply sent another sixty-two to work on the surface they, too, struck after only one day's work . . . I understand that they are being punished to the limits of legal liability by being put on bread and water, but that isn't getting any stone up!'[12] The stubborn behaviour of those prisoners did achieve something, as was admitted confidentially several months later: 'Our very bad experience with prisoners in the lead mines at Penrith forced us shortly after that to the conclusion that it would be no help to production to have [250 POWs] in West Cornwall [for tin mining], and we therefore withdrew our application for a Camp in that area.'[13]

In so far as the number of Italian prisoners brought over to Britain increased more rapidly than the satisfactory accommodation available, their spirits and discipline 'left somewhat to be desired' as an ICRC observer noted on a visit to a camp in Essex early in 1943. At the time of the visit, 'twenty-four prisoners [were] in detention, having refused to perform certain tasks which, in their view, would contribute to the war effort'. But the camp authorities were not regarded as blameless: 'There are certainly a few characters in this Camp who do not willingly co-operate with the authorities, but the impression is that a more indulgent attitude towards the prisoners and a more active interest in their welfare would greatly contribute to improve the atmosphere in this Camp.'[14] Considering that the ICRC reports were couched in the most cautious language, the above statement barely concealed strong criticism of the camp commandant and his men.

Sometimes the low spirits and depressive mood pushed prisoners beyond the limits of endurance, and the way out would be suicide. A month after the case of indiscipline just quoted, it was reported that a prisoner in a camp in Kent hanged himself at the infirmary – apparently after he was told that he was to be transferred to a different camp.[15]

Many Italians had been held in captivity for over two years, as was mentioned at the beginning, when the dramatic series of events that punctuated the summer of 1943 appeared to take a giant stride towards the end of the war, albeit at the awful price of turning Italian soil into a battlefield. Three days after Italy's capitulation, the prisoners read in the *Il Corriere del Sabato*, the Italian-language weekly paper that the British government circulated in the camps as a means of propaganda, the following notice in huge characters: 'ITALY IS NO LONGER AT WAR WITH GREAT BRITAIN, THE UNITED STATES AND RUSSIA.'[16]

The War Office was not taken unawares by the September events, or by their implications for the holding of Italian prisoners in Britain. As early as June 1943, Major-General Cyril Gepp, the director of the War Office's Directorate of Prisoners of War (DPW), had considered what should happen to the prisoners 'should Italy pack up and cease fighting'. He submitted that: 'While in some parts of the Empire, such as India and South Africa where Italian POWs are not employed, we may be glad to get rid of these prisoners . . ., in other parts, and certainly in this country, we shall not be in a position to let them go.'[17]

When Italy did 'pack up and cease fighting' the Ministry of Agriculture did not have to utter many words to persuade the War Office that 'the prisoners constitute an appreciable part of our labour force, and it would be very disturbing indeed to lose their services, especially at this time', when the planned invasion of France required the maximum war effort. So the prisoners were to be told in all frankness that they would not be repatriated for the time being, and that 'by helping to increase our food supplies they will be hastening the date of Germany's defeat and thus the date on which they can expect to return home'. Some vague suggestions as to the incentives to be offered were also indicated, but in the end what they were not to be told was that: 'As soon as the British prisoners have been returned from Italy (so that there can be no fear of reprisals) stricter disciplinary measures should be taken against prisoners who refuse to work or misbehave.'[18]

As for the prisoners' attitude to the events of the summer of 1943, their morale was monitored early in October by an officer of the Political Warfare Executive (PWE) in twenty-two camps. At the news of Mussolini's fall, it was written in the report that there was 'a great shock' and some incredulity, and then 'a reaction set in', of widespread apathy but also with apprehension and despondency in a small minority.

'A feeling of distress and depression' followed Italy's surrender, and 'for two or three weeks the general atmosphere in the camps was definitely "Grey" (neither fascist nor anti-fascist)'. This changed after Mussolini's liberation, with an 'ever-increasing divergence of opinion which is fast developing into disputes and quarrels between the "royalists" and the "fascists"'. When the 'Fascist Republic' was set up a degree of hope was revived amongst the pro-Mussolini, if not pro-Hitler, prisoners. A politico-social classification of the Italians was then attempted by a Foreign Office official:

> The POWs now appear . . . to be divided into the following categories: 1) The purely peasant type with no pronounced political tendencies, ready to side with any regime which could guarantee peace in Italy; 2) Men who are definitely in favour of the House of Savoy, with either Victor Emmanuel or Prince Humbert as King. These men appear to be subdivided into: (a) Men willing to fight with the Allies; (b) Men whose chief desire is to obtain suitable work in British factories to help our war effort. Amongst these are masons, mechanics, electricians, joiners, fitters, and all kinds of artisans; 3) Fascists and pro-Germans (including malcontents) who are definitely against any form of cooperation with the Allies. It is certainly not easy to estimate proportions or percentages; I should say, however, that the categories are now as follows: 1) 50%; 2) 35%; 3) 15%. It should be noted that category 1) is gradually being absorbed by one of the other categories (principally category 2).[19]

Despite the initial opposition of Washington and the persistent criticism of Sir Robert B. Lockhart, director of the PWE, the British government held firm on the view that the status of the Italians would still be that of 'prisoners of war', even if Italy was no longer at war with Britain – and, indeed, had become a 'co-belligerent' with the Allies. At the same time, in order to make the fullest use of the Italians' labour, it was necessary for the restrictions imposed by the Geneva Convention to be lifted. This could only be achieved with the consent of the Italian government; but the negotiations for that purpose dragged on for months, and came to nothing, as Badoglio did not deflect from his request that their status of 'prisoners' should be removed, as their unreserved support towards the war effort was now being sought.

D-Day was fast approaching, and the intensive and wide employment of Italian labour was becoming a compelling need. With mixed feelings of urgency, frustration and calculation, it was then decided that the British proposals simply to grant improvements to the prisoners' conditions were to be implemented, come what may, without Badoglio's acceptance. So, on Sunday 30 April 1944, all Italian POWs were paraded in their camps, with the exception of those in rural billets, for whom different arrangements were provided. The camp commandants addressed the prisoners to explain the advantages of co-operation. Volunteers would be organized into 'Italian Labour Battalions', to be run by Italian officers and NCOs, although under British command and supervision;[20] they would be allowed to walk freely outside the camp boundary during the day, within a radius of two miles; barbed wire and sentries would be removed from around the camp (but the main perimeter fence would remain); the minimum pay for unskilled work would be raised from 2s to 7s per week; their uniform would no longer have distinctively coloured patches, nor bear any inscription indicating the condition of POWs – instead, a flash with the word 'Italy' would be attached to their shoulders.

Less than 60 per cent of the prisoners volunteered. This was disappointing, as most camp commanders had reported that they expected between 75 and 90 per cent of the men to become co-operators.[21] It was also disturbing because unrestricted employment of Italians was necessary to sustain the service operations in connection with the invasion of France, mainly loading of materials and ammunition, which required them 'to work very long hours (some times 12 or 14 hours a day)'.[22]

The alarm was raised amongst farmers when Sir James Grigg, the Secretary of State for War, stated in Parliament that it was 'quite likely' that many Italians would be withdrawn from agriculture, now that they could be employed in work directly connected with the war effort. But there was some confusion as to any such transfer, and, pressed on that point, Colonel H. E. Chandler of the War Office reassured his colleagues at the Ministry of Agriculture that 'the great majority of [their] prisoners [would] remain [in] agriculture'. The rumours and possibly the misinformed statement by Sir James, added Chandler, had to do with the 19,000 Italians who had been moved so that co-operators and non-co-operators could be separated. Furthermore, since it was equally important to 'cut out every possible long distance journey', the whole operation became a 'complicated jig-saw puzzle'.

Chandler also attempted to answer the question as to the relatively low number of co-operators. 'The reasons for non-co-operators have been many and varied', he wrote, 'and for the most part were due to the fear of northern Italians that their families would be victimised.'[23] Another reason, suggested by Ivor Thomas MP (on the same day on which Sir James Grigg had alarmed the farmers) was: 'Is the Minister aware that the improvements are so negligible as to offer practically no inducement to these men to volunteer?'[24] No answer was forthcoming.

If the minister was unaware at the time, he would soon realize that there was great concern on that issue. This also had to do with the fact that many Germans captured in France were now being shipped across the Channel,[25] and for them to be accommodated in POW camps more Italians had to be moved out, which in turn could be best achieved by inducing more of them to co-operate, so that they could be either sent to hostels or billeted with farmers (for security reasons these options were not open to non-cooperators). Furthermore, the more Italians who volunteered, the more guards could be released to attend to the new and irksome prisoners.

The entire package offered to co-operators was therefore revised and improved at the beginning of August 1944. The minimum pay for unskilled work was raised to 9s a week; and up to half of the prisoners' earnings could be exchanged for sterling (until then the financial reward consisted of token money, which could only be used in the camp canteen); but probably more important in the eyes of the POWs was the concession to remit some money to their families in Italy (albeit at the punishing and by now unrealistic rate of 72 lire per pound sterling): this is the first glimpse of a more fitting role for the Italians – that of resuming their traditional and proud task as their families' breadwinners, in one way or another. Other new privileges were access to shops and cinemas, and the freedom to talk to civilians and to accept invitations to their homes; but it was still prohibited to 'fraternise' with civilians (which was really meant as a ban on association with women), although the new partial enfranchisement made that prohibition very difficult to enforce.

A side-effect of the concessions allowing the volunteers to be partially paid with real money and to be able to spend it in town was the creation of a desire to improve on their inadequate purchasing power. The prisoners achieved this by selling anything they managed to make in their spare time with the meagre raw materials accessible to them. In particular, Italians were judged to be 'extremely adept at making baskets [which they sold] in great number on the black market'.[26] Guards and supervisors often colluded, for a profit, by closing one eye or two to the traffic. Other illegal petty business was carried on thanks to the active participation of the surveillance personnel, possibly with farcical results, as in the alleged case of the British sergeant who wanted to buy one prisoner's watch and suggested that the transaction be executed outside the camp. The Italian accepted, but became suspicious at the suggestion and handed the coveted money over to a fellow-prisoner for safe keeping. When they returned to the camp the 'dealer' was thoroughly searched by an unusually eager corporal, who appeared to show surprise at not finding any money on him. As the plot became clear, the prisoner masterminded his lucrative revenge. The next day he approached the sergeant, pretending to have been 'robbed' by the corporal, showing anger and threatening to tell everything to the camp commandant. Caught between his own bad conscience and his greater distrust of the corporal than of the prisoner, the sergeant gave in and paid twice for the watch. Or so the story was told in one of the few published memoirs of Italian POWs in Britain.[27]

All in all, again, the outcome of the new set of incentives fell short of expectations, even though from then on there was a continual trickle of non-cooperators who volunteered. When the war ended some 70 per cent of Italians had volunteered, and by the end of 1945, when their repatriation began, only about 10 per cent still refused to co-operate. However, the fact that there was no rush to volunteer after the liberation of northern Italy, in April 1945, suggests that Colonel Chandler was wrong in singling out as the main cause for the Italians' reluctance to co-operate the fear that their families might be victimized. In March 1945 he enlarged a little on his earlier diagnosis by commenting that the likely principal cause was 'political indifference resulting from several years' captivity, coupled with a fear that there would be a "catch in it somewhere"'.[28]

Not even the 'catch' theory is fully persuasive, although in the early days of co-operation there was the suspicion among prisoners that volunteers might be sent back to fight. It is more likely that POWs were reasonably happy to be engaged in agriculture, and feared that, as co-operators, they would be transferred to different work. But two more plausible reasons must be mentioned.

First, the resistance to severing personal links of camaraderie and friendship, which were often strengthened by two – to some extent overlapping – loyalties: that to their army corps and shared military campaigns, and that to the province of origin (a strong sentiment, for which Italians have invented the word 'campanilismo' – attachment to one's own 'belltower', the symbol of a town or village – but this also extended to include the region and its distinct language). This is borne out by the names chosen for the football teams formed in the camps, as indicated (with an abundance of details about the matches) in the *Corriere del Sabato*: 'Fanteria' (infantry), 'Folgore' (the name of a famous parachute division), 'Tunisini' (obviously including men captured in Tunisia); but also: 'Romana', 'Lombarda', 'Adriatica', 'Alessandria' and 'Savona'.

Secondly, a reason which the War Office would not readily admit had already been pointed out by the PWE when they observed that, as a consequence of the unsatisfactory conclusions over their status, the prisoners were showing 'disillusionment, resentment and hostility'.[29] This view was shared by external observers such as A. Vulliet, a Swiss citizen who visited camps on behalf of the YMCA in March 1944. He reported that:

whereas four months ago the average POW seemed fairly contented with his lot – pleased that he [was] out of danger and happy to get abundant food and be well treated – the present scene has entirely changed now that they are [*sic*] no longer hungry. They are extremely disgruntled and full of bitter attacks against the Allies.[30]

Since the launching of 'co-operation' and the setting up of the 'Italian Labour Battalions', more space in the *Corriere del Sabato* was devoted to articles by pro-Allies prisoners expressing political views. This often aroused polemical discussions, which were suitably tailored and sometimes commented upon by the editors. Up to two pages of the eight-page weekly might consist of contributions under the sententious heading *Tutte le campane* ('Everyone's views'), in which the anti-fascist rather than the pro-Allies keynote was sounded.

To what extent this mode of persuasion was effective, it is impossible to gauge. One would have thought that throughout 1944 the impending defeat of Germany would be a most powerful, if indirect, instrument of successful propaganda for the majority of prisoners. But that was not necessarily so. Commenting on the information that during June 1944 (a significant month even in the Italian theatre, as the Allies at last entered Rome and pushed the Germans further north) 'a further 540 POWs have declared themselves fascist', Air Commodore P. R. C. Groves of the PWE wrote 'In view of the military situation in Italy this is on the face of it a remarkable statement, though not surprising to those who know how the whole issue of Italian POWs has been handled, or mishandled, since the Italian collapse last year.'[31]

Such an act of defiance, born out of disillusionment and bitterness, was one of the various forms of hostility prisoners manifested in a collective fashion. Others engaged in a go-slow at work, or all-out strikes and escapes, although there was never any hope that they could go very far. Individual displays of alienation and anguish ranged from the mild feigning of illness to the extremes of violence, derangement and suicide.

A selective (and contemptuous) account of the Italians' best-known misdeeds is provided by R. Jackson in his *A Taste of Freedom*. He reports, in particular, on the 'Tiverton mutiny'. This was when, in July 1944, all the 650 prisoners at Camp #92 in that part of Devon went on strike in sympathy against the punishment meted out to twenty-eight fellow-POWs who had refused to unload coal at Exeter railway station. They argued that the station was exposed to German air attack, and that employing prisoners there contravened the Geneva Convention. The other case of collective hostile action investigated by Jackson is the short-lived mass escape from Camp #112 at Ayr in December 1944, involving 97 prisoners.[32] Interestingly enough, there is no mention in Jackson's book of the one instance of a strike by Italian prisoners at Camp #155, in December 1942, already mentioned.

By the end of 1944, with the Allies' victory in sight, one might have thought that the attitudes of the Italian co-operators and non-co-operators towards their condition would have been markedly different. But a report in early 1945 revealed that this was not the case. It was compiled in February 1945, and was based on a survey of POWs' letters to their families carried out by the Postal and Telegraph Censorship.[33] The 27,000 letters examined came from both categories of prisoners in equal measure, and represented 11 per cent of the total mail censored in January and February of that year (16,500 letters were considered 'un-informative').

The most common complaint was the lack of mail received from either German-occupied Italy (4,898 cases), or Allied-occupied Italy (2,865 cases). In 1,671 instances the conditions in camps were praised (co-operators: 1,078; non-co-operators; 593), against merely 63 complaints (co-operators: 20; non-co-operators: 43). Only 175 prisoners praised the work they were doing (co-operators: 113; non-co-operators: 62), which may suggest a lack of enthusiasm amongst co-operators. There were many more cases of anti-Allies than pro-Allies remarks: 585 against 218. The breakdown of these two figures is particularly revealing, as the anti-Allies expressions were almost entirely found amongst non-co-operators (561 against 24 by co-operators), but the pro-Allies notes were much less unequally split (131 from co-operators and 87 from non-co-operators).

Two points need to be made here. First, when it comes to any ideological position, antagonistic feelings were more likely to be vented, as a means to soothing one's own frustration, than were expressions of accord. Consequently, there was probably an over-representation of opposition. Second, the lukewarm showing in favour of the Allies' cause was not monopolized by the co-operators; indeed, this was the sentiment with the smallest difference between the two categories of prisoners, which confirms that in several cases the refusal to volunteer did not mean support for the fascist cause.

A succinct comment on co-operators contained in the report was that they 'in general have settled down to a normal routine of life, but there is still a minority who are dissatisfied with their conditions. A few even state that they have exchanged their [POW] status for that of slave. Others resent the hostility of civilians towards them.'[34]

The observation that criticism was more likely to be expressed than appreciation also applies to the attitude of the public towards the Italian prisoners, which can be dealt with here only briefly. As soon as co-operators were given some freedom to move about and enter shops and cinemas (but not pubs), more numerous letters of complaint were written by ordinary citizens. To these the stock reply was that the Italians notably contributed by their work to the national interest and were thus earning their limited freedom. But the most recurrent denunciation (well preceding the beginning of co-operation) concerned the prisoners' 'fraternization' with women – whether in the form of consenting association or alleged pestering. The local press never missed an opportunity to make mountains out of molehills, according to government observers, while they ignored the fact that 'the approach [was] usually from the civilians and not the POWs'.[35]

An elaborate, condescending defence of the passionate Italian temperament was written (by a woman):

> Because of the southerner's instinctive inclination to the more sensual enjoyment of life; because the Italian cooperators were not prevented from meeting women at their work or being taken home by them and coming under the immediate influence of feminine attraction; because they were allowed to visit cinemas and suffer the disturbing excitement of sexy films; and more than all else, because some women seemed to enjoy prisoner-baiting as a sport, whilst others again fell sincerely and deeply in love with individual Italians, and desired to marry them – with the approval of their families – the order concerning fraternisation appeared extremely hard to the cooperators themselves, and extremely unimaginative to all who had contact with them, except the most stony-hearted. The cooperator's penalty for consorting varied from six months' to two years' imprisonment, the women were not punished.[36]

Punishment might even be meted out by the public, as happened in a Welsh village when a schoolgirl ran away from home for a few days: anti-Italian feeling spread in Llanrwst as the leader of the POW hostel was accused of associating with the girl, although 'no conclusive proof of this' existed. Two prisoners were hit by 'Marines the worse for drink', and 'two women at Dolgelley [*sic*] complained about [the hostel leader], apparently out of revenge'. The Italian was eventually transferred 'for his own protection', and his fellow-prisoners were not allowed 'out of the hostel after 7 p.m. on Saturdays as Dolgelley is a very rough place on Saturday nights'.[37]

A more complex fear of the Italians' fraternization with women was manifested by W. G. Goss, the Secretary of the Transport and General Workers' Union, when a particular employment of them was suggested on the eve of co-operation:

The proposed introduction of Italian POWs in the Admiralty Stores and Depots is bound to result in difficulties. There is not the least doubt in my mind that the workpeople will resent these men being brought in to work with them, and having regard to the number of women employed [there] the proposal is in my opinion unwise.[38]

The main concern of the union was obviously not so much with morality, as with the proposed employment of prisoners beside, perhaps even in replacement of, ordinary workers. Equally evident was the fact that the Trades Union Congress (TUC) would represent an obstacle to the unrestricted use of co-operators.

The unions' attitude was first tested as early as January 1944, when it was suggested that a survey should be carried out of the number and types of skilled workers among the POWs, in view of what was regarded as the imminent signature of the 'Agreement' by Badoglio. The purpose was to employ men skilled at their trades as long as the shortage of manpower persisted and security considerations allowed.[39] The idea was welcomed by government departments and employers, but rejected by the TUC, which was even reluctant to see Italians in unskilled work. The battleground where the government and employers' representatives confronted the unions' leaders was the Joint Consultative Committee (JCC). At one of their meetings late in 1944 the General Secretary of the TUC, Sir Walter Citrine, went as far as suggesting that 'Italian POWs should be returned to their own country to undertake non-combatant duties there rather than [be] employed in this country in order to release British workers for the services'.[40]

But a compromise was reached at that same meeting of the JCC. The document stated in the preamble that 'the continued employment of Italian POWs [was] essential in the national interest', and then indicated the conditions for their use on civilian work: first, prisoners could be employed on unskilled work where British labour was not available, and subject to consultation with the local representatives of the unions concerned; secondly, Italians were not to be employed on skilled work, with the exception of those working for Service departments, without whom 'it would have been impossible to provide sufficient labour for the mounting of the operations last summer', that is, the invasion of France. It was then added, to counter Sir Walter's statement, that 'no British civilians have been displaced on account of the employment of Italians'.[41]

When three months later the Minister of Labour, Ernest Bevin, was asked in Parliament how many skilled Italians were employed in building work of a civil character, he mentioned the figure of 2,000 'engaged on building work for the Service Departments', and also a further 1,500 'allocated for building work in London in connection with war damage repairs'.[42] He unwittingly revealed, therefore, that a major turning-point had been reached in the use of Italian labour. Now that the end of the war was clearly imminent, the necessity to employ volunteers and non-cooperators in – respectively – the direct and indirect war effort was giving way to the urge to employ them as a workforce for the reconstruction of the country and for its economic recovery. This course appeared to be endorsed by the TUC, which in April lifted the ban on the employment of skilled Italian prisoners. This was now possible, in case of labour shortage, provided that the unions gave their consent both at headquarters and local levels. It was also the blueprint for the post-war series of government-sponsored schemes that aimed at the 'importation' (as it was normally called) of Italian industrial workers to Britain, both males and females.

Fearing that the Italian POWs would be repatriated soon after the end of the war in Europe, the War Office received many applications from farmers for the prisoners to be permitted to remain in Britain and continue to work for them. The Aliens Department of the Home Office firmly rejected that idea with a spurious and sneering argument. First, it was stated that 'it has always been assumed that the presence of POWs here is due only to [. . .] their being brought here temporarily for custody in order to disembarrass our forces in operational zones'; and it was then added, with reference to the applications, 'I cannot imagine that anybody, except a few of their girl friends, would view favourably a suggestion that any of them should be allowed to stay here . . . except possibly on a temporary basis while they are required to supplement our manpower.'[43]

But if nobody (except the 'girl friends') wanted Italian ex-POWs in Britain, everybody wanted them to stay for the time being, disregarding the pressure from the Italian government for their repatriation, or at least for their release from POW status. The excuse was the lack of ships, but the truth was different and yet the same: 'In view of the continuing manpower shortage in the United Kingdom, and of the world food situation it was decided to take no steps to repatriate Italians from this country until after the [potato and sugar-beet] harvest.'[44] So it was only at the end of the year that the first Italian prisoners were to be sent home. Furthermore, the Cabinet agreed with the Ministry of Agriculture that it would have been desirable if up to 30,000 Italians had been induced to remain in Britain and continued to work in agriculture.

Eventually, 1,430 Italian POWs were allowed to stay on in Britain. The concession was only made to those engaged in agriculture, because of the much stronger opposition from the unions in the case of industrial employment. Farmers had to apply making a persuasive case for their retention. The contract was for one year in the first instance, but the Italians were restricted to agricultural activities.[45]

By the time the Italians began to be slowly repatriated, their place was taken by German prisoners, so that even future harvests were secured. No concession was made for repatriated Italians whom farmers wished to re-employ; the standard reply was that priority was to be given to the Poles and 'European Volunteer Workers' who were settling in Britain. Only after much lobbying by MPs on behalf of their rural constituents was a relaxation introduced, by which individual cases would be considered – notably cases in which sentimental and economic considerations would apply. Still, for most of the ex-POWs whose former employers would have been happy to have them back, there was rejection on the grounds that they had 'no special skills or qualifications'.[46]

The Italians may have been at the bottom of the pile of desirable foreign labour, but sometimes it became necessary to resort to them. The first and trend-setting case emerged at the end of 1945 in the iron foundry industry, which had about 10,000 unfilled vacancies. Attempts to bring in French and Belgian men failed, as work and pay conditions were not attractive. It was then that the Labour Attaché at the British Embassy in Rome, W. H. Braine, suggested that Italian workers should be approached, as there was high unemployment in Italy and their government was keen to encourage emigration. In February 1946, the Italian Ambassador in London, Count Nicolò Carandini, was informed of the proposal, and suggested that Italian workers might be recruited from the POWs still in Britain. Perhaps the government now regretted not having proceeded two years earlier with the classification of Italian POWs by their trades, so as to pick those who had any experience in iron foundries. But the unions' opposition, which had forced that proposal to be abandoned, was still there, whether the Italians were already in Britain as POWs or to be signed on in Italy.

As with the war effort before, a serious obstacle to the reconstruction drive was now a manpower shortage. In trying to overcome the difficulty the Attlee cabinet was 'at first reluctant to give up the powers of direction which the government had assumed in wartime'.[47] So the unions were pressed on the issue of Italian immigration for iron foundries, resorting to the familiar argument that had succeeded – albeit not without difficulties – in seeing that Italian co-operators, both unskilled and skilled, could be employed in any type of 'work of national importance'.

By the time the unions gave their consent in August 1946 to the employment of up to 2,800 Italians in iron foundries, most POWs had returned to Italy. But there were further problems. On the Italian side, in addition to the slowness of Italy's administrative machinery, there was the not entirely unjustified concern that the package was not attractive enough. The main objection was the limit on the amount of money the would-be emigrants were allowed to send to their families, who, incidentally, would be prohibited from joining them in Britain. The British government had to give in on this up to a point.

Initially, it was decided that only northern Italians were to be 'imported',[48] but not enough came forward who were regarded as suitable (more of this later), partly because industries in northern Italy were quickly recovering, and partly as a result of the competing and more alluring prospects of emigrating to France, Belgium and Switzerland, where families could soon join the workers. The recruitment of Italians was then extended to the southern half of the country.

Second – again a striking reminder of the attitude displayed in connection with the transfer of the POWs to Britain, the Home Office insisted on thorough vetting. This time the fear did not concern bringing over dangerous fascists, but dangerous communists. Security screening was to be adopted for all government-sponsored 'bulk recruitment' of Italians up to the 1960s,[49] despite persistent criticism as to its effectiveness from the British Labour Attachés in Rome, and notwithstanding the fact that almost from the beginning the majority of Italian workers came to Britain outside those schemes, through the mechanism of individual labour permits for which no screening was contemplated. Yet this was not the only inconsistency in a general policy that regarded the use of Italian labour as a cheap device for temporary adjustment of the manpower shortage, only to be tapped when the reservoir of the Poles, 'European Voluntary Workers' and 'Displaced Persons' was exhausted.[50]

Peter Thorneycroft had a point when he censured the government because they were 'prepared to use the slave labour of a conquered nation, to bolster up the restrictionist economy that they want'.[51] The reference – in November 1946 – was to German POWs, who at that time were legion; but the Conservative MP was disingenuous in passing off the supposed virtues of deregulating the post-war labour market as a moral indictment. If ethics are brought to bear, had the PWE not been right in condemning the way the issue of the status of Italian POWs had been dealt with? But then, had it not also been naïve in expecting an 'outcry in this country when the British public discovered the facts'?[52]

Notes

1. *The Times*, 10 and 12 July 1943.
2. In his classic study on the effects of prolonged and forced detention by 'total institutions', E. Goffman provides perceptive considerations on POWs. See his *Asylums*, New York, 1961, *passim*.
3. Colonel Stevens's ancestors had been wine merchants in Naples, and his family maintained contacts with southern Italy. He acted as Military Attaché in Rome and Durazzo (Albania) in the early 1930s, but became a well-known voice in Italy as the leading BBC commentator for broadcasts in Italian during the war.
4. PRO, Foreign Office Papers (hereafter FO), FO 916/176, 'Notes by Colonel Stevens on visit to Italian POW Camp, Royston, 23 Sept. 1941'.
5. Ibid., extract from a letter written by an English interpreter, 19 Sept. 1941. The camp involved was #31 at Ettington Park, Newbold-upon-Stour, Warwickshire.
6. Ibid., ICRC report by J. Zimmerman on visit to Camp #27, Ledbury, Herefordshire, 27 Oct. 1941. For 'Boccia', read 'Bocce' – bowls.
7. See J. MacDonald, *Churchill's Prisoners. The Italians in Orkney, 1942–44*, Kirkwall, 1987.
8. *The Times*, 1 Aug. 1941.
9. Ibid., 21 Nov. 1941.
10. This is an excerpt from Robina Herrington's memoirs, which she is writing for her grandchildren. I am grateful for her information. The site referred to was Camp #35, called Boughton Hall or Boughton Park Camp.
11. *The Times*, 9 Apr. 1943.
12. PRO, War Office Papers (hereafter WO), WO 32/9904, R. I. James, Ministry of Labour, to Major J. J. Sheppard, 31 Jan. 1943.
13. PRO, Ministry of Labour Papers (hereafter LAB), LAB 8/126, V. Rossiter to E. Maplesden, Ministry of Works, 26 Oct. 1943.
14. PRO, FO 916/581, ICRC report on visit to Camp #78, High Garrett, Braintree, Essex, 12 Feb. 1943.
15. Ibid., ICRC report on visit to Camp #40, Somerhill, Tonbridge, Kent, 1 Apr. 1943. The suicide had been committed on 8 March.
16. The weekly was published and edited by the Political Intelligence Department of the Foreign Office. It was launched in June 1942 with the undiplomatic title of *Il Corriere del Prigioniero* (The Prisoner's Courier), later changed into *Il Corriere del Sabato* (The Saturday Courier). Some prisoners were secretly collaborating in the production of the paper, which acquired more importance when

the prisoners' views were solicited after the process of co-operation began in May 1944.

17. PRO, WO 32/10755, W. L. Gorell Barnes, Privy Council Office, 8 June 1943.

18. PRO, Ministry of Agriculture and Fisheries (hereafter MAF), MAF 47/54, copy of a letter sent by W. C. Tame to Colonel H. E. Chandler, War Office, 9 Sept. 1943. Badoglio's pledge to free all the Allied prisoners held in Italy could not be substantially observed, as the Germans removed to their country those who did not manage to escape. A recent book has told the story of the adventurous and lucky ones who did escape and were sheltered by Italian peasant families. See R. Absalom, *A Strange Alliance. Aspects of Escape and Survival in Italy, 1943–45*, Florence, 1991.

19. PRO, FO 939/357, 'Political reactions in Italian POW Camps resulting from the downfall of the fascist regime', by N. H. Andreoni, 2 Oct. 1943.

20. This was intended to mitigate Badoglio's resistance rather than to win over the prisoners, as there was no longing amongst the POWs to be returned under Italian officers' control. Still, not every POW shared the sanguine desire of a seaman captured early in the war, who, when reminded that only 'gentlemen officers' were reasonably well paid in captivity despite their statutory idleness, confided to a fellow-prisoner: 'Yes, we're just sons of servants, lousy blighters, ragamuffins, to be cast aside as soon as we have served their purpose. By God! It makes one become revolutionary. They had better not put me together with the officers, or there'll be trouble. We're in England now, not Italy. One never knows how things will turn out in Italy after the war. There might be a soldier's tribunal. I don't like officers.' PRO, WO 208/4189, 'Interrogation reports on Italian POWs', no. 43, 3 Jan. 1941. These are contemporaneous translated transcripts of secretly recorded conversations between prisoners; they were carefully paired after the first interrogation: see R. Garrett, *POW. The Uncivil Face of War*, 2nd edn, Newton Abbot, 1988, p. 169.

21. In what is perhaps a reflection of this disappointment, Harold Macmillan's memory of that process was that 'though encouraged to [volunteer], few of the [Italian POWs] did', *War Diaries: Politics and War in the Mediterranean, January 1943 – May 1945*, London, 1984, p. 374, footnote 29.

22. PRO, WO 32/11131, minutes, circular memo. by W. H. Gardner, 15 July 1944.

23. PRO, MAF 47/54, Chandler to Tame, 15 May 1944.

24. *Hansard*, House of Commons, fifth series (1943–4), vol. 399, col. 1717, 9 May 1944.
25. The presence of German POWs in Britain has been studied by M. B. Sullivan, *Thresholds of Peace*, London, 1979. Almost entirely focused on the Germans is M. Koch, *Prisoners of England*, London, 1980.
26. PRO, Board of Trade Papers (hereafter BT), BT 168/84, F. H. Clinkard, Ministry of Supply, to F. Pickford, Ministry of Labour, 9 Nov. 1944. See also *Hansard*, House of Commons, fifth series (1943–4), vol. 403, col. 2229, 17 Oct. 1944 and vol. 404, col. 642, 31 Oct. 1944.
27. A. Berretta, *Prigionieri di Churchill*, Milan 1951, pp. 291–2. It is quite possible that the story was coloured, if not invented so as to show that Italians could outwit the British, against whom Berretta was bitter. He was not, of course, a co-operator.
28. PRO, FO 916/1279, letter to A. J. Gardener, Foreign Office POW Department, 23 Mar. 1945.
29. PRO, FO 916/971, 'Memorandum by PWE on the proposal to employ Italian POWs on work prohibited by the Geneva Convention', 14 Apr. 1944.
30. PRO, FO 939/356, report by Vulliet, 13 Mar. 1944.
31. PRO, FO 939/356, memo. by Groves, 8 July 1944.
32. R. Jackson, *A Taste of Freedom. Stories of the German and Italian Prisoners Who Escaped from Camps in Britain during WW II*, London, 1964, pp. 180–2 and 141–5, respectively.
33. PRO, FO 916/1275, 'Postal and Telegraph Censorship. Report on Italian POWs in Great Britain (compiled by Enemy Prisoners of War Branch)', 23 Feb. 1945.
34. Ibid.
35. PRO, WO 32/10737, communication by Major-General D. E. Dickinson (Western Command), 5 Jan. 1944.
36. W. Percival, *Not Only Music, Signora!*, Altrincham, 1947, p. 156. The writer was a pianist who volunteered to entertain Italian POWs in their camps; she was accompanied in many acclaimed performances by her husband, a violinist with the Hallé Orchestra.
37. PRO, WO 166/16295, War Diary, Camp #119, Pablo Hall, Llandudno, 30 Sept., 7–9 Oct. 1944. It was not only in Wales that POWs would complain about youngsters' obscene gestures and verbal abuse addressed at them, especially if there was a safe distance between the two parties. Dolgelley is the town named, but it is probably Dolgellau.
38. PRO, LAB 8/781, letter to N. J. Abercrombie, Labour Branch, Admiralty, 27 Apr. 1944.

39. Although the unions often muttered, with good reason, that the farmers took advantage of prisoners' cheap labour, they did not raise the issue of the notable financial benefit for the Treasury. Farmers employing POWs had to pay the War Office 48s per week per unskilled man (37s if he was billeted); the minimum wage for agricultural labour was 60s at first, and 70s by the end of the war; but the figure of 48s remained unaltered. The government fared even better, considering that the maximum amount paid by the War Office to individual co-operators was 9s a week. Nobody calculated the overall revenue, but there were 'allegations that His Majesty's government makes thousands of pounds monthly out of cooperators' and POWs' wages'. PRO, FO 916/1275, J. W. D. Davidson to Gardner, 2 Oct. 1945.
40. PRO, LAB 8/781, minutes of the 49th meeting of the JCC, 12 Dec. 1944.
41. Ibid., meeting of 12 Dec. 1944 and final document, JCC 146.
42. *Hansard*, House of Commons, fifth series (1944–5), vol. 409, col. 963, 22 Mar. 1945.
43. PRO, Home Office Papers, HO 213/1130, H. H. C. Prestige, Aliens Department, to Chandler, 18 May 1945.
44. PRO, WO 32/10753, memo. by DPW on repatriation of Italian POWs, 23 June 1945.
45. See in particular, PRO, Ministry of Labour Papers (hereafter LAB), LAB 8/91, 'Conditions under which Italian ex-POWs have been employed in Agriculture in this country', Apr. 1948.
46. This was a common formula used to indicate the reason for the refusal to issue labour permits to foreign applicants. See PRO, LAB 8/1670, 'Analysis of industrial and commercial refusals from 1st Oct. to 31st Dec., 1946', c.Jan. 1947.
47. A. Cairncross, *Years of Recovery. British Economic Policy, 1945– 51*, London, 1985, p. 386.
48. Perhaps the idea of recruiting only from northern Italy revealed a degree of prejudice about the working quality of southern Italians. The same view was expressed when the possibility of bringing over to Britain Italian POWs was first discussed in connection with *unskilled agricultural* work. If there was any such prejudice, it was not confined to Britain. Up to some 55,000 Italian rural labourers volunteered to work in Germany, between 1938 and 1943: only northerners were required. See B. Mantelli, 'L'emigrazione di braccianti italiani nel Terzo Reich, 1938–43', *Studi Storici*, vol. 3, 1990, pp. 739–69.
49. These included, between 1948 and 1950: young women for the cotton industry and domestic service in hospitals; men for masonry,

coalmining, the tinplate industry, brickmaking, and railway track maintenance and repair. Some projects were aborted because of the unions' opposition. The most successful scheme involved the brick industry, but bulk recruitment was soon superseded by the system based on labour permits.

50. See, for the government policies towards immigration in post-war years, C. Holmes, *John Bull's Island*, London, 1988, Ch. 5.
51. *Hansard*, House of Commons, fifth series (1946–7), vol. 430, col. 1038, 21 Nov. 1946.
52. PRO, FO 939/357, secret minute by PWE, n.d., but probably 10 Feb. 1944.

—9—

Captors and Captives on the Burma–Thailand Railway

Sibylla Jane Flower

There have been numerous first-hand accounts published by POWs on the Burma–Thailand Railway, but few have come from men who held positions of responsibility within the camps in which the prisoners employed on the project were held. Perhaps as a result of this, very little attention has been paid to the Allied officers who planned and maintained the administration of these camps, and who were responsible for negotiating directly with their captors. The prevailing interpretation has been to disparage the officers as a caste, an ideologically inspired approach which, it can be argued, has distorted both the history of POWs on the railway, and the general history of Allied servicemen in Japanese hands during the Second World War.

The main purpose of this chapter is to correct the obvious distortions that pervade both the popular and scholarly literature on the subject. To do this we should emphasize the role played by officers in helping their men to survive the privations and extreme conditions of life on the railway, particularly during the period of construction between June 1942 and October 1943. The Japanese decision to keep together all officers up to the rank of lieutenant-colonel and other ranks in the labour camps of Burma and Thailand enabled the POWs to maintain their military hierarchy. No one who saw the confusion and desolation of the camps of Asian labourers on the railway doubted that there was an advantage in being part of a predetermined military order. It was also an arrangement that the Japanese accepted and were prepared to work through. A further point to be stressed is that the experience of individual prisoners on the railway varied so considerably as to make any general conclusions invalid. The factors affecting this disparity of experience included the widely differing terrain and location of the camps themselves, with the problems of supply that these might entail, and the personality and effectiveness of those in authority – both Japanese and Allied.

The appraisal can be divided into three sections. First, an analysis of the existing published literature and its limitations, together with a survey of the many unpublished sources that provide a much more coherent picture of the railway's history. Secondly, an assessment of the way in which the Japanese captors operated on the railway project, drawing attention to the inconsistencies and local variations in command structures and behaviour that served to make each camp along the line different. Finally, we should evaluate the role of the officers, and the positive and negative effects of their behaviour, both collectively and individually, on the men under their command.

I

In spite of the high profile of the Burma–Thailand Railway in the accounts of Allied POWs in Japanese hands, the secondary literature is arguably deficient in a number of respects. It is constructive to consider three books that have achieved wide distribution: Ernest Gordon, *Miracle on the River Kwai* (1963), Leo Rawlings and Bill Duncan, *And the Dawn Came up like Thunder* (1972) and Eric Lomax, *The Railway Man* (1995). Gordon's book, with its strong evangelical message, was read for its British publishers by two officers who were POWs with Gordon in Thailand. One dismissed it as 'full of misrepresentations and inaccuracies' and the second made the comment that 'so much is embroidered and exaggerated'. The publishers nevertheless excused these deficiencies on the grounds that the manuscript had been ghost-written and altered by several editorial hands in the United States.[1] The book by Rawlings and Duncan, which has a foreword by Lord Mountbatten and was translated into Japanese, contains many of the powerful drawings made by Rawlings in Thailand; but it suffers from a defect that has subsequently been revealed. Duncan, despite his claims, was never a POW in the Far East, and the description of his experiences on the railway is imaginary.[2] Lomax entrusted the telling of his story to another hand, but the text has little value from a historical point of view. A lieutenant in the Royal Signals, Lomax was interrogated by the *Kempeitai* (Japanese Military Police) after the discovery of radios at a camp near Kanchanaburi in August 1943. His decision to retain a carefully drawn map of the railway even after his detention, and the map's discovery by the Japanese, led to predictable reprisals. Lomax uses very few of the surviving documents on what is a key episode in the history of the railway. Moreover, he had not spoken to any men from the British Intelligence network (of which he had no knowledge as a POW) that was put at risk, but miraculously not compromised, by the investigations he describes. The significance of the Japanese search has apparently entirely eluded Lomax.

Many of these reminiscences, written years after the events described, no doubt fulfil a personal need to make sense of the bitter years of captivity; but they lack the authentic detail and intensity of feeling that lend such power to the contemporary and near-contemporary narratives. Surviving journals written during captivity are very scarce. Writing materials were virtually impossible to replace, and many of the uncompleted journals were found and confiscated by the guards. At the end of 1944 the possession of paper and pencils was prohibited by the Japanese unless authorized for official use. The penalties for keeping any sort of record became so severe that most POWs buried their papers or destroyed them. At least two POWs began to collect information for projected books while still in captivity. Rohan D. Rivett, an Australian journalist who published *Behind Bamboo* in 1946, is illuminating on conditions at the Burma end of the line; Sir Edward 'Weary' Dunlop regarded this as the classic account of POW life under the Japanese. C. F. Blackater, a planter in Malaya before he was commissioned in the Indian Army, followed Rivett into print two years later with *Gods Without Reason*, in which he includes contributions from some of his fellow POWs in Thailand. Both books reveal the advantages and disadvantages of publishing so soon after the events they describe.

It could be argued that the wide circulation of certain memoirs and books on the history of the railway has served to distort the record. Most authors of published accounts were not officers, and so the officers' role tends inevitably to be subordinated, both in the public perception of what took place and also in the scholarly literature on the subject. The treatment of such officers' material as there is raises the more serious possibility that there may be a conscious intention to leave it out of the reckoning so as not to prejudice the record of the other ranks. Overall there is an unbalanced portrait of the military hierarchy, which is often taken at face value. On the other hand neither the officers collectively, nor the British government have done much to set the record straight.

While many officer-captives of the Japanese fulfilled their military obligations after their release and furnished reports of group, camp or battalion experiences, only one officer who held wide authority and influence on the railway chose to publish his diary. Sir Edward 'Weary' Dunlop (Lieutenant-Colonel, Australian Army Medical Corps), whose work appeared in 1986, occupied the dual role of commanding officer and principal medical officer of his force. He was unique in this respect. Quite apart from his medical knowledge, he had a wide understanding of military procedure, and his diary gives a vivid portrayal of the dilemmas he faced in attempting to exercise his two commands within the confines of the POW camps.[3] Beyond this important source, other officers who kept detailed diaries have been reluctant to publish the record of their spontaneous reactions to events and personalities in the overwrought atmosphere of POW life. Dunlop himself admitted in his preface 'I have shrunk from publishing these diaries for over forty years . . . I have distrusted the judgements I made at the time under harsh circumstances.'[4] He nevertheless decided to publish with the minimum of annotation or explanation, even at the risk of upsetting some of his fellow POWs. One can see why he 'distrusted' some of his judgements, such as his dismissal of that most courageous of British camp commanders, Lieutenant-Colonel H. H. Lilly (1/5th Sherwood Foresters), with the words 'he co-operates with the Nipponese'.[5]

Dr Roy Mills (Captain, AAMC), was the sole medical officer to a party of 718 men sent to jungle camps near the Burma–Thailand border. In publishing his diary in facsimile, he, unlike Dunlop, preferred to add a commentary in hindsight on the harrowing circumstances and the personalities mentioned in the text, including an assessment of his relationship with his commanding officer, Lieutenant-Colonel S. A. F. Pond (2/29th Battalion Australian Imperial Force), a man he held in high esteem.[6] The association between commanding officer and medical officer was pivotal in units engaged in the building of the railway; a point well illustrated by Dr Rowley Richards, whose book, *The Survival Factor* (1989), describes the cruel dilemma faced day after day by Lieutenant-Colonel C. G. W. Anderson VC, (2/19th Btn AIF) and himself when forced by Japanese demands to include sick men in the work parties.[7]

Another important text is the diary kept by Dr Robert Hardie, published by the Imperial War Museum ten years after the author's death. Hardie was in private practice in Kuala Lumpur before the Second World War and was captured serving as a medical officer with the Federated Malay States Volunteer Force (FMSVF). This is as much a personal as a medical record, reflecting the author's broad learning and artistic gifts in coming to terms with POW life. However, its main contribution is in providing a vignette of the civilians of pre-war Malaya: civil servants, scientists, planters, traders and businessmen, who generally formed their own society as POWs. They also played key, but necessarily clandestine, roles on the railway, primarily because of their knowledge of Thailand and the Thai and Chinese languages. Many of the Volunteers, though holding positions of responsibility in civilian life before the Allied surrender, went into captivity as private soldiers or NCOs, because it was customary in the Volunteer Forces for everyone to progress through the ranks before being commissioned. A number of their unpublished diaries provide the most authoritative, informed and objective commentaries in English on POW life on the railway, and their evidence on the fate of Asian labourers is especially valuable, coming as it does from men who had worked with Tamils, Malays and Chinese and spoke their languages.[8]

The surviving accounts reflect the differing circumstances of individual POWs on the railway. For example, the Japanese made better provision for officers than for other ranks; the base camps were tolerable compared with those in the jungle; some POWs were transported to their camps up river by barge, while others had to march; there were good and bad POW camp administrations; and some POWs adapted to the prevailing conditions more quickly than others. Two of the best published diaries of the captivity provide an instructive contrast between the perceptions of a fairly typical young British officer, Captain John T. Barnard (2nd Btn East Surrey Regiment), and an Australian, Sergeant Stan Arneil (2/30th Btn AIF), who survived the 'F' Force holocaust in the camps on the Burma border.[9] A New Zealand POW commented on Arneil's text when it appeared.

> It is written so close to the day's events that it contains an excess of what [we] used to call 'latrinograms' whose truth would not be accepted for more than a week or so. Nevertheless it showed up quite strongly the Aussie 'mates system' in healthy operation, and much more of value. How different was the experience of one man from another. It is appropriately named 'One Man's War'.[10]

Arneil himself states that he makes no apology for his own recollections, which fail to support much of what has been published by other authors. He is adamant that the criticism he (as a sergeant) makes from time to time of the officers 'follows an army pattern which began before Hannibal fought in the Punic Wars', and is not to be taken as a condemnation.[11]

It is also the case that some of the published reminiscences are disappointing when compared with their authors' original papers. For example, the lengthy report written on release by a medical officer, Captain Stanley S. Pavillard, Straits Settlements Volunteer Force, is of far greater historical value than his book, *Bamboo Doctor* (1960). Similarly, the account produced late in life by the distinguished Australian surgeon Sir Albert Coates gives little hint of the quality of Coates's papers and the evidence he presented to the post-war trials.[12] Other accounts include two by interpreters, important witnesses considering the problems encountered by the POWs with languages. Cornelius Dirk Punt (Ensign in the *Koninklijk Nederlands-Indisch Leger*) gives a compelling description of his experiences,[13] and a British officer with the Australians, William Mortimer Drower, a captain in the Intelligence Corps, includes twenty pages on his time as a POW in his autobiography.[14] Ian Watt (Lieutenant, Royal Artillery) who became an academic after the war, has also written extensively on POW life.[15] However, the principal fault in many of the personal accounts is that one of the staples of POW life – rumour – seeps so frequently into the narratives. Proper names are omitted or altered to protect fellow POWs or, indeed, to guard against libel actions. This can be seen as a very necessary precaution given the number of reputations that were lost during captivity. Some authors have felt the need to adapt texts written in diary form, no doubt under pressure from publishers. For example, Chaim Nussbaum, who was rabbi to the Jewish community in Jakarta and Bandung, and later an Army chaplain, published what is perhaps the only work of literature to figure in the bibliography of the railway. In his book, he is at pains to point out that, though the book is based on his diary, he had made the decision 'to freely adapt the dialogue' and thereby enhance 'the truth value'.[16] A different form of 'editing' can be seen in the book by Reginald Burton (Lieutenant-Colonel, Royal Norfolk Regiment). He was still a serving officer at the time of its writing, and submitted his text as required to the War Office, only to have it shorn of any matter that could give offence to the Japanese. As an 'H' Force survivor, he naturally felt aggrieved.[17]

There are, however, qualified exceptions to this rather depressing picture. Two Australian survivors of the railway, E. R. Hall and Don Wall, have each produced books that contain considerable research. Wall's volume is particularly valuable, as he has collected and collated original testimony of the Australian component of 'F' Force, which he intersperses with contemporary commentaries.[18] There are also two collections of oral interviews with surviving Australian and American prisoners in the Pacific theatre. The general Australian volume, edited by Hank Nelson, is carefully put together;[19] but the more directly relevant American collection is less satisfactory. It consists of edited versions of twenty-two interviews conducted between 1972 and 1990 with survivors of the 131st Field Artillery and the USS *Houston*. The majority of the POWs interviewed worked on the Burma end of the line, but two are included from the twenty-six Americans who went to Thailand with 'H' Force from Singapore in May 1943. Almost the only editorial tool employed on the interviews themselves is the roster of the Lost Battalion Association. None of the original testimony of the American survivors is used, which, as it was recorded immediately after the war, would have established a tighter chronology and background.[20] The best general survey of the railway's construction, and an evaluation of the project in terms of strategy, logistics and manpower, is Clifford Kinvig, *River Kwai Railway* (1992). In his preface, Kinvig laments the lack of documentation, yet makes only scant use of the rich resources available in the Public Record Office. Beyond this, there are a number of biographies of leading figures from the railway,[21] and a few interpretative works;[22] but the whole subject, apart from the medical aspects, has received very little scholarly attention. A research group comprising scholars from various Japanese universities has no counterpart outside that country.

Another contributory factor to the paucity of the literature is possibly the decision of the post-war British government to close the principal reports on Allied POWs of the Japanese for seventy-five years. (For some reason the medical reports came under the thirty-year rule, and have been in the public domain for many years.) These reports have recently been opened, and were used to compile the official history. However, although detailed chapters on some aspects of British POWs in Japanese hands exist in draft form, only an outline appears in the final published version.[23] The Australian official history does contain a far more comprehensive and competent survey of the general and medical aspects of the captivity. The only documentary evidence relating to the railway to appear under British government auspices was the result of the interrogations, research and personal observations made over a seven-month period immediately after the war by Lieutenant C. C. Brett (Canadian Intelligence Corps).[24] Given the number of British officers in Japanese captivity on the railway, the refusal to allow access to the documents, coupled with the reluctance of the officers to publish their own accounts, has prevented the full story from being made available.

Finally, the transcripts of proceedings in British Military Courts in the Far East were released between 1977 and 1981. These seem to have been an under-used, yet essential, source, and comprise the records of more than twenty trials of Japanese and Koreans accused of committing war crimes on the railway. When this is supplemented by the transcript of the major Australian trial relating to the Burma end of the line, which includes the evidence of American and Dutch witnesses and was opened in the late 1980s, these two collections provide the documentary core for any historical assessment of the railway. It should be noted that the affidavits and signed statements obtained from the liberated POWs were taken from men of all ranks and provided evidence on almost all the major incidents relating to Japanese treatment of prisoners, including specific information against individuals who were arraigned after the war.[25]

II

The proposal to build the Burma–Thailand Railway as a means of supplying the Japanese Army in Burma was initiated by Headquarters Southern Army soon after the fall of Singapore on 15 February 1942, although formal instructions to proceed were not issued by the Imperial General Headquarters in Tokyo until June. These instructions specified that the workforce would comprise POWs and Asian labourers. The Japanese decision to use POWs as forced labour was discussed by the Minister of War, General Tōjō Hideki, at a meeting in Tokyo in late April. Apart from the obvious advantages of utilizing the unexpectedly large number of POWs that had fallen into Japanese hands, Tōjō pointed out the propaganda value of using white POWs in a way that he believed could help banish the sense of racial inferiority among people of the occupied territories, and thereby instil 'a feeling of trust towards Japan'.[26]

In Tokyo, two offices were established within the War Ministry to handle matters concerning POWs: the POW Information Bureau, set up in December 1941, was intended to act as a registry and clearing-house in line with the requirements of Article 77 of the Geneva Convention; and the POW Control Bureau, formed at the end of March 1942, had charge of administrative matters relating to POWs. These two bureaux appeared to be separate, but were in fact run by the same personnel drawn from the retired list of the Army.[27] The International Committee of the Red Cross in Geneva described in their report the difficulties of negotiating with these officers, whom they found to be secretive and distrustful of foreigners.[28]

Other Japanese officers also holding commissions dating from before the First World War were seconded to command the POWs. These commandants received their orders at a conference at the Imperial General Headquarters in Tokyo on 7 and 8 July 1942. This conference, presided over by Lieutenant-General Uemura Mikio, senior officer of both the POW Information and Control Bureaux, was attended by the general officers appointed to command the principal POW areas and their staffs, amounting to about fifty officers in all. Major-General Sasa Akira, General Officer Commanding Burma and Thailand POW Administration until June 1943, was present, with at least three of the lieutenant-colonels who became group commandants on the Burma–Thailand Railway: Ishii Tamie, Nagatomo Yoshitada and Yanagita Shōichi, and one major, Chida Sotomatsu.

At this conference Uemura distributed a printed pamphlet listing the rules and regulations governing the treatment of POWs. The problem of policing the POWs gave rise to much discussion, because so many of them would be employed on work such as the railway project, where conventional prison bounds would be few. Uemura explained that all POWs without exception were to sign a parole form, a specimen of which he produced. Should a POW refuse to sign, Uemura added, he should be regarded as implying an intention to escape. One of the officers asked Uemura what action should be taken if a POW escaped after he had signed a parole form. Uemura is said to have replied that 'the prisoner could be shot on the spot, either during his escape or after his recapture and with or without court martial', but that the order to execute or to hold a court martial should be made by the Area Commander. Colonel Yanagita, the only senior officer in the Railway Administration whose word the POWs found in any way dependable, recalled after the war the instructions he was given at this conference on the handling of POWs. 'We were told that though there [was] an International Law . . . there might be some cases which must be handled in accordance with the circumstances and not exactly according to the International Law.'[29] These subjects were discussed again at meetings in Bangkok in August and December 1942, when Sasa briefed Chida, Nagatomo and Yanagita on practical matters relating to the supervision of POWs. On one of these occasions, Nagatomo asked for clarification of Uemura's order about escapees, and Sasa told him unequivocally that all were to be shot.[30] At the beginning of 1942, the Japanese government had informed the Allies of its agreement to apply *mutatis mutandis*, and subject to reciprocity, the provisions of the Geneva Convention to POWs in its power. Although these provisions were not incorporated in the training of either officers or other ranks of the Imperial Japanese Army (IJA), it appears from Colonel Yanagita's statement that the subject was at least considered by the POW Control Bureau, if only to be dismissed.

During August and September 1942 these commandants took over the four (later seven) groups into which the POWs were divided in Burma and Thailand. The technical aspects of the railway construction were, however, in the hands of two Railway regiments – the 5th (in Burma) and the 9th (in Thailand) – so that, until drastic alterations were made to the chain of command in July 1943 to hasten the completion of the work, labour on the track and the POW camp administration were the responsibility of two separate Japanese authorities. They were frequently at loggerheads with each other. The engineers, under the command of the two colonels of the Railway Regiments and the commander of construction, had a prodigious engineering feat to accomplish in an ever-decreasing amount of time. There was a gulf between the professional engineers, particularly the skilled and highly motivated young company or platoon commanders, and the flotsam and jetsam of the IJA collected together in the POW Administration. The headquarters of the latter was initially at Banpong, near the southern base of the railway, with more than 50,000 POWs in its charge scattered over the 400 kilometres to Thanbyuzayat in Burma. The camps ranged from a bivouac in the jungle to the highly complex social establishments that evolved on the plains of central Thailand, such as Chungkai (which in February 1944 held 9,000 POWs). The total manpower of the POW Administration at the start was 40 officers, 85 NCOs and 1,280 Korean guards, which, given the distances and the number of camps, had the effect of devolving considerable authority on individuals of lowly rank.[31] For example, in May 1943 Nagatomo had under his command in POW Group III a labour force of nearly 10,000: 4,500 Australians, 4,500 Dutch, 500 British and 200 Americans. To guard and supervise these men, distributed at any one time through a minimum of ten camps, over a 100-kilometre stretch, he had a staff of only 8 officers, 20 NCOs and 325 Korean guards.[32]

Lieutenant-Colonel Nagatomo was the most effectual of the Japanese group commanders, although he was based at his headquarters at Than-byuzayat during the construction period and his periodic inspections of the railway achieved nothing. The POWs found him impossibly contrary in character, his attitude changing with unnerving rapidity 'from friendliness to cold-blooded ruthlessness'. Ensign Cornelius Punt, the Dutch interpreter, who knew him well, wrote: 'Nagatomo . . . hated with intensity all that was Western and white. . . . Yet . . . he was drawn to their ways, culture and civilization.'[33] Unlike most senior Japanese officers, he was prepared to discipline his subordinates, most famously Lieutenant Naitō Tomoji. In July 1943, alerted to the fact that Naitō in a drunken fury had shot and wounded a POW at Retpu, Nagatomo arrived, and according to his own account, confiscated Naitō's collection of arms and sent him to Moulmein as a mental patient.[34]

Major Chida, unlike Nagatomo, Yanagita or Ishii, tended to remain in the background. At Tarsao, he left all the negotiations with the Senior British Officer to his adjutant, Lieutenant Tanaka Shigeaki, and later absented himself when his then adjutant, Lieutenant Komai Mitsuo, conducted the investigations after the discovery of radios at the camp near Kanchanaburi that resulted in two British officers being beaten to death. Having failed to restrain Komai, Chida did his best to conceal the consequences from his superiors.[35]

The Japanese of the POW Administration with whom the POW officers had to negotiate on a daily basis were the subalterns such as Naitō, Tanaka and Komai. The capabilities of these men and their attitude to the POWs varied considerably. Naitō was always unpredictable; he offered no concessions to the POWs, and was prepared to order the execution of escapees in the absence of his superior, Nagatomo. Tanaka was militarily arrogant, and enjoyed taunting the British officers at Tarsao over what he considered to be their lack of fighting spirit. Conversely, there were other lieutenants, such as Takasaki Shinji and Sannomiya Myōji, of whom many officer POWs spoke well.

When Sannomiya took over from Tanaka at Tarsao, the headquarters of Group IV, he at once ordered the rebuilding of POW accommodation and the erection of hospital huts near the river so that the sick from up-river camps could be removed more readily from barges, a concession which Tanaka had refused. The timing of this was fortunate, because by April 1943, a month after the change in command, the sick from Kanyu and Tonchan were pouring into Tarsao, reaching a total of 2,000 by September. The British officers at Tarsao found that, despite his vicious temper, Sannomiya was generally 'approachable and reasonable'.[36] Although generally well thought of, Takasaki's record was seriously flawed by his role in the executions of a British officer and an American journalist who had attempted to escape from Tamarkan. The camp commandant at Wampo between November 1942 and February 1943 was Lieutenant Hattori Hiroshi, a middle-aged lawyer who took no interest in the Emperor's war. He spoke excellent English (with a *penchant* for reciting Gray's *Elegy*), and at an early stage attempted to counteract the culpable Japanese decision to send thousands of POWs into the jungle without medical supplies by escorting one of the Allied medical officers to Kanchanaburi to buy drugs. At Wampo, he had a good relationship with the Senior British Officer, Lieutenant-Colonel Lilly, to whom he gave a fairly free rein as far as administration was concerned. Moreover, he controlled the behaviour of his subordinates. The engineer in charge of railway work in the early stages did not object to being 'pushed and bullied' by Lieutenant-Colonel Lilly, so that from the vantage point of mid-1943, those POWs who had experienced Hattori's Wampo looked back upon that camp with feelings approaching nostalgia.[37]

Most of the Japanese NCOs, if not all the younger officers, had seen active service in the brutal wars of the 1930s. As such, they took a much harder line with the POWs. Sergeant Ejima Nobuo (an architect's clerk by profession), who was hanged after the war for his role in the Kanchanaburi radio investigations, had served in Manchuria, and his partner in crime, Sergeant Watanabe Seikichi, had been dismissed from the IJA in China. Staff-Sergeant Hiramatsu Aitarō (known to the POWs as 'The Tiger') was proud of his service in the China War, but his ruthless and violent temper fuelled by alcohol struck terror into the POWs. 'Nobody ever saw the Tiger smile', observed one POW at Tonchan. '[He] had one overriding obsession: the railway must go forward, fast and regardless.'[38] However, as an efficient operator himself, Hiramatsu could appreciate the same quality in others. When Captain R. W. J. Newton (2/19th Btn AIF) arrived at Tonchan South and insisted on setting up his own camp without interference from the Japanese, Hiramatsu did not object then, or at subsequent camps under his command.[39]

Hiramatsu was feared by the Koreans and even by some of the Japanese officers. Thus when a benevolent officer such as Hattori came within his orbit (as happened at Tonchan Spring Camp), Lieutenant-Colonel Lilly described the change that came over Hattori as 'unbelievable'.[40]

Again, there were exceptions to this rule. Sergeant-Major Saitō, whom British POWs described as 'a credit to anyone's army', had seen several tours of active service in Manchuria and China. He knew how to handle troops, and his presence in the POW Administration puzzled POWs such as Lieutenant-Colonel Philip Toosey (RA), who had dealings with him over a long period. Saitō was neither an alcoholic nor wounded, two obvious reasons for being pushed into this backwater of army life. In fact, he later explained that this unwelcome posting had come about largely because he had fallen victim to service rivalry.[41]

It was a common POW complaint that the Japanese officers and NCOs did not control their subordinates. This was particularly true of the lowest form of life in the Japanese hierarchy, the Korean guards, who were despised by the Japanese themselves and hated and feared by the POWs. The unit of POW camp guards, numbering 3,000 Korean and Taiwanese youths, was raised in June 1942, just after the order for the railway project was issued. The guards were classed as civilian auxiliaries of the IJA, with an initial contract for two years. As there were quotas for districts, they were in effect conscripted. During their two months' training at Pusan, they were grounded in the ethos of the IJA and given elementary training in fieldwork and weaponry. At his post-war trial, Kim Chang Sik stated that 'it was not actually taught at the school that we could beat prisoners of war, but we were told that we should not be too soft with them as otherwise they would not respect us'.[42]

Languages did not form part of the tuition. The great majority of these Korean guards were teenage peasants; older ones were clerks or merchants. Two of the most notorious Koreans of POW Group IV were Hong Jong Mok (Tokuyama Mitsui), a barber by trade, and Cho Un Kuk (Kumoi Eiji), who had practised as a dentist in India until forced to leave in 1941. These circumstances had inculcated in the latter a hatred of the British which he expressed forcibly on the railway. Another guard gave evidence to the War Crimes Tribunal that, at Tarsao in 1943, Colonel Ishii empowered him to use force if necessary to get the POWs 'to do their best'.[43] At some of the smaller camps, Korean guards were in sole charge of the POWs. Not atypical was a guard named Kim Yong (Motoyama Kinzō), who oversaw a satellite camp of Tarsao in early 1943, and who had 'a ferocious temper and on the slightest pretext hit out at prisoners with bamboo poles or with his belt'.[44] Similarly, there was Ch'en Kwang-In (Chiba Kōrin) at Tonchan

Bridge camp, who ordered the sick to parade for work, belabouring those who were physically unable to comply and exacting fearful revenge on Captain John Rae (Singapore Royal Artillery) when he complained of this disgraceful behaviour to the Japanese.[45]

The average POW had more day-to-day experience of the Korean guards than he did of the Japanese officers, and the guards were in any case far more numerous. Perhaps this has given the Koreans an unduly prominent place in the demonology of the railway. When Tanaka, for instance, refused to allow the POWs to extend their hospital, his decision would have been known only to the Allied POW administrators in the camp, whereas the Koreans' misdemeanours were familiar and obvious to all personnel. There are many examples of Koreans who did give assistance to the POWs, demonstrating that this lay within their power. But there is very little evidence to mitigate the evil reputation of the Koreans as a group.

The medical section of the POW Administration was negligible, and most clearly reflected the Japanese contempt for physical frailty. From August 1942 until the surrender there were three successive medical officers at headquarters with the rank of captain or major, and 'medical conferences' were held by them for all Japanese medical personnel on the railway in January, March and October 1943, October 1944, and January and June 1945. Lieutenant Muraoka Shiegeo, the medical officer of POW Group IV, had qualified as a doctor in 1935; but his job on the railway was, he said, solely 'to forward opinions concerning the sanitary conditions'.[46] The Senior British Officer of this group reckoned that Muraoka was the most tolerable Japanese that he encountered on the railway, more doctor than soldier, but a lone wolf in that there was no effectual medical chain of command in the POW Administration. Certainly, during the cholera epidemic at Tonchan South in June 1943, the Japanese managed one half-pint bottle of lysol and two waterlogged sacks of chlorate of lime for a camp of 2,500 POWs placed near a large concentration of Asian labourers. The POWs also noted the wide apron of lime around each of the Japanese huts.[47]

In POW Group II, the senior Japanese medical officer (from January 1943) was Lieutenant Nobusawa Hisashi, who claimed to be a paediatrician but evinced no clinical experience, though he once surprised the POW medical officers by citing the Latin name for yaws. Nobusawa was called up in September 1941 and served in French Indo-China before being posted to Thailand. Lieutenant-Colonel H. C. Owtram described him as 'consciously callous'. As a group medical officer based initially at Chungkai, Nobusawa had under him Warrant Officer Eda Asaichi, who had received only five months' medical training when he joined the IJA in 1930, two sergeants, and six medical orderlies. In

Burma, the POWs fared no better. Major W. E. Fisher (AAMC) remarked that 'we rarely saw any Japanese practice far removed from the level of witch-doctoring'. He also noted that Lieutenant Higuchi Tomizō, who as senior medical officer was in charge of the health of approximately 15,000 men, revealed no knowledge of medicine. Perhaps not surprisingly, 'a personal appeal from one medical man to another', sent to him by Lieutenant-Colonel Hamilton (AAMC), remained unanswered.[48]

III

Approximately 64,000 Allied POWs worked on the Burma–Thailand Railway, and of these, more than half were British.[49] They were a far more diverse collection of men than the other national groups – American, Australian and Dutch. They belonged either to the Indian Army, the Regular Army, the Territorial Army, the Royal Air Force or the local Volunteer Forces. The largest contingent was the 18th Division, an East Anglian Territorial Army formation with significant additions from the North (9th Btn Northumberland Fusiliers) and the Midlands (1/5th Btn Sherwood Foresters), which had arrived just before the surrender of Singapore. Most of the Regular Army units, such as the 1st Btn Manchester Regiment, 2nd Btn Gordon Highlanders, 2nd Btn Argyll and Sutherland Highlanders, and 2nd Btn The Loyal Regiment, had been stationed in the Far East for some years and were well acclimatized. Indeed, some 200 other ranks of the Manchesters had not returned to England since the battalion left for service overseas in 1934. A large number of British officers went into captivity without their troops, including the Indian Army officers of more than thirty units that had fought in Malaya, and the officers of the three regiments of the Hong Kong and Singapore Royal Artillery, whose troops were Indians, and who were immediately removed by the Japanese in Singapore. The Anglo-Indian officers, and the Anglo-Indians of the Indian Medical Department, were sent with the British into Changi. Of the Volunteer Forces, the Chinese and Malay troops had been disbanded before the surrender, and the expatriates – British, New Zealand and Australian – went to Changi, as did one company of Singapore Eurasians, on the recommendation of their senior officer, Captain C. B. Webb, whose foresight almost certainly saved them from massacre. It is therefore unsafe to employ popular national stereotypes when writing of British POWs on the railway: the men involved came from a wide variety of military units and backgrounds.[50] The same was true of the Dutch, who, brought from the Netherlands East Indies, fell into three main groups. First, there were the Hollanders, born and raised in the Netherlands, who were serving in the Netherlands East Indies (NEI) as government officials, planters, miners and businessmen. Secondly, there were those who had been born in the NEI and either remained there or had spent some time in the Netherlands at college or university before returning to the colonies. Finally, there were the so-called *indische jongen*, those of mixed race. Only the Americans could really be described as a cohesive group. Numbering just under 700, they consisted of men from the 131st Field Artillery, a Texan unit captured in Java, and survivors from the USS *Houston* and an army transport vessel, the MS *Sawokla*.

The Japanese gave strict instructions to the Allied commands in Changi to make up labour battalions of between 500 and 600 POWs, but placed severe limits on the number of officers to accompany them. This presented particular difficulties to the British, who decided to divide up units, retaining in Singapore for as long as possible the nucleus of a fighting force. Thus the Japanese-designated 'B' Battalion (549 POWs), which left Changi for the railway in November 1942 under the command of Lieutenant-Colonel Lilly (Commanding Officer 1/5th Btn Sherwood Foresters), comprised:

Officers (including medical officer)	22
Other Ranks: Sherwood Foresters	275
1st Cambridgeshires	62
5th Bedfords	70
4th Suffolks	45
9th Northumberland Fus.	54
RAMC	6
Miscellaneous units	15[51]

Although all these men belonged to the 18th Division, and had more in common with each other than with the troops of Regular Army units, this was still a very mixed bag. The Australians, having fewer units, were not obliged to break them up. Indeed the two largest Australian contingents leaving Changi, 'A' Force and part of 'F' Force, kept two infantry brigades more or less intact. To take one Australian battalion as an example:

2/19th Btn Personnel leaving Changi:	'A'Force	144
	'D'Force	321
	'F'Force	38
	'H'Force	35

As Captain R. W. Newton commented, 'we were fortunate that the bulk of the unit kept together in the various "Forces" under the command and leadership of our well tried, senior officers'.[52]

The ratio of officers to men in the Australian labour battalions was much lower than in the British. When the Australians of 'D' Force left Changi for Thailand in March 1943, there were only 29 officers to over 2,000 other ranks. Furthermore, the 2/3rd Machine Gun Battalion AIF sailed from Java to Singapore, leaving behind most of their officers, a factor which was to prove a significant disadvantage on the railway.[53] The British, however, had a large surplus of officers in their lines, so that two entire battalions, each comprising approximately 400 officers, left Changi for Thailand at the end of 1942. These variations had a considerable effect on officer POW life on the railway. Unlike the British, the Australian officers, being so comparatively few in number, were not called upon to do manual labour, camp administration and the supervision of work parties occupying their time.[54] British officers began in similar fashion, but in a series of showdowns with the Japanese up and down the railway, in some cases at gunpoint, they were forced to form themselves into labour gangs. By the beginning of 1943, *all* British officers below field rank, with the exceptions of a small staff to administer each camp, medical officers and the elderly and infirm, were labouring on the track. At Chungkai, the officers made up a labour battalion numbering 200, and at Tarsao, the 100 Indian Army officers accepted the concept of officers' work parties in return for an (unfulfilled) promise from Tanaka, the Japanese adjutant, to give aid to the sick.[55]

The large number of British officers had one unforeseen but crucial effect on POW life. Without their funds, the group and base hospitals in Thailand would have been unable to function as they did. Finances were a problem from the earliest days at Changi, and for much of 1942 the POW battalion commanders were dependent on the resources they had taken with them into captivity. When each battalion left Changi for Burma or Thailand, the commanding officer drew on these; but changing money into local currency – rupees or ticals – was difficult. Senior Representative Donald Murchison, acting on behalf of the Australian Red Cross Society, arrived in Burma with 750 Straits dollars, which he found impossible to convert, though the Japanese allowed him an advance of 200 rupees, which constituted the sole Red Cross resource through two dysentery epidemics.[56]

These financial pressures were to some extent alleviated by a Japanese decision of August 1942 that officers would be paid at IJA rates in the appropriate local currency. This unexpected provision clearly reflected Article 23 of the Geneva Convention, which directed that 'officers ... who are prisoners of war shall receive from the detaining Power the same pay as officers of corresponding rank in the armed forces of that Power'. By the end of 1942, all officers were paid, at least in theory, on a sliding scale ranging from the equivalent of 220 Straits dollars for lieutenant-colonels down to eighty-five for lieutenants. In practice, the Japanese handed over only a fraction of these sums. One part was retained in lieu of lodging, food and clothes – the so-called 'rent, rice and rags' deduction – and another was placed on deposit with the Yokohama Specie Bank, allegedly for repayment after the war. For reasons that remain obscure, officers in Burma were better paid than those in Thailand. While there were far fewer of them, this is unlikely to have been the sole reason for the discrepancy.[57]

Officers, regardless of the state of their health, received regular pay (except for some in certain isolated forces whose pay was sometimes delayed). This gave them a great advantage over the other ranks, who were paid a mere pittance by the Japanese if they worked on the railway itself, or as authorized camp staff, but were given nothing if sick. Initially, a working private soldier received in canteen money the equivalent of 10 cents a day (the price of one egg in the jungle camps in 1942, or two eggs at base). From February 1943, the rate was 40 cents for warrant officers, 30 cents for NCOs and 25 cents for privates. Thus at Tonchan South in June of that year, a private soldier could afford one egg and four cigarettes a day *if* he was working.[58] In most camps a levy system operated to provide money for the hospital and for extra food such as eggs and fruit, and a typical contribution by a private soldier in Thailand between 1942 and 1943 was two days' pay out of thirty.[59] As duck eggs were such a rich source of protein, vitamins and fat, all in pitifully short supply on the railway, the extent of the officers' advantage over the other ranks in having money to buy them in quantity, at least when they were available, is obvious.

In Burma, Brigadier A. L. Varley (2/18th Btn AIF), in command of Group III, laid down that officers should contribute all pay in excess of 20 rupees per month to the common purse. From January 1943, between 7,000 and 8,000 rupees were made available monthly for the camps in Burma for the purchase of extra food for other ranks and the sick, and for what little was available in the way of medical supplies. (A typical fortnight's issue by the Japanese of bandages for a POW hospital of 1,000 patients was six two-inch rolls.) But Group III was fortunate to have a brigadier in command, for Varley had left Changi before the Japanese decided to remove all officers over the rank of lieutenant-colonel to Formosa. Among the British officers in Thailand there was a plethora of lieutenant-colonels, some of who ranked in seniority above the (Japanese-appointed) group and camp commanders.

Thus if one senior lieutenant-colonel refused to contribute to a common purse, this refusal had to be accepted by the others. In Thailand, for instance, when the jungle camps based on Tarsao (POW Group IV) were formed in November 1942, there was an uneven distribution of officers. A suggestion that all officers' subscriptions should be equalized and a pool fund formed to pay for the group hospital at Tarsao was turned down by the senior officer at Kanyu, who at that time had the larger income.[60] As he was a senior Regular Army officer, his decision was final. Although there were notorious examples of selfishness among the officers, this attitude was rare in the Territorial Army, with its strong paternalistic tradition. Largely through officers' subscriptions, Territorial Army lieutenant-colonels such as Philip Toosey at Tamarkan and Cary Owtram at Chungkai, were able to finance the hospitals at the base camps in Thailand to which all POWs were withdrawn after the completion of the railway. In October 1943, the hospital at Chungkai, for example, received its 10,000th patient.[61] Although there were other sources of funding, including profits from canteens and other enterprises, the officers' pay remained the most dependable source of revenue, in spite of its purchasing power being gradually eroded by inflation.

IV

The response to Japanese attitudes was handled with widely varying degrees of success by individual Allied camp commanders. The qualities needed began with endless patience, calm authority and the ability to ignore the humiliations heaped upon the officers by the lowliest camp guards. It was necessary 'to negotiate, procrastinate, plead [and] haggle' as one of the interpreters explained. Those who could do so won many concessions, not least the limitation of Japanese interference in the running of a camp.[62] Nevertheless, mental adjustments had to be made, and these took time, although the Japanese contempt for the act of surrendering was immediately apparent. The POWs were in the hands of an unknown enemy, alien in 'thought, word and deed'. It was, for instance, a profound shock to the Allied officers, soon after their arrival in Burma in May 1942, when eight POWs were executed for attempting to escape. Although Lieutenant-General Uemura's parole forms were not presented for signature until the POW Administration took over later in the year, the standing orders at Changi at the end of March had made it clear that punishment for infringing Japanese orders would be imposed 'without mercy'. The POWs in Burma were initially in the charge of front-line troops, and the Japanese in command of the firing squad, Lieutenant Shiina Hirayasu (Imperial Guards) dismissed with contempt the arguments advanced by Brigadier Varley and

Lieutenant-Colonel C. G. W. Anderson about the illegality and inhumanity of the execution. That a Japanese officer, a graduate of an élite military academy, could refuse to allow Varley and the chaplain, Captain F. H. Bashford, to speak with the condemned men except, as Shiina cynically suggested, 'after death', was a savage introduction to POW life under the IJA.[63]

Japanese efforts to undermine the authority of officer POWs had some success in the months following the surrender, when many junior officers and other ranks were highly critical of the conduct of the campaign. But in Burma and Thailand the punishments and humiliations inflicted by the Japanese on officer POWs such as camp commanders, officers in charge of work parties or medical officers endeavouring to protect the sick angered the rank-and-file POWs, some of whom became more sympathetic to the plight of their superiors.

The policy of 'limited co-operation' with the enemy, adopted by the most resourceful of the camp commanders as the only conceivable way of ensuring the survival of as many POWs as possible, did not find favour with every Allied officer. The dividing line between co-operation and collaboration was narrow, and appointment to the position of POW camp commander was generally made by the Japanese without regard to seniority. Owtram wrote in his diary shortly after taking over at Chungkai in July 1943: 'The whole system is Gilbertian. Here I am, a very junior Colonel, commanding 500 officers (who include 18 Lt. Cols.) and over 4,000 troops, endeavouring to run the show on British methods and according to King's Regulations and yet completely subject to the whims of one 2nd. Lt., 3 Sgts., and a handful of privates!'[64] Lieutenant-Colonel A. E. Knights, who was a camp commander in Thailand longer than any other British officer, thought of himself at Tarsao as 'a kind of Aunt Sally stuck up in the middle of No-man's land and fired at from both sides'. Knights was not, in fact, the senior officer at Tarsao, but had been selected as camp commander in November 1942 simply because of his capacity to impress Lieutenant Tanaka. Having brought his column of 600 men over seventy-five kilometres on foot from Kanchanaburi, Knights halted the main body outside the camp to wait for the stragglers to catch up. He then marched them into the camp with what Tanaka approved as considerable panache. From then until March 1943, when Tanaka left Tarsao for Kinsayok, all Knights's considerable ingenuity was spent in trying to cajole or outwit Tanaka, 'to box cleverly', as he himself expressed it. Discussions served only to highlight the mental gulf between captor and captive. To any request for assistance, Tanaka would reply that the POWs should remember their degraded position and their unwillingness to accept suffering and death. Humane feelings, he insisted, had no place in war.[65]

One of the most distasteful aspects of being a camp commander was the fraternization demanded from time to time by the Japanese. Knights was relieved that he received a summons to drink gin with Tanaka on only one occasion. Conversely, Lilly decided that the games of bridge he played with Hattori at Wampo long into the night contributed considerably to harmonious relations. Owtram was ordered to attend Lieutenant Osata Yoshio's dinner parties at Chungkai, and even to play poker with him; but Owtram was in no doubt that all the concessions he gained from the Japanese adjutant, such as food, medical supplies and an increase in paid jobs around the camp, stemmed directly from these contacts. At the end of June 1943, Owtram remarked in his diary: '[Osata] and I have now been associated for just over a year and as far as one can be on good terms with one's enemies, we are.'[66]

When Lieutenant Hosoda Yoshitarō took over the camp at Tanyin he arranged a party, commandeering what remained of the Australian orchestra and demanding that Lieutenant-Colonel Anderson and Lieutenant-Colonel J. M. Williams (2/2nd Pioneer Btn AIF) attend and drink brandy. By this time, the 'coolly imaginative' Colonel Anderson had studied his foe and did his utmost to turn the occasion to his advantage. Anderson, according to the interpreter who was with him for much of the three and a half years in captivity, was 'expert at the kind of verbal bridge where your opponent holds all the coloured cards, and you have a few twos and threes'. His manipulative approach to the Japanese was favourably compared with the sometimes 'damagingly blunt' style of Brigadier Varley and the 'obstructionist attitude' of Lieutenant-Colonel Williams 'which only brought more trouble than it prevented'.[67]

In the course of 1944 there was a perceptible change in the attitude of many of the Japanese and Koreans towards the POWs. At the hospital camp at Nakhon Pathom, built by the Japanese as a result of increasing international pressure but not supplied with medical equipment or drugs, Major Fisher was appalled to re-encounter Higuchi, the medical officer in Burma. The arrogance had disappeared; the Allied medical officers were invited to sit down at interviews and offered cigarettes. As a result, Fisher found it hard to convince his colleagues that the now obsequious Higuchi was the same man who had reviewed 900 sick men in ninety minutes at a work parade and had been unmoved by his visit to the dysentery hut at Thanbyuzayat.[68] In June, the Japanese made a unique formal announcement at all POW camps that an Allied landing had been made in France, promoting 'a wonderful air of confidence and cheerfulness'. Regimental Quarter-Master Sergeant J. K. Gale (Singapore Royal Artillery) noted the beneficial effect this had on the Korean Kim Yong, who began to express his resentment at the manner in which

Japanese officers such as Lieutenant Usuki had behaved towards him. A high-ranking Japanese officer made an inspection that was more than routine. In September, a protest made at Tamuang over men being forced to load munitions was heeded, and the order rescinded.[69] But men still starved, medical supplies were delayed, and the POWs were used as human shields to protect the railway installations at Nong Pladuk and the bridge at Tamarkan from Allied bombing. In January 1945, the Japanese separated the officers and men. At Tarsao during the construction of the railway, Knights had mused on the inexplicable manner in which the Japanese abused their workforce. Mechanically literate himself, he estimated that had the building of the railway been competently organized, particularly with regard to the health of the POWs, the casualty rate would have been reduced by three-quarters, yet the work completed in the same amount of time. As it was, over 12,000 POWs died.

V

In conclusion, it seems clear that, in the existing literature on the Burma–Thailand Railway, too much attention has been given to a relatively narrow range of sources. These have tended to become the classic stories against which all other experiences have been measured. Yet the POW experience on the railway was far from homogeneous, either between nationalities, between ranks, between camps or even within the same camps over a period of time. Moreover, the 'popular' sources have tended to ignore or play down the role of the Allied officers and their relationships with the Japanese captors; yet a reading of the available sources demonstrates the importance of the personalities involved. The attitudes of both Allied and Japanese commanders, and their relationships, were crucial factors in explaining the differences between one camp and another. This, combined with a better understanding of the origins and structures of the Japanese POW Administration, goes a long way to providing a more coherent picture of the history of the POWs on the railway. Conversely, there are many questions about Japanese behaviour that remain unanswered. Lieutenant-Colonel Knights could see no efficiency in the Japanese attitude to the POW workforce, and, even after fifty years, no one has produced a satisfactory explanation of precisely why, on at least one occasion, the Japanese sent POWs into the virgin jungle during the monsoon season, without medical supplies or cooking equipment, to build a camp for a thousand men with two axes, two billhooks, one pick and a broken shovel.[70] Until all these questions are answered, the Burma–Thailand Railway will remain a subject for scholarly attention, both in its own right, and as part of the wider history of POWs in the Pacific theatre during the Second World War.

Notes

1. Correspondence, Lieutenant-Colonel W. A. D. Innes (report) and Lieutenant-Colonel W. D. H. Duke MC (letter) with Collins, Publishers, London, January–February 1962, in the possession of Lieutenant-Colonel Duke.
2. For information on Duncan, Scottish Far Eastern POW Association (Welfare Officer), who established the fact that Duncan was never a POW of the Japanese.
3. E. E. Dunlop, *The War Diaries of Weary Dunlop*, Wheathampstead, 1987.
4. Ibid., xv.
5. Ibid., p. 284.
6. Roy Mills, *Doctor's Diary and Memoirs*, New Lambton, 1994.
7. Rowley Richards and Marcia McEwan, *The Survival Factor*, Kenthurst, 1989.
8. Robert Hardie, *The Burma–Siam Railway: The Secret Diary of Dr. Robert Hardie 1942–45*, London, 1983. Examples of Volunteers' diaries can be found at the Imperial War Museum, London. See those of J. K. Gale, C. H. Lee and J. T. Rea.
9. John T. Barnard, *The Endless Years*, London, 1950; Stan Arneil, *One Man's War*, Sydney, 1980.
10. R. J. P. Garden to Reverend Gerard Bourke, *c*.1980 (in the possession of R. J. P. Garden).
11. Arneil, *One Man's War* (see Note 9 above), p. 3.
12. Dr S. S. Pavillard, *Bamboo Doctor* London, 1960; PRO, War Office Papers (hereafter WO), WO 32/14551, report by Pavillard, 1945; Albert Coates and Newman Rosenthal, *The Albert Coates Story*, Melbourne, 1980; Albert Coates Papers, Australian War Memorial (hereafter AWM), PR 89/186; PRO WO 235/964, fos. 591–5, testimony of Lieutenant-Colonel A. E. Coates to Australian War Crimes Board of Inquiry, 29 Oct. 1945; R. John Pritchard and Sonia M. Zaide (eds), *The Tokyo War Crimes Trials: The Complete Transcripts of the Proceedings of the International Military Tribunal for the Far East*, New York, 1981, vol. 5, pp. 11,403–16, 11,425–49, 11,449–55, 11,458–526.
13. Cornel Lumière (pseud. Cornelius Dirk Punt), *Kura!*, Brisbane, 1966.
14. William Mortimer Drower, *Our Man on the Hill: A British Diplomat Remembers*, Berkeley, 1993.
15. See, for example, 'The Liberty of the Prison', *Yale Review*, vol. 44, 1956, pp. 514–32.

16. Chaim Nussbaum, *Chaplain on the River Kwai*, New York, 1988, p. 272.
17. Reginald Burton, *The Road to Three Pagodas*, London, 1963.
18. E. R. 'Bon' Hall, *The Burma–Thailand Railway of Death*, Armidale, 1981; Don Wall, *Heroes of F Force*, Mona Vale, 1993.
19. Hank Nelson, *Prisoners of War: Australians under Nippon*, Sydney, 1985.
20. Robert S. La Forte and Ronald E. Marcello (eds), *Building the Death Railway: The Ordeal of American POWs in Burma, 1942–45*, Wilmington, 1993.
21. James Bradley, *Cyril Wild: The Tall Man Who Never Slept*, Fontwell, 1991; Peter N. Davies, *The Man Behind the Bridge: Colonel Toosey and the River Kwai*, London, 1991; Sue Ebury, *Weary, The Life of Sir Edward Dunlop*, Ringwood, 1994.
22. Of special note is the invaluable compendium assembled by Captain David Nelson (Singapore Volunteer Corps and HQ Malaya Command) during the time he served with the Bureau of Record and Enquiry in Changi, and published under the title *The Story of Changi*, West Perth, 1974. Nelson lists the groups leaving Changi for the railway and much else of interest. For the most recent interpretative essays, see Gavan McCormack and Hank Nelson (eds), *The Burma–Thailand Railway: Memory and History*, St Leonards, 1993. This includes three essays by members of the Japanese research group on the railway, Murai Yoshinori and Aiko Utsumi.
23. These drafts can be found in PRO, Cabinet Office Papers, CAB 101/199.
24. C. C. Brett, 'The Burma–Siam Railway', historical bulletin published by the South-East Asia Translation and Investigation Centre, no. 246, 8 Oct. 1946.
25. An edition containing selected proceedings of the British Military Courts in the Far East is being prepared for publication.
26. Aiko Utsumi, 'Prisoners of War in the Pacific War: Japan's Policy', in McCormack and Nelson (eds), *Burma–Thailand Railway* (see Note 22 above), p. 73.
27. PRO, WO 325/121, *Laws, Rules and Regulations pertaining to Prisoners of War*, translated from the Japanese by Legal Section, GHQ, Supreme Commander for the Allied Powers, 1946.
28. *Report of the International Committee of the Red Cross on its Activities during the Second World War*, vol. 1, *General Activities*, Geneva, 1948, p. 446.
29. PRO, WO 235/1109, fo. 22, evidence of Lieutenant-Colonel Yanagita Shōichi to Military Court, Singapore, 21 Jan. 1947.

30. Interrogation of Lieutenant-Colonel Nagatomo, Australian Archives, Canberra (hereafter AA), CRS A471/1, item 81655, by Colonel C. H. D. Wild, Changi Jail, Singapore, 11 May 1946. Also Pritchard and Zaide, *War Crimes Transcripts*, vol. 22, pp. 49–52, 136–7, 142–3; PRO, WO 235/1109, fos. 22, 23, 26, Yanagita testimony, 21 Jan. 1947.

31. PRO, WO 235/963, fo. 290, testimony of Colonel Nakamura Shigeo to Military Court, Singapore, 12 Nov. 1946.

32. AA, CRS A471/1, item 81655, part 1, fo. 41, testimony of Lieutenant-Colonel Nagatomo to Australian Military Court, Singapore, 8 Aug. – 16 Sept. 1946.

33. Lumière, *Kura!* (see Note 13 above), p. 65; AWM 3 DRL/2691, Brigadier A. L. Varley, typescript diary, June 1942.

34. AA, CRS A471/1, item 81655, part 1, fo. 42, Nagatomo testimony.

35. PRO, WO 235/822, *passim*.

36. Lieutenant-Colonel A. E. Knights, *Reminiscences of a Camp Commander*, typescript memoirs, Royal Norfolk Regiment Museum, Norwich.

37. IWM 67/142/1, typescript diaries J. T. Rea; IWM 82/32/1, J. K. Gale, typescript diary and memoirs; IWM PP/MCR/249, P. H. Romney, typescript memoirs.

38. IWM, Romney memoirs, 23 June 1943.

39. R. W. Newton, *The Grim Glory of the 2/19th Battalion AIF*, Sydney, 1975, p. 588.

40. PRO, WO 235/963, statement by Lieutenant-Colonel H. H. Lilly, 31 Jan. 1945.

41. Davies, *Man Behind the Bridge* (see Note 21 above), pp. 99–100, 102, 205; also information concerning Saito obtained from E. R. Sherring.

42. AA, CRS A471/1, item 81641, evidence of Chang Kim Sik (Kaneshiro Masao); Yi Hak-Nae, 'The man between: a Korean Guard looks back' and crucially, Aiko Utsumi, 'The Korean Guards on the Burma–Thailand Railway' both in McCormack and Nelson (eds), *Burma–Thailand Railway* (see Note 22 above), pp. 120–6, 127–39.

43. PRO, WO 235/918, fo. 480, sworn statement of Choi Muang San (Matsumoto Meizan), Bankwang Gaol, near Bangkok, 14 Mar. 1946.

44. Ibid., fo. 102, affidavit signed by Gunner James Davie, 9th Coast Regiment, RA, 31 Mar. 1946.

45. Colonel H. J. Rae, diary and papers (a copy in the author's possession); also Rae's statement, AA, CRS A471/1, item 81242; IWM, Gale diary, pp. 132–3, 135, 137–8.

46. PRO, WO 235/957, testimony of Muraoka Shiegeo to Military Court, Singapore, 17 June 1946.
47. Knights, *Reminiscences* (see Note 36 above); IWM, Gale diary, 12 June 1943.
48. AWM 54, item 554/2/7, typescript, W. E. Fisher, 'Medical Experiences', pp. 40–1.
49. An American POW, J. C. Reas (USN) was summoned to the POW Administration HQ at Kanchanaburi on 28 Nov. 1944 and ordered to type the complete nominal roll of all POWs who had been employed on the railway. The figure of 64,000 included 'F' and 'H' Forces, PRO, WO 235/964, fo. 868.
50. Gavan Daws, *Prisoners of the Japanese*, New York, 1994. The list of source material is impressive, but many of the facts and opinions in the text relating to the railway (pp. 183–251) are apparently based solely on oral evidence gathered in the period 1982–93.
51. 'B' Battalion Records, in the possession of Captain J. S. Cook, 1st Btn Cambridgeshire Regiment.
52. Newton, *Grim Glory* (see Note 39 above), pp. 389 and 401.
53. AWM 54, item 554/2/1, Brigadier C. A. McEachern, report on Burma and Siam 1942–1945. Information about 2/3rd MG Btn AIF from R. Allanson.
54. For a discussion of Australian officers and work on the railway, see Joan Beaumont, 'Rank, Privilege and Prisoners-of-War', *War and Society*, vol. 1, 1983, pp. 67–94. Exceptionally, most of the Australian officers in 'H' Force were required to do manual labour.
55. Knights, *Reminiscences* (see Note 36 above).
56. AWM 54, item 554/2/7, Fisher typescript, 'Medical Experiences', p. 46.
57. Hall, *Burma–Thailand Railway* (see Note 18 above), p. 63; IWM 66/222/1, Lieutenant-Colonel H. C. Owtram, diary entry, 20 Jan. 1943.
58. IWM, Gale diary, p. 120.
59. IWM, Rea diary, p. 95.
60. Weary Dunlop Papers, memo by Lieutenant-Colonel D. R. Thomas to Lieutenant-Colonel E. E. Dunlop, Tarsao, 31 May 1943. Access to these papers was courtesy of Sue Ebury.
61. IWM, Owtram diary, 20 Dec. 1943.
62. Drower, *Our Man on the Hill* (see Note 14 above), p. 67.
63. AA, CRS A471/1, item 81655, Lieutenant-Colonel C. G. W. Anderson, report, part 4, p, 2 and Captain F. H. Bashford, affidavit, part 5, p. 32; Varley describes the incident in his diary as well.
64. IWM, Owtram diary, 11 July 1943.
65. Knights, *Reminiscences* (see Note 36 above).

66. IWM, Owtram diary, 25 June 1943.
67. Drower, *Our Man on the Hill* (see Note 14 above), p. 67; Richards and McEwan, *The Survival Factor* (see Note 7 above), pp. 124–5.
68. Fisher, 'Medical Experiences' (see Note 56 above), pp. 41–2.
69. IWM, Gale diary, pp. 186, 188–9, 191; PRO, WO 235/918, fo. 50, evidence of J. K. Gale to Military Court, Singapore, 13 Aug. 1946; IWM 86/35/1, E. W. Markham, narrative typescript, 1946, p. 106.
70. Knights, *Reminiscences* (see Note 36 above); IWM, Gale diary, p. 25. The camp was Kanyu 3.

10

From Consideration to Contempt: The Changing Nature of Japanese Military and Popular Perceptions of Prisoners of War Through the Ages

Ikuhiko Hata

From the Old Testament to the Field Service Code

In the history of prisoners of war (POWs) the earliest written record is the Psalmist's 'By the waters of Babylon we sat down and wept: when we remembered thee, O Sion.' There he set down the feelings and yearning for their native land of some thousands of Israelites captured and taken into exile in the sixth century BC. These were fortunate: after sixty years their prayers were answered and they returned to Israel. But the lot of POWs from antiquity until quite recent times was bitter. Their fate – death, slavery, or ransom – lay in the hands of the victorious general, who wielded the power of life or death. It was only in the nineteenth century that the practice of recognizing and protecting the human rights of POWs emerged – as part of international law acknowledged by advanced nations – in the Lieber Code of the US Army (1863), the Geneva Convention of 1864, the Brussels Declaration (1874) and the Hague Conventions dealing with land warfare (1899 and 1907). This was roughly at the same time as Japan first emerged on the world scene.

The Meiji leaders who pressed ahead with building the modern state in Japan were enthusiastic in their adoption of the legal systems of the advanced countries of Europe and the United States. They sought to secure recognition as a civilized nation by introducing international law, almost in direct translation, and affording it strict enforcement. The Geneva Convention and the Brussels Declaration were translated and introduced with singular dispatch; and Japan participated at the second Hague Conference and signed and ratified the instruments that emerged from it. Although the provisions in both relating to POWs subsequently took on a separate existence in the 1929 Geneva Convention, their essentials remained almost unchanged, namely:

1. POWs are in the power of the hostile government, but not of the individuals or corps who captured them.
2. They must be treated humanely and, as regards rations, quarters and clothing, on the same footing as the troops of the government which captured them.
3. The state may employ the labour of POWs, other than officers; but the work shall not be excessive, shall have no connection with the operations of war, and shall be paid for.
4. Their right to escape shall be recognized.
5. They may be set at liberty on parole if the laws of their country allow it.
6. Each belligerent shall establish a POW Information Bureau to receive from each of the armed services full information about POWs and to reply to all questions about them.[1]

Japan gained a good reputation internationally by faithfully carrying out these obligations – in the Sino-Japanese war (1894–5) according to the Brussels Declaration, in the Russo-Japanese war (1904–5) according to the first Hague Convention (1899), and in the First World War according to the second Hague Convention (1907). She did not, however, adopt the 1929 Geneva Convention. Among the reasons given for this was the following: 'Although to be taken prisoner is contrary to the ideology of the Japanese serviceman, those of foreign nations may think differently. Accordingly, although this Convention in form appears to impose reciprocal obligations, in actual fact it would impose duties only on us.'[2] When, immediately following Japan's entry into the Second World War, the United States and British Commonwealth governments raised the question of the applicability of the 1929 Geneva Convention, Foreign Minister Tōgō replied that Japan, although not bound by the Convention, would apply its provisions *mutatis mutandis*.[3] As a result, many Japanese were tried by 'B' and 'C' Class war crimes tribunals for violations of the 1929 Geneva Convention and sentenced to death or imprisonment. These tribunals, however, did not deal with violations where the victims were Japanese POWs.

From the above we can deduce that in the interval between the Russo-Japanese war and 1929 a change had taken place in the attitude of the Japanese government to the legitimacy of any of its own troops' accepting capture. This was not embodied in any legislation or formal declaration. It did, however, ultimately receive formal expression in the *Senjinkun* or Field Service Code issued by the Minister for the Army.

This received Royal Assent on 8 January 1941. The relevant article reads: 'You shall not undergo the shame of being taken alive. You shall not bequeath a sullied name.' From the outset, the authority and interpretation of this precept was the subject of dispute. It was addressed to the Army only, and not to the Navy. And even within the Army there were those who argued that it was contrary to the precepts of the Imperial Rescript to Servicemen (1882), and hence invalid. In the short period of only four and a half years that were to elapse between its promulgation and the war's end this principle had not completely permeated Japan's armed forces. Be this as it may, one should nevertheless recognize that this idiosyncratic attitude of the Japanese Armed Forces towards being taken prisoner was in existence before the promulgation of the Field Service Code, and one should seek its origins earlier than the Russo-Japanese war.

Japanese POWs in the Pre-Modern Period

Thanks to her location as an island kingdom and the closure of the country under the Tokugawas, Japan in the thousand years preceding the Meiji Restoration of 1868 was engaged in large-scale military operations against a foreign enemy on only three occasions: the Kudara (Korean) Expedition (661–7); the Mongol Invasion (1274–81); and Hideyoshi's Korean Expeditions (1592–8). There were, accordingly, few occasions when Japanese were taken prisoner.

The first Japanese POW to be mentioned is Otomobe-no-Hakama, who was captured at the battle of Hakusukinoe (663), when the Korean armies routed those of Japan and Kudara. When he returned to Japan twenty-seven years later, he was rewarded with 30 rolls of cloth, 1,000 bales of rice and 4 chō (1 hectare) of arable land. Besides this, all that the *Nihon Shoki* (compiled in 720) tells us is that Hakama was a native of Tsukushi (the north-west of Kyūshū), and that some other prisoners had been repatriated before him.

There continues to be controversy among historians about the composition of the 2,000 people who arrived in Japan aboard 47 vessels from China late in 671. There is agreement that 600 of them were the entourage of envoys from China. It is about the remaining 1,400 that scholars differ. Some argue that they were refugees from Kudara, others that they were political conspirators, and others that they were Japanese POWs captured at Hakusukinoe. Among the last group is Professor Naoki, who remarks that the treatment accorded to Hakama indicates an attitude to captives quite different from what we have observed in post-Meiji Japan.[4]

In the Mongol invasion, when Tsushima was occupied, about a thousand Japanese were captured, but it seems that almost none of them were removed.[5] On the other hand, when the ships of the invading armies were sunk by a typhoon off Hakata, some of the survivors were taken into captivity and the rest were beheaded beside the Nagara River.

In Hideyoshi's Korean wars it appears from the Chronicles of the Yi Dynasty that from the beginning of the first expedition many of the troops (including a number of their commanders) went over to the enemy, fought alongside them, and settled there. And in Hideyoshi's second expedition, in which he lost 50,000 out of 300,000, many deserted in Korea and in Kyūshū.[6] Among the commanders that surrendered was one who, as Kim Chung-Son, became famous.[7] In these expeditions the Japanese captured many Koreans – some say 20,000, some say 50,000 – and took them to Japan. Many of them were potters, taken to introduce their skills into Japan. It is well known that the Japanese Arita and Satsuma pottery derives from them.

The Sino-Japanese War (1894–5)

This was the first war fought by the Japanese under the constraints of international law. Since this was one succession of Japanese victories, the number of Chinese prisoners captured was very large – 1,790 (in addition to 5,000 who surrendered at Wei-Hai-Wei and 600 in the Pescadores, all of whom were released in return for undertakings not to engage in further hostilities). Of these Chinese POWs, 1,545 were distributed among nine internment camps in Japan, most of which were Buddhist temples. About a hundred (including a Major-General and a Naval Captain) were at the Chōkenji at Matsuyama. There the POWs received the same pay and subsistence allowances as Japanese troops, and, although there was an external bamboo fence, their movements within the temple grounds were unrestricted. In addition, they were not required to do any work.[8]

When, four months after the Peace Treaty, the POWs of both countries were repatriated it was found that the Japanese numbered only eleven, of whom ten were middle-aged men from labour battalions. The other was an infantry private, Goda Aikichi, taken just before the armistice. He had been captured by a troop of Chinese cavalry while returning alone from dispatching a money order at a field post office.[9] When his divisional commander asked the Chinese military police what had become of the other prisoners captured by the Chinese, he received the following irresponsible reply: 'During the period since winter our forces captured about 70. Some escaped. Some were probably killed by the locals. We are encountering difficulties in our investigations . . . We don't speak their language . . .'.[10] Such difficulties must have continued; for in the statistics issued by the Japanese Ministry of the Army in 1902 the figure still stands at eleven.[11] In the regional armies of China at that time central authority was weak, communications were poor, and there was no concept of protecting prisoners. The outlying units had probably killed them out of hand.

The Russo-Japanese War (1904–5)[12]

In comparison with the Sino-Japanese war, the Russo-Japanese war was a bitter and costly struggle, with casualties and expenditure increasing tenfold. There were 2,000 Japanese and 80,000 Russian POWs. This was Japan's first experience of prisoners in such numbers, and it made a considerable impact. On the outbreak of hostilities the Japanese government established a POW Information Bureau in the Ministry of the Army and issued regulations prescribing humane treatment of prisoners.[13] The Russian prisoners were distributed among twenty-nine camps at Matsuyama and elsewhere. In fact, their good treatment was praised at an International Red Cross Conference by the renowned jurist, diplomat, international arbiter and former director of Russia's POW Information Bureau, F. F. Martens, who after the war addressed a letter of thanks to the Japanese government. Similarly, the Russians treated their Japanese prisoners well.

After their repatriation, the Japanese prisoners were interrogated by the military authorities but were not court-martialled. Most of the officers, however, had to quit the service. And when the prisoners returned to their homes, many were subjected to traditional village ostracism by their neighbours and had to move elsewhere. The military authorities, who for future wars were seeking to enshrine the experience of the Russo-Japanese war in a distinct, national strategic and tactical doctrine and code of behaviour different from that adopted from the West, chose to resort to public opinion – in their regiments and in their villages – to punish those who had allowed themselves to be taken prisoner.

At Medved, where the greater part of the Japanese prisoners were held, they performed no labour except cooking for themselves and maintaining their quarters. Moreover, they were at liberty to walk within the confines of the village. Nevertheless, their biggest problem was boredom, although the conditions were much the same for the Russian prisoners at Matsuyama (the latter were victualled at about twice the cost of Japanese troops, and were permitted to bathe at the nearby hot springs and use the brothels). The Russians allowed the Japanese POWs to administer themselves and maintain their existing rank structure, with Colonel Murakami, the highest-ranking prisoner, in command. As a result, discipline was maintained, and mutinies and escapes were virtually unknown.[14] This contrasts with the succession of riots and disturbances by Japanese POWs in the Pacific War of 1941–5. There, however, the attendant circumstances were different. At Medved the prisoners did not feel that they were regarded as criminals by the authorities at home; they were permitted to correspond with their families, and there was the prospect of being able to return home in the not too distant future. The prisoners at Cowra (Australia), Featherston (New Zealand) and Camp McCoy (USA), however, knew that by becoming POWs they had severed all links with their native land. From this could stem only hopelessness and desperation.

Let us examine how the military authorities dealt with these 2,000 repatriated in 1905. The Imperial Ordinance establishing the POW Information Bureau stipulated that 'when notification is received that a member has become a prisoner in enemy territory and the particulars regarding his name, rank, etc. have been confirmed, this shall be published, . . . and if requested, details shall be supplied to the next-of-kin'.[15] Throughout the war this was faithfully observed. As the names and personal details of the POWs were received, via the German Embassy, they were published in the official *Gazette* and in the newspapers. Similarly, when the returning Medved prisoners disembarked at Kobe in February 1906 the newspapers reported this in detail. On their journey home they had at Berlin received flowers and cigarettes from the German Emperor and Empress, and at Singapore the Japanese community (including the prostitutes) had turned out with flags and fired a salute to welcome them. After being met by their families at Kobe they proceeded by train, with a military escort, to Tokyo. At each station *en route* large crowds assembled and showered them with presents. At Hamamatsu they were greeted by a military band.

They were not, however, allowed to return to their homes until they had been examined by the military authorities. In the case of the Army the procedure for this had been laid down in Regulations for the Processing of Repatriated POWs issued on 5 July 1905. These provided that a Court of Inquiry should be convened in the member's unit, which should examine the circumstances of his capture (Article 3) and report to the Minister of the Army whether these were honourable or whether he should be court-martialled or incur administrative sanctions (Article 9). In the case of the other ranks, these inquiries were usually quite routine. For example, on 15 February 1905 the Court of Inquiry, which had convened in the Narashino Cavalry Brigade depot, reported after sitting for two hours that Corporal Ishibashi 'has in no way besmirched his honour as a soldier and should, accordingly, return to his unit forthwith'.[16] In the case of officers the inquiries were somewhat more rigorous. They were examined first by a unit, and then by a central Court of Inquiry presided over by a Major-General. In the case of Shiina Mitsuzō, who surrendered the *Kinshū Maru*, and a group of severely wounded officers and men (including Colonel Murakami) who surrendered at Mukden, its findings were that since they had not committed suicide they should be court-martialled.[17] The minister, however, after consultations with the Adjutant-General's department, decided that no specific offence in military law had been committed, and applied administrative sanctions instead. Colonel Murakami was placed on the Unattached List, and his military career thereby terminated. The reason why he was dealt with so lightly was probably that he had distinguished himself at Port Arthur in the bitter fighting on Hill 203. Among the other officers some were placed under house arrest, and a major and two captains received decorations. For example, Second-Lieutenant Koga, who was captured during a scouting foray behind the enemy lines but escaped after several hours and brought back important information, was mentioned in dispatches.[18] In short, the military authorities in conducting these inquiries focused their attention not on whether or not the subject had been taken prisoner, but rather on whether in the circumstances he had done everything that was possible. They bestowed praise and censure over a wide spectrum. No one was court-martialled.

On the Russian side, General A. M. Stessel, who surrendered at Port Arthur, and Admiral Z. P. Rozhestvenski, who was captured, severely wounded, after Tsushima, were both court-martialled. The former was sentenced to death (later commuted); the latter was acquitted. In comparison the Japanese were the more lenient. But among the Japanese military, hatred of the prisoner was on the rise, propelled by pride in victory and public opinion.

How were the 2,000 Japanese POWs treated when they returned to their homes? Among seamen of the blockading fleet captured at Port Arthur, one was fêted by a civic reception and invited to address the pupils at the local primary school. Another from the same district wrote: 'I was overcome with shame and as much as possible stayed at home to avoid meeting other people.'[19] In one village in Saitama prefecture, when a severely wounded soldier was captured his children were persecuted at school and his wife was told by village elders to move elsewhere. As a result, he abandoned his farm, moved to Tokyo and became a baker.[20] In another village the POW received from the local Servicemen's Auxiliary an illuminated letter of thanks with money enclosed.[21] Goda Aikichi, the only combat soldier captured in the Sino-Japanese War, died in Hokkaido on 30 July 1911. A native of Tokushima prefecture, he too was probably forced out of his village. It would appear that hostility to former POWs was strongest in the countryside, and that not a few fled to the cities or overseas to avoid further opprobrium.[22]

To determine when the shamefulness of capture became part of the samurai ethic is not easy. Hasegawa Shin cites numerous examples from the Kamakura era up to the civil war at the beginning of the Meiji era; but they are of great variety and there is no consistent pattern among them. One can say at the most that the fate of the prisoner was determined by the political environment and conditions under which the two sides fought.

It is well known that after the Battle of Hakodate (1869), Enomoto, the defeated general, though he had decided on death, was prevailed on to surrender by the new regime's army, and that within a few years he and other rebel leaders received amnesties and were given office in the new government. Similarly, in the Seinan War (1877), although Saigō's generals were put to the sword, the junior officers and the rank and file were spared. The aim of the new government was speedily to establish a modern state. In so doing it was necessary for it to bear no grudges and use the able men available. At the same time, the defeated rebels were straight away absorbed in the new nationalism.

When this new nationalism was faced with foreign wars before its physical war potential had been developed, it had to depend upon the martial spirit of the troops and the tactics of 'human bullets'. It was not by chance that an ideology that spurned surrender and capture emerged and developed in parallel with kamikaze-type tactics in the Japanese Army after the Sino-Japanese war, in the Russian Army after the October Revolution of 1917, and in the Chinese People's Army of Liberation after the Second World War.[23]

The lessons that the Japanese Army learnt from the Russo-Japanese war were that it was strong in attack but weak in defence, and that a withdrawal in which the commanders had been lost tended to develop into a rout in which many were taken prisoner. The Army manuals issued after the war, such as the *Tōsui Kōryō* (Elements of Command) and the *Hohei Sōten* (Infantry Manual), were introduced as promulgating distinctive Japanese tactics and rules of conduct in the field. They were full of devices to remedy the kind of weaknesses that have been described above.[24]

In both the Army and the Navy's criminal codes and disciplinary regulations there was at no time any explicit provision prohibiting or disparaging capture. Indeed, there was legislation in force that was premised on some Japanese being captured. For example, the *Daitōa Sensō Rikugun Kyūyō Rei* (Greater East Asia War, Army Pay Regulations) issued in August 1943 stipulate that the payment of war zone allowances shall be suspended for the period that the soldier is a POW. Such legislation remained in force throughout the Second World War. Similarly in the training manuals, although some provisions dealing with the welfare of POWs were removed, there were never any provisions that directly forbade being taken prisoner.

After the outbreak of hostilities in China in 1937, legislation was enacted enlarging the ambit of the offence of desertion and increasing the punishments for it, and there were cases where recovered prisoners were 'advised' to commit suicide. There was, however, no legal foundation for such 'advice'. Accordingly, when Vice-Admiral Fukudome and his party were captured by guerrillas in the Philippines and escaped (the 'Otsu Incident') charges could not be brought against him and he continued in his posting. Hence one may say that the distinctive Japanese attitude to being taken prisoner originated as a moral precept at the individual level, progressively spread in the Army, and finally became a social norm that bound the whole community. This is not unconnected with the process whereby moral precepts that under the name *bushidō* spread through one section of the old samurai class, also permeated the attitudes of the rural conscripts (and their families) in Meiji Japan, which relied on a conscript Army largely recruited in the countryside.

Contradictions

Self-evident truths and political policies are liable to be overwhelmed by myths, and there have been many occasions where attempts to harness myths constructively have been swept away by them. We have seen how the military conferred a decoration on a repatriated POW while his home community subjected him to village ostracism. The Court of Inquiry exonerated Colonel Murakami; but when he returned to his regiment he was subjected to similar ostracism – the junior officers refused to salute him. On his retirement he returned to his village in Yamaguchi prefecture, but within three years had to move to Hyogo prefecture, where he died. In his case the military authorities were forced to go along with his condemnation.

In the First World War the Japanese were little more than spectators. They were shocked not only by the heavy casualties but also by the large number of prisoners, about eight million. Quite early in the war this prompted the writer Sasagawa Rimpu to publish an article 'Their Attitude to Surrender and Ours – The Differences' in the serious and widely read journal *Nihon oyobi Nihonjin*. 'In this war', he wrote, 'there has emerged the practice of large groups surrendering. If it spread to here it would be a national disaster.'[25] Later in the war Major-General Nara, the Director of the Military Affairs Bureau at the Ministry of the

Army, wrote that in waging war the European powers relied too heavily on *matériel*; in the Japanese Army, which had to fight with moral force, becoming a prisoner was not an option; its members believed capture to be shameful and fought to the death. As he wrote this in a journal addressed to serving officers, this would have been received as official Army doctrine.[26] The only land operation in which the Japanese were engaged in during the First World War was the capture of Shantung. Throughout this campaign not a single Japanese was taken prisoner, but 4,500 Germans surrendered after a token struggle and spent the next four years in POW camps in Japan. In this manner we observe the condemnation of surrender becoming a degree firmer during the Taishō era (1912–25).

In the Shōwa era (1926–45) there was the case of Major Kuga, who was taken prisoner during hostilities which broke out in Shanghai in 1932. Evidently he was captured when unconscious. When he was repatriated after the cease-fire, he returned to the spot where he was captured and there committed suicide. This made a great impact through the mass media, and he became a national hero. It has been argued that with the Kuga incident the shamefulness of capture became established as a self-evident truth to soldier and civilian alike.

And so by the time of the Second World War this tenet was so widely held that, as Ruth Benedict observed, it 'had no need of special official indoctrination'.[27] One can say that the Field Service Code of 1941 merely afforded ratification to a nation-wide belief. As this principle became established, new contradictions emerged. It became necessary to treat the enemy's POWs and Japan's own POWs according to different rules, which could not be reconciled. Here are some examples.

As we have already seen, in the Sino-Japanese war of 1894–5 the ratio of enemy to Japanese prisoners was 15:1. In the Russo-Japanese war it was 40:1, with Japanese good treatment of POWs so well known that Russian troops were alleged to surrender shouting 'Matsuyama! Matsuyama!' (see Table 10.1). As a result, Japan's expenditure on POWs in that war was ¥36,490,000, or 2 per cent of her total war budget. Inevitably this was a subject of criticism. In the First World War it cost ¥17 to maintain each POW, and they were made to defray part of this by work outside the camps.[28] By the time of the Second World War the wheel had turned full circle. In that struggle the Japanese Army earned an evil reputation for its ill-treatment of prisoners; and for this many of its members were punished by war crimes tribunals.

One of the reasons given for Japan's decision not to ratify the 1929 Geneva Convention was that it was argued that ratification would bring Japan itself within the range of enemy air raids. The enemy might be tempted to launch raids at the extreme range of his bombers if he

Table 10.1

Conflict	Japenese POWs	'Enemy' POWs
Sino-Japanese War, 1894–5	11	1,790
Russo-Japanese War, 1904–5	2,088	79,367
First World War	0	4,461
		(German)
Nomonhan Incident, 1939	159	89
		(Russian)
Second World War	50,000	*132,134

Source: Hata Ikuhiko, 'Japanese POWs in the Pacific Theatre', *Takushoko University Review*, no. 207 (1994), p. 302
* This figure does not include those soldiers of indigenous origin who were captured and imprisoned by the Japanese.

believed that the aircrews on ditching would receive the protection of the 1929 Convention. When despite this the Doolittle Raid took place on 1 April 1942, in revenge and as a warning some of the US airmen were executed (under retrospective legislation).

Adopting rules regarding capture that differed from those of the enemy rebounded on Japan. Under the Hague Conventions a prisoner has a duty to divulge only his name, rank and number. In foreign armies this was instilled into the troops before they were sent on operations. Japanese troops believed that by accepting capture they had severed all links with their native land; and many of them, once they opened their mouths, poured forth masses of military information. When, at the end of the Pacific War, Imperial Headquarters issued the order 'all hostilities will cease', to ensure that the armistice was effected smoothly it included among the implementing instructions the following: 'servicemen who come under the control of the enemy forces after the proclamation of the Imperial Rescript will not be regarded as POWs'.[29] This achieved its objective. It also gave rise to hostility between those who surrendered before and those who surrendered after 15 August 1945, and to tragedy for those who surrendered to the Russians. The attitude to POWs moulded by the unique processes of the post-Meiji years was shattered only by the destruction of the Empire.

Application of the Convention *'Mutatis Mutandis'*

In December 1941 Japan declared war against the United States, Great Britain and Holland. She coined the name Greater East Asia War to apply to this and to the fighting in China in which she was already engaged. Although in China many had been taken prisoner on both sides, neither the Japanese government nor the military authorities had established a policy on how to deal with the problem. As a result it had been left largely to be determined by the authorities on the spot. There had been no declaration of war. There was also, no doubt, the attitude that in China there was no necessity to apply the rights and duties of international law, which was a European product. In the Pacific War, however, the Japanese government decided that to handle the prisoners of the advanced countries in the same manner as those of China would be not only difficult to justify but also to Japan's disadvantage. Consequently, they adopted the policy of dealing with them, by and large, according to the established principles of international law. For example, 5th Division's regulations regarding POWs, issued as it embarked for the Malayan campaign, read: 'The regulations governing the China theatre shall not apply [but instead] . . . [i]n accordance with international law . . .'.

When war broke out the Hague Conventions were in force between Japan and the Allies. When the British government enquired through the Protecting Power and the International Committee of the Red Cross (ICRC) whether Japan intended to apply the provisions of the 1929 Geneva Convention, which Japan had signed but not ratified, the Foreign Ministry conveyed the reply that Japan would apply the Convention *mutatis mutandis*.[30] Within the Ministry of the Army in the POW Information Bureau this was in practice interpreted to mean: 'that we shall apply it with any necessary amendments: not that we shall apply it strictly'.[31] The Allies, however, interpreted it as tantamount to ratification. Therefore, where the 1929 Convention conflicted with Japanese domestic law, the former would prevail. On this basis the Allies unrelentingly, throughout the war, addressed 83 protests or references on the subject to Japan through the Protecting Power and the ICRC, and after the war in war crimes courts passed severe judgement on many people associated with POW camps. On the other hand, the Japanese government, although in incidents like Cowra and Featherston where many prisoners were killed it duly complained about the 'slaughter', issued no complaints regarding the general treatment of Japanese prisoners. This was not entirely because the surprisingly good treatment of Japanese prisoners at the front was well known through the reports of the Protecting Powers and the ICRC: even if they had been ill-treated, the Japanese government would have turned a blind eye.

The administration of POWs has two dimensions: enemy troops captured by one's own forces and one's own troops captured by the enemy. However, they are mutually interacting; for although the 1929 Convention was based on the principle of humanity, there was also underlying it the tacit assumption of reciprocity. But if, when they have been captured, one treats one's own troops as deserters and treats the enemy's troops well, then contradictions and difficulties are bound to arise.

On 27 December 1941 the Japanese government issued Imperial Ordinance 1246 setting up the POW Information Bureau, and in March the following year the Directorate of POWs was established – both under the Ministry of the Army. The Bureau's function was to provide information regarding Japanese troops and enemy troops who had been captured; the Directorate's function was to superintend the administration of the latter. The head and principal officers were common to both. The regulations governing these organizations followed closely those establishing their predecessors in the Russo-Japanese war and the First World War, except that the provisions requiring the names of captured Japanese to be published and notified to their next of kin were omitted.[32] Although the provisions regarding mail between prisoners and their next of kin were retained, they had become virtually meaningless; for capture was not reported to the next of kin and the great majority of prisoners refused to write. A report on its wartime activities eventually issued by the Bureau in 1955 reads as follows:

> The Japanese Government did not vigorously seek information about captives. Nevertheless when information arrived (either in the form of cables from the International Committee of the Red Cross or notifications and photographs from its Delegate in Japan) the Bureau translated it and compiled name cards and rolls for each camp and sent these rolls to the Army Ministry and the Navy Ministry for their reference. When it received enquiries from next-of-kin it *replied appropriately in the light of Japanese traditional concepts.* And in the case of communication with the POW himself, it was vigorous in providing *assistance and good offices.*[33]

What does 'replied appropriately' mean? Probably a reply that neither confirmed nor denied that he was a prisoner. Perusal of a Ministry of Foreign Affairs file, 'Handling of Enemy Nationals and POWs by the Belligerents', indicates that some 'assistance and good offices' with communications must have been afforded. It contains a notification from the ICRC that 190 items of mail had been delivered to Japanese POWs in Australia and a report from the police that some POWs in China had requested and received money from their families.[34] When one considers, however, that in the course of the war some 50 million messages from belligerent countries were passed through the ICRC, Japanese use of these facilities appears minimal. Therefore it is not surprising that such severance from their native land should have affected the group psychology of Japanese POWs.

Ill-Treatment of Allied POWs

In so far as they denied the existence of their own POWs, the Japanese came to regard time, effort and money spent on the large number of enemy POWs as a one-way burden. For example, albeit he was distinguished in the field of international law, Dr Shinobe Jumpei soon after the outbreak of hostilities published an article on 'The Greater East Asia War and the Handling of POWs' in which he was critical of the treatment Japan had afforded to Russian and German prisoners in the past. 'Prisoners of war', he wrote, 'are not honoured guests and must not be treated as such.'[35] Tōjō, who as Prime Minister and Minister for the Army issued the Field Service Code, always took a hard line on this subject. So did the first director of the POW Information Bureau, Lieutenant-General Uemura Mikio, who laid down two simple principles: within the limits prescribed by humanity enemy POWs must be treated severely; and POWs must be used to expand production. 'In the war with Russia', he wrote, 'we gave them excellent treatment in order to gain recognition as a civilized country. To-day such need no longer applies.'[36] He continued to issue precepts of this nature at conferences of camp commandants and similar venues: 'Not a man amongst them must be permitted to eat the bread of idleness' (30 May 1942); 'We shall use the POWs to make the native peoples realize the superiority of the Japanese Race' (25 June 1942);[37] and finally, at a conference of Heads of Army Ministry Directorates (22 July 1942) the following conversation was recorded:

Uemura: We rejected a British offer to send relief goods to the POWs at Hong Kong and now the Americans are making a similar offer for the POWs at Bataan.

Tōjō: Where Japanese troops are facing hardships . . . there is no need to pamper [the] POWs.

Uemura: The Red Cross wants to send quinine . . .

Tōjō: Reject them all. There's no knowing where this might end.

Uemura: The Red Cross want to send their Delegates to the areas that we have occupied. We'll turn that down, too.[38]

In the Japanese POW camps the food, the medical facilities and the conditions of labour were very bad. The International Military Tribunal for the Far East noted that, whereas the death-rate among the United States troops captured by Germany and Italy was only 4 per cent, it was 27 per cent among those captured by Japan.[39] In fact, the POW Bureau was unaware of many of these deaths. For instance, the number of

Allied prisoners captured up to December 1943 and registered with the Bureau was about 110,000, but the subsequent deaths of less than 4,000 were actually reported to it.[40]

This ill-treatment of Allied POWs was grievous and widespread and, as a consequence, many camp commandants and their subordinates were tried and convicted by the war crimes tribunals of the various Allies. However, to blame this on deficiencies in the legal sphere is incorrect. Regulations were in being, but they were not being properly implemented. Rather than blaming camp commandants and their subordinates, it should be recognized that the responsibility clearly lay with Tōjō, Uemura and the other senior military leaders. For at the heart of the matter lay their belief that their own troops on being taken prisoner should forfeit all human rights. Inevitably, this attitude was applied with equal vigour towards enemy POWs.

The Field Service Code and its Environment

Although the Field Service Code is well known as the instrument laying down the attitude of the Army to capture in the Second World War, different views were held regarding its binding force and the extent of its influence. Some saw it merely as the confirmation of an existing attitude. Some laid stress on its influence on the young – on the next generation of soldiers. Some have ventured the view that it was a spell that bound the military leadership rather than the rank and file: for eventually they could think only of 'to the last man' defences and 'kamikaze' attacks. It can also be argued that these same attitudes, especially concerning the humiliation of capture, contained in the Field Service Code flourished among and had more of an impact upon Japanese non-combatants and quasi-combatants than on the combatants to whom it was addressed. For example, at Saipan there was mass suicide among the Japanese residents (including the women and children) and the Army nurses. The same tragedy was repeated in other theatres. By that stage of the war the spirit of the Field Service Code, which forbade being taken prisoner, had been expanded into a moral precept binding combatant and non-combatant alike.

In the Criminal Code of each of the armed services there were no clear provisions that made being taken prisoner an offence. The Army Criminal Code was amended in 1942, and some new offences like 'rape in an area of military operations' were added; but not 'being captured'. As a result, when prisoners were recovered the Japanese military authorities were always in a quandary as to how to deal with them. In practice they adopted a technique like 'administrative guidance', in which the unit would first examine the recovered prisoner's motives, then consult higher authority, and then take action. Attempts were made to draw up appropriate guidelines. The first time that this was done was after the settlement of the Nomonhan Incident (the Russo-Japanese border conflict that took place in Manchuria in 1938–9), when the Russians handed back 159 Japanese prisoners. It seems that the Kwantung Army proposed to deal leniently with them. The central military authorities, however, took a different line, and ordered that 'each case is to be investigated and if there is evidence of guilt charges are to be laid'. What happened was that, after considering such factors as the severity of their wounds, they were either charged with desertion under the Army Criminal Code (Rikugun Keihō) or awarded a minor punishment under the Disciplinary Regulations (Rikugun Chōbatsurei), and, after the sentences were served, steps were taken to ensure that they resided outside Japan.[41] In the case of officers 'different measures' were to be taken. Whether these were stated in writing or orally is not clear. However, all the Japanese officers captured at Nomonhan were made to commit suicide.

These guidelines were also sent to the China Expeditionary Force. In that theatre an unforeseen phenomenon was appearing – as well as deserters and recaptured prisoners, there were prisoners released by the enemy (principally by the Communist armies) after 'brain-washing'. A copy of guidelines issued by the Force HQ in March 1941 classified as top secret has survived.[42] It advised that if by any mischance one was taken captive one should immediately escape or commit suicide – by starvation if other means were not to hand; if a recovered prisoner was permitted to return to his unit, he should there seek death in battle; for officers suicide was the only solution. In actual practice these guidelines were not always followed. There were cases of suicide being forced on other ranks, of deserters who killed their guards and returned with captured secret documents being punished, of prisoners returning to their units without censure or being found jobs locally after serving their sentences.

Except for a few recovered at the end of the opening campaigns, very few Japanese POWs were recovered during the Second World War. Furthermore, at the time of the exchange of diplomats and other non-combatants by sea in the summer of 1942, the Japanese government rejected the Allies' proposal to include POWs in the exchange.[43] The Japanese POWs held by the Allies were of two kinds – those who hoped to return home even if it meant being sentenced to death by a court martial, and those who hoped to survive under assumed names. It is somewhat ironic that Japan's defeat exorcized this taboo and all were able to return. Meanwhile, vast numbers of troops had died in last-ditch defences prolonged solely in order that no prisoners should be taken.

Among these the most tragic fate was that of the seriously wounded in field hospitals. During the Meiji and Taishō eras Field Service Regulations contained a provision that these, like medical personnel, were under the protection of the Red Cross Convention of 1864. In the 1940 edition, however, this was replaced by a provision enjoining them not to fall into the hands of the enemy. And so it came about that they were either poisoned by the Medical Officers or given hand-grenades with which to kill themselves.

POWs in a Shame Culture

During the Pacific War, in the US Office of War Information the cultural anthropologist Ruth Benedict set herself to analysing the culture of the Japanese, 'the most alien enemy the United States had ever fought'. Using among her source material the interrogation reports of Japanese POWs, she characterized Japanese society as a 'shame culture'. One thing that drew her attention was the very low ratio of POWs to troops killed in action, and the fact that almost all the Japanese POWs were either wounded or unconscious when captured: in the armies of Occidental nations the proportion of the captured to the dead ran at about 4:1; among the Japanese troops in North Burma it was 1:120.[44] In the closing stages of the war this ratio increased somewhat. But if we accept the Japanese POW Information Bureau's total of 42,543 Japanese troops captured it remains about 1:40 for the war as a whole (cf. 1:55 in the Russo-Japanese war)[45] – still a low ratio. Benedict saw the POW's feeling of shame, that he 'could not hold up his head in Japan' again, as the driving force behind the principle of 'no surrender'.

As Benedict noted, this shame sometimes gave rise to a sense of obligation or debt to be repaid. Many POWs, after the immediate agony of capture had passed, experienced strong feelings of this nature. Experienced interrogating officers were able to capitalize on this to gain valuable information. The feeling that they had ceased to be Japanese turned some into active collaborators. For example, there was one who flew in an Allied bomber to guide it to its target. Under the Hague Conventions and the 1929 Geneva Convention a prisoner was required to disclose only his name, rank and number, and he could not be compelled to divulge military information or to co-operate. In the armies of other nations these rights and their duty to maintain security were instilled into the troops as part of their training; but in the Japanese armed forces such training could not be given. As a result, Japanese POWs were not security-conscious, and provided much valuable intelligence. For example, even such a high-ranking officer as the captain of the destroyer, *Asagumo*, when captured after the Battle of the Surigao

Strait (24–25 October 1944), answered all questions freely, in a 'cour-teous, friendly, co-operative manner', providing detailed and accurate information on subjects ranging from the Order of Battle of the Com-bined Fleet to the capacity of its radar installations.[46] It was the same with the diaries and notebooks that Japanese troops often carried with them. These were an important source of intelligence.[47]

Although it varied a little according to time and place, the treatment given to Japanese POWs was generally good (except, perhaps, in some Kuomintang camps). They were not required to perform any labour. There were a number of deaths from malnutrition; but this would appear to have been the result, not of deliberate cruelty, but of the misappro-priation of rations by commandants or their subordinates. In American and British Commonwealth camps they were not required to do even the work permitted under the 1929 Convention. Once the customary interrogation was completed, they lived a life of idleness, left to their own devices – albeit behind barbed wire. This was because the Japanese POWs regarded any work as assisting the enemy, while the Allied authorities feared that the prisoners' protests would take the form of mass suicides or riots. There were some among the Allied commandants who at times took a firm line with the Japanese POWs; but as this produced confrontation and non-co-operation they tended to try and placate them in a manner that parents would employ when their children were throwing a tantrum. When the prisoners made frivolous demands, like requiring that rice be available at every meal, that musical instruments be issued, that Japanese public holidays be recognized and that they be permitted to cultivate Japanese vegetables, these were usually acceded to. When 'in order to impede the enemy's war effort as best we can by such means as are at our disposal' they destroyed their surplus rations, the authorities turned a blind eye. Many of the Japanese POWs assumed false names, often choosing the name of some national hero or contemporary public figure. The authorities treated this with unconcern. On Hawaii about 1 per cent registered under the name of Hayakawa Kazuo, the film star. One former US prison camp official, Otis Cary, recounts how when addressing each new draft of prisoners he used to relieve the tension by beginning with, 'Have we Hayakawa, Kazuo with us to-day?'[48] Despite such circumspect treatment, riots and mass suicides occurred at Featherston, Cowra and Paita (New Caled-onia), and were narrowly averted at Camp McCoy and Bikaner (India).

It would be hard to imagine a more difficult society to manage than a group of people who used false names to mask their wish for suicide. Nevertheless, they formed self-governing societies sufficient to carry on life from day to day. Whereas many of the POWs in Japanese hands had been taken captive along with their units, this was not the case with

Japanese prisoners. They had usually been captured singly. The camps were conglomerates of unconnected individuals who, for the most part, concealed their true identities (and often even their military rank) from each other. Hence organization on the basis of unit and rank was impossible. A system of self-government appropriate to the new situation, however, emerged remarkably quickly.

In the camps the POWs were usually organized under their own headquarters into huts and within huts into squads. The leaders and their staffs were usually selected by election, with an admixture of direct nomination. In camps where the officers had been separated from the other ranks, the leadership among the latter usually fell to those among the veteran NCOs who had skills appropriate to their new situation and knew how to negotiate with the camp authorities. At the senior or headquarters level, the leaders were often the Japanese 'boss' types that one so often saw elected to village and town councils. The qualities required of these new leaders appear to have been of a type quite different from those required either in civil life or in combat. Recounting the experience of his own unit's two years' captivity in Rangoon after the war's end, Professor Aida writes that the new leaders were not the inspiring and capable NCOs in battle or the educated men, but the archetypal 'bosses'.[49] The Allies as a general rule did not interfere in the internal management of the camps. As a result the leaders that emerged were sometimes rather disreputable types. In Ōoka Shōhei's *Furyoki* (*Diary of a POW*) the leader at Leyte #1 Camp was a private soldier (a carrier in civil life) masquerading as a staff-sergeant. At Cowra it was one of these camp leaders, bearing the assumed name Minami Tadao, who spearheaded the break-out.

In these self-governing camps factions emerged and contended for the leadership: Army versus Navy, new arrivals versus originals, those who had surrendered versus those who had been captured. And as the war entered its final phase the principal line of cleavage was between those who believed in a Japanese victory and those who saw defeat approaching. This was a continuation of existing divisions between those who insisted on non-co-operation with the Allied camp commandant and his administration and those who advocated co-operation; and between those whose lifestyle was markedly Japanese and those who were more Westernized. The 'defeat' faction appeared to be ingratiating themselves with the Allies and to be preparing opportunistically to change sides. This drew upon them the hatred of the 'victory' faction. The attitude of the camp authorities to the struggle between these two factions varied from country to country and from place to place. The Americans, the Russians and the Chinese restrained the activities of the 'victory' faction and gave protection to the 'defeat' faction and to the democratic movements that the latter's radical elements were fostering. As a result, the factional struggles there did not erupt into violence. The British, however, adopted a policy of non-intervention. In India, at Bikaner, they moved the 'defeat' faction into a separate camp; and at the civilian internees' camp at Deoli there was a riot in which seventeen of the 'victory' faction were shot.

Almost all the Japanese POWs were repatriated before the end of 1946. Perhaps because fresh trouble was feared from them they were with a few exceptions kept separate from the 'surrendered personnel' who came under Allied control at the war's end. Unlike the latter, they escaped forced labour and the hunt for war criminals. They also, for the most part, adapted more quickly to civilian life than did the 'surrendered personnel'. This is hardly surprising; for Japan under military occupation was much the same as a POW camp. It is perhaps for reasons such as these that the atmosphere pervading most chronicles of POW life (and some dozens of these have been published) is generally cheerful but torpid. In a sense, with food, accommodation and clothing provided, every day was a Sunday and time hung heavy on their hands. One of the best of these accounts is Ōoka's *Furyoki*. When he was captured on Leyte in January 1945 he found the POW camp full of idle men, with much more food than they could eat, passing their days and nights in quarrelling, gambling and drunken carousals (they were adept in distilling 'jungle juice'). 'The Americans', he wrote, 'provisioned us on the same scale as their own troops and, because their lines of communication were fully established, they had no need of our labour. These factors led to our corruption.'[50] With the end of the war, he noted, the tempo of corruption increased. It was probably because he continued to believe that to be taken prisoner was to forfeit one's honour for all time that in later years he, to everyone's surprise, declined election to the Geijutsuin, the Japanese Academy of the Arts. There were many others who through feelings of shame concealed their past, left their pensions unclaimed and shunned their unit associations. It appears that, although the ancient traditions of Japan lost their binding force, they nevertheless remained alive at the level of the individual.

But the prisoners were not just a burden to their captors. The cost of maintaining them was more than offset by the value of the intelligence gained from them. Interrogation in the Japanese Army usually amounted to nothing better than off-the-cuff questioning by whatever officer with a smattering of English happened to be in the vicinity. In contrast to this, interrogation in the Allied armies was systematic and scientific. Initially prisoners were very few. Charles A. Lindbergh, the famous American aviator and wartime consultant to the United Aircraft Corporation, noted that in the front-line areas he visited, US troops tended to kill any POWs that came into their hands until orders were issued offering additional recreational leave to anyone who brought in a prisoner.[51] The intelligence sections of the Allied armies produced results by patiently collecting and piecing together scattered pieces of information and, when they had found the right prisoner, pursued the matter with the untiring efforts of skilled interrogators. Often the Allied victories have been called 'victories in the intelligence war'. Along with cryptanalysis the principal source of intelligence was the interrogation of prisoners.

Notes

1. *Hague Regulations Respecting the Laws and Customs of War* (1907), Articles 4 to 14.
2. International Military Tribunal for the Far East (hereafter IMTFE), Exhibit 3043.
3. IMTFE, *Judgment*, p. 1099.
4. Naoki, Kōjirō, 'Hakusukinoe no Horyo to Nihon Shoki', *Nihonshi Kenkyū Tsūshin*, no. 6 (1984). See also Inoue, Hideo, 'Hakusukinoe no Tatakai' in Obayashi, Tarō (ed.), *Ikusa*, Tokyo, 1984 and Suzuki, Osamu, *Hakusukinoe*, Tokyo, 1972.
5. Hasegawa, Shin, *Nihon Horyoshi*, Tokyo, 1979, vol. 1, p. 23. Tsushima is located on Honshu island near the city of Nagoya.
6. Nakajima, Kawatarō, 'Horyo Samazama', *Seiron*, June 1991.
7. He died in 1642 at the ripe age of 72, leaving an autobiography; but some say that this is a forgery produced in a later period. The fourteenth generation of his descendants are thriving to-day.
8. Saikami, Tokio, *Matsuyama Shūyōjo*, Tokyo, 1969, pp. 11–21.
9. Muneta, Hiroshi, *Heitai Hyakunen*, Tokyo, 1968, pp. 138–46.
10. National Defence Institute, Tokyo, General Officer Commanding 44th Division to Governor, Occupied Areas, 27 Sept. 1895.
11. Rikugunshō, *Meiji 27-28-Nen Seneki Tōkei*.
12. For Japanese POWs in the Russo-Japanese war see, in addition to the overall war history, Sambo Hombu, *Meiji Sanjūshichihachi-nen Nichiro Senshi*, Tokyo, 1914; Rikugunshō, *Meiji Sanijūshichihachi-nen Seneki Furyo Toriatsukai Temmatsu*, Tokyo, 1907, Ch. 3; Rikugunsho, *Meiji Sanjūshichihachi-nen Seneki Tōkei*, vol. 2, 1911; Rikugunshō, *Meiji Sanjūshichihachi-nen Seneki Rikugun Seishi*, vol. 8, 1911, Ch. 17. In English see Stewart Lone, *Japan's First*

Modern War: Army and Society in the Conflict with China 1894–95, New York, 1994.

13. See *Rikugun Horyo Toriatsukai Kisoku*, the *Furyo Toriatsukai Saisoku*, the *Furyo Rōeki Kisoku* and the *Furyo Jiyū Sampo oyobi Minka Kyojū Kisoku*.

14. Saishin, Tokio, *Medoveiji-mura no Nihonjin Bohyō*, Tokyo, 1983.

15. Chokurei 44 of 21 Feb. 1904, Article 11. In the corresponding ordinance issued in 1941 this provision is omitted. Chokurei 1246 of 27 Nov. 1941.

16. Saimami, *Matsuyama Shuyojo* (see Note 8 above), p. 202.

17. Sambō Hombu (ed.), *Meiji Sanijūshichihachi-nen Himitsu Nichiro Senshi*, Tokyo, 1978, p. 420.

18. Kaikosha (ed.), *Sensō Hiwa (Nichiro Seneki)*, Tokyo, 1935, p. 248.

19. Saishin, *Medoveiji-mera* (see Note 14 above), p. 116.

20. Kibe, Keiji, *Nichiin no Zansho*, Tokyo, 1989 and discussions with the author.

21. Hayashi, Hideo, 'Nichiro Sensō no Nihonjin Horyo Gaisen Nikki', *Shinchō*, Oct. 1985.

22. For example, Shimada Kazuo writes that in 1934 when he was a journalist on a Manchurian daily newspaper he met some former POWs who had settled near Dairen and had taken out local citizenship. According to one of them (a former corporal who had become a village headman) there were about 200 of them living in four or five places nearby; they were mostly wounded men who had escaped from a Russian field hospital. Shimada Kazuo, 'Wakai Hi no Watashi', *Mainichi Shimbun*, 16 Apr. 1987.

23. Russia, like Japan, did not adopt the 1929 Geneva Convention; and, because refusal to accept capture was inculcated in the training of the Soviet Army, suicide was quite common, and most of the recovered POWs were sent to forced labour camps. In the Chinese Communist Army similar principles were instilled, and recovered prisoners in the Korean War were demoted, with many of them being banished to farms.

24. In the 1909 edition of the Infantry Manual the provision that the wounded should be evacuated from the forward defended localities was deleted in 1923.

25. Sasagawa, Rimpu, *Nihon oyobi Nihonjin*, 15 Dec. 1914.

26. *Kaikōsha Kiji*, no. 527, June 1918.

27. Ruth Benedict, *The Chrysanthemum and the Sword*, New York, 1946, p. 38.

28. Rikugunshō, *Taishō Sannen naishi Kunen Seneki Furyo ni kansuru Shorui*, Oct. 1916, statement by Major-General Nara, DCGS.

29. Dairikurei 385; Daikairei 50.
30. IMFTE, *Judgment*, p. 1099.
31. 'Furyo wa Ika ni Toriatskawareta ka', Feb. 1946.
32. See Rikutatsu 44 of 1904 and 30 of 1914.
33. Furyojōhōkyoku, *Furyo Toriatsukai no Kiroku*, Dec. 1955. Author's emphasis.
34. Ministry of Foreign Affairs Archives, file 'Kōsenkoku-kar, Tekikokujin oyobi Furyo Toriatsukaiburi': Legation in Switzerland to Foreign Minister, 13 July 1945; 'Gaiji Keisatsu Gaikyō – Shōwa 17-nen', fos. 296–8.
35. *Gaikō Jihō*, 15 May 1942.
36. Furyojōhōkyoku, 'Nihon Furyojōhōkyoku to Furyokanribu no Gaikan Dec. 1941 – Aug. 1945'.
37. Chaen, Yoshio, *Dainippon Teikoku Naichi Furyo Shūyōsho*, Tokyo, 1986, p. 78.
38. National Defence Institute, diary of Kimbara, Setzuzō, 14 July 1942.
39. IMTFE, *Judgment*, pp. 1002–3.
40. Furyojōhōkyoku, *Furyo Toriatsukai no Kiroku*.
41. Ministry of Foreign Affairs Archive, file, Rikuman (Army in Manchuria): Mitsu (secret) nos. 854 & 855; File, Rikushi (China Expeditionary Force): Mitsu (secret) no. 3553. The US *War Weekly Intelligence Review*, no. 79, 14 Feb. 1945 cites an instruction to the latter to the same effect dated 7 Aug. 1942.
42. National Defence Institute, Shina Hakengun, Sambōbu, 'Furyo ni kansuru Kyōkun', Mar. 1941.
43. Ministry of Foreign Affairs Archives, file A.700–9–30.
44. Benedict, *Chrysanthemum* (see Note 27 above), p. 39.
45. Nakamura, Teiji, *Horuo Mondai ni kansuru Kōsatsu*, Tokyo, 1982, p. 35.
46. Allied Translation and Interpretation Service, Interrogation Reports, 50–IR–7, 31 Dec. 1944.
47. Richard Storry, an intelligence officer on the Burma front, wrote that: 'Every prisoner carried a wad of photographs – of his parents, of his wife and children, and so on. He had on him also either a national flag, signed by his relatives and containing heartening messages – usually a *senninbari* ("belt stiched by a thousand") – many had diaries and note-books' (from an unpublished manuscript by G. R. Storry, 'Notes on Japanese Prisoners of War', 1948). Japanese prisoners were few; but, thanks to their disclosures and their diaries, the intelligence value of each exceeded that of a score of Allied prisoners.

48. O. Cary, *Yokoito no Nai Nihon*, Tokyo, 1976, pp. 43–4.
49. Y. Aida, *Prisoner of the British*, London, 1966, pp. 148–69.
50. Ōoka, Shōhei, *Furyoki*, Tokyo, 1952, p. 293.
51. C. A. Lindbergh, *The Wartime Journals of C. A. Lindbergh*, New York, 1970, pp. 853–7, 902, 915.

11

Protecting Prisoners of War, 1939–95

Joan Beaumont

Today the prisoner of war is a spoilt darling; he is treated with a solicitude for his wants and feelings which borders on sentimentalism. He is better treated than the modern criminal ... Under present-day conditions, captivity ... is no sad sojourn by the waters of Babylon; it is usually a halcyon time, a pleasant experience to be nursed fondly in the memory, a kind of inexpensive rest-cure after the wearisome turmoil of fighting. The wonder is that any soldiers fight at all: that they do so, instead of giving themselves up as prisoners, is a high tribute to the spirit and the discipline of modern armies.[1]

The date of this quotation? 1911. The author? The contemporary authority on the law of war, J. M. Spaight, reflecting on the Russo-Japanese war of 1904–5 and the internment of prisoners of the Boer war in Ceylon and Bermuda.

For anyone familiar with the history of prisoners of war (POWs) during the Second World War and later armed conflicts it is hard to find any resonance with Spaight. Deep pessimism might seem more appropriate – pessimism about the record of this century, such as has been expressed by the eminent British social and economic historian, Eric Hobsbawm. The material achievements of the twentieth century, Hobsbawm argued in 1994, have been astonishing, but these have not been matched by a comparable moral progress. With the onset of the First World War the precedent was set for killing on a massive scale; for the blurring of the age-old distinction between combatant and civilian. Once even war had rules, but with the evolution of 'total war' the world has entered an 'age of catastrophe. We have become relatively insensitive to atrocity; our voice of moral outrage has been silenced and we have been "brainwashed into accepting barbarity"'.[2]

In many respects the history of POWs during the Second World War reinforces this judgement. In certain theatres of war millions of captured military personnel and civilian internees died as a result of physical abuse, execution, starvation, disease and neglect. Millions more worked in conditions that were dangerous, debilitating and damaging to their long-term health. With the conclusion of the conflict many Axis prisoners lingered in captivity in former enemy territories for up to a decade. Yet this record of maltreatment has to be balanced against the comparatively humane treatment of prisoners in other theatres of the war, where the Third Geneva Convention of 1929 protecting POWs was generally observed. Moreover, the Second World War, by virtue of its very barbarity, provided a critical momentum for further reform in international humanitarian law. With the revision of the Geneva Conventions in 1949, POWs had their protected status reaffirmed in law. In practice, as a review of major international conflicts since 1945 shows, the treatment of POWs has rarely, if ever, sunk again to the depths of that global conflict.

The problem for POWs in the Second World War was not so much the scope of international law as the failure of major belligerents to observe it. When war broke out in 1939, there was a well-developed international legal regime that aimed at guaranteeing humane treatment for POWs. The keystone of this regime was the 1929 Geneva Convention, which was the distillation of over sixty years of international discussion of the issue. Building on the Hague Conventions of 1899 and 1907, and especially the experience of the major European powers in handling over 5 million prisoners during the First World War,[3] the 1929 Convention covered many practical aspects of captivity, as well as confirming general principles of protection. It confirmed, for example, the principle that prisoners should not be punished for the simple fact that they had borne arms and killed in the name of the state. Nor could they be viewed, as they had been in earlier centuries when they were prized for their potential for ransom, as the captives of individuals rather than governments.

The 1929 Convention covered in considerable detail all those enduring preoccupations of POWs throughout modern warfare: namely, food, work, pay, discipline, escape, religious freedom, rights under interrogation and access to external support. The humanitarian role of the International Committee of the Red Cross (ICRC), whose activities had expanded dramatically during the First World War, was also acknowledged in the 1929 Convention, while provision was made for Protecting Powers, appointed by the belligerents, to visit and consult with POWs. Both these measures were considered essential if the Convention was to be applied.

All this edifice of international law, however, was shaken to its foundations by the Second World War. As already mentioned, this conflict witnessed great extremes in the treatment of prisoners. At one end of the spectrum were the generally acceptable conditions in camps in Western Europe, the United States and the British dominions. The

German government, in stark contrast to its behaviour in Eastern and Central Europe, generally respected the 1929 Convention so far as prisoners of the Western Allies were concerned. Though there was often great hardship, particularly when living conditions in Germany deteriorated under the impact of the Allied strategic bombing offensive and when prisoners were turned out of their camps in the winter of 1944–5 to escape the advancing Allied armies, the death toll among Western prisoners was comparatively low: for example, only 265 of the more than 8,000 Australians who were captured in Europe, the Mediterranean and the Middle East died.[4]

The Western Powers, in turn, motivated by that combination of self-interest and idealism which has always underpinned international regulations concerning POWs, treated Axis prisoners on the whole well. In the United States, conditions were so good that there were complaints at every public level from the local press up to Congress that German POWs were getting a better diet than many Americans![5] In the British dominions, Italian prisoners, working as rural labourers, were often befriended by the local population, and even sponsored as immigrants after the war.[6]

Of course, there *were* major breaches of the 1929 Convention in Western Europe, one of the most notorious being the tit-for-tat manacling of prisoners which followed on the Germans discovering in late 1942 that their surrendered personnel had had their hands tied during the Dieppe raid of August.[7] (The 1929 Convention prohibited using prisoners in reprisals.) German prisoners who fell into Allied hands in late 1944–5 also suffered appalling privations. Though they were to all intents and purposes POWs, the Western Allies denied them this status by declaring them to be 'surrendered enemy personnel' (the British term) or 'disarmed enemy forces' (the American).[8] The most critical account of conditions in the makeshift camps in the Rhineland and France puts the German death toll at over a million.[9] This is almost certainly a gross exaggeration; but even the fiercest defenders of the US authorities – who attribute the deaths to the logistic problems of handling over three million prisoners rather than to malice – put the minimum number of deaths at 56,000.[10]

On the Eastern front and in the Asia–Pacific theatre conditions were far worse. Probably over three million Soviet POWs were executed or died of starvation or overwork at the hands of the ideologically and racially obsessed Nazi regime. The conditions in which they were interned were appalling. To quote an account written shortly after the war by an Hungarian tank officer:

We were stationed at Rovno. I woke up one morning and heard thousands of dogs howling in the distance . . . I called my orderly and said: 'Sandor, what is all this moaning and howling?' 'Not far from here' he said, 'there's a huge mass of Russian prisoners in the open air. There must be 80,000 of them. They're moaning because they are starving. . . . I went to have a look. Behind wire there were tens of thousands of Russian prisoners. Many were on the point of expiring. Few could stand on their feet. Their faces were dried up and their eyes sunk deep in their sockets. Hundreds were dying every day, and those who had any strength left dumped them in a vast pit.[11]

The record of the Japanese was not significantly better. Although there were greater differences between prison camps throughout Asia than is often conceded, generally Allied prisoners suffered from malnutrition, overwork, disease, harsh disciplinary regimes and often gratuitous brutality from their Japanese and Korean guards. One in four of the 140,000 Allied personnel captured died.[12] Of the over 22,000 Australian prisoners nearly 36 per cent died in captivity.[13]

In both the Soviet and Japanese theatres of war the problem was not the content of international law, nor indeed whether it was applicable. Although neither the Soviet Union nor Japan were parties to the 1929 Convention, they had the option of declaring their willingness to abide by it. In any case, the Convention embodied essential principles of customary international law that all states were bound to observe. The appalling record of the Second World War was rather the result of those persistent enemies of humanitarianism: mutual incomprehension of alien cultures, ideological fanaticism, and racial hatreds. These were compounded by the progressive elimination of neutral countries, who could play the role of Protecting Powers, and by the logistical chaos intrinsic to such a vast and inherently uncontrollable conflict.

Even before the Second World War had ended international negotiations had begun to revise the Geneva Conventions, a movement inspired initially by the United States, which has always prided itself on its role in the development of humanitarian law from the time of the Lieber Code of 1863 on.[14] The 1949 Prisoner of War Convention resolved some of the ambiguities in the earlier regulations and clarified, in the light of the experience of 1939–45, the details of a whole range of practical and health issues: for example, disciplinary and judicial procedures within the prison camp; the finances of prisoners; and their right to immunity from medical experimentation, such as had been inflicted on prisoners of the Japanese and Germans.[15]

A few examples suffice to illustrate the innovations in 1949. In the case of food, it was agreed to substitute national standards for an 'absolute' standard. Food rations now had to take account of the prisoners' habitual diet and to be sufficient in quantity, quality and variety to prevent loss of weight or nutritional deficiencies. The obsessive struggles of Allied prisoners in the Pacific to make something palatable of the endless rice served to them, or the battles of Central and Eastern Europeans to digest white bread, were meant to be a thing of the past.

Work was another key issue. The 1929 prohibition on labour that had 'a direct relation with war operations' had proved to be inadequate and ambiguous in 1939–45. In the modern 'total war' what economic activity was *not* related to the war effort? Few Westerners had any difficulty in denouncing the construction of the Burma–Thailand railway, as much for its appalling working conditions as for its strategic purpose: but what about the Alaskan highway? The US Advocate General had declared that it was inappropriate work for German POWs on strategic grounds, but his advice had been overruled.[16] After a long, and at times bitter, debate, the 1949 conference agreed to list six specific classes of work, in addition to camp maintenance, on which prisoners could be employed.[17] These categories did not include clearing mines laid by the prisoners' own armies, despite strong arguments in favour of this by the British. Even though it could be argued that belligerents would be far more cautious about keeping records of where they laid mines if they knew their own personnel might be obliged to clear them, the issue was resolved 'signally to the POW's advantage – and by necessary implication to the civilian's disadvantage [who would have to clear them instead]'.[18]

The Second World War had also shown more graphically than ever before the vulnerability of prisoners in transit: two glaring examples were Greece in 1941, when 25,000 British commonwealth troops were crowded into staging camps with primitive sanitation, and then into cattle trucks for journeys of up to seven days to Austria and Germany; and south-east and east Asia in 1942–4, when Allied prisoners were transported to various destinations in stifling 'hell ships'. Events in France in 1944–5 had also shown how prisoners being handed from the custody of one ally to another could suffer a worsening of their conditions. The 1949 Convention therefore made the original captor government responsible for ensuring adequate treatment for the prisoners, even after their transfer – a provision that was to prove important in the Vietnam war, when the US handed prisoners over to South Vietnamese control. Neither the 1949 nor any later conference, however, was able to agree on how to protect prisoners being transferred by sea. The ICRC's estimate for the number of prisoners and civilian internees killed by their own submarine forces in the Mediterranean, Atlantic and Pacific oceans between 1939 and 1945 was 15,000.[19] Nearly forty years later, during the Falklands/Malvinas war, there were still no internationally approved guidelines for the transferring of prisoners by sea.[20]

Finally, the 1949 Convention strengthened the regulations on what has always been a profoundly contentious issue: the repatriation of prisoners. At the time the conference met, many thousands of Axis prisoners still languished in Soviet labour camps; those in the United Kingdom had only recently been allowed home, in 1948.[21] This was partly punitive; partly because the European victors claimed they needed POW labour for post-war reconstruction; and partly because conditions in the devastated cities of Germany and elsewhere in Europe made it difficult to accommodate yet more people seeking homes, food and employment. But the Allies had a legal cover for their pragmatic retention of POWs in the 1929 Convention's wording that prisoners should be repatriated as soon as possible 'after the conclusion of *peace* [my emphasis]'. The revised Convention changed the wording to 'after the cessation of active hostilities'. Even this did not ensure prisoners in later conflicts speedy repatriation.

Significantly, the 1949 Convention did not prohibit one of the most appalling tragedies of the Second World War: the repatriation of prisoners against their will. With the tragedy of the forcible repatriation by the Allies of the Cossacks and other Soviet citizens in mind,[22] the ICRC tried to get this item on the agenda;[23] but many governments resisted the notion that there should be any exceptions to repatriation.[24] Any 'escape clause', even one with a liberal intent, it was feared, might be exploited to prevent captives from returning home; and no government, either Western or Communist, wanted to be under any obligation to provide asylum to prisoners who might number millions.

The wording of the 1949 Convention on repatriation was therefore sufficiently ambiguous as to be the cause of fiercely competing interpretations during the Korean War. The Soviet Union, North Korea and China insisted that the refusal by the United States forcibly to repatriate prisoners at the end of this conflict was a flagrant violation of international law. A literal interpretation of Article 118 of the 1949 Convention, the Soviet spokesman, Andrei Vyshinsky, said, made it mandatory to repatriate prisoners without exception. The United States disagreed. Motivated in part by a desire to prove the superiority of the democratic system — surely no prisoner offered the choice between communism and the West could choose communism! — the US argued that the Convention's primary purpose was to protect prisoners. Forcible repatriation to a regime that denied their human rights was inconsistent with this.[25] Embryonic though human rights law was at this stage, the US interpretation progressively prevailed after 1953. In conflicts such as the Iran–Iraq War of 1980–8 and the Gulf War of 1990–1 the ICRC insisted on the right to interview prisoners, without witnesses, to ensure they were willing to return home.[26] Some 13,000 Iraqi prisoners decided in 1991 not to do so.[27]

At the same time as refining the rights of prisoners, the 1949 Convention grappled with another issue that the Second World War had thrown into sharp relief: the question of who is entitled to prisoner-of-war status. Under international law in 1939–45 combatants were defined[28] essentially as those belonging to the armed forces of a belligerent (including their ancillary units), and to militia and volunteer corps, providing that they fulfilled certain conditions. They had to be commanded by a person responsible for his subordinates; they had to have a fixed emblem recognizable at a distance; they needed to carry their arms openly and to conduct their operations in accordance with the laws and customs of war. In addition, civilians who rose spontaneously to take up arms against an invading power – the classic *levée en masse* – were recognized as combatants if they fulfilled the last two conditions.

This definition, however, did not cover the kinds of resistance movements that had emerged in France, Yugoslavia and elsewhere *after* these countries had been occupied by Nazi Germany. The *Maquis* and Tito's partisans were treated like the *francs-tireurs* that had so angered the Prussians in 1870–1 and were executed summarily. So, too, were the Italian troops who went over to the Allies in 1943 when Marshal Badoglio had not declared war on Germany. Tens of thousands were shot, and 600,000 deported to slave labour camps.[29] With the shadow of these experiences hanging heavily over the 1949 conference, which included delegates who had lived through German occupation, it was agreed to extend the definition of combatant to cover 'organized resistance movements' in occupied territory.[30] The Convention also defined as combatants those members of regular armed forces who owed allegiance to a government or authority not recognized by the detaining power.[31] This aimed to protect personnel in forces like the Free French under De Gaulle's command.

The definition of a combatant, however, still remained comparatively narrow. Like all the Geneva Conventions of 1949, the Third Convention encompassed only international conflicts. Fighters in civil wars, which were the conflicts that became endemic in the post-1945 period, were covered only by one article in the 1949 Convention, the so-called common article 3.[32] This guaranteed fundamental human rights to anyone rendered *hors de combat* in a civil conflict, regardless of whether they could claim POW status or not. It prohibited all those practices which had characterized Nazi rule in Europe and the Soviet Union: violence, murder, torture and mutilation, the taking of hostages, humiliating and degrading treatment and the sentencing and execution of captured personnel without due processes of law.

It was not until 1977, with the signing of two Protocols additional to the Geneva Conventions, that the international community extended the definition of a combatant – who was thereby entitled to POW status – beyond the essentially Second World War context of 1949. Recognizing that the guerrilla or freedom fighter of the national liberation movements of the post-war era could not conform to the conditions specified in the 1949 Convention, Protocol I added to the traditional definition of combatants in international conflicts[33] those who distinguish themselves from the civilian population 'while they are engaged in an attack or in a military operation preparatory to an attack'. Even if they cannot so distinguish themselves, 'owing to the nature of hostilities', they retain combatant status so long as they carry arms openly 'during each military engagement' and 'during such times as [they are] visible to the adversary while [they are] engaged in military deployment preceding the launching of an attack'. Leaving aside the vexed question of how to define certain key phrases in this convoluted article, which one critic has described as 'obscure to the point of incomprehensibility and therefore irrelevance',[34] this definition was widely criticized, at the time and later, because of its potential for blurring irreparably the distinction between combatant and civilians – one of the central concerns of international humanitarian law.

The development of international humanitarian law in response to the disasters of the Second World War in essence gave POWs the privileged status in law that Spaight claimed they had fifty years earlier. As Geoffrey Best says in his recent subtle and sophisticated account of war and law, in 1949:

> [p]risoners of war took a giant stride along the road to becoming the most favoured category of war victim: more popularly favoured by far than the wounded and sick, on whose account the series of Geneva Conventions began. The 1949 POW Convention, so much enlarged beyond the 1929 bridgehead, was made up of 143 articles and five annexes. Apart from the articles that were common to all the Conventions, the POW Convention was simply a comprehensive code for the humane treatment of prisoners from the moments of capture and interrogation through all facets of the internment (not a detail escaped the expert legislators' notice) up to their return to normalcy through the gates of release, repatriation, or death. None of the three other Conventions possessed as concentrated a character or invited such concentrated attention.[35]

But what difference has the 1949 Convention made in practice to the treatment of POWs in the conflicts of the post-1949 world? Does the record of the latter half of the century suggest that the Second World War was an aberration; or, in any significant practical sense, a watershed in the treatment of POWs?

The record of treatment of prisoners in the past fifty years, it has to be said, has been a mixed one. When the Korean War broke out, the 1949 Conventions had only just been signed. North Korea was not even party to the 1929 Convention. Yet it was generally agreed that at least the principles of current international humanitarian law should apply to the conflict. In practice, however, the North Koreans consistently refused to supply lists of the United Nations troops they captured or to allow the ICRC access to the camps they controlled.[36] Conditions in these camps varied dramatically.[37] At some stages of the war, notably during the initial North Korean offensive and during the truce negotiations, conditions for prisoners bordered on the acceptable. But during the UN advance to the Yalu River and the subsequent Chinese offensive, prisoners suffered forced marches, summary executions, inadequate diet (which took no account of national taste), disease, and chronic shortages of medicine and medical supplies: 38 per cent of the 2,730 US troops captured died.

The camps controlled by the UN Command had problems of overcrowding, poor rations and inadequate sanitary conditions, especially in the first year of the war, when the logistical problems of handling the 170,000 prisoners that fell into UN hands (95 per cent of the total taken during the whole war) were acute. The major problems for the UN Command, however, were controlling the violent tensions between communist and non-communists within the camps and managing, both within the camps and globally, the major international controversy over repatriation already referred to.

In the Vietnam war, the governments of South Vietnam, the United States and their allies agreed to apply the Geneva Conventions in respect to both North Vietnam and the Viet Cong.[38] But this did not guarantee humane treatment for prisoners – especially for the Viet Cong, whose guerrilla tactics precluded their carrying arms openly and distinguishing themselves from the civilian population. On occasions they were tried as terrorists and executed. Conditions in established internment camps appear to have been reasonable, at least after 1967 when the ICRC was allowed access to them; but at the point of capture prisoners were regularly maltreated. During interrogation they were threatened, abused and tortured in what appears to have been an officially condoned policy of extracting intelligence by violence. Eventually the US evacuated its prisoners to the rear before handing them over to the South Vietnamese.[39]

The Viet Cong, for its part, argued that it was not bound by the Geneva Conventions, since its political arm, the National Liberation Front, had not ratified them. It kept its prisoners in the primitive conditions imposed by its reliance on mobile military operations. At times it claimed to have killed Americans in reprisal for the execution of Viet Cong terrorists. As in Korea, prisoners were subjected to political indoctrination.[40]

The North Vietnamese, meanwhile, denied the American airmen they captured POW status on the grounds that they were war criminals, targeting civilians in their bombing. Like the Soviet Union, North Vietnam had entered a reservation to Article 85 of the third 1949 Convention, which stated (in what might be considered an excess of generosity) that prisoners prosecuted for acts committed prior to their being captured retained, *even if convicted*, the benefits of the Convention. Hanoi interpreted their reservation to mean that even prisoners who were *alleged* to have committed war crimes were not entitled to be considered as POWs.[41] The result is well known: Hanoi refused to communicate to the US full details of their prisoners and missing in action; and the ICRC was consistently denied access to camps in North Vietnam.[42] Americans reported on repatriation many instances of torture, solitary confinement and brutality. Yet, according to one commentator, this does not appear to have been the dominant theme of captivity;[43] and it can be argued that once the rhetoric of observing international law has been peeled away, the differences between the treatment of prisoners by the North and South Vietnamese were not as dramatic as Western polemicists would have it.[44]

In the Afghanistan conflict from 1980 the record for international humanitarian law was just as qualified. Although legal opinion judged that it was an international conflict from 1980 on,[45] the Soviet authorities and their client Afghan government denied the relevance of the Geneva Conventions. One Soviet spokesman even claimed with breathtaking disingenuousness that the humanitarian problems caused by the Afghan conflict did not concern the Soviet Union, because its forces had not participated in the conflict! The ICRC, having had access to the country before the Soviet intervention, was forced to leave in June 1980 and could not return until 1987. In the interim extensive human rights abuses by Soviet forces were reported by refugees and credible international organizations.[46]

The Iran–Iraq war of 1980–8 saw even greater abuses of international law. Despite the fact that both countries were party to the Geneva Conventions, there were summary executions and torture of POWs, indiscriminate targeting of civilians and the use of chemical warfare. Twice the ICRC took the unusually politicized step of calling on the community of states that were party to the 1949 Geneva Conventions to act to enforce humanitarian law.[47]

Both Iran and Iraq made wide use of their prisoners for propaganda purposes, and Iran, in particular, practised systematic indoctrination of prisoners with the aim of turning them against the Iraqi regime and the United States. The ICRC, unable to gain assurances that it could carry out its visits on acceptable terms, was forced to suspend visits to Iran for prolonged periods.[48] Even at the war's end it had not been notified of the identity of all soldiers killed or captured at the front.[49] Prisoners became pawns in the political game when their repatriation was delayed. Not until the invasion of Kuwait in 1990 did Saddam Hussein, now needing Iran's support in the new Gulf conflict, execute a dramatic *volte face* and expedite the return of prisoners.

Few of the other international conflicts of the 1970s and 1980s produced quite so consistent a denial of prisoners' rights. The unending Arab–Israeli dispute has raised a plethora of legal tangles – most notably over the status of the conflict and the PLO – that need not concern us here. In the unambiguously international conflicts of 1967 and 1973 all parties agreed that the 1949 Conventions applied. In the Six Day War Israel had the upper hand, given the extraordinary disparity in the number of prisoners taken: in one repatriation exchange, 360 Syrian prisoners and 328 civilians were returned for one Israeli prisoner and three civilians.[50] The logistical problems of handling returned numbers of prisoners led the Israelis, so it was learnt in 1995, to execute some Egyptians who fell into their hands, not only in this war but also in the earlier 1956 Sinai campaign.[51] Other prisoners of the 1967 war were repatriated quickly. In the Yom Kippur War, which had a much less decisive outcome, the repatriation of POWs from Syria became central to the bitter haggling and shuttle diplomacy over a political settlement.[52]

In the brief Indo-Pakistan war of 1971 more than 76,000 Pakistanis were captured.[53] Conditions of internment seem to have been generally acceptable, but the Pakistani prisoners were detained for over twenty months after the cessation of hostilities, thanks to the Indians' and Bangladeshis' insistence that they needed time to assemble evidence against those responsible for the slaughter of tens of thousands of civilians in East Pakistan before the war.[54] The legal justification for detaining all 76,000 prisoners when possibly as few as 195 were guilty of war crimes was thin; but there were considerations of *realpolitik* also which delayed repatriation.[55] The inevitable tensions of prolonged captivity led to escape attempts and violence within the camps; but the needs of the prisoners were monitored regularly by the ICRC, which fulfilled its traditional role of providing relief supplies and tracing services. The vast majority of prisoners survived to be repatriated in 1973–4.

The Falklands/Malvinas War of 1982 could hardly have been in starker contrast to many of the post-1945 conflicts. After Margaret Thatcher's initial gaffe in claiming that personnel taken during the fighting would not be POWs because 'a state of war did not exist between [Britain] and the Argentine',[56] the Convention was generally well applied.[57] Both Britain and Argentina, confronted with logistical difficulties in holding POWs in the harsh terrain, released prisoners very quickly, in some instances before the end of hostilities.[58] No internment camps were set up.

What distinguished the Falklands was the fact that it was a short war and subject to intense international media scrutiny. The Gulf conflict of 1990–1 shared these qualities, though of course it was profoundly different in other respects. Conscious of the vital importance of generating and maintaining a broad international consensus about the legitimacy of its intervention, the United Nations Command paid great attention to questions of the law of war. A battery of lawyers advised UN commanders about legitimate targets of attack, and although the US and Britain had not ratified either of the 1977 Protocols, the pronouncements of the UN commanders were resonant with the language of these agreements. According to General Colin Powell, chairman of the US Joint Chiefs of Staff, 'Decisions were impacted by legal considerations at every level.'[59]

Consistently with this, the ICRC was able to play a major – and unprecedented – consulting role in the long lead-time to UN intervention. It advised the UN forces on how to handle POWs and where to site camps. The Geneva Conventions, according to the ICRC Head of Operations in Saudi Arabia, became almost 'Book Choice of the Month'.[60]

Notwithstanding this, the age-old problems of logistics made it impossible to prevent overcrowding, shortages of food and water and delays in registering prisoners when something like 65,000 Iraqis fell into UN hands within three days of fighting. There were also some incidents during the war when UN troops attacked Iraqis in controversial circumstances, raising a question that remains as contentious now as it was on the islands of the Asia–Pacific theatre in 1941–5:[61] what is proper evidence that troops wish to surrender?

The Iraqi government's record, predictably, was far less impressive. Despite its having come to have some trust in the ICRC during the 1980s conflict, it refused its delegates access to POWs throughout the land war. Coalition prisoners in Iraqi hands appear to have been tortured, and captured airmen were paraded on television. Only when it needed to effect an efficient and smooth transfer of POWs in the aftermath of the war did Baghdad again turn to the ICRC.[62]

From this all-too-brief review of international conflicts it is clear that the regime of international law established in the aftermath of the Second World War has often been only partially effective. On the positive side, the 1949 Convention and the Protocols of 1977 succeeded in establishing international standards of treatment for POWs that have universal acceptance, at least formally. By mid-1994, Protocol 1 had been ratified by 135 of the 184 states in the United Nations. Protocol 2, the more limited convention covering civil conflicts,[63] has been ratified by 125 states. The 1949 Geneva Conventions have almost universal acceptance. The long-standing accusation that international law is a European creation has been invalidated, not least by the extremely activist and effective role of the Third World countries in shaping the agenda of the diplomatic conferences that drafted the Protocols. The Geneva Conventions can claim to be genuinely 'international' norms, reflecting custom in Islamic and Asian as well as Christian and Western cultures.[64]

There have also been changes in practice. If one accepts that there is some hierarchy of human rights, in which the right to subsistence – to life and health – is the elemental and fundamental need, then the treatment of prisoners has arguably improved in recent international conflicts. For all the infringements of international humanitarian law, there have been no disasters comparable, in terms of the loss of prisoners' lives, to the Second World War or Korea. Excluded from this judgement, of course are essentially civil conflicts, such as Rwanda and Bosnia, in which the predominant loss of life has been civilian.

There has also been an immeasurable strengthening since the Second World War of the role of the ICRC. Unglamorous, obstructed and, of necessity, unpublicized though much of its work has been, it has regularly performed the role of guaranteeing prisoners those rights that make captivity tolerable: the right to send and receive mail, to get relief parcels, to speak to someone objective about grievances, to know that one's family is aware of one's fate, to be repatriated in a humane way. One has only to compare prisoners who benefited from such rights (as did Allied prisoners in Germany in 1939–45, who even late in the war received food parcels that they could consume and trade with the civilian population) with those who did not (for example, most prisoners of the Japanese) to understand what a transforming impact Red Cross intervention may have upon captivity. The ICRC has also been able in many conflicts to bring about an improvement in prisoners' conditions by monitoring conditions in camps.

Yet on the negative side it is clear that the ICRC has often been prevented from playing this role. The most intractable problem confronting international humanitarian law now, as it was in 1941–5 when the ICRC was denied access to POWs in the Russo-German war, remains enforcement. How, given the nature of international law, which lacks a central power able to enforce the law and a central court that can resolve disputes about interpretation, can the victims of war be guaranteed protection?

The 1949 Geneva Conventions addressed the question of enforcement by requiring governments to enact legislation through which they could bring to trial in their own national courts anyone committing, or ordering to be committed, so-called grave breaches of the Conventions.[65] Alternatively they could hand suspected war criminals over to another High Contracting Party of the Conventions. Protocol 1 went further in 1977, obliging military commanders to make their subordinates aware of their obligations as *individuals* under international law. Moreover, commanders are now required to prevent violations of the Conventions when they become aware that their subordinates are going to commit them, and to take action against any offenders.[66] However, the limitations of national courts and national policing as instruments for enforcing international humanitarian law are obvious. Almost no government or defence force in the twentieth century, from the German in 1921 to the Serbian in 1994, has shown any enthusiasm for committing its own nationals to trial. The Calley trial during the Vietnam war was a highly contentious exception.

Other more traditional means of enforcement also have limitations. Like the Nazis and the British in 1939–45, governments of the post-war era have been tempted to use reprisals against breaches of international law by their enemy. But, if we leave to one side the fact that reprisals against POWs and civilians are forbidden in modern international law, this form of enforcement is essentially self-defeating; and, given the intense public agitation aroused by any issue concerning POWs, reprisals are contrary to the self-interest of the governments that initiate them.

International public opinion, or as it has been called, 'the mobilisation of shame',[67] might appear to offer more scope. Although its utility was minimal in a conflict like the Second World War, when almost all neutral powers were eventually engulfed in the conflict and no longer able to be courted or swayed by violations of international law, in the age of 'war by television' and articulate human-rights monitoring organizations, international public opinion may have a growing role. It seems that the closure of the terrible internment camps, such as Omarska, in Bosnia was the result of international outrage. The omnipresence of the press in both the Falklands and the Gulf War of 1991, as we have seen, sensitized the belligerents to legal issues. However, it must be acknowledged that there is always the potential for international public opinion to be manipulated. Far from having humanitarianism as its main concern, it may rapidly descend into what Geoffrey Best has called 'the fog of lies, rumours, myths, and misunderstandings which darkens the thinking of peoples at war'.[68]

The need for a more effective means of enforcement than any of the above has led in the 1990s to the revival of one of what appeared for many decades to be one of the more discredited legacies of the Second World War, the bringing to justice of war criminals at Nuremberg and Tokyo. At the time of writing, the prospects for the international tribunal set up to prosecute war crimes in the former Yugoslavia, and the future of plans for a similar tribunal in Rwanda, are uncertain. In its favour the Yugoslav tribunal has the legitimacy of being established by the United Nations Security Council, unlike the Nuremberg and Tokyo international military tribunals, which were undeniably the creations of the victorious Allies and vulnerable to the charge of exacting vengeance (though their principles were later confirmed by the UN).

However, there are many obstacles in its path. As of mid-1995 the Yugoslavia tribunal had accused of war crimes twenty-two Serbians, but had obtained custody of only one, a former guard in a prisoner-of-war camp, Duško ('Dule') Tardič. The prosecution will face difficulties in collating admissible evidence: much of the material gathered by journalists, is not. It might be argued that the intensive media coverage of the war will make a fair trial impossible. Future defendants might exploit, with a view to minimizing the charges against them, the intricate question of when the conflicts in the former Yugoslavia acquired an international character.[69]

The major problem, however, will be obtaining custody of those senior government officials who were responsible for the policies of ethnic cleansing and brutality that individuals like Tardič implemented. The tribunal was established as part of a wider United Nations initiative to restore peace and security within the former Yugoslavia. Should the demands to prosecute leading Serbian and Croatian politicians seem to be frustrating peace negotiations, then the tribunal might lose the international support and funding essential to its effectiveness.[70]

If the tribunal for the former Yugoslavia fails to prosecute senior government officials – something that Nuremberg, for all its controversy, at least achieved – it quite clearly will have failed. This would be an undeniable blow to the already battered reputation of the United Nations and to the prospects of international humanitarian law's providing effective protection in the future for POWs and other victims of war.

However, the development of international humanitarian law, as we have seen, has never been an uninterrupted or linear one. Rather it has been a case of 'two steps forward; one step backward', with the international community responding to the obvious fragility of international law that conflicts such as the Second World War have revealed. With each painful reassessment of the efficacy of the law, however, there has emerged some new, and more broadly accepted, consensus about what is acceptable behaviour in armed conflict. The international community, torn in rather Wagnerian tension between chaos and order, continues to pursue the objective of a world in which the excesses of the Second World War cannot be repeated.

Notes

1. J. M. Spaight, *War Rights on Land*, quoted in J. V. Dillon, 'The Genesis of the 1949 Convention Relative to the Treatment of Prisoners of War', *Miami Law Quarterly*, vol. 5, 1951, p. 40.
2. Quoted in the *Times Higher Educational Supplement*, 4 Mar. 1994.
3. Allan Rosas, *The Legal Status of Prisoners of War*, Helsinki, 1976, p. 75. For the First World War see Geoffrey Best, *Humanity in Warfare: The Modern History of the International Law of Armed Conflicts*, London, 1980, Ch. 4, *passim*; Gerald H. Davis, 'National Red Cross Societies and Prisoners of War in Russia, 1914–18', *Journal of Contemporary History*, vol. 28, no. 1, 1993, pp. 31–52; Daniel J. McCarthy, *The Prisoner of War in Germany*, London, 1917; British Parliamentary Papers, Cmd. 8988, *Report on the Treatment by the Enemy of British Prisoners of War behind the Firing Lines in France and Belgium*, 1918.
4. See Joan Beaumont, 'Prisoners of war', in Peter Dennis, Jeffrey Grey, Ewan Morris and Robin Prior (eds), *Oxford Companion of Australian Military History*, Melbourne, 1995.
5. Geoffrey Best, *War and Law since 1945*, Oxford, 1994, p. 139.
6. See, for example, Alan Fitzgerald, *Italian Farming Soldiers: Prisoners of War in Australia 1941–1947*, Melbourne, 1981.
7. See C. P. Stacey, *Official History of the Canadian Army in the Second World War*, vol. 1, *Six Years of War*, Ottawa, 1955, pp. 396–7.
8. This practice, incidentally, the 1949 Geneva Convention took care to prohibit. Article 5 states that the Convention applies 'from the time [POWs] fall into the power of the enemy until their final release and repatriation'.
9. James Bacque, *Other Losses*, Toronto, 1989.
10. This figure is that of A. E. Cowdrey in Günter Bischof and Stephen E. Ambrose (eds), *Eisenhower and the German POWs*, Baton Rouge, 1992.

11. Quoted in Alexander Werth, *Russia at War 1941–1945*, London, 1965, pp. 635–6. For a similar account from a camp in Germany see Donald Edgar, *The Stalag Men*, London, 1982, Ch. 6.

12. This is the estimate of Gavan Daws, *Prisoners of the Japanese: POWs of World War II in the Pacific*, New York, 1994.

13. Gavin Long, *The Final Offensives*, vol. 7, series 1, *Australia in the War of 1939–1945*, Canberra, 1963, pp. 633–4.

14. *These Instructions for the Government of Armies of the United States in the Field*, drafted during the American Civil War, provided the inspiration for later nineteenth-century international declarations on prisoners of war and the law of war.

15. Useful summaries of the changes in the 1949 Conventions can be found in Dillon, 'Genesis of the 1949 Convention' (see Note 1 above); Joyce A. C. Gutteridge, 'The Geneva Conventions of 1949', *British Yearbook of International Law, 1949*, London, pp. 294–326; Josef L. Kunz, 'The Geneva Conventions of August 12, 1949', in George A. Lipsky (ed.), *Law and Politics in the World Community*, Berkeley, 1953, pp. 279–373. The most comprehensive account of the rights of prisoners is Howard S. Levie, *Prisoners of War in International Armed Conflict*, Naval War College, International Law Studies, vol. 59, Newport, 1978.

16. Dillon, 'Genesis of the 1949 Convention' (see Note 1 above), p. 52.

17. These are (1) agriculture; (2) industries connected with the production or extraction of raw materials and manufacturing industries, with the exception of metallurgical, machinery and chemical industries, public works and buildings; (3) transport of handling of stores; (4) commercial business and arts and crafts; (5) domestic service; (6) public utility services. Categories (2), (3) and (6) are to have 'no military character or purpose'. The 1949 Convention, unlike that of 1929, allows prisoners to work on unhealthy or dangerous work if they volunteer to do so.

18. Best, *War and Law* (see Note 5 above), pp. 138–9.

19. *Report of the International Committee of the Red Cross on its Activities during the Second World War*, vol. 1, *General Activities*, Geneva, 1948, p. 320.

20. Sylvie-Stoyanka Junod, *Protection of the Victims of Armed Conflict: Falkland–Malvinas Islands (1982)*, Geneva, 1984, p. 31.

21. For prisoners in Britain, see Miriam Kochan, *Prisoners of England*, London, 1980; Matthew Barry Sullivan, *Thresholds of Peace: German Prisoners and the People of England, 1944–1948*, London, 1979.

22. See Nicholas Bethell, *The Last Secret: Forcible Repatriation to Russia 1941–7*, London, 1974. For more controversial works, see Nikolai Tolstoy, *Victims of Yalta*, London, 1977, and *The Minister and the Massacres*, London, 1986.
23. *ICRC, Summary Report of the Work of the Conference of Government Experts for the Study of the Conventions for the Protection of War Victims*, Geneva, 1947, p. 95.
24. See Best, *War and Law* (see Note 5 above), pp. 140–2.
25. See Jan P. Charmatz and Harold M. Wit, 'Repatriation of Prisoners of War and the 1949 Geneva Convention', *Yale Law Journal*, vol. 62, no. 3, 1953, pp. 398–405.
26. See the *Age* (Melbourne), 14 Nov. 1988; ICRC, *Annual Report 1991*, Geneva, 1992, pp. 111–12; *Annual Report 1992*, Geneva, 1993, pp. 141–2; *The Gulf 1990–91: the ICRC at work*, Geneva, 1991, pp. 25–6.
27. ICRC, *Annual Report, 1991*, p. 102.
28. The 1929 Convention had adopted the definition in Article 1 of the 1907 Hague Convention, but extended it to maritime and aerial warfare.
29. Richard Lamb, *War in Italy, 1943–45: A Brutal Story*, reviewed in the *Australian*, 2–3 Apr. 1994.
30. However, these had to fulfil essentially the conditions of the Hague Conventions. It was also agreed in 1949 to extend combatant status to merchant seamen and the crews of civil aircraft.
31. Article 4.
32. In that it was common to all four 1949 Geneva Conventions dealing with the wounded, sick, shipwrecked and civilians in occupied territory as well as prisoners of war.
33. As a result of Third World pressure, Protocol 1 also extended the definition of international conflicts to include a number of essentially civil conflicts with an international dimension: that is, armed conflicts in which 'peoples are fighting against colonial domination and alien occupation and against racist régimes in the exercise of their right of self-determination' as defined by the United Nations. The literature on the negotiation of the Protocols is immense. A good coverage is provided in A. Cassese (ed.), *The New Humanitarian Law of Armed Conflict,* Naples, 1979.
34. Yoram Dinstein, 'The New Geneva Protocols: A Step Forward or Backward?', *The Year Book of World Affairs, 1979*, London, 1979, p. 271. Dinstein sees the relevant article of Protocol 1 (Article 44) as 'a dangerous retrogressive step in the evolution of *jus in bello*' (p. 272).

35. Best, *War and Law* (see Note 5 above), p. 135.
36. *Report on the Work of the ICRC (January 1 to December 31, 1952)*, Geneva, 1953, p. 44; *Report on the Work of the ICRC (January 1 to December 31, 1953)*, Geneva, 1954, p. 53.
37. See Richard I. Miller, *The Law of War*, Lexington, MA, 1975, pp. 118 ff.
38. Howard S. Levie, 'Maltreatment of Prisoners of War in Vietnam', *Boston University Law Review*, vol. 48, no. 3, 1968, pp. 323–4.
39. Ibid., pp. 340–2; Miller, *The Law of War* (see Note 37 above), pp. 169–72, 178–82.
40. Miller, *The Law of War* (see Note 37 above), pp. 172–4.
41. For a full discussion of the North Vietnamese position see 'The Geneva Convention and the Treatment of Prisoners of War in Vietnam', *Harvard Law Review*, vol. 80, 1966–7, pp. 859–68.
42. See ICRC *Annual Reports* for 1965–74, Geneva, 1966–75.
43. Miller, *Law of War* (see Note 37 above), pp. 174–5.
44. See Keith Suter, 'The Work of the ICRC in Vietnam', *Instant Research on Peace and Violence*, vol. 3, 1974, pp. 121–32.
45. See W. Michael Reisman and James Silk, 'Which Law Applies to the Afghan Conflict?', *American Journal of International Law*, vol. 82, 1988, p. 485.
46. Ibid., pp. 479–80, 459.
47. Paul Tavernier, 'Combatants and Non-combatants', in Ige F. Dekker and Harry H. G. Post (eds), *The Gulf War of 1980–1988: The Iran–Iraq War in International Legal Perspective*, Dordrecht, 1992, p. 131.
48. With the prospect of the ICRC being crippled, the United Nations Secretary General sent two missions in 1985 and 1988 to investigate the position of prisoners.
49. ICRC, *Annual Report 1989*, Geneva, 1990, p. 85.
50. See ICRC *Annual Report 1967*, Geneva, 1968, pp. 8–9.
51. *Sunday Age*, 3 Sept. 1995. Estimates of those killed are forty and 'a dozen' in the respective conflicts.
52. Egypt and Israel repatriated prisoners within weeks of the war's end; but it took months of shuttle diplomacy before the Syrians, playing on Israel's extreme sensitivity on this issue, would even release a list of prisoners in their hands. The ICRC was not allowed access to Syrian camps, and final exchanges of POWs took place in June 1974. See Ismail Fahmy, *Negotiating for Peace in the Middle East*, London, 1983, pp. 55, 64–5; Lester A. Sobel (ed.), *Peace-Making in the Middle East*, New York, 1980, pp. 24, 27; Matti Golan, *The Secret Conversations of Henry Kissinger*, New York, 1976, *passim*.

53. Possibly 14,000 of these were irregular forces. Although not technically prisoners of war under the 1949 definition they were granted this status.

54. Donald L. Zillman, 'Prisoners in the Bangladesh War: Humanitarian Concerns and Political Demands', *The International Lawyer*, vol. 8, no. 1, 1974, pp. 124–35.

55. Bangladesh wanted to pressure Pakistan for recognition; India was always looking for bargaining counters over Kashmir; and there was some fear of Pakistan's renewing hostilities. For this see P. Arnaud, 'Pak POWs and International Law', *India Quarterly*, vol. 28, no. 2, 1972, p. 110. Bangladesh also wanted to get back tens of thousands of its citizens and former soldiers marooned in Pakistan. See Best, *War and Law* (see Note 5 above), p. 357.

56. Quoted in Leslie C. Green, 'The Falklands, the Law and the War', *Year Book of World Affairs 1984*, p. 114. The Geneva Convention applies 'to all cases of declared war or of any other armed conflict . . . even if the state of war is not recognized by one of [the parties to the Convention]' (article 2). As Green points out, the British continued in some minor respects to ignore their legal obligations, and were willing to make the commander of the Argentine garrison of Grytviken, South Georgia, available for questioning by Sweden and France in relation to war crimes allegedly committed against their nationals in Argentina before the conflict. Had this been followed through it would have been in violation of Article 85 of the Convention.

57. For qualifications see Best, *War and Law* (see Note 5 above), p. 355.

58. Ibid., p. 115.

59. Quoted in Adam Roberts, 'The Laws of War in the 1990–91 Gulf Conflict', *International Security*, vol. 18, no. 3, 1993–4, p. 135.

60. Jean Rigopoulo, 'Tens of Thousands of Interviews without Witnesses', in *The Gulf, 1990–1991: The ICRC at Work*, Geneva, 1991.

61. See, for example, John Dower, *War without Mercy. Race and Power in the Pacific War*, New York, 1986, p. 64.

62. See Roberts, 'The Laws of War' (see Note 59 above), pp. 160–1.

63. Defined as conflicts that have crossed the subjective threshold of being more than 'riots' or 'isolated and sporadic acts of violence', but that are not international conflicts as defined by Protocol 1.

64. Tavernier, 'Combatants and Non-combatants' (see Note 47 above), p. 129.

65. Article 129.

66. This in part a legacy of the Second World War, reflecting the so-called 'Yamashita principle', after the Japanese commander who

was tried and sentenced to death by a US court in the Philippines, on the grounds that he had not brought to an end consistent committing of atrocities by troops under his command. Protocol 1 has also made provision for an International Fact Finding Commission to enquire into allegations of grave breaches of the Conventions or the Protocols. However, thanks to differences between the US and the Soviet bloc countries, the Commission is a compromise, almost entirely dependent in its undertakings on the consent of the parties to the dispute and with no power to make judgements. It appears to have little chance of developing into a major force for policing international humanitarian law. See J. F. Thomson, 'Repression of Violations', *Australian Yearbook of International Law,* vol. 9, 1985, pp. 326–8.

67. B. V. A. Röling, 'Aspects of Criminal Responsibility for Violations of the Laws of War' in Cassese (ed.), *New Humanitarian Law* (see Note 33 above), p. 200.

68. Best, *War and Law* (see Note 5 above), p. 383.

69. Once the republics of Yugoslavia had declared independence and established themselves as states, the hostilities between them were clearly international. But when, for example, *did* Croatia become a state? Its declaration of independence preceded its recognition by some six months. The resolution of such questions will affect whether the actions with which war criminals will be charged are grave 'breaches' within the meaning of the Conventions and Protocols or not.

70. See Christopher Greenwood, 'The International Tribunal for Former Yugoslavia', *International Affairs*, vol. 69, no. 4, 1993, pp. 641–55, for an excellent discussion of the tribunal.

Notes on Contributors

Joan Beaumont is Professor of History in the School of Australian and International Studies, Deakin University, Australia. She is the author of *Gull Force: Survival and Leadership in Captivity, 1941–5* (1990), and editor of *Australia's War, 1914–18* (1995) and *Australia's War, 1939–45* (1996). In addition, she has published a number of articles on various aspects of the British and Australian experience of the Second World War, especially the treatment of POWs.

Kent Fedorowich is a lecturer in British Imperial History at the University of the West of England, Bristol. Recent publications include *Unfit for Heroes: Reconstruction and Soldier Settlement in the Empire between the Wars* (1995) and articles on the disbandment of the Royal Irish Constabulary and British inter-war migration to the dominions. He is now working on a book with Bob Moore entitled *Britain, the Empire and Italian POWs, 1940–7*.

Sibylla Jane Flower is consultant on Archives to Christie's London. She is writing a history of Allied POWs in Burma, Thailand and Malaya, 1942–5.

Ikuhiko Hata is Professor of the History of Modern Japan, Chiba University, Chiba Prefecture, near Tokyo. Until 1976 he served as chief historian of the Japanese Ministry of Finance, and is the author of numerous works including *A History of the Japanese Military Fascist Movement* (1962) and *The Nanjing Incident* (1986). More recently, he has contributed to *The Cambridge History of Japan* (1988) and to a collection of essays on the Second World War in Asia and the Pacific edited by Saki Dockrill (1994).

David Killingray is Reader in History, Goldsmiths College, University of London. He has written books and articles on aspects of African, Caribbean, Imperial and English Local history.

Notes on Contributors

Bob Moore is senior lecturer in Modern History at the Manchester Metropolitan University. He has published extensively on twentieth-century Dutch history, including *Refugees from Nazi Germany in the Netherlands 1933–1940* (1986), and more recently on prisoners of war. Current projects include the preparation of a monograph on the persecution of the Jews in the occupied Netherlands.

Charles G. Roland (MD) is the Jason A. Hannah Professor of the History of Medicine at McMaster University in Hamilton, Ontario, Canada. For the past fifteen years he has researched and published extensively on the health conditions in POW camps in the Second World War. In 1992 he published *Courage Under Siege: Disease, Starvation, and Death in the Warsaw Ghetto*, and has a chapter in a forthcoming book on men captured at Hong Kong on Christmas Day, 1941.

David Rolf is an Honorary Research Fellow in the School of History at the University of Birmingham. Author of *Prisoners of the Reich: Germany's Captives, 1939–1945* (1988), he is at present working on a book about carrier warfare in the Second World War.

Lucio Sponza is Professor of Italian at the University of Westminster. He is the author of *Italian Immigrants in Nineteenth Century Britain: Realities and Images* (1988) and the co-author of *Italy – World Bibliography Series* (1995).

Martin Thomas is a lecturer in International History at the University of the West of England, Bristol. He is currently working on a history of the French Empire in the Second World War, and has just completed a book entitled, *Britain, France and Appeasement: Anglo-French Relations in the Popular Front Era* (1997).

Jonathan F. Vance is a research fellow at the Centre for Military, Strategic and Disarmament Studies at Wilfrid Laurier University. He is the author of *Objects of Concern: Canadian Prisoners of War through the 20th Century* (1994), and is currently researching Canada's collective memory of the First World War.

Index

Index

Blackater, C.F., 229
black prisoners, 91–2, 94, 98, 103, 108
  of Germany, 11, 182–3, 186–99
  of Italy, 182–3, 192–6, 199
  of Japan, 182–3, 186–9
Boisson, Pierre, 90, 93–5, 102, 106–7
Bosnia, 289
Bourdillon, Bernard, 95
Bowers, H.S., 50
Bowmanville camp, 59
Bracken, Brendan, 126–7
Brain, W.H., 220
Brazzaville, 99
Brett, C.C., 233
British Army, 121
British Broadcasting Corporation, 59,
  62, 121, 126, 129
British Expeditionary Force (BEF),
  21–2, 25, 48
British prisoners, 32–3, 55–60, 96–7,
  100, 108
  black troops, 192–3, 198–9
  of Germany, 11, 47–62
  of Japan, 1, 7, 92, 152, 165, 231–3,
    236, 240–2
  see also United Kingdom
British Red Cross and Order of St John
  of Jerusalem, 48–55, 62
British West African Governors, 95
Brittany, 188
Brooks, Dallas, 121, 133, 138
Broughton Rectory, 27
Bruce, Stanley, 60
The Bugle, 128
Brussels Declaration (1874), 253–4
Burma, 133–4, 269
  black troops in, 182, 185, 198
  labour camps, 227, 230–1, 233, 235,
    239–40, 243–6
Burma and Thailand POW
  Administration, 234–9, 244
Burma-Thailand Railway, 12, 227, 281
  administration of, 233–43
  and Allied officers, 228–30, 233, 237,
    240–5
  Korean guards, 233, 238–9
  literature on, 228–33, 247
  POW Administration, 235–9, 244
  war crimes, 233, 237, 238
  workforce, 233–6, 240–2
Burton, Reginald, 232
Bushidō, 171, 261
Butler, R.A., 53

Cabanatuan camp, 167

Cabinet War Committee (Canada), 72
Cairo, 121, 126
Calley, William Jr., 290
Cameroons, 91, 96
Campbell, Mrs. Ian, 55
Le Camp de Thiaroye, 191
Camp McCoy, 258, 270
Canada, 59, 183
  deportation of prisoners to, 24–5,
    28–9, 34, 36, 55–6, 73
  German prisoners of war, 9, 23–4,
    57–9, 81
  and prisoner exchanges, 6, 69–82
Canadian prisoners,
  of Germany, 9, 56–7, 60, 69, 71, 74
  of Japan, 9, 69, 75–7, 79–80, 152
Carabinieri, 127
Carandini, Nicolò, 220
Carnera, Primo, 196
Cary, Otis, 270
Cassels, Robert A., 123
Catroux, Georges, 95, 100–2
Cawthorne, W.J., 132
censorship, 50, 54, 61, 216
Ceylon, 277
Chad, 91, 96, 100, 108
Chamberlain, Neville, 24
Chandler, H.E., 212, 214
Changi camp, 240–4
Chan Pak, 168, 170
charitable associations, 49–56
Charité-sur-Loire, 187
Chartres, 187, 194
Chasselay-Montluzin, 187
Ch'en Kwang-In, 238–9
Chetwode, Phillip, 52–3
Chida sotomatsu, 234–6
China, 92, 237–8, 261
China Expeditionary Force (Japan), 268
Chinese People's Army of Liberation,
  260
Chinese prisoners of war, 7, 150, 230,
  240, 256
Chōkenji camp, 256
Choun Kuk, 238
Chronicles of the Yi Dynasty, 256
Chungkai camp, 236, 239, 242, 244–6
Churchill, Winston, 22–3, 25, 62,
  and Italian POWs, 28–9, 33, 120,
    122–3
  reciprocal agreements with Germany,
    35, 51, 57–60
  and Vichy France, 93, 95, 97
Citrine, Walter, 218
civilians,

Index

Index

Italian prisoners, 1, 3–4, 99–100, 109, 119–2, 130–4, 135–6, 140, 266
  of Britain, 1, 8, 10, 12, 119–41, 205–21, 279
  co-operator status, 12, 32–4, 140, 206, 212–9
  deportation, 27, 30–2, 34, 95, 124, 138–9, 141
  in India, 124–41
  as labour force, 10, 12, 20, 28–39, 99, 119, 123, 127, 129, 136, 138–40, 206–7, 209–12, 214–5, 218–21, 279
  morale, 12, 38, 124, 127, 131, 137, 205–12, 214–6
  re-education, 10, 120–41, 205
Italia Redenta, 135–6, 138–40
Italy, 69, 184
  black prisoners, 11, 182–3, 192–6, 199
Iwanami Hiroshi, 163–4, 170, 172
Iwasaki Yoshiho, 166–7

Jackson, R., 215
Jaipur camp, 134–8
Japan, 75–80, 150, 231
  American POWs, 7, 161–4, 167, 169, 232, 236, 240–1
  Australian POWs, 2–3, 92, 166–7, 169, 229, 232–3, 236, 240–1
  bacteriological warfare, 7, 150–2, 169
  black POWs, 182–3, 186, 197–9
  British POWs, 1, 7, 92, 165
  civilian prisoners, 2, 6–7, 10, 150, 168–9, 186
  policy on Japanese POWs, 3, 12–3, 75, 171, 253–70
  treatment of prisoners, 2, 6–8, 10, 12–3, 171, 186, 244, 247, 257–9, 262–7, 280, 289
  sick and injured prisoners, 152–7, 162–7, 230, 237, 239
  vivisection, 7, 10–11, 149–72, 254
Japanese prisoners of war, 1, 3, 12–3, 257–8, 265, 270–3
  shame, 13, 171, 255, 259–62, 269–70
  suicide, 13, 259, 267–8, 270
Java, 164, 241–2
Jersey, 188
Jerusalem, 100–1
Jeune, R.D., 102
Jews, 5, 35, 199
Jiheikai Medical College, 162
Johnston, A.C., 138
Joint Consultative Committee, 218
Joint Intelligence Committee, 126
Journal of Modern History, 4

Jowitt, Sir William, 52
Junod, Marcel, 52
Justice Pal, 160

Kagbo, David, 198
Kaikōsha Hospital, 158
Kamo Unit, 151
Kanchanaburi, 228, 236–7
Kanyu, 244
Keele camp, 195
Keitel, Wilhelm, 60
Kempeitei 150, 160, 228
Kent camp, 210
Kenya, 27
Keshner, Harold, 153–6
Kilwick Island, 166
Kim Chang Sik, 238
Kim Chung-Son, 256
Kim Yong, 238, 246–7
King, Mackenzie, 71, 75
King's African Rifles, 185
Kinoshita Hiroshi, 162
Kinsayok, 245
Kinshū Maru, 259
Kinvig, Clifford, 232–3
Kipling, Rudyard, 128
Knights, A.E., 245–7
Kobe, 258
Koga, Second Lieutenant, 259
Komoi Mitsuo, 236
Komoi Yoshirō, 168, 170
Komori Taku, 157–8
Kondō Hideo, 166–7
Koninklijk Nederlands-Indisch Leger, 231
Korea, 256
Korean camp guards, 233, 238–9, 280
Korean War, 282, 285–6, 289
Koufra, 100
Koulikoro camp, 99
Kriegsmarine, 22, 26
Kuala Lumpur, 230
Kudara (Korean) Expedition (661–7), 255
Kuga, Major, 262
Kuomontang camps, 270
Kuwait invasion (1990), 287
Kwantung Army, 268
Kwantung Army Epidemic Prevention and Water Supply Unit, 151
Kyūshū, 255–6
Kyūshū Imperial University, 156–7, 159, 170

Labour Corps, 138

Index

Munro, I.S., 126, 129–33, 137
Murakami, Colonel, 257, 259, 261
Muraoka Shiegeo, 239
Murchison, Donald, 242
Murphy, John, 161
Murray, S.S., 48
Mussolini, Benito, 8, 12, 100, 122, 128, 137, 139, 184, 205, 210–11
mutatis mutandis, 228, 254, 263–5

Nabetani, Surgeon Lieutenant, 163–4
Nagatomo Yoshitada, 234–6
Naitō Tomoji, 236
Nakagawa Kōichi, 159
Nakamura Hirosato, 168–72
Nakamura Kiyoshi, 164
Nakhon Pathom camp, 246
Namibia, 194
Naoki Kōjirō, 255
Naples, 196
Narashino Cavalry Brigade, 258
Nara Takeji, 261–2
Narvik, 22
National Farmers' Union, 28
National Liberation Front, 285
Native Military Corps (NMC), 183, 195
Naval Medical School (Japan), 163–4
Nehring, K., 186
Nelson, Hank, 232
Netherlands, 22, 70
Netherlands East Indies, 240–7
New Delhi, 126, 129
Newfoundland, 25
New Guinea, 78
Newton, R.W., 237, 242
Newton, Thomas Wodehouse Legh, 47
New Zealand, 77, 79, 231, 240
N'Guetta, Edmund, 187, 190
Nigeria, 95
Nihon oyobi Nihonjin, 261
Nihon Shoki, 255
Niigata, 153
Nobusawa Hisashi, 239
Nogaga, Nzamo, 194–6
Noguès, Charles, 103–4
Nomonhan Incident, 268
Non-European Army Services (NEAS), 183, 194
Nong Pladuk, 247
Normandy landings, 34, 184
North Africa, 32, 119, 123–4, 132, 136, 183–4, 192–3, 197, 199
Northern Rhodesia Regiment, 185
North Korea, 285
North Vietnam, 285–6

Norway, 22
N'Tchóréré, Charles, 187
Numata Kimio, 159
Nuremberg Code, 152
Nuremberg trials, 152, 291
Nussbaum, Chaim, 232
Nyasaland, 185

Odier, Mlle, 53
Ogdensburg agreement, 71
Okuyama, Surgeon Commander, 163–4
Omarska camp (Bosnia), 290
Ōoka Shōhei, 171, 271–2
Operation Menace, 91, 96, 102
Operation Torch, 88, 90, 95, 104, 106, 108
Oran, 102
Osata Yoshio, 246
Ōshiba Yoshifumi, 166
Oswestry camp, 26
Other Losses: An Investigation into the Mass Deaths of German Prisoners of War at the Hands of the French and Americans After World War II, 6
Otomobe-no-Hakama, 255
Otsu Incident, 261
Ōtsuka Yasumasa, 166
O.V.R.A., 127
Owtram, H.C., 239, 244–6

Paita camp, 270
Pak Taroeng, 168, 170
Palestine, 100–2
Palestine Liberation Organization (PLO), 287
Paris, 87, 191
Parti Communiste Français, 104–5
Pavillard, Stanley S., 231
Peace Treaty of 1952, 7
Pearl Harbor, 71
Pelauw, 165
Penrith camp, 209, 216
Pétain, Philippe, 88, 91, 94–5, 97, 107–8
Peyrouton, Marcel, 103, 107
Pingfan, 151
Platon, Charles, 101
Platt, William, 93, 103
Pleven, René, 105–6, 191
Poitiers, 189
Poland, 25, 35, 48–9, 194
Polish internees, 105, 220
political warfare, 10, 119–41
Political Warfare Executive (PWE), 10, 120–1, 126–7, 130–41, 210–11, 214–15

Index

Index